THE N-TOWN PLAY
Cotton MS Vespasian D. 8
VOL. I

EARLY ENGLISH TEXT SOCIETY
S.S. 11
1991

Ego sum alpha & oo principium et finis

Deus

My name is knowyn god & kynge
my werk for to make now wyl I wende
In my self restyth my reynenge
It hath no gynnyng ne non ende
And all that evyr xal have beynge
It is closyd in my mende
Whan it is made at my lykynge
I may it save I may it shende
After my plesawns
So gret of myth is my pouste
All thyng xal be wrouth be me
I am oo god in personys thre
knyt in oo substawns

I am the trewe trenyte
here walkyng in this wone
thre personys my self I se
lokyn in me god alone
I am the ffadyr of powste
my sone with me gynnyth gon
my gost is grace in mageste
wellyth welthe up in hevyn tron
O god thre I calle
I am fadyr of myth
my sone kepyth ryth
my gost hath lyth
& grace withalle

Myself begynnyng nevyr dyd take

Cotton MS Vespasian D. 8, f. 10r

THE N-TOWN PLAY
Cotton MS Vespasian D. 8

EDITED BY

STEPHEN SPECTOR

VOL. I
INTRODUCTION AND TEXT

Published for

THE EARLY ENGLISH TEXT SOCIETY

by the

OXFORD UNIVERSITY PRESS

1991

Oxford University Press, Walton Street, Oxford OX2 6DP
Oxford New York Toronto
Delhi Bombay Calcutta Madras Karachi
Petaling Jaya Singapore Hong Kong Tokyo
Nairobi Dar es Salaam Cape Town
Melbourne Auckland
Associated companies in Beirut Berlin Ibadan Nicosia

British Library Cataloguing in Publication Data
The N-town play: Cotton MS Vespasian D. 8.—(Early English Text Society, S.S., 11–12).
1. English drama
I. Spector, Stephen II. Early English Text Society
III. Series
822.0516

ISBN 0–19–722411–3 v. 1
ISBN 0–19–722412–1 v. 2

Set by Joshua Associates Ltd, Oxford
Printed in Great Britain
by Ipswich Book Company Ltd

PREFACE

The N-town manuscript contains a collection of mysteries indeed. This is true not only theologically and in terms of genre, but more broadly as well. For this stout little codex bristles with mysteries about its own makeup and history, and is textually among the most challenging English literary documents of its time. Reliable external evidence about the cycle is almost wholly lacking. Internal testimony, by contrast, is abundant but extremely complex, owing to the eclecticism of the text. The Introduction and Commentary of the present edition are intended to describe, interpret, and contextualize much of the information in the Proclamation and forty-one plays that constitute the collection. More conjectural solutions to the mysteries of the cycle are presented in the appendices.

In preparing this edition, I have been unusually fortunate in my teachers, colleagues, and friends. Professor Marie Borroff's learning and judgement made her advice invaluable during the entire course of this project. Professors E. Talbot Donaldson and John C. Pope offered bold and persuasive solutions to cruces, teaching in the process essential ways to address textual and linguistic problems. Professor Martin Stevens reviewed and strengthened many aspects of this edition, and demonstrated the highest standards for editing religious drama. Professor A. C. Cawley offered very generous advice about problematic textual and linguistic issues. Professor Norman Davis commented on my early efforts to extract meaning from the watermarks and make sense of the manuscript, and he and Professor George Kane each graciously helped solve recalcitrant linguistic problems in the cycle.

For their advice on palaeographic issues, I am indebted to the late Professor T. J. Brown, Professor Davis, Dr A. I. Doyle, and Dr M. B. Parkes. Dr Doyle's generous assistance also led to key findings about the transmission of the codex. Professors Angus McIntosh and Michael Samuels provided valuable dialectal information about the principal scribes, and Professor McIntosh gave detailed advice distinguishing eccentric but legitimate dialect forms from scribal errors. Dr Richard Beadle reviewed the Glossary and the Commentary, and enriched this edition in many ways. And Mr R. A. Waldron's advice in preparing this edition for publication was extremely helpful and appreciated.

I am indebted to Miss Joan Gibbs for her assistance in historical research, and to Mr Richard Proudfoot for his advice about analytical bibliography. I wish to thank Professors Dewey Faulkner and Traugott Lawler, who offered valuable suggestions about editing the text, Professor Nicholas Hammond, who commented on the Greek motto and cipher, and Professor Rufus Hendon, who concorded the plays. Further thanks for friendly assistance are due to Professors Sherman M. Kuhn and Robert E. Lewis, Dr P. O. E. Gradon, Mrs Linda Drury, Mr Hilton Kelliher, Professor Anne Hudson, and Professor Phillip Pulsiano. I am grateful to Professor David Bevington for his generous comments during the course of my work. For my wife Jeri's patient toleration and support of this project over the nineteen years that it took to complete, no thanks can suffice.

I am also indebted to the immense labours of the other scholars who have attempted to disclose the secrets of this cycle. Two recent books, Peter Meredith's *The Mary Play from the N.town Manuscript* and Martin Stevens's *Four Middle English Mystery Cycles*, reached me after I had submitted this edition. I have tried, however, to cite relevant findings and arguments in these books that I had not included at the time of submission.

I wish to thank the officials of the British Library, the Bodleian Library, and the libraries of Corpus Christi College, Oxford, St John's College, Cambridge, and the University of Durham for allowing me to examine materials relating to this study, and for providing photographic copies of relevant documents. I am also grateful for the financial assistance I was awarded in support of this project from the National Endowment for the Humanities, the American Council of Learned Societies, and the SUNY Research Foundation, and for the research fellowship appointments I held at the Center for Humanities, Wesleyan University, and the National Humanities Center.

The plates are reproduced from Cotton MS Vespasian D. 8 by permission of the British Library.

CONTENTS

ABBREVIATIONS

Briquet	C. M. Briquet, *Les Filigranes.* 4 vols, Geneva, 1907; *The New Briquet*, gen. ed. J. S. G. Simmons. Amsterdam. 1968.
DNB	*Dictionary of National Biography*
EETS	Early English Text Society OS Original Series ES Extra Series SS Supplementary Series
ELN	*English Language Notes*
JEGP	*Journal of English and Germanic Philology*
LSE	*Leeds Studies in English*
ME	Middle English
MED	*Middle English Dictionary*
MLN	*Modern Language Notes*
MLR	*Modern Language Review*
MP	*Modern Philology*
OE	Old English
OED	*Oxford English Dictionary*
OF	Old French
PMLA	*Publications of the Modern Language Association*
PQ	*Philological Quarterly*
RORD	*Research Opportunities in Renaissance Drama*

INTRODUCTION

MANUSCRIPT

Provenance and history

BL MS Cotton Vespasian D. 8 contains one of the four surviving English mystery play cycles, a composite and in many ways unique dramatic collection of unknown origin.[1] The paucity of information about its provenance and auspices has resulted in conflicting conjecture, which has in turn inspired different names for the cycle: it has been variously referred to as the Coventry Plays, the Cotton Plays, the Hegge Plays, the Lincoln Plays, the *Ludus Coventriae*, and the N-town Plays. Some of these names are based on mistaken or uncertain assumptions, as noted below. And only the last has textual authority: Pr 526–7 refer to the production as the 'play' that will be presented in 'N-town'. 'N-town' therefore seems the best title for the collection. The 'N' is generally considered to be an abbreviation of *nomen*, standing for the name of the site of performance. This may indicate that the play was itinerant, at least at some point in its history (see the note to Pr 527, however).

The name *Ludus Coventriae* derives from a description written on the flyleaf of the codex by Richard James, Sir Robert Bruce Cotton's librarian:

Elenchus contentorum in hoc codice
Contenta novi testamenti scenicè expressa· et actitata olim per monachos sive Fratres mendicantes· vulgò dicitur hic liber Ludus Coventriae· sive ludus corporis Christi· scribitur metris Anglicanis.

Though the evidentiary value of this description is now generally

[1] Much of the remarkable textual and linguistic character of the cycle is noted throughout the apparatus of this edition. N-town is thematically unique among the extant English mystery plays in its depiction of Lamech's killing of Cain (Play 4), the Jesse Tree (Play 7), the story of Joachim and Anna (Play 8), the Presentation of Mary in the Temple (Play 9), the Parliament of Heaven (Play 11), the Trial of Joseph and Mary (Play 14), the Cherry Tree episode (Play 15), Death's slaying of Herod (Play 20), the appearance of Veronica (Play 32; cf. York 34), the Harrowing of Hell segmented into two plays (33 and 35) surrounding the Burial, the risen Christ's appearance to the Virgin Mary (Play 35), etc. Radical conflations of scriptural episodes, such as the Burning Bush and the giving of the Decalogue (Play 6), and the Last Supper and the dinner with Simon the leper (Play 27), are also unexampled in English drama.

discounted, it may merit attention. James' notation may be a traditional account of the plays, and it does square with the earlier inscription atop f. 1^{r}, 'The plaie called Corpus Christi'.[1] The allusion to production by religious is consonant with several features of the manuscript, including the learned marginal genealogies and the absence of any reference to civic auspices.[2] James did not refer to the book as the *Ludus Coventriae*, but said only that it was commonly spoken of by that name; the term may in any event have been a generic designation for mystery plays.[3] None the less, William Dugdale, influenced by James' description, wrote in 1656 that the manuscript contains New Testament plays performed by the Grey Friars of Coventry.[4] In the Cottonian catalogue of 1696, however, Dr Thomas Smith omitted the reference to Coventry, and mentioned both Old and New Testament plays.[5] Thomas Sharp noted in 1825 that the

[1] James Orchard Halliwell suggested that James' description derived from a colophon on the last leaf, now lost (ed. *Ludus Coventriae*, Shakespeare Soc. Publications no. 4 (1841), p. viii), but W. W. Greg doubts that James was passing on an existing tradition about the manuscript, and cites James' inaccuracy in noting the presence of only New Testament plays (*Bibliographical and Textual Problems of the English Miracle Cycles* (London, 1914), p. 109). K. S. Block observes that the connection with Coventry is not supported by any evidence, but wonders if James' omission of Old Testament plays may indicate separate storage of the Passion plays (ed. *Ludus Coventriae*, EETS ES 120 (1922), p. xxxviii); see p. xviii in the present edition, however.

[2] See E. K. Chambers, *English Literature at the Close of the Middle Ages* (New York and Oxford, 1945), p. 49; Block, p. xxxiv; Martial Rose, 'The Staging of the Hegge Plays', Stratford-upon-Avon Studies, 16 (London, 1973), p. 221; Mary Lampland Tobin, 'A Study of the Formation and Auspices of the *Ludus Coventriae*' (Rice Ph.D. thesis, 1973), *passim*; and note 5 below.

[3] Greg (p. 109) says that James used the terms 'Ludus Coventriae' and 'Ludus Corporis Christi' as though they were synonymous. Thomas Sharp in 1825 cited a passage in Heywood's *Four P's* showing that Coventry was peculiarly celebrated for the Corpus Christi play. But Sharp concluded that the present cycle was intended for exhibition at a Corpus Christi festival *generally*, rather than expressly at Coventry (*A Dissertation on the Pageants or Dramatic Mysteries Anciently Performed at Coventry* (Coventry, 1825, photographic reproduction, 1973), pp. 6–7). Block (pp. xl–xli) reviews the evidence that the term 'Corpus Christi play' had a broad frame of reference and that such plays were popularly associated with Coventry.

[4] William Dugdale, *The Antiquities of Warwickshire Illustrated* (London, 1656), p. 116. Scholars as early as Sharp (p. 5) questioned the claims about the Coventry Grey Friars' connection to the manuscript, and Greg asserts that 'the Conventry Greyfriars' plays . . . are almost certainly an invention of seventeenth century antiquaries' (*Problems*, pp. 109–10). Alfred W. Pollard (*English Miracle Plays Moralities and Interludes* (Oxford, 1909), p. xxxviii) and Hardin Craig ('Note on the Home of *Ludus Coventriae*', appended to Esther L. Swenson's *An Inquiry into the Composition and Structure of Ludus Coventriae*, Univ. of Minnesota Studies in Language and Literature, 1 (Minneapolis, 1914), pp. 73–4) observe that early allusions to the Grey Friars at Coventry indicate the place of performance, not the actors.

[5] Smith's description reads: 'Vespasianus D. viii. A collection of plays in old English

plays of Vespasian D. 8 were not those of the Coventry guilds, and other nineteenth-century scholars recognized that the language of the plays indicates a more easterly provenance than Coventry.[1] Several studies documented affinities to the dramatic records of Lincoln, but modern dialectologists have established that the language of the plays is East Anglian.[2] The fact that the principal constituents of the cycle were copied out by East Anglian scribes, evidently writing at various times, argues strongly for compilation and transcription in East Anglia. And the appearance of East Anglian dialect words, several

metre, i.e. Dramata sacra in quibus exhibentur historiae veteris et N. Testamenti, introductis quasi in scenam personis illic memoratis quas secum invicem colloquentes pro ingenio fingit Poeta. Videntur olim coram populo sive ad instruendum sive ad placendum a Fratribus mendicantibus repraesentata' (cited by Block, p. xxxviii).

[1] Sharp, p. 7. Halliwell accepted the attribution to Coventry, and supported it in his edition of 1841 with a brief and incorrect discussion of the dialect (p. viii). Bernard ten Brink thought that the language shows a northeast midlands colouring, however (*History of English Literature*, trans. William Clarke Robinson (New York, 1892), II: 283). Max Kramer argued for an origin perhaps near Wiltshire, but observed that the cycle in its current form belongs to the northeast midlands (*Die Sprache und Heimat des sogenannten Ludus Coventriae* (Halle, 1892)).

[2] Arguments associating the cycle with Lincoln were advanced by Charles Mills Gayley, *Plays of Our Forefathers* (New York, 1907), p. 136; Hardin Craig, 'Note on the Home of *Ludus Coventriae*', pp. 72–83, and *English Religious Drama of the Middle Ages* (Oxford, 1967, rpt. of 1955 edn.), pp. 265–80, which includes unfortunate misstatements about the language of the cycle; H. Hartman, 'The Home of the "*Ludus Coventriae*"', *MLN* 41 (1926), 530ff.; R. S. Loomis, 'Lincoln as a Dramatic Centre', *Mélanges d'histoire du théâtre du moyen âge* (Paris, 1950), pp. 241–7; Kenneth Cameron and Stanley J. Kahrl, 'The N-Town Plays at Lincoln', *Theatre Notebook* 20 (1965–6), 61–9, and 'Staging the N-Town Cycle', *Theatre Notebook* 21 (1967), 122–38, 152–65; and Claude Gauvin, *Un cycle du théâtre religieux anglais du moyen âge* (Paris, 1973), ch. 3. Kahrl's examination of the Lincoln dramatic archives produced no new records bearing on the provenance of N-town (*Records of Plays and Players in Lincolnshire, 1300–1585*, Malone Soc. 8 (Oxford, 1974), p. x). Alan H. Nelson questions the degree of dramatic activity at Lincoln in *The Medieval English Stage* (Chicago and London, 1974), pp. 100–18. The language of the N-town main scribe was identified as East Anglian by Greg in 1914 (*Problems*, p. 110), and the East Anglian character of the language in the cycle was confirmed by E. J. Dobson, 'The Etymology and Meaning of *Boy*', *Medium Ævum* 9 (1940), 152–3; Alarik Rynell, *The Rivalry of Scandinavian and Native Synonyms in Middle English* (Lund, 1948), p. 108; Mark Eccles, '*Ludus Coventriae* Lincoln or Norfolk?', *Medium Ævum* 40 (1971), 135–41; and Jacob Bennett, 'The Language and Home of the "*Ludus Coventriae*"', *Orbis* 22 (1973), 43–63, all of whom affirm that Norfolk was the home of the cycle. Angus McIntosh and Michael Samuels have confirmed the East Anglian nature of the language, and Richard Beadle has recently provided a detailed dialectal analysis of the cycle. See LANGUAGE below. No contemporaneous East Anglian archival references to N-town or its constituents have yet been identified. Peter Meredith cites a payment for an interlude, recorded in the East Harling church-wardens' accounts, as well as payments to performers at Thetford priory and allusions to 'games' in the area (*The Mary Play* (London and New York, 1987), pp. 9–10. See *Records of Plays and Players in Norfolk and Suffolk, 1330–1642*, eds David Galloway and John Wasson, Malone Society Collections, Vol. XI (Oxford, 1980/81)).

times in rhyme, confirms the notion of composition and performance in that region (see *Handwriting* and LANGUAGE). Whether or not the plays were ever itinerant, the eclecticism and revision of the text imply a permanent home that served as the base for compilation and alteration over time. Several scholars have suggested Norwich as this home, though a case has recently been made for Bury St Edmunds.[1]

The codex was probably transcribed between *c.* 1468 and the early years of the sixteenth century. Marginal notations show that the plays continued to be revised and expanded after the manuscript was copied out (see *Handwriting* and DATE below). Around 1540, N-town may have exerted some literary influence on the poet Nicholas Grimald. According to George Coffin Taylor, Grimald apparently either read or saw acted parts of the cycle portraying the Resurrection, and incorporated elements from N-town in his *Christus Redivivus.*[2] Despite substantial differences between the texts, that poem does exhibit several parallels to the depiction of the four guards in N-town 34 and 35. Taylor proposes that Grimald's access to the manuscript was in some way connected with Myles Blomefylde, an early owner of the Digby plays, who came to Cambridge at about the same time that Grimald left there to go to Oxford. It is worth noting that Grimald wrote *Christus Redivivus* at Oxford, for it is there that the N-town manuscript next appears.

A century or more after its transcription, the codex came into the possession of Robert Hegge (*c.* 1597–1629), a Durham man who became a prominent member of Corpus Christi College, Oxford.[3]

[1] Though offering no opinion on the question of dialect, Chambers suggested in 1903 that the 'N' might stand for Norwich (*Mediaeval Stage* 2: 421; by 1945, in *Literature at the Close of the Middle Ages*, p. 47, he supported the idea that the dialect is East Anglian). Dobson (p. 153) called Chambers' suggestion 'as certain as such things can ever be', and Norman Davis ('The Language of the Pastons', *Proc. of the British Academy* 40 (1954), 133) and Bennett (p. 43) concur. Cf. Nelson, pp. 119–37. On admittedly slight evidence, Madeleine Hope Dodds tentatively suggested Bury St Edmunds as the home of the manuscript ('The Problem of the "Ludus Coventriae"', *MLR* 9 (1914), 91). Chambers dismissed the tradition that John Lydgate, monk of Bury, was the author of the plays (*Mediaeval Stage* 2: 145 and *Literature at the Close of the Middle Ages*, p. 49), and Block (p. xlvii) cited points of disagreement between Lydgate's *Life of Our Lady* and N-town. The cycle does bear many linguistic and thematic affinities to Lydgate's work, however. Gail McMurray Gibson has recently reopened the case, linking the cycle to Bury St Edmunds and citing Lydgate's possible influence on the plays ('Bury St. Edmunds, Lydgate, and the N-Town Cycle', *Speculum* 56 (1981), 56–90).

[2] George Coffin Taylor, 'The *Christus Redivivus* of Nicholas Grimald and the Hegge Resurrection Play', *PMLA* 41 (1926), 840–59. See also Patricia Abel, 'Grimald's *Christus Redivivus* and the Digby Resurrection Play', *MLN* 70 (1955), 328–30, and Ruth H. Blackburn, 'Nicholas Grimald's *Christus Redivivus*: A Protestant Resurrection Play', *ELN* 5 (1968), 247–50.

[3] See my 'Provenance of the N-town Codex', *Library*, 6th ser., 1 (1979), 28–33.

Hegge may have received the manuscript from his father, Stephen Hegg, a Durham notary public who gave him at least two other medieval manuscripts. Or he may have obtained it from Thomas Allen, who befriended him at Oxford, and who included in his large collection of manuscripts one written by Hegge.[1] K. S. Block (p. xxxvii) writes that the codex 'is supposed to have been acquired in 1629 by Sir Robert Bruce Cotton's first librarian, Richard James, on the death in that year at Oxford of Robert Hegge, a member of James' own college, Corpus Christi'. James may have acquired the book for the Cottons, but not necessarily in 1629, since the transfer would presumably have had to have taken place between June, the month of Hegge's death, and November, when Cotton and James were imprisoned and the library was sealed. In view of the suddenness of Robert's death and the legal entanglements that ensued, it is unlikely that his possessions could have been dispersed in so short a time. In addition, a seventeenth-century inscription on f. 111[v] indicates that the manuscript may not have passed directly to Cotton. It may instead have remained in the Hegge family for a time, having perhaps been acquired by Robert's brother Stephen, who bought Robert's possessions after his brother's death. The inscription (which was misread by Block) says 'Tho: Kinge the yownger / Hath demised'.[2] Sharp MS 13 in the Durham Cathedral Library contains a reference to a Thomas Kinge who married the daughter of Stephen Hegg. The Thomas Kinge the younger of the N-town inscription may very well have been their son, who died in the middle of February 1633/4; this may be the *terminus ad quem* for the inscription.[3]

The catalogue of the Cottonian collection dated at 1621 omits the N-town codex, but the next catalogue, of between 1631 and 1638, includes it. The manuscript was first catalogued not as Vespasian

[1] Allen bequeathed most of his manuscripts to his former student Sir Kenelm Digby, owner of the Digby plays (Andrew G. Watson, 'Thomas Allen of Oxford and his manuscripts', in *Medieval Scribes, Manuscripts and Libraries*, eds M. B. Parkes and Andrew G. Watson (London, 1978), p. 279). Donald C. Baker *et al.* say that the codex containing those plays is a typical Allen–Digby book, but note that the plays are not mentioned in Bryan Twynne's catalogue of the Allen library (*The Late Medieval Religious Plays of Bodleian MSS Digby 133 and E Museo 160*, EETS os 283 (1982), p. x).

[2] Block, p. xxxvi. I am grateful to Dr A. I. Doyle for his generous assistance in identifying Kinge.

[3] Norman Davis thinks it probable that this inscription consists of Kinge's signature followed by the unrelated 'Hath demised', and observes that Kinge would probably not have signed the book while it belonged to Robert Hegge. Read as a single clause, Davis notes, the inscription could refer to a bequest by Kinge, and so imply his death ('Provenance of the N-town Cycle', *Library*, 6th ser., 2 (1980), 333–4).

D. 8, but as D. 9, with the manuscript now known as Caligula A. 2 having been labelled Vespasian D. 8. The Caligula manuscript bears the mark 'Vespasian D. 8' on f. 3r, and was given that shelf-mark in the Cotton library catalogue of sometime before 1654 (Add. MS 36682, B). Immediately below this entry in the catalogue comes the description of the N-town codex, opposite a mark that originally read 'D. 9'. The '9' was altered in a different coloured ink to an '8', the present number of the codex, presumably after the earlier D. 8 was moved to the Caligula shelf and its entry as a Vespasian manuscript was cancelled. This appears to resolve the long-standing question of why William Dugdale referred to the N-town codex in the *Antiquities of Warwickshire Illustrated* (1656) as 'Vesp. D. 9'. Block (p. xxxix) thought that this was either an error or an indication that the manuscript was stored in two parts, as D. 8 and D. 9. But the simple truth seems to be that Dugdale examined the manuscript before the 'D. 9' had been altered to 'D. 8'. And in fact, Sharp (p. 6) reports that Dugdale was introduced to the Cotton manuscripts in 1638, and the *DNB* records that Dugdale used the Cotton library in 1652.[1]

Physical make-up

The codex is a quarto in a British Museum binding of 1907,[2] with leaves cut and separately mounted on guards, save for a few bifolia, which are mounted on single guards. It comprises a flyleaf and 225 leaves consisting of at least seven kinds of paper, trimmed to approximately 200–205 mm. by 135–40 mm. Folios 92 and 93 are much narrower, 124 mm. and 118 mm. wide respectively. Quires A and B consist of paper with a Bunch of Grapes watermark measuring about 61 × 11[26.5|27]10; its twin measures 68 × 14[25|32]4.5 and its design is in part horizontally inverted.[3] The paper of quires C-D, F-M (with the

[1] See Craig, 'Note on the Home of *Ludus Coventriae*', p. 73. Dr. Richard Beadle has brought to my attention the fact that the N-town codex appears to have been one of eight manuscripts from the Cotton Library that were on loan to John Selden (see D. M. Barratt, 'The Library of John Selden and Its Later History', *Bodleian Library Record* 3 (1950–51), 135.

[2] In their introduction to the facsimile of N-town, Peter Meredith and Stanley J. Kahrl quote correspondence from W. H. Kelliher, who notes the date of the binding and reports that there is no record of an earlier binding or of the original collation (*The N-town Plays* (Leeds, 1977), p. xiv).

[3] The watermark measurements indicate (in millimeters) first the mark's height, then, within square brackets, its width. Vertical bars within square brackets denote that the mark is split by chain lines; in such instances, the numbers surrounding the vertical bars indicate the width of the mark on each side of the chain lines. The numbers to the right and left of the square brackets measure the distance of the mark from the surrounding chain lines. See *Essays in Paper Analysis*, ed. Stephen Spector (Washington, London, Toronto, 1987), pp. 10–11.

exception of the interpolated ff. 95, 96, and 112), V, and W (except for the interpolated Assumption of Mary play, on ff. 213–22) contains a YHS in a Sun watermark measuring about 42 × 2[36.5|5]; its twin measures 44.5 × [3.5|37.5|2]. Quire E bears the mark of a one-armed Pot surmounted by a cross, measuring about 40 × 5[15]5. Folios 95 and 96, mounted uncut as a bifolium, bear a long, graceful Hand watermark surmounted by a pentangle, with a 'B' or some similar form at the palm and a bit of lacing at the wrist. It measures about 70 × 1[20]7. Folio 112, which seems to have been interpolated along with ff. 95–6, is unwatermarked, but its chain lines are similar to those of the two earlier leaves. The paper of quires N and P-R in Passion Play 1 has the mark of a Bull's Head surmounted by an 'X'. It measures about 74 × 2[32]8, while the twin, which differs slightly in design, measures about 70 × 7[29]6. Folio 151 in the interpolated O quire carries a portion of a Bunch of Grapes watermark, and the entire quire appears to consist of this paper stock. The paper of quires S and T, constituting Passion Play 2, bears a Two Crossed Keys watermark. One of the twins measures about 47 × 14.5[16.5|25.5]4.5, the other (which differs in minor details) about 51 × 6[24|18]15. Folios 143 and 184–5, interpolated in Passion Plays 1 and 2 respectively, are unwatermarked, but their chain lines resemble those of the Bunch of Grapes or YHS in a Sun paper. The ten leaves of the interpolated Play 41, the 'Assumption of Mary', carry a Two-Wheeled Cart watermark. The twins, which differ slightly in design, measure about 69 × 12.5[19|22]8 and about 69 × 12[20|20]10.[1] For the dates of similar designs in watermark albums, see DATE below.

Most of the original signatures have been cut away. Signatures that survive include *b* on f. 42, *d* on f. 70, +*1* on f. 164, +*2* on f. 165, +*4* on f. 167, +*5* on f. 168, +*6* on f. 169, and *a4* on f. 183.[2] Catchwords appear on the final leaves of quires B (f. 40^{v}), N (f. 148^{v}, see the note to 27/141–268), S (f. 179^{v}), and T (f. 189^{v}). Foliation runs from 1–225.[3] Verso-sides

[1] Block (p. xii) mistakenly observed that the Shield watermark on the flyleaf of the codex is the same as that on the paper of the 1621 Cotton library catalogue. The design of this mark, which Meredith and Kahrl (p. xvi) compare to Heawood 1218, is similar to the one in the catalogue, but they are not the same.

[2] First reported by Meredith and Kahrl (p. xiv), who read *d4* on f. 70. I cannot confirm their reading of a *c* on f. 56, which would be the only signature that does not correctly indicate its place in its quire.

[3] Block (p. xi) says that the foliation is in a modern hand. Meredith and Kahrl (p. xxvii n. 2) reject Gauvin's conclusion (p. 18) that the folio numbers were written by the same hand as 'The plaie called Corpus Christi' on f. 1, considering it more probable that the numbering is contemporary with the quire lettering.

are numbered by tens in another hand. Blank leaves are ignored in this sequence, resulting in progressively larger discrepancies between these numbers and those on the recto-sides: ff. 9^v–49^v are numbered 10–50, 60^v–110^v are numbered 60–110, 121^v–161^v are numbered 120–60, 172^v–212^v are numbered 170–210, and 223^v is numbered 220.[1]

Later, perhaps Cottonian, quire-marks appear (A–W, excluding I and U), but the quiring they indicate is very odd: according to these marks, six gatherings contain only two leaves each, while others consist of three, eight, ten, thirteen, fourteen, sixteen, seventeen, nineteen, and twenty leaves. Much of this irregularity was caused by interpolation and the loss of leaves, as indicated by the pattern of watermark distribution within gatherings.[2] The collation may be represented as: π^1 A–B^{20} C^8 D/F^{16} E^2 (interpolated) G^{20} (–G16) H^{15} + two (ff. 95–6 interpolated after H9) J^{20} + one (f. 112 interpolated after J9; wants J10, 11) K–L^2 M^{10} N^{12} + one (f. 143 interpolated after N7) O^3 P–Q^2 R^8 S^{16} T^8 + two (ff. 184–5 interpolated after T4) V^{20} W^6 + ten (ff. 213–22, the 'Assumption', interpolated after W3).[3]

The insertion of E quire divided the existing gathering into two, now designated as D and F, with two leaves and fourteen leaves respectively. Before this, D/F contained at least sixteen leaves, and the watermark distribution suggests that it originally may have been a twenty. The watermark pattern within H indicates that that gathering may have lost four leaves after the Shepherds play (enough room to include a play, possibly the 'Purification of Mary') and one leaf where the interpolated ff. 95–6 now stand. The reconstruction of the original quire may be represented as follows:[4]

[1] The blank leaves occurring before each shift in the verso numbering are ff. 52, 120, 164, and 213. The verso-enumerator evidently counted the blank f. 105 by mistake. See Meredith and Kahrl, p. viii.

[2] See my 'Symmetry in Watermark Sequences' (*Studies in Bibliography* 31 (1978), 162–78) for a discussion of the analysis of watermark sequences, with specific application to the present manuscript.

[3] The pattern in the watermark sequence permits Meredith and Kahrl's hypothesis (p. xiv) of a single quire KL, but other conclusions are possible. In the case of quires D and F, for example, a two-leaf interpolation separated two leaves from the rest of the quire, resulting in a pattern similar to this one. The same may apply to quires P, Q, and R (see p. xxii n. 3).

[4] 'WM' here signifies the watermark. As is typical of quartos, the marks are split, with the complementary portions represented here by 'W' and 'M' and the twins distinguished by the subscripts '1' and '2'. Dashes indicate unwatermarked leaves. Asterisks signify hypothetical elements. The 'r' and 'v' above folio numbers show which side, the recto or verso, is the mould side. See Spector, 'Symmetry in Watermark Sequences', pp. 163–8.

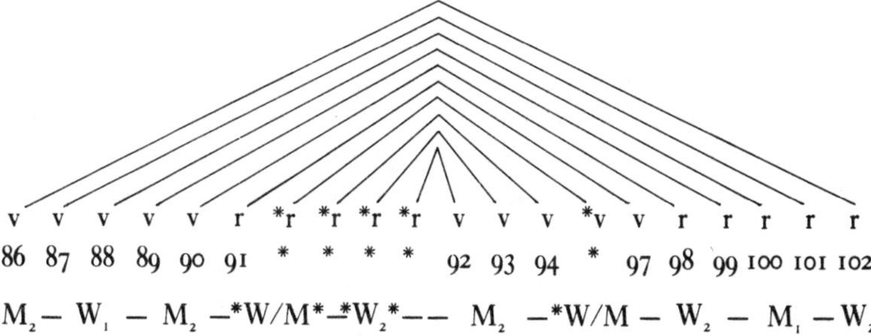

The loss of four leaves would account for the absence of a Play 17.[1] It would also explain the extreme cropping of ff. 92 and 93, which in this arrangement would have stood at the centre of the gathering, and might well have come loose when the four leaves immediately preceding them (including their two conjugate leaves) were excised; when the manuscript was trimmed, the outer margins of ff. 92 and 93 would have been cut away more drastically than those of other leaves. The watermark patterns also suggest that quire N may want four leaves, O may want an initial leaf, and W and the Assumption play may each want initial and final leaves.

In sum, two paper stocks, Bunch of Grapes and YHS in a Sun, constitute most of the gatherings, several of which (A, B, J, V, also possibly D/F and H) are twenties.[2] The Passion Plays, which appear to be additions to the codex, and the interpolated 'Assumption of Mary', consist of different paper types in shorter gatherings. Their inclusion, along with the minor interpolations, created the patchwork effect that now exists.

Stains and wear on the following folios indicate that they were once stored separately, probably as outside leaves: 136, the first leaf of Passion Play 1 (rubbed and soiled); 151[v], the final leaf of the interpolated O quire (three elongated triangular stains); 164, the flyleaf of Passion Play 2 (a similar triangular stain); and 213, the flyleaf of the interpolated Assumption of Mary play (a stain that penetrates several leaves into the play).

[1] See the headnote to Play 17. Folios 95–6 contain more text than would typically have fit on a single leaf, but see the note to 18/221–302.

[2] Of the short quires not yet discussed, C and M occur at points of textual transition, and W is the final gathering. See Spector, 'Symmetry in Watermark Sequences', pp. 175–6.

Handwriting

Scribe A, the main scribe, wrote in an Anglicana hand that most experts consider typical of the mid-fifteenth century or slightly thereafter, though one authority suggests a date several decades later.[1] The main scribe employed both *þ* and *th* in initial position, and, though he preferred initial *ȝ*, he very occasionally used *y* (for discussion of the scribes' orthographic practices, see LANGUAGE below). He normally wrote *þ*^{t}, and *w*^{t}, which are here expanded to *þat* and *wiþ*. He often raised a letter above the line without indicating omission, as in *þ*^{e}, *þ*^{i}, and words like *boþ*^{e}; I treat *þ*^{u} as *þu* in consideration of the scribe's preference when writing the word in full. He placed the vowel above the line when omitting *r*, as in *p*^{i}*de*, *p*^{i}*se*, and *p*^{a}*yth*, and a *t* above the line as a pr. 3 sg. marker in *cheu*^{t} for *cheuyth* (32/158). He used the common abbreviations of the period, including signs for *and*, *per* or *par*, *pre*, *pro*, *ur*(*e*), *us*, *yr* or *er*, and *ys*. The flourish on *r* appears to render *re*. A dotted circumflex or horizontal stroke typically signals omission of a nasal or of *y* in *-cyon*, as well as contraction of Latin words, though these signs are sometimes otiose. Other abbreviation marks appear to be without significance. Meredith and Kahrl observe that the tag on final *d* seems to be functional only in *viridi* (4/249 s.d.).

This scribe copied out most of the codex, and is thought to have rubricated the entire manuscript, including the interpolated 'Assumption of Mary', which he may also have corrected.[2] The markedly more untidy and irregular quality of his writing in the Passion Plays indicates that he copied them out at a different time from the bulk of the manuscript, a conclusion confirmed by evidence adduced below (see pp. xviii–xxi, xxxiv, and 541 note 1). Block (p. xv) notes that he used exceptionally large capitals in Passion Play 1, as well as a few especially tall letters in top lines,[3] and that he wrote *þe* instead of *þ*^{e} more often

[1] Greg considers the hand compatible with the date 1468 on f. 100^{v} (*The Assumption of the Virgin. A Miracle Play from the N-town Cycle* (Oxford, 1915), p. 6). Block (p. xv) takes the hand to be probably of the third quarter of the fifteenth century, and C. E. Wright concurs (*English Vernacular Hands from the Twelfth to the Fifteenth Centuries* (Oxford, 1960), plate 23). M. B. Parkes, however, dates the main scribe's hand no earlier than the 1490s ('s. xv ex or s. xv/xvi': private correspondence and Meredith and Kahrl, p. xxvii n. 4).

[2] Greg, *Problems*, p. 114, *Assumption of the Virgin*, p. 7; Block, pp. xvii, xix, and 361. Parkes concurs in identifying the main scribe's hand in a marginal notation in this play (correspondence). See Peter Meredith's 'A Reconsideration of Some Textual Problems in the N-town Manuscript', *LSE* 9 (1977), 42–7. The line attributed to the main scribe is 41/214.

[3] This practice may be functional on ff. 153^{v} and 154, where the tall top lines may note

than was his practice elsewhere in the manuscript. His writing is slightly more regular in Passion Play 2. The interpolated leaves 143 in Passion Play 1 and 184–5 in Passion Play 2 are written in the firmer hand typical of the main scribe's work in the bulk of the codex. This scribe also seems to have written the Textura script in several speaker headings and Latin passages, notably in Plays 9, 11, 13, and 19, and in the marginal genealogies on ff. 16ᵛ–18, 21–22ᵛ, and 37–37ᵛ.

Three other scribes, here designated B, C, and D, made substantial contributions. B wrote the interpolated f. 51 in a rough business or clerical Anglicana hand that probably dates from the late fifteenth or early sixteenth century.[1] B employed *y* rather than *ȝ*, and *th* rather than *þ*. Several of his abbreviation marks are similar to the main scribe's, others are mere appendages.

C's writing is of the same sort as B's, and is perhaps of similar date.[2] His *v* and *w* are Secretary forms, and his single-compartment *a* is a current version of the Secretary form. This scribe used initial *y* frequently, but normally *ȝ* in *ȝe*, and *þ* (in the *y* form) as well as *th.* He made the only use in the codex of the abbreviation for *com*, in *company* (22/19 on f. 112).[3] C took a particular interest in the Shepherds, Magi, and Innocents plays (16, 18,and 20), altering patches of words in each (often apparently in order to ameliorate the diction), and interpolating ff. 95–6 into the Magi play in the place of earlier text (see p. xxxviii note 1 and the note to 18/221–302). C also interpolated f. 112, the first leaf of the Baptism play (see note to 22/1–53). And he wrote several marginal revisions and additions later in the manuscript. Interestingly, he drew upon an expanded version of the Harrowing of Hell plays (33 and 35), referring to at least one character and to text that are not represented in the plays as we have them: he apparently incorporated a part for Anima Caym in Play 35, and referred to text not recorded by the main scribe. C may also have written the marginal note introducing Anima Latronis into Play 33. In addition, C seems to have referred to an expanded version of the Three Marys play (36): the

the juxtaposition of two unusually short quires. Q quire may in fact be an interpolation; see Spector, 'Symmetry in Watermark Sequences', pp. 173–4.

[1] Parkes dates B's hand as 's. xviⁱ' (correspondence).

[2] Block (p. xvi) considers C's hand to be from the same period as the main scribe's. But Brown and Doyle say that it may be of the late fifteenth or early sixteenth century, and, as Meredith and Kahrl (p. xxvii n. 6) report, Parkes puts it in the first quarter of the sixteenth century.

[3] Block (p. xliii) suggests that a misreading of this contraction in the word 'considerynge' may have resulted in the unintelligible 'hese juge' of 13/34. Meredith's emendation to 'he, seynge' is far more persuasive, however ('A Reconsideration', pp. 35–9).

lines he wrote for the Marys on ff. 197^{v} and 198^{r} in that play, and the alterations he made in existing speeches, make the women refer to the risen Christ's personal appearance to them, a scene that is not depicted in the text (cf. Matt. 28: 9–10). C also may have been the scribe who wrote 'finem 1^{a} die Nota' on f. 196, evidently denoting a break in the performance, and perhaps an attempt to segment the cycle.[1] And C apparently wrote the notations 'vade worlych' and 'nota worlych', presumably references to an actor, in Play 38 (f. 207).

D wrote the 'Assumption of Mary', Play 41. His Anglicana hand is mixed with Secretary elements (cf. the single-compartment *a* and the horned *g*), and may be at least as early as the main scribe's. He never used *ȝ*, the only instance of this letter in Play 41 being found in line 214, which may have been added by the main scribe. D normally wrote *th*, using *þ* (in the *y* form) in only a few instances, and the earlier form (*þ*) even less often.[2] He made less use of abbreviation than did the other scribes.

Minor revisions and additions by other hands appear throughout much of the manuscript. Speaker headings, stage directions, and text are altered or supplied, and portions of text are copied. A reviser wrote the speaker heading 'Mulier' on f. 124^{v} in Play 24, for example, to clarify the fact that the contrition in lines 209–16 is uttered by the adulteress rather than by Scriba, the preceding speaker. Possibly the same reviser wrote the speaker heading 'Doctor' on f. 126, thereby attributing the closing speech to an expositor rather than the original speaker, Jesus.[3] 'Angelus' has been written in the margins of ff. 97^{v} and 101^{v}, shortly before the angel's appearances in the Purification and Innocents plays (19 and 20). A reviser's marginal notes evidence still another reference to a different version of a play from the one in the codex: this reviser wrote the stage directions 'here enterith (?) þe fyrst prophete' and 'here entreth þe parte off þe ij^{de} prophete' at the feet of ff. 144^{v} and 145 respectively in the 'Entry into Jerusalem', a play that includes no prophets. The introduction of prophets may have grown

[1] Meredith and Kahrl (p. xxiv) propose that C tried to divide the Resurrection plays into two units, with the first day's presentation running from C's 'nota Incipit hic' on f. 189 to the present notation. The 'nota Incipit hic' occurs in the midst of a play (at 34/158), however, and it may pertain instead to the parts of Cayphas, Pylat, *et al.*, whose action begins at that point, following the Burial scene.

[2] The earlier form appears in *þat* (41/242) and *þi* (41/342). Block (p. xvii) observes that this form occurs elsewhere in the manuscript only in the marginal notes by a reviser on ff. 144^{v} and 145.

[3] A similar change seems to have occurred at the opening of Play 11: see the note to 11/1–32.

out of the apostle John's reference on f. 144^{v} to Jesus' entry on an ass as fulfilling 'þe prophetys prophesé' (26/426). Of the text that has been copied by other hands, the most substantial is the section of Magdalene's speech on f. 200^{v}, which someone has rewritten on the next page. There are also many scribblings, some of which Block (p. xxxvi) attributes to irreverent schoolboys. A cipher is written on f. 119^{v}; the first letters look like *πίστα τε* with the accent misplaced or *πυστα τε* 'things trustworthy' or 'things learnt' (Professor Nicholas Hammond, correspondence).

Several names are inscribed in the margins, including: of þe Vyn / R. Wych(e?) (f. 57^{v}); William (Wylliam) Dere (ff. 91^{v}, 136); Polerd, John Hasycham, and John Taylphott of Parish / Bedonson, with the motto 'wee that will not / when we paie when we would / we shall saie (?) nay' on f. 91^{v}; John and hary Hol(l)ond on ff. 151^{v}, 153^{v}, and 155^{v}; hollond on f. 152^{v}; and the names John and Wylliam (sometimes incomplete) on ff. 21^{v}, 91^{v}, 147^{v}, 164^{v}, 179, 180^{v}, 210^{v}, 213^{v}.[1] The name Worlych, mentioned above, is written in the margins of the *Peregrini* play. Richard Beadle notes that all of the fifteenth- and sixteenth-century instances of this name cited in P. H. Reaney's *Dictionary of British Surnames* are from East Anglian sources, and adds that virtually all appearances of the name in wills registered at Bury St Edmunds and Norwich for that period are restricted to a narrow area of south central Norfolk and north Suffolk.[2]

A sixteenth-century hand wrote 'The plaie called Corpus Christi' at the head of f. 1. Robert Hegge's name followed by 'Dunelmensis' appears on f. 10. Though largely cropped, the original inscription may have read 'Liber Roberti Hegge Dunelmensis', like that in another of Hegge's books, MS Titus D. 5. His initials are written on f. 164, the flyleaf of Passion Play 2: 'Ego R. H. Dunelmensis possideo' above the motto, *οὐ κτησις ἀλλὰ χρησις*. Meaning 'Not possession but use', this motto appears in Aristotle's *Nicomachean Ethics*. As noted above, the

[1] Block (p. xxxvi) suggests that the oddness of John Taylphott's name throws doubt on the name of the parish, and notes that no record of a parish Bedonson has been found. She adds that the name John Holland of Brabant and a motto similar to the one on f. 91^{v} appear among the scribblings in the Chester plays, MS Add. 10305. Meredith and Kahrl (p. xxv) read the name Evosund (?) on f. 91^{v}. McIntosh, Samuels, and Michael Benskin associate the name John Hasycham with Hassingham, which is 7½ miles from Norwich (*A Linguistic Atlas of Late Mediaeval English* (Aberdeen, 1986), 3: 339).

[2] H. R. L. Beadle, 'The Medieval Drama of East Anglia: Studies in Dialect, Documentary Records and Stagecraft', York Ph.D., 1977, 1: 89–90. Cameron and Kahrl identify this name with William Worleyge of Weston ('Staging the N-Town Cycle', pp. 133–4).

description of the cycle on the flyleaf of the codex was written by Richard James, Sir Robert Bruce Cotton's librarian. The mark 'Vespasian D. 8.' was inscribed on the flyleaf, apparently by the same hand that wrote 'Caligula A. 2' in that manuscript (see p. xviii above).

Layout

Most plays begin on a fresh page, but plays 2, 3, and 5 follow immediately after preceding plays, as do all plays within the Passion Play segments (except for the 'Procession of Saints'), as well as the Harrowing and Resurrection plays up to Play 37. Plays 4–6 begin with 'Introitus' and a title; 24–5, 38–9, and 42 start with 'Hic' or 'Hic incipit' and a title; 21 is preceded by 'Modo de doctoribus disputantibus . . .', and 40 by 'Modo de die Pentecostes'. Plays 5–7 and 37 conclude with 'Explicit', in all instances but the first with a title. Rubricated play numbers normally mark the beginning of each play, but the play-number '10' appears twice, both at Contemplacio's speech on f. 48 and at the head of the play proper on f. 49. The Summoner's prologue to Play 14 appears prior to the play-number for the body of the play on f. 75. Since ff. 95–6 and 112, written by C, are not rubricated, Play 22, which begins with f. 112, is the only play in the collection that lacks a play-number.

There is no visible line ruling. Most complete pages contain 26 to 30 lines each, though the number varies from fewer than 20 to above 30. The Proclamation, for example, averages over 29 lines per page, while Play 11 averages fewer than 23, with only 17 lines on f. 63^{v}. The main scribe normally wrote each verse as a distinct line, but in thirteeners and tail-rhyme stanzas he often wrote the bob at the right; Scribe C also occasionally followed this practice in recording tail-rhyme. In several instances the main scribe wrote short-lined stanzas two lines as one, or even three as one, divided by double virgules or by a tick and comma. Speaker headings normally appear at the right of the verse throughout the manuscript, and at the foot of the preceding page when a speech begins at the top of a page. Some speaker headings in the Passion Plays are written above the speeches, however, as are the rubricated speakers' names at the start of the Pentecost play (40). A few brief extrametrical utterances are written to the right of speaker headings (8/116, 9/73, 10/237). Rhyme brackets are written at the right, and a large tick and comma is sometimes used to indicate that the stanza is continued on the following page (e.g. on ff. 63^{v}, 185, 189^{v}).

Stage directions are usually written across the page, though they too sometimes appear at the right.

Various reference marks are drawn in the left margins to indicate the proper placement of interpolations, as for example on ff. 48ᵛ and 51 in Play 10. Letters appear in the left margin to signal the proper order of speeches, such as the Bishop's speeches in Play 10 and the Shepherds' in 16. The letters 'a' and 'b' are sometimes written at the left to indicate that lines are inverted in the manuscript (e.g. Pr 356–7, 41/149–50, 216–17). Pointing appears in many plays. Block (pp. xxvi–xxvii) observes that it is especially frequent in the Contemplacio group of Marian plays (8, 9, 11, 13), the Purification play (19), the Passion Plays up to f. 184, and segments that she identifies as additions to the original cycle: the Lamech episode in Play 4, the cherry tree scene in Play 15. She also notes systematic pointing in certain speeches of a declamatory character. Pointing indicates internal rhyme within an octave in 10/186–90. Meredith and Kahrl (p. xxii) note that the main scribe used pointing to indicate natural speech pauses, after exclamations, to divide lists, to mark contrastive words and phrases, to divide Latin from English, and to clarify awkward readings.

Rubrication

Rubricated lines appear beneath most stage directions and play titles, and looped red lines normally underscore speaker headings.[1] Play numbers are also rubricated, as are the numbers of the Commandments in Play 6. Occasional whole words are written in red, notably in 27/381, which the main scribe wrote at the foot of f. 154, and the speaker headings at the beginning of Play 40. The genealogies at the feet of ff. 16ᵛ–18, 21–22ᵛ, and 37ᵛ also contain rubricated words. Initial capitals are rubricated at the opening of many plays, and in the Gradual Psalms (Play 9), the 'Magnificat' (Play 13), and the 'Procession of Saints'. Red capitals are used in a few other instances as well, including the speaker's name 'Gabriel' in 11/213 and the words 'Ave', 'Benedictus', and 'Magnificat' in Contemplacio's conclusion (13/152A, 171A, 172A, and 185A). Block (p. xxv) observes that the red capitals of the 'Procession of Saints' are drawn more carefully than is most of the rubrication in the codex. She adds that the rhyme-brackets

[1] Initial speaker headings in plays are often underscored by a simple red line or are not underlined when preceded by capitula or written in decorative script. The speaker's name in 23/1 is enclosed by a red line and square bracket rather than the normal loop.

there are neatly drawn in red, in contrast to the dark ink normally used to link rhyme in the cycle.[1] Red strokes are frequently added to the initial letters in lines, to some letters in other positions, and often to the double virgules and tick and comma marks used when two or three lines are written as one. Rubrication is also used in corrections, for the three crosses in 8/115, and for reference marks, such as the signs which stand before 1/39 s.d., 2/282 s.d., 8/97 s.d., and two couplets spoken by Jesus (31/133 and 135).

Rubricated capitula precede new stanzas, though such marks are sometimes inaccurate or wanting. Couplets in Passion Play 2 and the Assumption of Mary play (41) are marked by a marginal red a, and versicle marks in the Assumption play, and in 33/24 s.d. (f. 185v) are also in red.[2] A red sign is used in Play 41 to mark single lines concatenated by rhyme to contiguous stanzas. Capitula appear in other capacities as well, especially at the start of plays: they stand before many initial speaker headings, before the stage direction at the opening of Play 10, before 'Introitus Moyses' in Play 6, 'Modo de Pentecostes' in 40, and 'Hic incipit' in 42. A capitulum marks the first line of Play 24, which is written on the same line as the title, and other capitula set off words whose proper location might otherwise be unclear (e.g. 'testimonium' in 6/154a, 'Veryly' in 8/245). Capitula also stand before some speaker headings written atop speeches (rather than in the normal position at the right) in the Passion Plays.

Rubrication sometimes testifies to stages in the development of plays. At the opening of Play 11, for example, the rubricated '1us' and '2' evidently recall that Contemplacio's lines had originally been spoken by two prophets (see the note to 11/1–32). Very interestingly, rubrication also keeps track of the octaves and quatrains that make up the Marian plays (8, 9, 11, and 13; see p. 539 below). Beginning with 'Joachim and Anna' (Play 8), red dots are drawn in the loops of the capitula preceding such stanzas. In the Marriage play (10), the dots continue to appear in the capitula preceding octaves and quatrains, but never in the ones that stand before the thirteeners. This confirms

[1] Rubricated rhyme-brackets occasionally appear elsewhere in the manuscript, as in 10/61 and 65, 11/48a, and 41/53–6.

[2] A mark precedes quatrains at 13/162A and 26/65, an octave at 26/25, and four tail-rhyme stanzas at 34/302–25. (The tail-rhyme, written three lines as one, may have appeared to be couplets.) A similar black sign stands before many stage directions in Passion Plays 1 and 2. The couplet at 31/131 is preceded by a large capitulum; a mark stands before the subsequent two couplets, as noted above. A couplet in Play 41 (lines 151–2) is also preceded by a large capitulum.

the theory that the octaves and quatrains in Play 10 are connected with the surrounding Marian plays, and represent a different stratum from the thirteeners.[1] The rubrication, as noted above, is attributed to the main scribe.

LANGUAGE

The linguistic evidence indicates that the codex was recorded principally or exclusively by scribes trained in East Anglia. Rhymed dialect words suggest that some or all of the cycle was also composed in that region.

The reflex of OE *ā* is normally written *o* or *oo*, and typically rhymes on itself, though in several instances it appears in rhyme with the reflex of OE *ō* and occasionally with the reflex of OE *ēo*. Thus *gon* rhymes on *don* (5/254) and on *sone* 'soon' (12/118); *home*: *dome* (18/325), *non*: *don* (42/80) and *schon* (22/30); *rowe*: *growe*, *flowe*, *trowe* (5/220); *snowe*: *growe* (14/307), and *wo(o)*: *do* and *to* (2/277, 22/135, 27/142, etc.). Shortened *a* is retained in *haly* and *halwe* (6/100, 108, 111); cf. *halwyd* (10/449, 22/92). *Gan* in the sense 'to go', rhymes with *man*, *certayn*, *tan* (4/96). The minority form *knawe* rhymes several times on *lawe*, also on *awe* (9/234, 11/145, etc.), while *thrawe* appears once, also rhyming with *lawe* (26/240). Despite its spelling, *more* in Pr 122 rhymes with *Abyacar* and *war*, as well as *sore.* Scribe B wrote *knowyth* (10/170), C wrote *know* (18/242), *oon*, *oo* (18/249–50), and *euerychone* (22/34). D wrote *alon* rhyming on *Syon*, *on*, *Jordon* (41/20) and on *anon*, *fon* (41/43); *gone*: *done*, *anone*, *one* (41/212); and *more*: *thore*, *bore* 'borne' (41/219), but *euyrmare*: *declare*, *fare*, *care* (41/260).

OE *a* is normally retained, though it is written as *e* in *credyl* (14/198, 20/16; cf. OE **credel*) and in *qweke*: *freke*, *breke* (2/272, but see the note

[1] The dotting starts with C quire on f. 41 and continues until f. 62 in Play 11. Thereafter it occurs irregularly in Plays 11 and 13. Probably through a misunderstanding of the nature of the stanza, the capitulum before one octave in Play 10 lacks a dot (10/417). One quatrain in the play of Joseph's Doubt (12/17) has a dotted capitulum, perhaps indicating its source (see p. 540 n. 1). Dots appear in the capitula of 10-line stanzas at 12/137 and before the initial stanza of the Purification play (19), which, like the Marian plays, may be a late addition to the cycle (see p. 540); also in 19/187. The loop of the initial capitulum in Play 36 is decorated and dotted. The dotted capitula are noted in my 'Genesis of the N-Town Cycle' (Yale Ph.D. thesis, 1973), pp. 49–51, and 'The Composition and Development of an Eclectic Manuscript: Cotton Vespasian D. VIII', *LSE* 9 (1977), 71; they are also reported by Meredith and Kahrl, p. xvii. I have been unable to examine John Marshall's 'Staging of the Marian Group from the N-town Cycle', Leeds MA thesis, 1974.

to this line). In lengthening groups the sound is most often written *o*, and sometimes rhymes with the reflex of OE *o* (e.g. *hond*: *husbond* in 2/109, 128). But in 'hand(s)', the spelling with *a* occurs more than twice as often as *o*, and *hang*(*e*) and related spellings with *a* appear frequently, while *honge* and *hongyn* occur only once each (32/224: *longe*, 27/129). The minority form *lambe* occurs only twice (22/47, 27/349, neither instance in rhyme), and *stand*(*e*) and related forms with *a* appear 13 times (never in rhyme) as against 37 spellings with *o*, most often rhyming on *londe*, *sonde*, and *honde* (though *stond*: *ground* in 10/162). C wrote *old*: *tolde*, *bolde*, *kold* (18/221), *cold* (18/235), and *Beholde* (22/41). D wrote *hald*(*e*) (41/88, 473), *hand* (41/442), and *lond* (41/30).

OE *ī* is represented by *y* and sometimes *i*, but is lowered to *e* in *bete* (apparently meaning 'bite' 2/138), *lech* 'like' (21/40: *mech*; see the note to this line), *leke* 'like' (31/57 s.d.), and *thretty*(*e*) (Pr 492, 11/11). The spelling *ey* appears occasionally, as in *stey* (37/47, 39/47, beside *stye*), *vntey* (25/429: *wey*), and *wheyle* (26/173, beside *whyle*, *wyle*, *qwyle*, *wel*). C wrote *wese* 'wise' in 18/238. D often used spellings with *i*.

The reflex of OE *i* is usually written as *y*, sometimes as *i* or *u*, and frequently as *e*. 'Bring' is regularly spelled with *y*, with the exception of *brenge* (27/465), and 'find' is spelled with *y* except in the case of *fende* (19/91: *mankende*, *mende* 'mind', *kende* 'kind'). Spellings with *y* also dominate in *qwyk*(*e*) and its variants, while *qweke* appears twice (26/86, 29/172). 'Hither' and 'thither', by contrast, are spelled exclusively with *e*, as *hedyr* (D wrote *heder*) and *thedyr*, both rhyming on *togedyr* (15/157, 30/92, etc.). 'Live, lived', etc. are most often spelled with *e*, though spellings with *y* are common. The plural of 'limb' is spelled *lemys* twice (19/35, 36/29), while *lyme*, the singular form, occurs once (18/276). Spellings with *e* appear in the infinitive and other forms of *wete* 'to know', in rhyme with *fete* 'feet', *mete* 'meet', *suete* 'sweet', etc. (*o* and *oo* spellings also appear in the present indicative). In addition to *wyl*(*l*), *wol*(*e*), *woll*, and *will*, *wele* occurs several times, along with three instances of *wul*. The main scribe spelled 'bishop' only with a *u*, B wrote *beschoppys* (10/163), and D wrote *byschop* (41/397). In the pp., *dreve*, *drevyn*, *smet*(*e*), and *wrete*, *wretyn* appear. *i* is also lowered to *e* in words of French origin, such as *ceté*, *cetye* (along with *cyté*); *cevyle*, *sevyle*; *contenue*; *peté*, *pety* (but also *pyté*); *prevely*, *preuyly*, etc.; *prevy*; *velany*, *velony*(*e*); and *vesage*. B wrote *beschoppys* (cited above), C wrote *velany* (18/283) and *levyng* (22/7), and D wrote *byschop* (cited above), *levyng* (41/60, 69), *sengler* 'singular' (41/177), *heder* (41/207), *peler* 'pillar' (41/245), *peté* (41/291, 470), *prevely* (41/378), etc.

The reflexes of $\bar{\ae}^1$ and $\bar{\ae}^2$ are normally written *e* or *ee* and usually rhyme on each other and on the reflexes of OE *ē*, *$\overline{eo}$*, *ēa*, and *ȳ*, and very rarely *e*. *Dede* 'deed' rhymes on *dred*, *reed*, *spede* (2/143); also on *heyd* 'heed' (5/211), on *possede*, *sede*, *mede* (5/231), on *forbede*, *lede*, *rede* (6/180), etc. *dred(e)* rhymes on *hede* 'hide' (Pr 333); also on *dede* 'deed', *vnhede*, *hede* 'hide' (2/169), on *spede* (3/40), on *dede* 'dead', *brede* 'bread' (3/154), etc. It rhymes on *sted* (OE *stede*) as well as *ded* 'dead' and *reed* in 2/157. *lede* rhymes on *dede* 'deed', *forbede*, *rede* (6/183), on *spede*, *indede*, *kynrede* (13/165), and on *dede* 'deed', *drede*, *blede* (27/224). *mene*: *clene*, *bene*, *sene* (22/175), and *se* 'sea': *be*, *fle*, *me* and on *degré*, *powsté* (Pr 71, 2/105, 4/84). *rede*: *forbede*, *dede* 'deed', *brede* 'breed' in 4/58 as well as *dede* 'dead', *drede*, *Godhede* (25/399).

Many words containing the OE $\bar{\ae}^1$ and $\bar{\ae}^2$ are spelled with *a*, in some cases with shortening. The normal development of OE *ǣnig* is *any*, though *ony* occurs frequently. In addition to the majority form *led(de)*, a single instance of *lad* appears in rhyme with *had*, *sad*, *glad* (Pr 8). *las(se)* 'less' occurs as a minority form three times, rhyming on *Cleophas*, *pas*, *was* (Pr 470), and on *gres*, *pas* (36/22, cf. lines 17–19); in 14/376, *lesse* represents the majority spelling but rhymes with *grace*, *place*, *trespace.* Eight instances of the verb *last(e)* appear, with rhymes on *fast*, *cast*, *hast* 'haste' (27/105, 30/242, etc.); compare the nine instances of *lest(e)* (:*best* 'beast', *rest*, *west* in 2/47 and :*brest(e)* 'burst' in 8/170 and 28/162) and *lestyth.* Along with the majority forms *let(e)*, *lett* are eighteen instances of *lat(e)*, *latt*, none in rhyme. *Sprad* 'spread', pp., occurs twice, rhyming on *glad*, *fad* 'fed', *bad* (2/78) and on *glad* (38/299). A single instance of *þare* 'there' appears in 8/104, with rhyme on *are*, *bare*, *ware* 'were'; *þer(e)*, and *ther(e)* are the majority forms, but *thore* and *þore* occur several times in the Marian plays (D also used this form), often in rhyme with *bore*, *sore*, *beffore*, and *res(s)tore* (9/92, 11/61, 173, etc.). Along with *were*, the majority spelling of 'were', and beside *wore* and *worn*, there are three examples of *ware* rhyming on *are*, *bare*, *þare* (8/102) and on *care* (32/281, 35/181). *Wrastele* appears in 20/187. C wrote *clene* (22/46), *drede* (22/12), and *tech*: *spech*, *lech* (18/271). D wrote *bere* 'bier' (41/222, 364, etc.), *clennesse* (41/330), *helthe*: *felthe* 'filth' (41/465), *ony* (four times), *rede*: *nede* (41/317), *sprede*: *sede* (41/311), and *thore* rhyming on *lore* (41/139) and on *bore* (41/220).

The reflex of OE *ȳ* is usually written *y*, though often *e*, and occasionally *i* or *ey*. The main scribe usually spelled 'fire' as *fyre*, and three times *fyer(e)*, but twice he wrote *feyr* (Pr 57, 28/80 s.d.), and five times *fer(e)*, with rhymes on *prayere*, *cler*, *her* 'here' and on *presoner*, *daunger*, *here* 'hear' (8/174, 42/112). He wrote *fylth* twice, and usually spelled the verb 'hide' with a *y*, but he spelled it *heyde* once (4/197) and *hede* twice, rhyming on *drede* (Pr 329) and on *dede* 'deed', *vnhede* 'reveal', *drede* (2/171). He spelled 'pride' only with *y* and *i*, as *pryde* and *pride.* C wrote *drey* 'dry': *saye*, *eye* (18/228), *fyere* (22/9); and *hyde* (22/26). D wrote *hide* (41/84), but also *felthe* 'filth': *helthe*, *welthe* (41/469), and *fer* 'fire' (41/479).

The reflex of OE *y* is most often written *y*, but very frequently *e*, in several instances *i* or *u*, and sometimes *o*. *bylde* and *byldyd* appear once each (1/32, 4/93), while *belde* occurs once (1/35). 'Busy' is only spelled *besy* (8 instances); *besyly*, *besily*, and *bisyli* also occur. 'Bury' is most often *bery*(*e*), but also *burry* (cf. *burryenge*, *buryed*). The dominant spelling of 'did' is *dede*, though *dyd* and *dude* also appear. *dent* is the majority form of 'dint', with rhymes on *present*, *bent*, *rent*, and on *omnypotent* (18/63, 36/57); *dynt* appears once (31/2: *flynt*), and *dyntys* once (34/225). *fyrst* occurs 60 times, against only twice for *ferste* (both times written by D, in 41/18, 106). *kend*(*e*) and *mankend*(*e*) appear twice as often as the spellings with *y*; *kend*(*e*) rhymes on *fynde*, *blynde*, *bynde* (26/229), as well as on *sende* (11/191) and *ende* (9/266, 11/242, etc.). 'Kin' is usually *kyn*(*ne*), but in one instance *ken*: *men* (27/200). In addition to the majority form *lyst*(*e*) 'listen' appear three instances of *lest*(*e*), rhyming with *hest*, *prest*, *areste* (10/33), and with *brest*, *best*, *rest* (21/44). Thirty-six instances of *mend*(*e*) 'mind' occur, rhyming on words like *bynde* and *fynde* as well as *ende* and *frende* (*meende* occurs once, in 28/174: *rende*); *mynde* appears only nine times, and rhymes on words like *fynde* and *blynde*, but also on *wende*, *frende*, *ende* (25/274). 'Worm' and its inflected forms are spelled five times with *e* in the stem, four times with *o*, once with *u*, and once with *y*. Along with *kys*(*se*), *myrth*(*e*), and *shytt* 'shut' appear the less frequent spellings *cus*, *merth*(*e*), and *schet*. *knett* is one of the pp. forms of 'knit' (35/279: *fett*, *ssett*), and the pp. of 'stir' is written *steryd* (2/212, 9/125, etc.). 'Buy' is most often written *by*(*e*), rhyming on *mercy*, *ey*, *dye* (24/13) and on *glorye*, *deye*, *Caluarye* (25/453); in one instance it is *bey*: *deney* (26/106). C wrote *fyrst* (18/245) and *kynde* (18/259: *fende*, *defende*). D wrote *beryed* (41/20), *dede* 'did' (41/8, 290, 313), *dentis*: *ententis*, *schent is* (41/77), *ferste* (cited above), *kende*: *fende*, *hende*, *pretende* (41/159), *mende*: *kynde* (41/151), *mynde* (41/342), and *pet* (41/482, 487).

The reflex of earlier initial *hw* is most often *wh*, several times *w*, occasionally *h*, and frequently *qw*, *qwh*, or *qu*. Thus *qwall* 'whale' (7/72) occurs along with *whallys* (38/116); *whan* and *when* appear, but also *quan*, *qwhan*, *qwan* (12/16, 19/146 s.d., etc.); *what*(*h*) and *whatt*, beside *qwhat* and *qwat* (8/173, 27/515, etc.); *whelpe* along with *qwelp* (5/72); *wher*(*e*) and *were* 'where' beside *qwere* and *qwher* (11/149, 29/215, 37/35); *why* and *whi*, but also *qwy* and *qwhy* (12/100, 20/90, 25/171); *which*(*e*), *wech*(*e*), *whech*(*e*), etc., along with *qwych*(*e*), *qwhich*, *qweche* (25/197, 27/501, etc.); *whyl*(*l*), *whyle*, *wyle*, etc., but also *qwyl*(*e*) and *qwhyl* (8/100, 170, 31/1st s.d.); and *white*, *whyte*, *whyght* beside *qwyte* (2/23). 'Whether' and 'whose' are spelled only with *wh* and *w*, and 'who' and 'whoso' are only written with *h* and *wh*; but the only instance of 'whence' is spelled *qwens* (9/109). Compare *qwyppys* 'whips' (31/196). Such spellings with *q* appear very rarely early in the MS but are commoner in the Marian and Passion plays. They do not occur in text written by B and C. D wrote many words with *wh*, but also *qwyche* for 'which' (41/116, 167, 221).

OE *sc* is normally *sch* or *sh* initially, except in 'shall' and 'should', which are written *xal*, *xall*(*e*), *xul*, etc. in over a thousand instances. Fewer than one hundred spellings of 'shall' and 'should' with *sch* and *sh* appear, and most of these were written by D in Play 41, which includes no instances of initial *x*. Two other words in the text begin with *x*: *xad* ('shed', 27/485) and *xamefullest* (29/61). OE *sc* is sometimes represented in medial position by *ch*, *sc*, or *s*, as in *flescly*, *flesly* (beside *fleschly*, *fleshe*, etc.), and *lordchep* (6/8, 18/3, 20/254). These spellings also occur in some words of OF origin: *cheryse* (but also *cherysch*), *norch*, *norchyth* 'nourish' (along with *norsshere*), *parochonerys* 'parishioners', and *punchement*, *punchyth* 'punishment, punish'. *sc* also represents OE *s* initially in *scle*, *scloo*, *sclayne*, etc., (beside *sle*, *slo*, etc.), *sclepe* 'sleep', *sclepyr*, *sclyde* (but also *slyde*). 'Shall' and 'should' are not represented in the work of B. C wrote *xall*, *xulde*, etc., but *Shall* in 18/227. D, as noted above, never wrote initial *x*; he did write the two instances of *flech* in the cycle (41/230, 302).

An interesting orthographic development within the codex involves the reflex of OE *ht*, which shifts in the course of the MS from a preponderance of regional forms to *ght*. This spelling change occurs gradually, and so may be an example of progressive translation.[1] In the Proclamation and plays 1 to 3, the regional spellings *th*, *ht*(*t*), *t*(*t*), and *tht* prevail decisively over *ght*, which is scarcely represented. Thus in words with front vowels, *Almythy* and *Almyhtty* appear (Pr 46, 3/62),

[1] See Michael Benskin and Margaret Laing, 'Translations and *Mischsprachen* in Middle English manuscripts', in *So meny people longages and tonges*, Michael Benskin and M. L. Samuels, eds. (Edinburgh, 1981), pp. 55–106.

along with *bryth*, *bryht* 'bright' (Pr 17, 1/32, 78, etc.), *flyth* 'flight' (Pr 31), *knyth*, *knythtys*, *knyt(t)ys* 'knight(s)' (Pr 219, 228, etc.), *lyth* 'light' (1/25, 30, 37), *myth*, *myht* 'might' (Pr 15, 27, etc.), *mythty* (1/59), *nyth*, *nyht*, *nygthtys* 'night(s)' (Pr 268, 472, etc.), *ryth*, *ryht* 'right' (Pr 19, 78, 2/283, etc.), and *syth*, *ssyht* 'sight' (Pr 29, 229, 3/195, etc.). Toward the conclusion of Play 3, *ght* spellings become more frequent, in *bryght*, *syght*, *dyght*, *Almyghty*, etc. By Play 4, such spellings are firmly established as the majority forms, and remain so in the bulk of the MS. The regional orthography again prevails in the Passion Plays, which appear to have been written at a different time from the rest of the MS; only in the interpolated ff. 143 and 149–51 do *ght* forms preponderate in Passion Play 1. A similar pattern obtains after back vowels. Thus the Proclamation, plays 1–3, and the Passion plays contain all thirteen instances of *wrowth* and *wrougth* and three of the five occurrences of *wrouth*, but only 9 of the 53 *ght* spellings of this word. (This pattern is less emphatic in some words, such as 'daughter', which is spelled with *ght* only once, by B in 10/172). The spellings *tȝ*, *twh* and *twth* occur in *notȝ*, *notwh*, *notwth* (26/252, 28/144, 32/104, 284), and *gth* appears (as in *wrougth*, noted above). In addition, 'right' is spelled *rygh* four times (14/97, 23/25, 25/19, 36/41; cf. similar verbal inflexions discussed below). B wrote *ght* in *Doughter* but also *wt* in *dowty* on f. 51; C used the Standard *ght* spellings in *bryght*, *cawght*, etc.; and D employed regional spellings in Play 41. Many of the regional spellings suggest that the fricative had become silent, a conclusion supported by inverted spellings like *abought* 'about' (20/134, 21/55), *fryght* 'frith' (16/103), and *smyght* 'smite' (:*forthryght* 5/168), and by rhyme (e.g. *byth* 'bite': *myth* 'might', 2/125).

The main scribe wrote *g* as well as *ȝ* in words like *ageyn(e)*, *aȝen*, *ageyns*, *aȝens*, *ȝeve*, *gyf(f)*. He wrote *ȝit(t)*, *ȝet(t)*, and *ȝyt*, but also, in one instance, *yet* (26/107); also *ye* (2/278). B wrote *ye*, *you*, and *yis* on f. 51; C wrote *ageyn(e)* and *gyff* 'give', and also *yon*, *yong*, *yow*, *ye*, etc., but several times *ȝe*; D employed *g* and *y* in words like *agayn*, *yer(e)*, *yit*, *yon(e)*, and *you*. The main scribe several times wrote *w* and *v* in variation: *dowe* 'dove', *knove* 'know', *show(e)* 'shove', *stewyn* 'voice' (beside *stevene*, *stevyn*), and *vyl* 'will' (Pr 77, 4/251, 28/144, 34/100, 3/129, 10/244, 28/32). In Pr 77 *dowe*: *flowe* and *crowe*, and in 34/100 *show* 'shove': *anow*. D also wrote *dowe* (41/510), as well as *dewelys* (41/484), *lave* 'law' in rhyme with *knawe*, *awe*, *blawe* (41/40), etc.

The main points of verbal inflexion are:

Infin. is usually without ending or followed by *e*, but the main scribe and D wrote many verbs with *-n*, as confirmed in rhyme by, for example, *asayn*: *mayn*, *certeyn*, *fayn* (2/119); *bene*: *bedene*, *sene*, *wene* (Pr 34); *gon*: *echon*, *on*, *alon* (11/164), also rhyming on *anon*, *non*, *mon* (12/35) and on *ton* (14/258), etc.[1] B wrote *spede*: *lede*, pr. 1 sg. (10/157), *enbrace*: *place* (10/161), etc. C wrote *rech*: *lech* (18/233), *dwell*: *hell* (22/13), etc.

Pres. indic. 1 sg. is uninflected or followed by *e*, but cf. *trostyn* (14/322) and *plyghtys*: *knyghtys* (20/38).

2 sg. ends in *st*, which also appears in the pa. t. of weak verbs: *answeryst* (29/162), *askyst* (27/266), *byddyst* (2/118), *dedyst* (12/123), etc., and, in the work of D, *ascendist* (41/216), *pretendist* (41/217), etc. But *dwellys* (9/117) is marked by a sibilant, *wace*: *place* (28/104), and *brest* (32/97) is uninflected.

3 sg. normally ends in *th*, though sometimes in *t*, occasionally in *s* or *ce*, several times in *ght* or *ht*, and very rarely in *gh*; 3 sg. verbs are also sometimes uninflected. Thus the main scribe wrote *abydyth* (10/415, 11/264, etc.); *askyth* (24/36) but also *Askyht* (3/169); *beryth* five times but in one instance *beryght* (15/47); frequently *byddyth* but once *byddyt* (28/16 s.d.); *doth(e)* (Pr 98, 107, etc.) beside *do* (Pr 150); *etyth* (27/204 s.d.) along with *ete* (27/76 s.d.) and *etyht* (27/257), etc. Other 3 sg. verbs ending in *ght* or *ht* include *blomyght* (15/29), *chargight* (10/146), *eylight* and *heylyght* (25/55, 14/263), *grevyht* (4/94, 103, 5/183), *growyht* (8/143), *haht* (35/21), *hatyht* (3/145), *hattyht* (16/31), *lestyght* (10/312), *lyght* (15/160), *longyht* (6/176), *makyht* (10/434), *menyht* (4/92), *overthrowyht* (8/141), *shewyght* (16/25), *syttyht* (10/300), *smytyht* (9/81), *sowyht* (8/138), *werkyht* (6/135), and *wonyght* (16/9); also the impers. *us helpyht* (25/446) and *methynkyht* (4/160, 10/236, 14/365).[2] The inflexion *gh* marks 3 sg. verbs in *folwygh* (24/55), *lokygh* (18/75), *longygh* (23/178), *stynkygh* (25/393), and *weldygh* (10/248); also *methynkygh* (20/143). Final *t* occurs chiefly but not exclusively in the Passion Plays, in *byddyt* (28/16 s.d.), *dystroyt* (26/180), *fortefyet* (27/400), *seyt* (26/453 s.d., 27/268 s.d.), and *waxit* (38/162). 3 sg. verbs end in a sibilant in *asaylys*: *bedellys*, *merveyllys*, *provaylys* (26/39); *has*, rhyming on *glas* (21/99) and on *grace* (24/291); *lyce*: *wyse*, *servise* (10/85); *lyse*: *paradyse*, *ryse*, *devyse* (Pr 430) also rhyming on *avyse* (11/168); and *syttys* (12/174). B wrote *lyth* (10/156). C wrote *spekyth* (22/3), but interlined *wonyt* on f. 93v (18/131).[3] D employed *th* in *abidyth* (41/128), *autorysyth* (41/13), etc., but *s* in *louris* (41/400: *prechours*, *schouris*, *touris*).

[1] The infin. *neyth* (26/49) is presumably a form of *neyȝ*.
[2] Cf. *gohth*, part of a cancelled portion of 27/204 s.d.
[3] Cf. *bere*, possibly 3 sg. in 18/238.

Pl. verbs usually have no ending or *-e*, though the main scribe ended several with *n*, including *abydyn* (26/385 s.d.), *faryn* (9/292), and, in rhyme, *don*: *polucyon* (15/230), and *gon*: *bon*, *echon*, *alon* (2/20). He also ended several pl. verbs with *th*, e.g. *apperyth* (29/41) and *befallyth*: *callyth*, 3 sg. (29/68);[1] cf. *-s* in *provaylys* (26/37, rhymes listed above) and *stondys* (31/179). B wrote *doth* (10/161), C wrote *beleuyn* (18/73) and *rysyn* (18/297), beside *goo* (18/297), and D wrote uninflected forms and *-e* along with *-n* in *seyn* (41/69), *beryn* (41/386), etc.; he also wrote *was* (41/284, see the note).

Pr. pples. normally end in *ng*(*e*) for the main scribe, though he wrote several instances with *nd*(*e*), chiefly in the Marian and Passion plays: *applyande*, *declinande*, and *plesande* in rhyme with each other and *hande* (26/134); *neyhand* (19/4); *pleand* (8/3); and *knelende* (8/146: *amende*). D mixed forms with *ng*(*e*) and *nd* (the latter rhyming only on themselves).

Past pples. of strong verbs are very often followed by *n*(*e*) but in many instances are marked by *e* or are uninflected. Thus *bore* occurs along with *born*(*e*), *chose* with *chosyn*, *do* with *don*(*e*), etc. C wrote *fownde* (18/265) and *bownde* (18/267), but *borne* (18/272 and 22/46: *beforne*, *forlorne*, *to-torne*). D wrote *bounden* (41/46) and *sprongyn* (41/383) but also *betake* (41/244).

Imp. pl. is usually uninflected or followed by *e*, but often ends in *th*: thus *Attende* (27/89) appears beside *attendyth* (39/57). The endings *ght* and *ht* occur in *folwyht* (39/29), *goht* (34/263), *heryght* (36/2), *makyght* (20/106), *Shapyht* (20/31), *takyght* (20/82), and *takyht* (30/41). *-s* appears in *thynkys* (13/147), and *-n* occurs in *gon* (20/25) and *seyn* (30/256). B wrote *knowyth* (10/170), C wrote *Beth* (22/7) beside several instances with *-e*, and D wrote *beth*, *takyth* (41/271, 332), etc., as well as *aray*, *go* (41/390, 395), etc.

Dialect

The East Anglian character of the main scribe's language is evidenced by his writing *xal*, *xuld*, etc.; *qu*, *qw*, etc. for OE *hw*; *th*, *ht*, etc. for OE *ht*; his use of regional pr. 3 sg. markers; and the appearance of several other typically and perhaps exclusively East Anglian forms of the period.[2] Among these are *kure* 'to cover' (5/179), *recure* (10/106:

[1] *askyght* in 15/270 appears to be pr. plural.

[2] For discussion of the East Anglian nature of these features in N-town, see Greg, *The Assumption of the Virgin*, pp. 6–21; Dobson, pp. 152–3; Eccles, pp. 135–41; Bennett, pp. 43–63; and Beadle, *passim.*

Scrypture, 27/75: *sewre*), *recuryd* (26/38), and *swem*(*e*) 'grief, pity' (8/78, 11/127: *qweme*, *deme*, *seme*), *swemful* 'distressing' (8/66) and *swemyth* (15/98).[1] The fact that these dialect words appear in rhyme illustrates the East Anglian colour of the language of the poet or poets of those portions of the text. Eccles (p. 140) points out that *serge* for 'search' (29/80) is cited by *OED* only in texts assigned to East Anglia, and Baker *et al.* (p. xxxvii) note that *therkeness* (10/436, *thyrknes* PS 27) is a spelling usually considered characteristic of Norfolk; cf. Dobson, pp. 152–3. Edward Wilson proposes that *'tys* 'it is' (28/106 s.d., in Passion Play 1) may have arisen in Norfolk and occurred only there in Middle English.[2] Beadle observes that *nyn* for 'nor', which occurs only in the Marian plays (8/15, 9/149, 13/66), and *hefne* and *sefne* for 'heaven' and 'seven' (Pr 434, 7/81, etc.) were probably restricted to East Anglia. He adds that *erdon* 'errand, petition' (28/46), which, like *serge*, occurs in the Passion plays, was also probably restricted to that region. In addition, *MED* cites *amat* (29/115), *auantorysly* in the sense 'by chance' (34/100 s.d.), *brybe* meaning 'bribe' (24/67), *cessacyon* (11/55), *dwere* in the sense 'amazement, awe' (Pr 484), *fop* (29/164), and *prongys* meaning 'pangs of distress' (28/176) only from texts assigned to East Anglia.

Beadle observes that the following forms in N-town, though not individually restricted to East Anglia, are found as a set only in texts copied in that region: *dede* 'death' (35/81: *rede*, *brede*), *erde* 'earth' (28/92 s.d.), *kend*(*e*) and *mend*(*e*), *werd*(*e*) for 'world' (Pr 11, 4/102, etc.), and *whow*, *whov* for 'how, why' (8/103, 11/263, 19/64, etc., chiefly in the Marian plays). He adds that several other spellings in the MS are typically though not exclusively East Anglian, e.g. *mech*(*e*) and *mekyl* 'much', *swech*(*e*) 'such', *w*(*h*)*ech*(*e*) 'which', and *ony* 'any'; also *w* spellings for *v*.

Beadle (1: 88) concludes that the main scribe was from Norfolk, as suggested by his use of *whow*, etc., *mekyl*, *dede* 'death', *erde*, *werd*(*e*), *wore/ware* 'were', *-and* in the pr. pple., and perhaps *Kyrke* along with *Cherche* and *Chirch.* He dates this scribe's work perhaps a generation after 1450, based in part on the appearance of *th* and *þ* forms of 'their' and 'them' (beside the majority forms *her*, *here*, and *hem*) and initial *g* in 'give' beside spellings with *ȝ*. Professor Angus McIntosh has kindly

[1] Norman Davis cites the East Anglian associations of *cure* and *swemful* in his linguistic analysis of the *Play of the Sacrament* in *Non-Cycle Plays and Fragments*, EETS ss 1 (1970). Cf. Beadle, 1: 65–6, 75–7.

[2] 'The Earliest 'Tis = "It Is"', *Notes and Queries*, 219 (April 1974), 127–8.

informed me that he and Professor Michael Samuels assign the main hand to the neighbourhood of Harling in south central Norfolk. Samuels adds that the main scribe's use of *loyn* 'lain' (Pr 428, 11/3, 29/111) and *nere* 'nor' (6/175, 176, etc.) are reminiscent of Bury but by no means impossible for a scribe writing in south central Norfolk (private correspondence).

B's limited text has no specifically East Anglian forms, except perhaps *dowty* 'doughty' (10/174), a spelling also employed by the main scribe. C's language is distinctively East Anglian in his use of *xall*, *xulde*, etc., and *mekell* (18/246), and his revision of the main scribe's *myrke* to *thyrke* (18/304).[1] Samuels locates C perhaps a bit east of the main hand. D's East Anglian usages include *curyng* 'covering' (41/284), *sweme* 'be overcome' (41/198: *teme*, *queme*, *seme*), *word* for 'world' (41/154), initial *q* in *qwyche*, and *mend(e)* and *kend(e)*. Beadle (1: 92–3) cites also his use of *hefne*, *Cherche*, *meche*, *mekyl*, *sweche* and *ony*, and takes D's mixing of *ng(e)* and *and* endings in pr. pples. to be characteristic of Norfolk. He adds that D's preference for *hem* and *here* over *them* and *ther* may suggest that he worked earlier than the main scribe. Samuels finds characteristics of Bury in D's spelling, perhaps indicating that the scribe was educated there before working in Norfolk.

DATE

'1468' is written, apparently by the main scribe, at the close of the 'Purification of Mary' (f. 100v). The unusual location of this date may suggest that it marks some specific event, perhaps the incorporation of the Purification play into the cycle (see pp. 473 and 540). In any case, it serves as a presumptive *terminus a quo* for the manuscript. The handwriting, watermarks, language, and other internal evidence confirm that the main scribe and the other principal scribes worked on the manuscript during the second half of the fifteenth century, and perhaps the early part of the sixteenth.

[1] Block (p. xvii) says that several of C's revisions, including *shene* to *bryght* (16/15), *selkowth* to *mervelus* (16/16), *carpynge* to *spekyng* (16/32), *barne* to *child* (16/34), *bale* to *sorow* (16/77), *buske* to *go* (16/79), *pap-hawk* to *paddoke* (18/88), *tholyn* to *suffyr* (18/63), *shaftys* to *sperys* (18/89), and *myrke* to *thyrke* (18/304), were intended to remove archaic or unfamiliar words.

Handwriting

As noted above (p. xxii), most authorities have concluded that the main scribe's hand is typical of the mid-fifteenth century or slightly thereafter, and so is consonant with a date of 1468. One expert, however, dates the hand closer to the end of the century, or later.[1] The hands of B and C probably date from the late fifteenth or early sixteenth century. D's hand may be at least as early as the main scribe's. Block (pp. xxvii–xxviii) observes that the rubricated *4*, *5*, and *7* in play-numbers and in the Commandments in Play 6 have the earlier Arabic form, which changed in the course of the fifteenth century.

Watermarks

Current theory argues that precise dating by watermarks requires locating *identical* marks in dated texts, and that comparison to similar tracings in watermark albums is far less valuable than following the life history of marks and moulds in their progressive states across different texts. In addition, as Allan Stevenson conceded, paper used in manuscripts could have been stored for some time between manufacture and use.[2] None the less, watermarks resembling those in the present codex date from the same period suggested by the other indications of date in N-town. When the resemblance is very close, as in the case of the paper of Passion Play 2, the date of the similar watermark is very near 1468.

The watermarks in the paper used by the main scribe are similar in design to marks dated in or near the third quarter of the century: the Bunch of Grapes mark is similar to Briquet 13055 and 13056, which are dated 1453 and 1460–77 respectively. The YHS in a Sun resembles Briquet 9477, which appears in texts dated 1466–79 (with one early sixteenth-century attestation). The Bull's Head paper of Passion Play 1 bears some resemblance to Briquet 14183, 14184, and 14189, which are dated 1447–60 (Briquet notes that variations on this sort of mark appear over much of the century); generally similar marks in Gerhard Piccard's *Ochsenkopf* album (section IX) run from the mid-1440s to mid-1470s. The Two Crossed Keys watermark of Passion Play 2 is very similar in design to Piccard III. 492 (*Wasserzeichen Schlussel*),

[1] M. B. Parkes suggests the later date; see p. xxii n. 1.

[2] Allan Stevenson, 'Paper as Bibliographical Evidence', *Library*, 5th Ser., 17 (1962), 201. See Spector, *Essays in Paper Analysis*, pp. 18–21.

which is dated 1469 (the less similar Briquet 3887 is dated 1461–70). Of the paper used by the other scribes, the one-armed pot on B's paper contains some similarities to Briquet 12496, 12498, and 12501; according to Briquet, these marks date from 1485–1519, which is consistent with the period assigned to B. The Hand watermark on C's paper is not similar enough to watermark tracings to allow comparison. D's paper in Play 41 bears a Two-Wheeled Cart watermark that resembles Briquet 3528, which is found in texts dating from 1429–61.

Language

Richard Beadle dates the main scribe's work at perhaps a generation after 1450, and considers D's to be perhaps a bit earlier, as suggested by their spellings of words like 'them' and 'give' (see LANGUAGE, pp. xxxvii–xxxviii). This agrees with the other indices of date cited above. One can go further and conjecture the date of *composition* by noting when each word in the plays first appeared in the same sense in other texts, as recorded in *MED*. The results show that N-town contains a large number of words and meanings that became current between 1425 and 1450. Many of these first appeared in the 1440s, often in East Anglian texts.[1] And several are first cited after 1450, as represented on p. xli.[2] As the chart indicates, the comparatively late words and meanings tend to cluster in the Marian plays, the Passion plays,

[1] Words and senses first cited by *MED* in the 1440s include *herty* (Pr 384, 4/89, 170), *veruently* (Pr 496), *dowcet* (2/77), *hevyly* (8/137), *clyne* (11/285), *punche* (36/30), and *chille* (41/483), all first cited in the *Promptorium Parvulorum* (1440); *carnall* (21/163), *erraunt* (22/152), and *brothel* (24/146), first cited in Capgrave's *St. Norbert* (1440); *cognysion* (21/63) and *moralysacyon* (26/141), in Bokenham's *Legendys of Hooly Wummen* (1447); *luminarye(s)* (PS 3, 17) in Lydgate's 'Ave Regina' (*a.* 1449); also *dyffuse* (10/103), *praty* (10/459), *prevayll* (27/528), *prate* (35/283), and *rejoyse* (42/114).

[2] For *stomachere* see the note to 26/65–108. The date of *dompnesse*, *c.* 1456, signifies a quarter century earlier or later than 1456. Words and senses that make their earliest appearance in N-town are irrelevant to the present purpose, and so are not listed in the chart. The same applies to words and senses that *MED* cites only in N-town; these include *appose* (Pr 245), *hardaunt* (Pr 418), *peynfulnes* (3/77, 22/8), *dyght* (3/164), *hest* (4/165), *dissponsacyon* (9/302), *celestly* (10/448, 41/360), *morny* (10/479), *pleson* (11/117), *maculacion* (14/240, 334), *reclyne* (14/313), *pap-hawk(ys)* (18/88, 20/11), *prosodye* (21/8), *lynyacyon* (21/19), *attrybute* (21/129), *desertnes* (22/123), *delyre* (22/163), *indute* (22/164), *pynne* (23/110), *accende* (24/31), *disteyne* (24/59), *fortyfye* (26/55), *perdure* (26/411), *obecyon* (30/81), *rochand* (31/1), *fortefye* (31/146), *bragge* (41/37), *craggyd* (41/38), *gratulacyon* (41/97), *desideracyon* (41/99), *extende* (41/111), *pretende* (41/113), *consorcyté* (41/116), *pretende* (41/161), *detent* (41/218), *sede* (41/313), *dodemvsyd* (41/390), *glabereris* (41/399), *louris* (41/400), *belthe* (41/471), *relesere* (41/515). This study was undertaken while *MED* was still in progress.

and the 'Assumption of Mary' (Play 41), all of which appear to be additions to the cycle.[1]

N-TOWN	*MED* CITATION	FIRST APPEARANCE
nowthty (3/172)	noughti adj. (b)	*c.* 1475
Jesse (7/49)	jesse n.	1463
parochonerys (8/56)	parishoner n.	1465
intelligence (13/33, 26/273, 434)	intelligence n. 2 (b)	1543 (1464)
dompnesse (13/35)	dombenesse n. (a)	*c.* 1456
howlott (20/15)	houlot n.	*a.* 1475
fytt (20/232)	fit n. 1 (b)	*a.* 1475
ortografye (21/6)	ortografie n.	*a.* 1460
stomachere (26/74)	–	1474
possyble (26/211)	possible adj. 2 (a)	*a.* 1460
seryattly (27/440)	seriatli adv.	*c.* 1484 (*a.* 1475)
assumpte (41/11)	assumpten v. (b)	(1464)
ierarchye (41/11)	jerarchi(e) n. 1 (c)	*a.* 1475
fise (41/83)	fis(e) n. (a)	*a.* 1500
assedually (41/174)	assiduel(l)i adv.	*c.* 1475
drag (41/486)	draggen v. (a)	?*a.* 1475

To the degree that this method provides a reliable test of date, it indicates that N-town was not composed before 1425–50. Much or all of the cycle may in fact date from no earlier than the 1440s, with substantial portions of text possibly having originated in the second half of the century.

Other indications of date

Satan's costume, as described in his prologue to Passion Play 1, fits with a date between the mid-1460s and about the 1480s (see the note to 26/65–108).

VERSE

The prosodic forms in the cycle include one principal type and several less common varieties of 13-line stanza; tail-rhyme in four rhyme-schemes (aaabcccb, aaabaaab, aabccb, aaaaaa), usually with four

[1] The concentration of late words in the 'Assumption' (Play 41) may contradict the indications cited above of a comparatively early date of transcription for this play. The present results may be confounded, however, by the rarity of the diction in this play (cf. the unique usages cited, p. xl n. 2).

stresses per line and three in the bob, but often with shorter lines; long- and short-lined varieties of octave rhyming ababbcbc and, less frequently, abababab; long- and short-lined forms of quatrain, couplet, and 9-line stanza (ababcdddc); 10-line stanzas rhyming aabaabbcbc; and 5-line stanzas rhyming abbba.[1] There are also some exceptional forms like the 17-line stanza in 3/45–61 (which may be a quatrain joined to a thirteener), and the octave that rhymes ababcbcb in 37/25–32. Several stanza fragments appear, and a few stanzas are divided: a thirteener is shared between plays 1 and 2, for example, and another thirteener has been segmented into a quatrain and a 9-line stanza by the interpolation of quire E after f. 50.[2] In the 'Assumption of Mary', single lines and couplets are frequently concatenated by rhyme to neighbouring stanzas. Latin lines are sometimes incorporated into stanzas, as in the Magnificat in Play 13, while English verses are occasionally ametrical.

I refer to three forms of thirteener by name. The 'proclamation thirteener', so named because it constitutes most of the Proclamation, also appears in fourteen plays, and is the principal variety of thirteener in the cycle. It rhymes ababababcdddc, with lines 1–8 and 10–12 normally containing four stressed syllables and seven to ten syllables in all; lines 9 and 13 typically have three stressed syllables.[3] The 'long thirteener' has the same rhyme-scheme as the proclamation thirteener but, by contrast, has much longer lines: lines 1-8 frequently have five or six stressed syllables and ten to fourteen syllables in total. Although

[1] Many stanzaic forms in the cycle typically have four stressed syllables in each verse, though lines are sometimes hypermetric. I refer to such stanzas as 'short-lined' when contrasting them with long-lined varieties that have the same rhyme-scheme but contain many verses with five or six stressed syllables. Some stanzas, especially in tail-rhyme, have exceptionally short lines (e.g. 34/262–325). Bob lines in the various stanzaic forms most often contain one or three stressed syllables, though exceptions occasionally appear. Swenson identifies tumbling metre in the Lamech scene (Play 4) and other portions of the cycle that she considers to have been reworked. Patch ('*Ludus Coventriae* and the Digby *Massacre*', p. 334) questions the extent to which this metre can be considered as a test of style, however. For a fuller discussion of the prosody in the cycle, see Greg, *Problems*, pp. 108–43, and *Assumption of the Virgin*, pp. 26–35; Swenson, *passim*; Spector, *Genesis of the N-town Cycle*, *passim*, and 'Composition and Development of an Eclectic Manuscript', pp. 62–83.

[2] Another thirteener may have been similarly divided by 10-line stanzas in Play 12 (see the headnote).

[3] Proclamation thirteeners appear in the Proclamation, plays 1–4, 10, 12, 16, 18, 20, 22, 23, on the interpolated ff. 143 and 149 in plays 26 and 27, and in Play 42. The metrics of proclamation thirteeners are occasionally irregular, as for example in Pr 191–203, in which the bob at 199 has only one stressed syllable and the subsequent three lines have only two.

the long thirteeners have been all but unnoticed in previous studies, they make up a substantial portion of the Proclamation and also appear in several plays.[1] And 'Herod thirteeners', rhyming abab ababbcccb and characterized by unusually dense alliteration, are spoken only by Herod in plays 18 and 20. Less common kinds of thirteener rhyme ababababcaaac in 2/126–38 (apparently intended as a proclamation thirteener), ababbabacdddc in plays 3 and 4;[2] and ababacacdeeed in Plays 3 and 10 (both possibly joined fragments).[3] Thirteeners in the rhyme-scheme ababbcbcdeeed make up most of plays 39 and 40.[4] And long-lined thirteeners rhyming ababababbcccb, ababababcdddc, and ababababaccca appear in Play 41.[5]

Octaves rhyming ababbcbc appear in several of the N-town plays, with the long-lined variety of this form serving as the basal stanza of the Marian plays. The less common abababab octaves are associated with revision, specifically in the 'Visit to Elizabeth' (Play 13). Tail-rhyme appears in the punishment scene in the Fall of Man play (2), Den's prologue to Play 14, the Shepherds, Magi, and Innocents plays (16, 18, and 20), and the Crucifixion, Harrowing, and Resurrection plays. Ten-line stanzas occur only in the plays of Joseph's Doubt and the Purification of Mary (12 and 19). The Passion plays comprise various prosodic forms, chiefly long- and short-lined octaves, quatrains, and couplets, but also 5-line stanzas and other forms. The 'Assumption of Mary' consists of several mostly long-lined verse forms, including three varieties of thirteener, as well as octaves, quatrains, and couplets, with the intercalation of single lines and couplets noted above. See the headnotes for more detailed discussion of prosody, and Appendix 1 for a reconstruction of the compilation of the cycle based in part on prosodic tests.

[1] Pr 27–39 is a typical proclamation thirteener, while the subsequent stanza is a long thirteener. Long thirteeners also appear in Pr 386–437 (see p. 541 n. 2), in Play 16, in Herod's and Death's speeches in Play 20, in John the Baptist's hortatory homily at the close of Play 22, and in the devils' speeches in Play 23. A few stanzas (e.g. Pr 1–13) are hybrid.

[2] A comparatively long-lined version of this form appears in 3/32–44 and 66–78, a short-lined version in 4/53–65.

[3] In 3/105–17 this thirteener has bad rhymes and irregular metre, in 10/14–26 it does not.

[4] This stanza tends to have 2- or 3-stress lines on the *e*-rhyme. Cf. 8/237–49 and the headnote to that play.

[5] Cf. 41/1–13 and the note.

SOURCES AND ANALOGUES

The plays derive principally from the Vulgate and the apocrypha, as well as from hagiographic, meditational, Patristic, homiletic, liturgical, dramatic, narrative, and iconographic sources.

Most plays are ultimately based on biblical accounts, though these are often substantially, even radically, revised and embellished. The chief New Testament apocryphal sources are Pseudo-Matthew, which provided, for example, the names of Mary's handmaidens in Play 10, and the *De Nativitate Mariae*, an important source of the Marian plays that was transmitted through the *Legenda Aurea.* The *Transitus Mariae*, also substantially incorporated in the *Legenda Aurea*, was a principal source of the 'Assumption of Mary'. The *Gospel of Nicodemus* inspired not only the Harrowing of Hell plays (33 and 35) but also the earlier diabolical dialogue in Play 31. The *Protevangelium of James* and other New Testament apocrypha had some influence, and a few plays show indebtedness to Old Testament apocrypha and pseudepigrapha, notably the *Life of Adam and Eve.*

The *Legenda Aurea* was a major source of the Marian sequence and the 'Assumption of Mary', and plays sometimes reveal specific indebtedness to this source rather than to the earlier apocrypha that it adopted. Other hagiographic texts, particularly Lydgate's *Life of Our Lady*, contain detailed similarities to N-town; the *Life of St. Anne* is especially close in content and structure, though the claim that it was the source of the Marian plays is overstated (see the headnote to Play 8).

Among meditational and instructional texts, the pseudo-Bonaventuran *Meditationes Vitae Christi* was an ultimate source of the Marian sequence, much of which closely follows Nicholas Love's *Mirrour of the Blessed Lyf of Jesu Christ*, a popular English translation and adaptation of the *Meditationes.* Some speeches in abababab octaves in those plays essentially versify the *Mirrour*, and several 10-line stanzas in 'Joseph's Doubt' and the 'Purification of Mary' (plays 12 and 19) also closely follow Love. The *Charter of the Abbey of the Holy Ghost* and two closely related manuscripts, Trinity College, Cambridge, B. 2. 18, and Trinity College, Dublin, 423, all texts ultimately derived from the *Meditationes*, offer extremely close parallels to the Parliament of Heaven in Play 11.

Patristic writings and other Christian commentary inform much of the cycle. The description of the Decalogue as consisting of three laws relating to God and seven pertaining to man, for example, appears in commentaries by Augustine and others (see the note to 6/61–4), and Jesus' exposition of the Last Supper (Play 27) closely agrees with that of Rabanus Maurus.

The division of the Ten Commandments is also recorded in Peter Comestor's *Historia Scholastica*, which may have been an immediate source of the killing of Cain in Play 4. Homily also influenced the cycle, and characters in several instances take on the role of homilist. N-town contains many liturgical hymns and prayers, especially in plays involving Mary, and the 'Assumption of Mary' sometimes follows formulations in liturgy rather than those in the main source, the *Legenda Aurea.* The Athanasian and Apostles' creeds also influenced the plays, doctrinally in the Creation and Doctors plays (1 and 21), for example, and perhaps structurally in the 'Jesse Tree' (Play 7).

The cycle participates in the rich tradition of English religious drama, exhibiting affinities not only to other mystery plays, but also to plays in other genres, including the morality play the *Castle of Perseverance.* Like the *Castle*, N-town has a prologue written in thirteeners and delivered by vexillatores, with the name of the town of performance unspecified. And like the *Castle*, N-town has a Debate of the Four Daughters of God, a personified Death, an alliterative geographical list, and an attack on sinfully fashionable dress (cf. Block, pp. liv–lv). N-town resembles Cornish and Continental plays in many ways as well. The Noah play, for instance, displays affinities to the Cornish *Creacion of the World*, and Rosemary Woolf and other scholars have linked N-town with French dramatic traditions.

The cycle recalls several motifs in narrative analogues, including the acrostic fashioned on the five letters in 'Maria' (9/262–7). Passion Plays 1 and 2 often agree very closely with the *Northern Passion.* And the Guarding of the Sepulchre has marked affinities to the same episode in MS Ashmole 61; Ernst Falke cites this as a source of N-town 34, but Woolf questions the direction of the indebtedness (see the note to 34/182–205).

There are many iconographic parallels to episodes in N-town: Play 7, for example, may itself be considered a conflation of the iconographic Jesse Tree with the dramatic *Prophetae.*

SELECT BIBLIOGRAPHY

BIBLIOGRAPHIES

Brown, Carleton, and Robbins, Rossell Hope, *The Index of Middle English Verse* (New York, 1943).

Hartung, Albert E. (ed.), *A Manual of the Writings in Middle English 1050–1500* (New Haven, 1975) XII. 'Miracle Plays and Mysteries' by Anna J. Mill.

Robbins, Rossell Hope, and Cutler, John L., *Supplement to the Index of Middle English Verse* (Lexington, 1965).

Stratman, Carl J., *Bibliography of Medieval Drama* (Berkeley and Los Angeles, 1954; 2nd edn., 2 vols., New York, 1972).

Wells, John Edwin, *A Manual of the Writings in Middle English, 1050–1400* (New Haven, 1916, and *First* to *Ninth Supplements*, 1919–51).

EDITIONS OF THE N-TOWN PLAYS

The cycle:

Ludus Coventriae: A Collection of Mysteries Formerly Represented at Coventry on the Feast of Corpus Christi, ed. James Orchard Halliwell. Shakespeare Society (London, 1841).

Ludus Coventriae: or The Plaie called Corpus Christi, ed. K. S. Block. EETS ES 120 (1922, repr. 1960).

The facsimile edition:

The N-town Plays, ed. Peter Meredith and Stanley J. Kahrl. Leeds Texts and Monographs (Leeds, 1977).

Individual plays:

Stevens, John, appendix to William Dugdale's *Monasticon Anglicanum* (London, 1722). Proclamation and plays 1–5.

Hone, William, *Ancient Mysteries Described* (London, 1823). Passages from plays 8–15.

Collier, John Payne, *Five Miracle Plays or Scriptural Dramas* (London, 1836). Play 10.

Marriott, William, *a Collection of English Miracle-Plays or Mysteries* (Basel, 1838). Plays 12 and 14.

Pollard, Alfred W., *English Miracle Plays, Moralities, and Interludes* (Oxford, 1890; 8th edn. 1927). Passages from Play 11.

Manly, John Matthews, *Specimens of the Pre-Shaksperean Drama*, 2 vols. (Boston and New York, 1897–8). Plays 4 and 11.

Hemingway, Samuel B., *English Nativity Plays* (New York, 1909, repr. 1964). Plays 11–13, 15–16.

Greg, W. W., *The Assumption of the Virgin: A Miracle Play from the N-town Cycle* (Oxford, 1915). Play 41.

Adams, Joseph Quincy, *Chief Pre-Shakespearean Dramas* (Cambridge, Mass., 1924). Stanzas from the Proclamation; Play 1; portions of Play 11 and the Passion Plays.

Tickner, F. J., *Earlier English Drama from Robin Hood to Everyman* (New York, 1929). Selections from plays 1–2, 7, Passion Play 2, and Play 42.

Browne, E. Martin, *The Play of the Maid Mary* (London, 1932). Adapts plays 8–11.

—— *The Play of Mary the Mother* (London, 1932). Adapts plays 11–13, 15–19.

Loomis, Roger Sherman, and Wells, Henry W., *Representative Medieval and Tudor Plays* (New York, 1942). Abridgement of much of the cycle.

Broadbent, Joan, 'An Edition of the Noah Pageant in the English Corpus Christi Cycles', Univ. of Leeds MA thesis (1955).

Browne, E. Martin, *Mystery and Morality Plays* (New York, 1958, repr. 1960). Portions of Play 11, Play 24.

Cawley, A. C., *Everyman and Medieval Miracle Plays* (New York, 1959). Plays 3 and 24.

Thomas, R. George, *Ten Miracle Plays*. York Medieval Texts (Evanston, 1966). The Proclamation and plays 4, 24, and 42.

Davies, R. T., *The Corpus Christi Play of the English Middle Ages* (Totowa, 1972). Most of the cycle.

Spector, Stephen, 'The Genesis of the N-Town Cycle', Yale Ph.D. thesis (1973). Plays 10, 12, 13, 20, and 32; published in revised form as *The Genesis of the N-town Cycle* (New York and London, 1988).

Fletcher, Alan, 'An Edition of the N-Town Conception of Mary', Leeds MA thesis (1974).

Bevington, David, *Medieval Drama* (Atlanta, Dallas, etc., 1975). The Proclamation, the Death of Herod from Play 20, plays 24, 26–8, 29–30.

Happé, Peter, *English Mystery Plays* (Middlesex, New York, etc., 1975, repr. 1980, 1984). Plays 11–12, 15, 20, 26–8, and 38.

Meredith, Peter, *The Mary Play from the N. town Manuscript* (London and New York, 1987). Plays 8–13.

EDITIONS OF RELATED PLAYS

The Ancient Cornish Drama, ed. and transl. Edwin Norris. 2 vols. (New York and London, 1859, reissued 1968).

The Chester Plays, ed. Hermann Deimling and J. B. Matthews. EETS ES 62 (1892, repr. 1926, 1959, 1968), 115 (1916, repr. 1935, 1959, 1968).

The Chester Mystery Cycle, ed. R. M. Lumiansky and David Mills, EETS SS 3 (1974), SS 9 (1986).

The Creacion of the World, ed. and transl. Paula Neuss (New York and London, 1983).

The Digby Plays, ed. F. J. Furnivall. New Shakspere Soc. (1882, repr. EETS ES 70 1896, repr. 1930, 1967).

The Late Medieval Religious Plays of Bodleian MSS Digby 133 and E Museo 160, ed. Donald C. Baker, John L. Murphy, Louis B. Hall, Jr., EETS OS 283 (1982).

The Macro Plays, ed. Frederick J. Furnivall and Alfred W. Pollard. EETS ES 91 (1904, repr. 1924).

The Macro Plays, ed. Mark Eccles. EETS OS 262 (1969).

Le Mistére du Viel Testament, ed. James de Rothschild. 6 vols. (1878–91).

The Non-Cycle Mystery Plays, together with the Croxton Play of the Sacrament and the Pride of Life, ed. Osborn Waterhouse. EETS ES 104 (1909).

Non-Cycle Plays and Fragments, ed. Norman Davis. EETS SS 1 (1970).

The Towneley Plays, ed. George England and Alfred W. Pollard. EETS ES 71 (1897, repr. 1907, 1925, 1952, 1966).

Two Coventry Corpus Christi Plays, ed. Hardin Craig. EETS ES 87 (1902, 2nd edn. 1957, repr. 1967).

The Wakefield Pageants in the Towneley Cycle, ed. A. C. Cawley. (Manchester, 1958, repr. 1968).

York Plays, ed. Lucy Toulmin Smith (Oxford, 1885, repr. New York, 1963).

The York Plays, ed. Richard Beadle. York Medieval Texts (London, 1982).

COMMENTARY ON THE N-TOWN PLAYS

Anderson, M. D., *Drama and Imagery in English Medieval Churches* (Cambridge, 1963).

Ashley, Kathleen M., '"Wyt" and "Wysdam" in the N-town Cycle', *PQ* 58 (1979), 121–35.

Baird, Joseph L., and Baird, Lorrayne Y., 'Fabliau Form and the Hegge *Joseph's Return*', *Chaucer Rev.* 8 (1973), 159–69.

Baker, Donald C., 'The Drama: Learning and Unlearning', in *Fifteenth-Century Studies*, ed. Robert F. Yeager (Hamden, 1984), pp. 202–6.

Baugh, Albert C., 'A Recent Theory of the *Ludus Coventriae*', *PQ* 12 (1933), 403–6.

Beadle, H. R. L., 'The Medieval Drama of East Anglia: Studies in Dialect, Documentary Records and Stagecraft', 2 vols. York Ph.D. thesis (1977).

Benkovitz, Miriam J., 'Some Notes on the "Prologue of Demon" of *Ludus Coventriae*', *MLN* 60 (1945), 78–85.

Bennett, Jacob, 'The Language and the Home of the "*Ludus Coventriae*"', *Orbis* 22 (1973), 43–63.

Block, K. S., 'Some Notes on the Problem of the "Ludus Coventriae"', *MLR* 10 (1915), 47–57.

Bonnell, John K., 'The Source in Art of the So-called *Prophets Play* in the Hegge Collection', *PMLA* 29 (1914), 327–40.

— 'The Serpent with a Human Head in Art and in Mystery Play', *American Journal of Archaeology* 21 (1917), 255–91.

— 'Cain's Jaw Bone', *PMLA* 39 (1924), 140–6.

Branham, Joel Scott, 'The Hegge Cycle in Relation to the Medieval Church', Columbia MA thesis (1947).

Brawer, Robert A., 'The Form and Function of the Prophetic Procession in the Middle English Cycle Play', *Annuale Mediaevale* 13 (1972), 88–124.

Brown, Carleton, 'Sermons and Miracle Plays', *MLN* 49 (1934), 394–6.

Bryant, Joseph Allen, Jr., 'The Function of *Ludus Coventriae* 14', *JEGP* 52 (1953), 340–5.

Cameron, Kenneth, and Kahrl, Stanley J., 'The N-Town Plays at Lincoln', *Theatre Notebook* 20 (1965–66), 61–9.

— 'Staging the N-Town Cycle', *Theatre Notebook* 21 (1967), 122–38, 152–65.

Campbell, Thomas P., 'The Prophets' Pageant in the English Mystery Cycles: Its Origin and Function', *RORD* 17 (1974), 107–21.

Cawley, A. C., 'Middle English Metrical Versions of the Decalogue with Reference to the English Corpus Christi Cycles', *LSE* 8 (1975), 129–45.

Chambers, E. K., *The Mediaeval Stage*. 2 vols. (London, 1903, repr. 1925, 1948, 1954, 1963, 1967, 1978).

— *English Literature at the Close of the Middle Ages* (New York and Oxford, 1945).

Clark, Thomas Blake, 'A Theory Concerning the Identity and History of the Ludus Coventriae Cycle of Mystery Plays', *PQ* 12 (1933), 144–69.

Coletti, Theresa, 'Devotional Iconography in the N-Town Marian Plays', in *The Drama of the Middle Ages*, ed. Clifford Davidson, C. J. Gianakaris, and John H. Stroupe (New York, 1982, repr. 1983, 1985), pp. 249–71.

— 'Sacrament and Sacrifice in the N-Town Passion', *Mediaevalia* 7 (1981), 239–64.

Collins, Patrick J., *The N-town Plays and Medieval Picture Cycles.* Early Drama, Art, and Music Monograph Series, 2 (Kalamazoo, 1979).

Craig, Hardin, 'Note on the Home of Ludus Coventriae', appended to Swenson (see below), pp. 72–83.

—— *English Religious Drama of the Middle Ages* (Oxford, 1955).

Daniels, Richard Jacob, 'A Study of the Formal and Literary Unity of the N-town Mystery Cycle', Ohio State Univ. Ph.D. thesis (1972).

Davidson, Clifford, *Drama and Art.* Early Drama, Art, and Music Monograph Series, 1 (Kalamazoo, 1977).

—— 'Gesture in Medieval Drama with Special Reference to the Doomsday Plays in the Middle English Cycles', *Early Drama, Art, and Music Newsletter* 6 (1983), 8–17.

Davis, Sister Marian, 'Nicholas Love and the N-Town Cycle', Auburn Univ. Ph.D. thesis (1979).

Deasy, Brother C. Philip, 'St. Joseph in the English Mystery Plays', Catholic Univ. Ph.D. thesis (1937).

Dobson, E. J., 'The Etymology and Meaning of *Boy*', *Medium Ævum* 9 (1940), 121–54.

Dodds, Madeleine Hope, 'The Problem of the "Ludus Coventriae"', *MLR* 9 (1914), 79–91.

Downing, Marjorie D. Coogan, 'The Influence of the Liturgy on the English Cycle Plays', Yale Ph.D. thesis (1942).

Dugdale, William, *The Antiquities of Warwickshire Illustrated* (London, 1656).

Dustoor, P. E., 'The Origin of the Play of "Moses and Tables of the Law"', *MLR* 19 (1924), 459–62.

Dutka, JoAnna, *Music in the English Mystery Plays*. Early Drama, Art, and Music Reference Series, 2 (Kalamazoo, 1980).

Eccles, Mark, '*Ludus Coventriae* Lincoln or Norfolk?', *Medium Ævum* 40 (1971), 135–41.

Erbacher, Sister Leo Gonzaga, 'Glossary of Two Plays from Ludus Coventriae'. Univ. of Kansas MA thesis (1926).

Falke, Ernst, *Die Quellen des sogenannten Ludus Coventriae* (Leipzig, 1908).

Fletcher, Alan J., 'The "Contemplacio" Prologue to the N-Town Play of the Parliament of Heaven', *Notes and Queries*, new ser., 27 (1980), 111–12.

—— 'The Design of the N-Town Play of Mary's Conception', *MP* 79 (1981), 166–73.

—— 'Marginal Glosses in the N-Town Manuscript', *Manuscripta* 25 (1981), 113–17.

—— 'Layers of Revision in the N-Town Marian Cycle', *Neophilologus* 66 (1982), 469–78.

Forrest, Sister M. Patricia, 'Apocryphal Sources of the St. Anne's Day Plays in the Hegge Cycle', *Medievalia et Humanistica* 17 (1966), 38–50.

—— 'The Role of the Expositor Contemplacio in the St. Anne's Day Plays of the Hegge Cycle', *Medieval Studies* 28 (1966), 60–76.

Foster, Frances A. (ed.), *The Northern Passion*. EETS OS 147 (1916), 2: 89–101.

Frost, Inez, 'Glossary of Five Plays from the Ludus Coventriae', Univ. of Kansas MA thesis (1927).

Fry, Timothy, 'The Unity of the *Ludus Coventriae*', *Studies in Philology* 48 (1951), 527–70.

Gauvin, Claude, *Un cycle du théâtre religieux anglais du moyen âge* (Paris, 1973).

Gay, Anne Cooper, 'A Study of the Staging of the N.Towne Cycle', Univ. of Missouri MA thesis (1961).

—— 'The "Stage" and the Staging of the N-Town Plays', *RORD* 10 (1967), 135–40.

Gayley, Charles Mills, *Plays of Our Forefathers* (New York, 1907).

Gibson, Gail McMurray, '"Porta Haec Clausa Erit": Comedy, Conception, and Ezekiel's Closed Door in the *Ludus Coventriae* Play of "Joseph's Return"', *Journal of Medieval and Renaissance Studies* 8 (1978), 137–56.

—— 'Bury St. Edmunds, Lydgate, and the *N-Town Cycle*', *Speculum* 56 (1981), 56–90.

—— 'East Anglian Drama and the Dance of Death: Some Second Thoughts on the "Dance of Paul's"', *Early Drama, Art, and Music Newsletter* (Fall, 1982), 1–9.

Greg, W. W., *Bibliographical and Textual Problems of the English Miracle Cycles* (London, 1914).

—— 'The N-town Plays', *Library*, 4th ser., 1 (1920–1), 182–4.

Hammer, M. L., 'The Saviour As Protagonist in the *Ludus Coventriae*', Univ. of N. Carolina MA thesis (1944).

Hanning, R. W., '"You Have Begun a Parlous Pleye"', in *The Drama of the Middle Ages*, pp. 140–68.

Harrison, Izola Curley, 'The Staging of the Ludus Coventriae', Univ. of Chicago MA thesis (1929).

Hartman, Herbert, 'The Home of the *Ludus Coventriae*', *MLN* 41 (1926), 530–1.

Hohlfeld, Alexander, 'Die altenglischen Kollektivmisterien', *Anglia* 11 (1889), 219–310.

Hussey, S. S., 'How Many Herods in the Middle English Drama?', *Neophilologus* 48 (1964), 252–9.

Jngram, R. W., 'The Use of Music in English Miracle Plays', *Anglia* 75 (1957), 55–76.

Kahrl, Stanley J., *Traditions of Medieval English Drama* (London, 1974). See Cameron, Kenneth.

Kelly, Ellin M., '"Ludus Coventriae" Play 4 and the Egerton "Genesis"', *Notes and Queries* 217 (1972), 443–4.

Kökeritz, Helge, '"Out Born" in *Ludus Coventriae*', *MLN* 64 (1949), 88–90.

Kolve, V. A., *The Play Called Corpus Christi* (Stanford, 1966).

Kramer, Max, *Die Sprache und Heimat des sogenannten Ludus Coventriae* (Halle, 1892).

Kretzmann, Paul Edward, *The Liturgical Element in the Earliest Forms of the*

Medieval Drama. Univ. of Minnesota Studies in Language and Literature, 4 (Minneapolis, 1916).

Leigh, David J., 'The Doomsday Mystery Play: An Eschatological Morality', in *Medieval English Drama: Essays Critical and Contextual*, ed. Jerome Taylor and Alan H. Nelson (Chicago and London, 1972), pp. 260–78.

Leonard, Robert Joseph, 'Patterns of Dramatic Unity in the N-town Cycle', SUNY, Stony Brook, Ph.D. thesis (1984).

Loomis, Roger Sherman, 'Lincoln as a Dramatic Centre', in *Mélanges d'histoire du théâtre du moyen âge* (Paris, 1950), pp. 241–7.

Luke, Brother Cornelius, 'The Rôle of the Virgin Mary in the Coventry, York, Chester and Towneley Cycles', Catholic Univ. Ph.D. thesis (1933).

Macaulay, Peter Stuart, 'The Play of the Harrowing of Hell as a Climax in the English Mystery Cycles', *Studia Germanica Gandensia* 8 (1966), 115–34.

Marshall, Mary Hatch, 'The Relation of the Vernacular Religious Plays of the Middle Ages to the Liturgical Drama', Yale Ph.D. thesis (1932).

Marx, C. W., 'The Problem of the Doctrine of the Redemption in the ME Mystery Plays and the Cornish *Ordinalia*', *Medium Ævum* 54 (1985), 20–32.

McNeir, Waldo F., 'The Corpus Christi Passion Plays as Dramatic Art', *Studies in Philology* 48 (1951), 601–28.

Meredith, Peter, '"Nolo Mortem" and the *Ludus Coventriae* Play of the *Woman Taken in Adultery*', *Medium Ævum* 38 (1969), 38–54.

— 'A Reconsideration of Some Textual Problems in the N-town Manuscript (BL MS Cotton Vespasian D VIII), *LSE* 9 (1977), 35–50.

— 'Scribes, Texts and Performance', in *Aspects of Early English Drama*, ed. Paula Neuss (Cambridge, 1983), pp. 13–29.

Meredith, Peter, and Muir, Lynette, 'The Trial in Heaven in the "Eerste Bliscap" and Other European Plays', *Dutch Crossing* 22 (1984), 84–92.

Mills, David, 'Concerning a Stage Direction in the *Ludus Coventriae*', *ELN* 11 (1974), 162–4.

Nelson, Alan H., 'On Recovering the Lost Norwich Corpus Christi Cycle', *Comparative Drama* 4 (1970), 241–52.

— 'Some Configurations of Staging in Medieval English Drama', in *Medieval English Drama*, pp. 116–47.

— 'The Temptation of Christ; or, The Temptation of Satan', in *Medieval English Drama*, pp. 218–29.

— *The Medieval English Stage: Corpus Christi Pageants and Plays* (Chicago and London, 1974).

Nelson, Sandra Robertson, '"Goddys Worde": Revelation and Its Transmission in the N-Town Cycle', Duke Univ. Ph.D. thesis (1976).

Nitecki, Alicia K., 'The N-Town Lamech and the Convention of Maximainus' [*sic*] First Elegy', *American Notes and Queries* 17 (1979), 122–4.

Owst, G. R., *Literature and Pulpit in Medieval England* (Cambridge, 1933).

Parker, Roscoe E. (ed.), *The Middle English Stanzaic Versions of the Life of Saint Anne*. EETS OS 174 (1928, repr. 1971), pp. xxxiv–liv.

—— 'The Reputation of Herod in Early English Literature', *Speculum* 8 (1933), 59–67.

—— '"Pilates Voys"', *Speculum* 25 (1950), 237–44.

Patch, Howard R., 'The *Ludus Coventriae* and the Digby *Massacre*', *PMLA* 35 (1920), 324–43.

Phillips, Elias Hiester, 'A Study of Some Epic Aspects of the Ludus Coventriae', Univ. of N. Carolina MA thesis (1931).

Poteet, Daniel Powell II, 'The *Hegge Plays*: An Approach to the Aesthetics of Medieval Drama', Univ. of Illinois Ph.D. thesis (1969).

—— 'Condition, Contrast, and Division in the *Ludus Conventriae* "Woman Taken in Adultery"', *Mediaevalia* 1 (1975), 78–92.

—— 'Symbolic Character and Form in the *Ludus Coventriae* "Play of Noah"', *American Benedictine Rev.* 26 (1975), 75–88.

—— 'Time, Eternity, and Dramatic Form in *Ludus Coventriae* "Passion Play 1"', in *The Drama of the Middle Ages*, pp. 232–48.

Prosser, Eleanor, *Drama and Religion in the English Mystery Plays: A Re-evaluation* (Stanford, 1961).

Reid, S. W., 'Two Emendations in "Passion Play II" of the *Ludus Coventriae*', *ELN* 11 (1973), 86–7.

Reiss, Edmund, 'The Story of Lamech and Its Place in Medieval Drama', *Journal of Medieval and Renaissance Studies* 2 (1972), 35–48.

Rendall, Thomas, 'Visual Typology in the Abraham and Isaac Plays', *MP* 3 (1984), 221–32.

Rose, Martial, 'The Staging of the Hegge Plays', in *Medieval Drama*. Stratford-upon-Avon Studies, 16 (London, 1973), pp. 196–221.

Rynell, Alarik, *The Rivalry of Scandinavian and Native Synonyms in Middle English, Especially Taken and Nimen* (Lund, 1948, repr. Nendeln, Liechtenstein, 1968).

Salter, F. M., 'The Old Testament Plays of *Ludus Coventriae*', *PQ* 12 (1933), 406–9.

Sharp, Thomas, *A Dissertation on the Pageants or Dramatic Mysteries Anciently Performed at Coventry* (Coventry, 1825).

Skinner, Frances Marie, 'Glossary of Five Plays from Ludus Coventriae', Univ. of Kansas MA thesis (1927).

Southern, Richard, *The Medieval Theatre in the Round* (London, 1957).

Spector, Stephen, 'The Genesis of the N-Town Cycle', Yale Ph.D. thesis (1973); published in revised form as *The Genesis of the N-town Cycle* (New York and London, 1988).

—— 'The Composition and Development of an Eclectic Manuscript: Cotton Vespasian D VIII', *LSE* 9 (1977), 62–83.

—— 'Symmetry in Watermark Sequences', *Studies in Bibliography* 31 (1978), 162–78.

—— 'The Provenance of the N-Town Codex', *Library*, 6th ser., 1 (1979), 25–33.

Squires, Lynn, 'Law and Disorder in the *Ludus Coventriae*', in *The Drama of the Middle Ages*, pp. 272–85.

Staines, David, 'To Out-Herod Herod: The Development of a Dramatic Character', in *The Drama of the Middle Ages*, pp. 207–31.

Stemmler, Theo, 'Typological Transfer in Liturgical Offices and Religious Plays of the Middle Ages', *Studies in the Literary Imagination* 8 (1975), 123–43.

Stevens, Martin, *Four Middle English Mystery Cycles* (Princeton, 1987).

Swenson, Esther L., *An Inquiry into the Composition and Structure of Ludus Coventriae*. Univ. of Minnesota Studies in Language and Literature, 1 (Minneapolis, 1914).

Tajima, Matsuji, 'The Gerund in Medieval English Drama with Special Reference to Its Verbal Character', *Studies in English Language and Literature* 32 (1982), 81–96.

Taylor, George Coffin, 'The English "Planctus Mariae"', *MP* 4 (1907), 605–33.

—— 'The Relation of the English Corpus Christi Play to the Middle English Religious Lyric', *MP* 5 (1907), 1–38.

—— 'The *Christus Redivivus* of Nicholas Grimald and the Hegge Resurrection Plays', *PMLA* 41 (1926), 840–59.

Thien, Hermann, 'Über die englischen Marienklagen', Kiel Ph.D. thesis (1906).

Thompson, Elbert N. S., 'The *Ludus Coventriae*', *MLN* 21 (1906), 18–20.

Tobin, Mary Lampland, 'A Study of the Formation and Auspices of the *Ludus Coventriae*', Rice Univ. Ph.D. thesis (1973).

Tomlinson, Warren E., *Der Herodes-Charakter im englischen Drama*. Palaestra 195 (Leipzig, 1934).

Traver, Hope, *The Four Daughters of God.* Bryn Mawr College Monographs, 6 (1907).

Tydeman, William, *The Theatre in the Middle Ages* (Cambridge, London, etc., 1978).

Vance, Sidney Jerry, 'Unifying Patterns of Reconciliation in the *Ludus Coventriae*', Vanderbilt Univ. Ph.D. thesis (1975).

Vriend, J., *The Blessed Virgin Mary in the Medieval Drama of England* (Purmerend, Holland, 1928).

Walsh, Sister Mary Margaret, 'The Judgment Plays of the English Cycles', *American Benedictine Review* 20 (1969), 378–94.

Watson, Thomas Ramey, 'N Town *Death of Herod*', *Explicator* 40 (1981), 3–4.

Wee, David L., 'The Temptation of Christ and the Motif of Divine Duplicity in the Corpus Christi Cycle Drama', *MP* 72 (1974), 1–16.

Wells, Henry W., 'Ludus Coventriae', *American Church Monthly* 22 (1927–8), 273–86.

—— 'Style in the English Mystery Plays', *JEGP* 38 (1939), 360–81.

Wickham, Glynne, *Early English Stages.* 3 vols. (London, Henley, New York, 1963–81).

—— *The Medieval Theatre* (London, 1974).

Williams, Arnold, *The Drama of Medieval England* (East Lansing, 1961).

Wilson, Edward, 'The Earliest 'Tis = "It is"', *Notes and Queries* (April, 1974), 127–8.

Woolf, Rosemary, 'The Effect of Typology on the English Mediaeval Plays of Abraham and Isaac', *Speculum* 32 (1957), 805–25.

—— *The English Mystery Plays* (Berkeley and Los Angeles, 1972).

Wright, Michael J., '*Ludus Coventriae* Passion Play I: Action and Interpretation', *Neuphilologische Mitteilungen* 86 (1985), 70–7.

Zisowitz, Milton L., 'New Testament Apocryphal Elements in Eight Plays of the *Ludus Coventriae*', Columbia MA thesis (1935).

TABLE OF CORRESPONDING LINES

The line numbers of the present edition agree with those in Block's *Ludus Coventriae* except as noted below:

SPECTOR	BLOCK	
2/1–334	2/83–416	
7/1–24	7/1–22	(misnumbered)
25–136	23–134	
8/1–25	8/1–25	(Contemplacio)
26–116	1–90	
117–245	91–218	
246–53	219–26	
9/1–17	9/1–17	(Contemplacio)
18–73	1–55	
74–293	56–275	
294–310	1–17	(Contemplacio)
13/1–81	13/1–81	
82–174	82–152	
147A–149A	–	
150A–185A	1–36	(Contemplacio)
14/1–33	14/1–32	(Summoner)
34–405	1–372	
15/1–6	15/1–6	
7–321	6–320	
16/1–61	16/1–61	
62–73	78–89	
74–89	62–77	
90–154	90–154	
22/1–40	22/1–40	
41–6	41–5	(misnumbered)
47–183	46–182	
26/1–124	26/1–124	(Lucifer)
125–64	1–40	(John the Baptist)
165–485	1–321	
27/1–571	27/322–892	
28/1–192	28/893–1084	

29/1–20	29/1–20	(Contemplacio)
21–224	1–204	
30/1–261	30/205–465	
31/1–212 s.d.	31/466–677 s.d.	
32/1–293	32/678–970	
33/1–48	33/971–1017	(misnumbered)
34/1–16	34/1018–33	
17–325	1035–1343	(misnumbered)
35/1–304	35/1344–1647	
41/1–26	41/1–26	(Doctor)
27–148	1–122	
149–50	124, 123	
151–201	125–75	
202–13	175–86	(misnumbered)
214	–	
215	187	
216–17	189, 188	
218–528	190–500	

THE N-TOWN PLAY

THE TEXT

The spelling of the codex is reproduced except for the correction of apparent errors and the conjectural restoration of passages made illegible or lost by revision or cropping of the manuscript. Emendations are enclosed by square brackets and indicated in the *apparatus criticus*, which cites the manuscript forms as well as the abbreviated names or initials of those who proposed emendations: *B* stands for Block, *Bev* for Bevington, *D* for Davies, *G* for Greg, *H* for Hemingway, *Hal* for Halliwell, *M* for Meredith (see pp. xlvi–li for full references). Editorial deletions and additions are signalled in the textual notes by the terms 'deleted' and 'supplied' respectively. Suspensions and contractions have been expanded silently according to each scribe's practice when writing the same or similar words in full (see pp. xxii–xxiv). The letters *u*, *v*, and *w* are as they appear in the manuscript; consonantal *i* is printed as *j*, and *ȝ* is replaced by *z* where warranted. Initial double *f* is printed as *F* where appropriate, but otherwise as *f*. Word division is regularized, and capitalization and punctuation are modern. An acute accent is added to final *e* when it is an alternative spelling to *-y*. Stanzaic structure is indicated by indented rhyming lines, and speaker headings are uniformly placed at the beginnings of speeches, on the left.

[THE PROCLAMATION]

f. 1r
'A quire'

PRIMUS VEXILLAT[OR]

Now, gracyous God, groundyd of all goodnesse,
As þi grete glorie nevyr begynnyng had,
So þu socour and saue all þo þat sytt and sese,
And lystenyth to oure talkyng with sylens stylle
and sad.
For we purpose us pertly stylle in þis prese
þe pepyl to plese with pleys ful glad.
Now lystenyth us louely, bothe more and lesse,
Gentyllys and ȝemanry of goodly lyff lad,
þis tyde.
We xal ȝou shewe as þat we kan
How þat þis werd fyrst began,
And how God made bothe molde and man,
Iff þat ȝe wyl abyde.

SECUNDUS VEXILLA[TOR]

In þe fyrst pagent we þenke to play
How God dede make þurowe his owyn myth
Hevyn so clere upon þe fyrst day,
And þerin he sett angell ful bryth.
Than angell with songe, þis is no nay,
Xal worchep God as it is ryth.
But Lucyfer, þat angell so gay,
In suche pompe þan is he pyth
And set in so gret pride,
þat Goddys sete he gynnyth to take,
Hese Lordys pere hymself to make.
But þan he fallyth a fend ful blake
From hevyn, in helle to a[byde].

On the flyleaf appears the shelf-mark Vespasian D. 8. *and a note by Richard James*: 'Elenchus contentorum in hoc codice * Contenta novi testamenti scenicè expressa· et actitata olim per monachos sive Fratres mendicantes· vulgò dicitur hic liber Ludus Coventriae· sive ludus corporis Christi· scribitur metris Anglicanis.' I *appears in left margin opposite* Contenta

The paper of A and B quires carries a Bunch of Grapes watermark. The plaie called Corpus Christi *written at the top of the page in an Elizabethan hand*

1 VEXILLATOR] Vexillat, *remainder cropped*   14 VEXILLATOR] Vexilla, *remainder cropped*   26 abyde] a, *remainder cropped*

TERCIUS VEXILLA[TOR]
In þe secunde pagent, by Godys myth,
We þenke to shewe and pley bedene
In þe other sex days, by opyn syth,
What þenge was wrought. Þer xal be sene
How best was made, and foule of flyth,
And last was man made, as I wene.
Of mannys o ryb, as I ȝow plyth,
Was woman wrougth, mannys make to bene,
And put in paradyse.
f. 1v Ther were flourys bothe blew and blake;
Of all frutys þei myth þer take,
Saff frute of cunnyng þei xulde forsake
And towche it in no wyse.

The serpent toke Eve an appyl to byte,
And Eve toke Adam a mursel of þe same.
Whan þei had do þus aȝens þe rewle of ryte,
Than was oure Lord wroth and grevyd al with
grame.
Oure Lord gan appose þem of þer gret delyte,
Bothe to askuse hem of þat synful blame.
And þan Almythy God for þat gret dyspite
Assygned hem grevous peyn, as ȝe xal se in
game,
Indede.
Seraphyn, an angell gay,
With brennyng swerd, þis is verray,
From paradise bete hem away,
In Bybyl as we rede.

PRIMUS VEXILLATOR
We purpose to shewe in þe thryd pagent
The story of Caym and of hese brother Abelle.
Of here tythyngys now be we bent
In þis pagent þe trewth to telle.
How þe tythyng of Abel with feyr was brent
And accept to God, yf ȝe wyl dwelle,
We purpose to shewe, as we haue ment,
And how he was kyllyd of his brother so felle.

27 VEXILLATOR] Vexilla, *remainder cropped* 44 delyte] *B* debyte

And than
How Caym was cursyd in al degré
Of Godys owyn mowthe þer xal ȝe se.
Of trewe tythyng þis may wel be
Exaw[m]ple to every man.

SECUNDUS VEXILATOR
The iij^{de} pagent is now ȝow tolde.
þe fourte pagent of Noe xal be,
How God was wroth with man on molde
Because fro synne man dede not fle.
He sent to Noe an angel bolde, f. 2^{r}
A shyp for to makyn and swymmen on þe se,
Vpon þe water both wood and coolde;
And viij sowles þer savyd xulde be,
And j peyre of everich bestys in brynge.
Whan xl^{ti} days þe flode had flowe,
þan sente Noe out a crowe,
And after hym he sent a dowe
þat brouth ryth good tydyng.

TERCIUS VEXIL[LATOR]
Of Abraham is þe fyfte pagent,
And of Ysaac, his sone so fre,
How þat he xulde with fere be brent
And slayn with swerd, as ȝe xal se.
Abraham toke with good atent
His sone Ysaac and knelyd on kne—
His suerd was than ful redy bent—
And thouth his chylde þer offered xuld be
Vpon an hyll ful ryff.
Than God toke tent to his good wyl
And sent an angel ryth sone hym tyl,
And bad Abraham a shep to kyl,
And sauyd his chyldys lyff.

PRIMUS VEXIL[LATOR]
The sexte pagent is of Moyses,
And of tweyn tabelys þat God hym took,

65 exawmple] exawple 79 VEXILLATOR] Vexil, *remainder cropped*
81 *one or more letters* (f.?) *canc. in red before* with 92 VEXILLATOR] Vexil, *remainder cropped*

In þe which were wrete, without les,
þe lawes of God to lerne and lok;
And how God charged hym be wordys these
þe lawes to lerne al of þat book.
Moyses than doth nevyrmore sese,
But prechyth duly bothe ȝere and woke
f. 2v The lawes, as I ȝow telle,
þe Ten Comaundementys alle bedene—
In oure play ȝe xal hem sene—
To alle þo þat þere wyl bene,
If þat ȝe thenke to duelle.

SECUNDUS VEXILLATOR

Off þe gentyl Jesse rote
þe sefnt pagent, forsothe, xal ben,
Out of þe which doth sprynge oure bote,
As in prophecye we redyn and sen.
Kyngys and prophetys with wordys ful sote
Schull prophesye al of a qwen,
þe which xal staunch oure stryff and moote,
And wynnyn us welthe withoutyn wen,
In hevyn to abyde.
They xal prophecye of a mayde,
All fendys of here xal be affrayde.
Here sone xal saue us, be not dismayde,
With hese woundys wyde.

TERCIUS VEXILLATOR

Of þe grete bushop Abyacar
þe tende pagent xal be, without lesyng,
þe which comaundyth men to be war
And brynge here douterys to dew weddyng;
All þat ben xiiij ȝere and more,
To maryage he byddyth hem bryng.
Wherevyr þei be, he chargyth sore
þat þei not fayle for no lettyng,

119 tende *written over an erasure* (viij?)

þe lawe byddyth so than.
Than Joachym and Anne so mylde,
þei brynge forthe Mary, þat blyssyd chylde.
But she wold not be defylyde
With spot nor wem of man.

In chastyté þat blysful mayde f. 3^{r}
Avowyd there here lyff to lede.
þan is þe busshop sore dysmayde
And wonderyth sore al of þis dede.
He knelyd to God, as it is sayde,
And prayth than for help and rede.
þan seyth an angel, 'Be not afrayde;
Of þis dowte take þu no drede,
But for þe kynrede of Dauyd þu sende.
Lete hem come with here offryng,
And in here handys white ȝerdys brynge.
Loke whose ȝerde doth floure and sprynge,
And he xal wedde þat mayden hende'.

PRIMUS VEXILLATOR

In þe x^{te} pagent, sothe to say,
A masangere forthe is sent.
Dauydis kynrede without delay,
They come ful sone with good entent.
Whan Joseph offeryd his ȝerde þat day,
Anon-ryth forth in present,
þe ded styk do floure ful gay,
And þan Joseph to wedlok went,
Ryth as þe angel bad.
Than he plyth to his wyff
In chastyté to ledyn here lyff.
þe busshop toke here iij maydonys ryff;
Som comforte þere she had.

126 serteyn *canc. before* than   144 x^{te}] *altered from* ix^{te} *by erasure of* i
156 had] hadde, *with* -de *crossed through and marked with deleting dots*

SECUNDUS VEXILLATOR

In þe xj^{de} pagent goth Gabryell
  And doth salute oure Lady fre.
Than grett with chylde, as I ȝow tell,
  þat blyssyd mayde, forsothe is she.
f. 3^{v} þo iij maydenys þat with here dwelle
  Here gret spech, but noon þei se.
Than they suppose þat sum angell,
  Goddys masangere þat it xuld be.
    And thus
      þe Holy Gost in here is lyth,
      And Goddys sone in here is pygth.
      þe aungell doth telle what he xal hyght
    And namyth þe chylde Jhesus.

TERCIUS VEXILLATOR

In þe xij pagent, as I ȝow telle,
  Joseph comyth hom fro fer countré.
Oure Ladyes wombe with chylde doth swelle,
  And þan Joseph, ful hevy is he.
He doth forsake here with hert ful felle,
  Out of countré he gynnyth to fle;
He nevyrmore thenkyth with here to dwelle,
  And than oure Lady, ryth sore wepyth she.
    An angell seyd hym ryf:
      'God is with þi wyff, sertayn,
      þerfore, Joseph, turne hom agayn'.
      þan is Joseph in herte ful fayn,
    And goth ageyn onto his wyff.

PRIMUS VEXILLATOR

The xi[i]ij^{te} pagent, I sey ȝow bedene,
  Xal be of Joseph and mylde Mary:
How they were sclawndryd with trey and tene,
  And to here purgacyon þei must hem hy.

157 *B notes that the writing becomes smaller and the ink colour changes in this stanza, but these changes are slight, if present at all* xj^{de}] *altered from an original* x^{de} 170 xij *interl. above* hellenthe, *which is canc. in red* 179 sertayn] a *written over an* e 180 agayn] *second* a *written over an* e 183 xiiij^{te}] xij^{te}ij, *altered from* xij^{te} *After 186, 55 mm blank on f. 3^{v}; 36 mm blank on f. 4^{r} before 187*

SECUNDUS VEXILLATOR

In þe xv pagent shewe we xal f. 4^{r}
  How Joseph went withoute varyauns
For mydwyuys to helpe oure Lady at all,
  Of childe that she had delyuerauns.

TERCIUS VEXILLATOR

In þe xvj pagent Cryst xal be born.
  Of þat joy aungelys xul synge
And telle þe shepherdys in þat morn
  The blysseful byrth of þat kyng.
The shepherdys xal come hym befforn
  With reuerens and with worchepyng,
For he xal sauyn þat was forlorn
  And graunt us lyff evyrmore lestyng,
    Iwys.
      þis gle in gryth
      Is mater of myrth.
      Now Crystys byrth
    Bryng us to his blys.

PRIMUS VEXILLATOR

[In] the xv^{te} pagent come kyngys iij f. 4^{v}
  With gold, myrre, and frankynsens.
Kyng Herowdys styward hem doth se
  And bryngyth all to his presens.
The kyngys of Coleyn with hert ful fre
  Tolde Kyng Herownde here dylygens,
That þei south in þat countré
  A kyng of kyngys from fere thens;
    A sterre led hem þe way.
      'The chylde is ȝoung and lyth in stall;
      He xal be kyng of kyngys all.
      Beffore hym we thynk on kne to fall
    And worchep hym þis day'.

187 xv *altered from* xiij 189 mydwyuys] *the third* y *smudged and perhaps written over another letter* *53 mm blank after 190* 191 xvj *altered from* xiiij 203 *A word* (No..?) *canc. in brown and red before* Bryng 204 In *supplied* the] h *unusually tall* 207 *an incomplete letter canc. before* all

SECUNDUS VEXILLATOR

In þe xvj pagent as wroth as wynde
Is Kyng Herownde, þe soth to say,
And cruel knytys and vnkende
To sle male chylderyn he sendyth þat day.
But Cryst Jesu þei may not fynde,
For Joseph hath led þat childe away
Vnto Egypth, as we haue mende,
As angel to Joseph dyd byd and say,
In hyȝht.
þo chylderyn þat syt in here moderys lap
To sowkyn ful swetly here moderys pap,
þe knythtys do sle hem evyn at a swap.
þis is a rewly syth.

TERCIUS VEXILLATOR

In þe xvij pagent þe knythtys bedene
Shull brynge dede childeryn befor þe kyng.
Whan Kyng Herownde þat syth hath sene,
Ful glad he is of here kyllyng.
Than Kyng Herownde, withowtyn wene,
Is sett to mete at his lykyng.
In his most pride xal come gret tene,
As ȝe xal se at oure pleyng.
f. 5r His sorwe xal awake.
Whan he is sett at hese most pryde,
Sodeyn Deth xal thrylle his syde
And kylle his knyttys þat with hym byde;
þe devyl þer soulys xal take.

PRIMUS VEXILLATOR

In þe xviij pagent we must purpose
To shewe whan Cryst was xij ȝer of age,
How in þe temple he dede appose
And answerd doctoris ryth wyse and sage.
The blyssyd babe, withowte glose,
Ouercam olde clerkys with suych langage
þat þei merveylyd, ȝe xal suppose,
How þat he cam to suche knowlage,
And in þis whyle.
Thre days he was oute
Fro his modyr, without doute.
Wepyng she sowth hym rownde aboute
Jheruselem many a myle.

SECUNDUS VEXILLATOR

In þe xix pagent xal Seynt Jhon
Baptyse Cryst, as I ȝow say,
In þe watyr of Flom Jordon.
With which devys as we best may,
The Holy Gost xal ouyr hym on.
þe Faderys voys xal be herd þat day
Out of hevyn, þat blisful tron;
þe Fadyr xal be herd, þis is no nay.
And forthwith pleyn
þe Holy Gost xal be his gyde
Into desert, þerin to abyde
xl^{ti} days, a terme ful wyde,
And xl^{ti} nygthtys to faste, sarteyn.

TERCIUS VEXILLATOR

In þe xx^{ti} pagent all þe deuelys of helle,
They gadere a parlement, as ȝe xal se.
They haue gret doute, þe trewth to telle,
Of Cryst Jesu, whath he xulde be.
They sende Ssathan, þat fynde so felle, f. 5^{v}
Cryst for to tempte in fele degré.
We xal ȝow shewe, if ȝe wyl dwelle,
How Cryst was temptyd in synnys thre
Of þe devyl Sathan.
And how Cryst answeryd onto alle,
And made þe fende awey to falle,
As we best may, þis shewe we xalle
Thorwe grace of God and man.

PRIMUS VEXILLATOR

The xxi^{ti} pagent of a woman xal be,
þe which was take in adultrye.
The Pharysewys falsed þer ȝe xal se,
Cryst to convycte how they were slye.
They conseyvyd þis sotylté:
Yf Cryst þis woman dede dampne, trewly,
Ageyn his prechyng than dede he,
Which was of peté and of mercy;

268 sarteyn] a *altered from an* e   273 *ascenders in this line are unusually tall*

And yf he dede here save,
þan were he aȝens Moyses lawe,
þat byddyth with stonys she xulde be slawe.
þus they thowth vndyr þer awe
Cryst Jesu for to haue.

SECUNDUS VEXILLATOR

The grettest meracle þat evyr Jesus
In erthe wrouth beforn his Passyon
In [þe] xxij^{ti} pagent we purpose vs
To shewe indede þe declaracyon.
þat pagent xal be of Lazarus,
In whos place and habytacyon
Cryst was logyd—þe gospel seyth thus—
And ofte-tyme toke þer consolacyon.
But ȝyt
f. 6^{r} Lazarus, as I ȝow say,
Was iiij days ded and beryed in clay.
From deth to lyve þe iiij^{te} day
Cryst reysed hym from þat pyt.

TERCIUS VEXILLATOR

In þe xxiij^{ti} pagent Palme Sunday
In pley we purpose for to shewe,
How chylderyn of Ebrew with flourys ful gay,
þe wey þat Cryst went þei gun to strewe.

PRIMUS VEXILLATOR

In þe xxiiij^{ti} pagent, as þat we may,
Cryst and his apostelys alle on rewe,
The Mawndé of God þer xal they play,
And sone declare it with wordys fewe.
And than
Judas, þat fals traytour,
For xxx^{ti} platys of werdly tresour
Xal betray oure Savyour
To þe Jewys, certan.

293 vndyr] n *smudged altered from other letters* 297 þe *supplied* 302 ofte] o *blotted;* oft *possibly* 320 certan] e *blotted*

SECUNDUS VEXILLATOR

For grevous peyn, þis is no les,
In þe xxv^{ti} pagent Cryst xal pray
To þe Fadyr of Hevyn þat peyn for to ses,
His shamful deth to put away.
Judas, þat traytour, befor gret pres
Xal kys his mouth and hym betray.
All his dyscyples than do dyscres
And forsake Cryst, þe soth to say;
For doute þei do hem hede.
Hese dyscyplys all, everychon,
Do renne awey and leve hym alon;
They lete hym stondyn amonge his fon
And renne away for drede.

TERCIUS VE[XILLATOR]

Than in þe xxvj^{ti} pagent f. 6^{v}
To Cayphas Cryst xal be brouth.
þo Jewys ful redy þer xul be bent
Cryst to acuse with worde and thouth.
Seynt Petyr doth folwe with good intent
To se with Cryst what xuld be wrouth.
For Crystys dyscyple whan he is hent,
Thryes he doth swere he knew hym nowth.
A kok xal crowe and crye.
Than doth Petyr gret sorwe make,
For he his Lord þus dede forsake.
But God to grace hym sone doth take
Whan he doth aske mercye.

PRIMUS VEXILLATOR

In þe xxvij pagent Sere Pylat
Is sett in sete as hy justyce.
Whan he is set in his astat,
Thre thevys be brout of synful gyse.
And Cryst, þat louyd nevyr stryff nor bat,
But trewth and goodnesse on every wyse,
As for a thef with ryth gret hat
Is browth to stondyn at þat same syse.

334 VEXILLATOR] Ve, *remainder cropped*

And þan, as I ȝow say,
The wyff of Pylat goth to rest
Coveryd with clothis al of þe best;
Than for to slepe she is ful prest.
All þis we thenke to play.

SECUNDUS VEXILLATOR
In þe xxviij^{ti} pagent xal Judas,
þat was to Cryst a fals traytour,
With wepyng sore evyr crye, Alas!
þat evyr he solde oure Savyour.
f. 7^{r} He xal be sory for his trespas
And brynge aȝen all his tresour,
All xxx pens, to Sere Cayphas—
He xal them brynge with gret dolowre—
For þe which Cryst was bowth.
For gret whanhope, as ȝe xal se,
He hangyth hymself vpon a tre,
For he noth trostyth in Godys peté.
To helle his sowle is browth.

TERCIUS VEXILLATOR
In þe xxix pagent to Pylatus wyff
In slepe aperyth þe devyl of helle.
For to savyn Crystys lyff
The devyl here temptyth, as I ȝow telle.
Sche sendyth to Pylat anon ful ryff
And prayth þat Cryst he xuld not qwelle.
þan Pylat is besy, and ryth blyff
Cryst for to savyn he ȝevyth councelle,
For he dede neuyr trespas.
The Jewys do crye fast for to kylle,
The rythful man þei aske to spylle;
A thef þei saue with herty wylle
þat callyd is Barrabas.

PRIMUS VEXILLATOR
In þe xxx^{ti} pagent þei bete out Crystys blood
And nayle hym al nakyd upon a rode-tre;

356 *and* 357 *are transposed; corrected by placement in left margin of a* b *opposite* 357 *and an* a *opposite* 356 365 *an* s *canc. before* tresour 382 *the writing is slightly less regular down to the bottom of this page* 383 ryff *canc. before* rythful

Betwen ij thevys—iwys, they were to wood—
They hyng Cryst Jesu, gret shame it is to se.
Vij wurdys Cryst spekyth hangyng upon þe rode, f. 7^{v}
þe weche ȝe xal here, all þo þat wyl þer be;
þan doth he dye for oure allther good.
His modyr doth se þat syth, gret mornyng makyth she;
For sorwe she gynnyth to swowne.
Seynt Johan evyn þer, as I ȝow plyth,
Doth chere oure Lady with al his myth,
And to þe temple anon forthryth
He ledyth here in þat stownde.

SECUNDUS VEXILLATOR

We purpose to shewe in oure pleyn place
In þe xxxj^{ti} pagent þorwe Godys myth
How to Crystys herte a spere gan pace
And rent oure Lordys bryst in ruly plyth.
For Longeus, þat old knyth, blynd as he was,
A ryth sharpe spere to Crystys herte xal pyth.
þe blod of his wounde to his eyn xal tras,
And þorwe gret meracle þer hath he syth.
Than in þat morn,
Crystys soule goth down to helle,
And þer ovyrcomyth þe fend so felle,
Comfortyth þe soulys þat þerin dwelle,
And savyth þat was forlorn.

TERCIUS VEXILLATOR

Joseph and Nycodemus, to Cryst trew servaunt,
In þe xxxij page[nt] þe body þei aske to haue.
Pylat ful redyly þe body doth hem graunt,
þan þei with reverens do put it in grave.
þe Jewys, more wyckyd þan ony geawnt,
For Crystys ded body kepers do þei craue;
Pylat sendyth iiij knytys þat be ryth hardaunt
To kepe þe blody body in his dede conclaue.

389 is *interl. above canc.* was 392 dye] e *written over an incomplete letter*
412 *to the bottom of the page, the writing is quite small* 413 pagent] page

f. 8[r]

And ȝit, be his owyn myth,
The body, þat was hevy as led,
Be þe Jewys nevyr so qwed,
Aryseth from grave þat þer lay ded,
And frayth than every knyth.

PRIMUS VEXILLATOR

In þe [x]xxiij pagent þe soule of Cryst Jesu
Xal brynge all his frendys from helle to paradyse.
Þe soule goth than to þe grave and, be ryth gret vertu,
Þat body þat longe ded hath loyn to lyf aȝen doth ryse.
Than doth Cryst Jesu onto his modyr sew,
And comfortyth all here care in temple þer she lyse.
With suche cher and comforth his modyr he doth indew
Þat joy it is to here þer spech for to devyse.
And than
Oure Lady of Hefne so cler,
In herte sche hath ryth glad chere.
Whan here sone þus doth apere,
Here care awey is tan.

SECUNDUS VEXIL[LATOR]

In þe xxxiiij[ti] pagent xal Maryes thre
Seke Cryst Jesu in his grave so coolde.
An aungel hem tellyth þat aresyn is he.
And whan þat þis tale to them is tolde,
To Crystys dyscyplis with wurdys ful fre
They telle these tydyngys with brest ful bolde.
Than Petyr and Johan, as ȝe xal se,
Down rennyn in hast ouyr lond and wolde,
The trewth of þis to haue.
Whan þei þer comyn, as I ȝow say,
He is gon from vndyr clay.
Þan þei wytnesse anoon þat day
He lyth not in his grave.

425 xxxiij] xxiij *cropped* 427 ryth *interl.* 438 VEXILLATOR] Vexil, *remainder cropped*

TERCIUS VEXILLATOR

Onto Mary Mawdelyn, as we haue bent, f. 8^{v}
Cryst Jesu xal than apere
In þe xxxv^{ti} pagent,
And she wenyth he be a gardenere.
Mary be name, verament,
Whan Cryst here callyth with spech ful clere,
She fallyth to ground with good entent,
To kys his fete with gladsom chere.
But Cryst byddyth here do way.
He byddyth his feet þat sche not kys
Tyl he haue styed to hefne blys.
To Crystys dyscyplys Mary, iwys,
Than goth, þe trewth to say.

PRIMUS VEXILLATOR

In þe xxxvj^{ti} pagent xal Cleophas
And Sent Luke to a castel go.
Of Crystys deth as þei forth pas
They make gret mornyng and be ful wo.
Than Cryst þem ovyrtok, as his wyl was,
And walkyd in felachep forth with hem too.
To them he doth expowne bothe more and las,
All þat prophetys spak, a[n]d of hymself also.
That nyth, in fay,
Whan þei be set within þe castell,
In brekyng of bred þei know Cryst well.
Than sodeynly, as I ȝow tell,
Cryste is gon his way.

SECUNDUS VEXILLATOR

In þe xxxvij^{ti} pagent þan purpos we,
To Thomas of Ynde Cryst xal apere;
And Thomas euyn þer, as ȝe xal se,
Xal put his hand in his woundys dere.

TERCIUS VEXILLATOR

In þe xxxviij^{ti} pagent up stye xal he f. 9^{r}
Into hefne, þat is so clere.

459 *a malformed letter* (*a* b *written over a* d?) *canc. before* byddyth 465 castel] c *apparently altered from another letter* 471 and] ad 474 know] *or* knew 481 *an unnecessary capitulum stands opposite this line*

All hese apostel þer xul be
And woundere sore and haue gret dwere
Of þat ferly syth.
þer xal come aungell tweyn
And comfforte hem, þis is certeyn,
And tellyn þat he xal comyn ageyn,
Evyn by his owyn myth.

PRIMUS VEXILLATOR Than folwyth next, sekyrly,
Of Wyttsunday, þat solempne fest,
Whych pagent xal be ix and thretty.
þe apostelys to apere be Crystys hest
In Hierusalem were gaderyd xij opynly,
To þe cenacle comyng from west and est.
þe Holy Gost apperyd ful veruently,
With brennyng fere thyrlyng here brest,
Procedyng from hevyn trone.
All maner langage hem spak with tung,
Latyn, Grek, and Ebrew among;
And affter þei departyd and taryed not long,
Here deth to take ful sone.

SECUNDUS VEXILLATOR The xl^{ti} pagent xal be þe last,
And Domysday þat pagent xal hyth.
Who se þat pagent may be agast
To grevyn his Lord God eyther day or nyth.
The erth xal qwake, bothe breke and brest,
Beryelys and gravys xul ope ful tyth;
Ded men xul rysyn, and þat þer in hast,
And fast to here ansuere þei xul hem dyth
f. 9v Beffore Godys face.
But prente wyl þis in ȝoure mende:
Whoso to God hath be vnkende,
Frenchep þer xal he non fynde,
Ne þer get he no grace.

493 to *deleted before* þe   507 brest] e *written over another letter*   *f.* 9v *marked* 10; *the* 10 *then crossed through*

TERCIUS VEXILLATOR

Now haue we told ȝow all bedene
The hool mater þat we thynke to play.
Whan þat ȝe come þer xal ȝe sene
This game wel pleyd in good aray.
Of Holy Wrytte þis game xal bene,
And of no fablys be no way.
Now God þem save from trey and tene
For us þat prayth upon þat day,
And qwyte them wel þer mede.
A Sunday next, yf þat we may,
At vj of þe belle we gynne oure play
In N-town; wherfore we pray
That God now be ȝoure spede.
Amen.

I

f. 10r

[THE CREATION OF HEAVEN; THE FALL OF LUCIFER]

Ego sum alpha et oo, principium et finis.

DEUS

My name is knowyn, God and kynge.
My werk for to make now wyl I wende.
In myself restyth my reynenge;
It hath no gynnyng ne non ende.
And all þat evyr xal haue beynge,
It is closyd in my mende.
Whan it is made at my lykynge,
I may it save, I may it shende
After my plesawns.
So gret of myth is my pousté,
Allthyng xal be wrowth be me.
I am oo God in personys thre,
Knyt in oo substawns.

527 N-town] N. town

[*Play 1*] *Several words, including* Roberti Hegge Dunelmensis, *partially cropped in top margin*

I am þe trewe Trenyté
  Here walkyng in þis wone.
Thre personys myself I se
  Lokyn in me, God alone:
I am þe Fadyr of Powsté;
  My Sone with me gynnyth gon;
My Gostis grace in magesté
  Weldyth welthe up in hevyn tron.
    O God thre I calle:
      I am Fadyr of Myth,
      My Sone kepyth ryth,
      My Gost hath lyth
    And grace withalle.

Myself begynnyng nevyr dyd take,
f. 10v   And endeles I am thorw myn owyn myth.
Now wole I begynne my werke to make.
  Fyrst I make hevyn with sterrys of lyth,
In myrth and joy euyrmore to wake.
  In hevyn I bylde angell ful bryth
My servauntys to be; and for my sake,
  With merth and melody [to] worchepe my myth,
    I belde them in my blysse.
      Aungell in hevyn evyrmore xal be
      In lyth ful clere, bryth [of] ble,
      With myrth and song to worchip me;
    Of joye þei may not mys.

Hic cantent angeli in celo: 'Tibi omnes angeli, tibi celi et vniuerse potestates, tibi cherubyn et seraphyn incessabili voce proclamant: Sanctus, Sanctus, Sanctus, Dominus Deus Sabaoth'.

LUCIFERE To whos wurchipe synge ȝe þis songe,
  To wurchip God or reverens me?
But ȝe me wurchipe ȝe do me wronge,
  For I am þe wurthyest þat evyr may be!

34 to *supplied;* my *written in right margin* 37 of] *D; MS* as 39 s.d. *The rubricated mark* precedes Hic. *A capitulum precedes the first* Tibi

ANGELI BONI We wurchipe God of myth most stronge,
Whiche hath formyd bothe vs and the.
We may nevyr wurchyp hym to longe,
For he is most worthy of magesté.
On knes to God we falle.
Oure Lorde God wurchyp we,
And in no wyse honowre we the!
A gretter lord may nevyr non be
Than he þat made us alle.

LUCIFERE A wurthyer lorde, forsothe, am I!
And worthyer than he euyr wyl I be.
In evydens þat I am more wurthy, f. 11r
I wyl go syttyn in Goddys se.
Above sunne, and mone, and sterrys on sky
I am now set, as ȝe may se.
Now wurchyp me for most mythty,
And for ȝoure lord honowre now me
Syttyng in my sete.
ANGELI MALI Goddys myth we forsake,
And for more wurthy we þe take.
Þe to wurchep honowre we make
And falle down at þi fete.

DEUS Thu, Lucyfere, for þi mekyl pryde
I bydde þe falle from hefne to helle,
And all þo þat holdyn on þi syde,
In my blysse nevyrmore to dwelle!
At my comawndement anoon down þu slyde,
With merth and joye nevyrmore to melle.
In myschyf and manas evyr xalt þu abyde,
In byttyr brennyng and fyer so felle,
In peyn evyr to be pyht!
LUCYFERE At thy byddyng þi wyl I werke,
And pas fro joy to peyne smerte.
Now I am a devyl ful derke,
Þat was an aungell bryht.

45 the] *the* e *written over another letter and another* e *interl. above it* 50 we *interl.*
59 wurthy *canc. in red before* mythty 74 *a word* (py..?) *canc. before* pyht

Now to helle þe wey I take,
In endeles peyn þer to be pyht.
For fere of fyre a fart I crake!
In helle donjoon myn dene is dyth.

f. 11v

2
[THE CREATION OF THE WORLD; THE FALL OF MAN]

DEUS Now hevyn is made for aungell sake
þe fyrst day and þe fyrst nyth.
The secunde day watyr I make,
The walkyn also, ful fayr and [br]yth.
The iij^{de} day I parte watyr from erthe;
Tre and every growyng thyng,
Bothe erbe and floure of suete smellyng,
The iij^{de} day is made be my werkyng.
Now make I þe day þat xal be þe ferthe.

Sunne, and mone, and sterrys also
þe forthe day I make in-same.
þe v^{te} day werm and fysch þat swymme and go,
Byrdys and bestys, bothe wylde and tame.
The sexte day my werk I do
And make þe, man, Adam be name.
In erthelech paradys withowtyn wo
I graunt þe bydyng, lasse þu do blame.

Flesch of þi flesch and bon of þi bon,
Adam, here is þi wyf and make.
Bothe fysche and foulys þat swymmyn and gon,
To everych of hem a name þu take;
Bothe tre, and frute, and bestys echon,
Red and qwyte, bothe blew and blake,
þu ȝeve hem name be þiself alon,
Erbys and gresse, both beetys and brake;

[*Play 2*] *A capitulum precedes 1. A figure* (N?) *is written in left margin before 2*
4 bryth] *Altered by rubbing and a hole in the leaf to* lyth

Þi wyff þu ȝeve name also.
Loke þat ȝe not ses
Ȝowre frute to encres,
Þat þer may be pres,
Me worchipe for to do.

Now come forth, Adam, to paradys; f. 12r
Ther xalt þu haue all maner thynge:
Bothe flesch, and fysch, and frute of prys,
All xal be buxum at þi byddyng.
Here is pepyr, pyan, and swete lycorys;
Take hem all at þi lykyng,
Bothe appel, and pere, and gentyl rys—
But towche nowth þis tre þat is of cunnyng.
Allthynge saff þis for þe is wrought.
Here is allþinge þat þe xulde plese
All redy made onto þin ese.
Ete not þis frute ne me dysplese,
For than þu deyst, þu skapyst nowth!

Now haue I made allthynge of nowth,
Hevyn and erth, foull and best.
To allthynge þat myn hand hath wrowth
I graunt myn blyssyng þat evyr xal lest.
My wey to hefne is redy sowth,
Of werkyng I wole þe vij^{te} day rest.
And all my creaturys þat be abowth,
My blyssyng ȝe haue both est and west.
Of werkyng þe vij^{te} day ȝe sees.
And all þo þat sees of laboryng here
Þe vij^{te} day, withowtyn dwere,
And wurchyp me in good manere,
Þei xal in hefne haue endles pes.

47 lest] e *interl. above an* a, *with a deleting dot below the* a   49 sefte *canc. in red before* vij^{te}

Adam, go forth and be prynce in place,
f. 12v For to hefne I sped my way.
þi wyttys wel loke þu chase,
And gostly gouerne þe as I say.

ADAM Holy Fadyr, blyssyd þu be,
For I may walke in welthe anow.
I fynde datys gret plenté
And many fele frutys ful every bow.
All þis wele is ȝovyn to me
And to my wyf þat on me lowh.
I haue no nede to towche ȝon tre,
Aȝens my Lordys wyl to werke now.
I am a good gardenere.
Euery frute of ryche name
I may gaderyn with gle and game.
To breke þat bond I were to blame
þat my Lord bad me kepyn here.

EUA We may both be blythe and glad
Oure Lordys comaundement to fulfyll.
With fele frutys be we fayr fad,
Woundyr dowcet and nevyr on ill.
Euery tre with frute is sprad,
Of them to take as plesyth us tyll.
Oure wytte were rakyl and ovyrdon bad
To forfete ageyns oure Lordys wyll
In ony wyse.
In þis gardeyn I wyl go se
All þe flourys of fayr bewté,
And tastyn þe frutys of gret plenté
þat be in paradyse.

f. 13r SERPENS Heyl, fayr wyff and comely dame,
þis frute to ete I þe cownselle.
Take þis appyl and ete þis same;
þis frute is best, as I þe telle.

62 *A blot obscures final* e *in* welthe *and* a *in* anow 65 ȝovyn] *B* ȝevyn
70 ryche] *B* rythe 85 plenté] t *interl. above a blotted letter* (d*?*)

EUA
That appyl to ete I were to blame!
From joy oure Lorde wolde us expelle.
We xuld dye and be put out with schame,
In joye of paradyse nevyrmore to duelle.
God hymself þus sayde.
What day of þat frute we ete,
With þese wurdys God dyd us threte,
þat we xuld dye, oure lyff to lete.
þerffore I am affrayde.

SERPENS
Of þis appyl yf ȝe wyl byte,
Evyn as God is, so xal ȝe be:
Wys of connyng, as I ȝow plyte,
Lyke onto God in al degré.
Sunne, and mone, and sterrys bryth,
Fysch and foule, boþe sond and se,
At ȝoure byddyng bothe day and nyth,
Allthynge xal be in ȝowre powsté:
Ȝe xal be Goddys pere!
Take þis appyl in þin hond
And to byte þerof þu fond.
Take another to þin husbond;
þerof haue þu no dwere.

EUA
So wys as God is in his gret mayn
And felaw in kunnyng, fayn wold I be.

SERPENS
Ete þis appyl and in certeyn, f. 13v
þat I am trewe sone xalt þu se.

EVA
To myn husbond with herte ful fayn
þis appyl I bere, as þu byddyst me.
þis frute to ete I xal asayn
So wys as God is yf we may be,
And Goddys pere of myth.
To myn husbond I walke my way,
And of þis appyl I xal asay
To make hym to ete, yf þat I may,
And of þis frewte to byth.

95 sayde] a *altered from an* e   109 hond] o *interl. above an* a, *with a deleting dot below the* a   117 *preceded by a capitulum*

Hic Eua reueniet Ade viro suo et dicet ei:

My semely spowse and good husbond,
Lystenyth to me, sere, I ȝow pray:
Take þis fayr appyl all in ȝoure hond,
þerof a mursel byte and asay.
To ete þis appyl loke þat ȝe fonde,
Goddys felaw to be alway,
All his wysdam to vndyrstonde,
And Goddys pere to be for ay,
Allthyng for to make:
Both fysch and foule, se and sond,
Byrd and best, watyr and lond.
þis appyl þu take out of myn hond;
A bete þerof þu take.

ADAM I dare not towch þin hand for dred
Of oure Lord God omnypotent!
If I xuld werke aftyr þi reed,
Of God oure Makere I xuld be shent.
f. 14r If þat we do þis synful dede,
We xal be ded by Goddys jugement!
Out of þin hand with hasty spede
Cast out þat appyl anon present
For fer of Goddys threte!

EVA Of þis appyl yf þu wylt byte,
Goddys pere þu xalt be pyht,
So wys of kunnyng, I þe plyht,
þis frute yf þu wylt ete.

ADAM If we it ete oureself we kylle.
As God us tolde, we xuld be ded.
To ete þat frute and my lyf to spylle,
I dar not do aftyr þi reed.

EUA A fayr aungell þus seyd me tylle:
'To ete þat appyl take nevyr no dred.
So kunnyng as God in hevyn hille
þu xalt sone be withinne a sted'.

151 ete] *final* e *smudged*

þerfore þis frute þu ete.

ADAM
Off Goddys wysdam for to lere,
And in kunnyng to be his pere,
Of thyn hand I take it here,
And xal sone tast þis mete.

Adam dicit sic:

Alas, alas for þis fals dede!
My flesly frend my fo I fynde.
Schameful synne doth us vnhede:
I se vs nakyd before and behynde.
Oure Lordys wurd wold we not drede,
þerfore we be now caytyvys vnkynde. f. 14v
Oure pore pryuytés for to hede
Summe fygge levys fayn wolde I fynde,
For to hyde oure schame.
Womman, ley þis leff on þi pryvyté,
And with þis leff I xal hyde me.
Gret schame it is vs nakyd to se,
Oure Lord God þus to grame.

EVA
Alas, þat evyr þat speche was spokyn
þat þe fals aungel seyd onto me!
Alas, oure Makers byddyng is brokyn,
For I haue towchyd his owyn dere tre!
Oure flescly eyn byn al vnlokyn;
Nakyd for synne ouresylf we se.
þat sory appyl þat we han sokyn
To deth hath brouth my spouse and me.
Ryth grevous is oure synne.
Of mekyl shame now do we knowe,
Alas, þat evyr þis appyl was growe!
To dredful deth now be we throwe,
In peyne vs evyr to pynne.

167 vnhede] v *perhaps altered from another letter* *letter* (l *or beg. of* h) 178 speche] c *written over another* 182 h *canc. before byn*

DEUS Adam, þat with myn handys I made,
Where art þu now? What hast þu wrought?
ADAM A, Lord, for synne oure flourys do fade.
I here þi voys but I se þe nought.

DEUS Adam, why hast þu synnyd so sone,
þus hastyly to breke my bone?
f. 15r And I made þe maystyr vndyr mone,
Trewly of euery tre.
O tre I kept for my owe,
Lyff and deth þerin I knowe.
þi synne fro lyf now þe hath throwe—
From deth þu mayst not fle.

ADAM Lord, I haue wrought aȝens þi wyll!
I sparyd nat mysylf to spylle.
þe woman þat þu toke me tylle,
Sche brougth me þerto!
It was here counsell and here reed;
Sche bad me do þe same deed.
I walke as worm, withowtyn wede,
Awey is schrowde and sho.

DEUS Womman þat arte þis mannys wyffe,
Why hast þu steryd ȝoure bothers stryffe?
Now ȝe be from ȝoure fayr lyffe,
And are demyd for to deye.
Vnwys womman, sey me why
þat þu hast don þis fowle foly.
And I made þe a gret lady
In paradys for to pleye.

EUA Lord, whan þu wentyst from þis place,
A werm with an aungelys face,
He hyth vs to be ful of grace,
þe frute yf þat we ete.

195 *lacks a capitulum* 212 stryffe] r *smudged and an* r *interl. above* 213 be *interl.*

I dyd his byddyng, alas, alas!
Now we be bowndyn in dethis las.
I suppose it was Sathanas;
To peyne he gan vs pete.

DEUS
Thou werm with þi wylys wyk, f. 15v
þi fals fablis, þei be ful thyk!
Why hast þu put dethis pryk
In Adam and his wyff?
Thow þei bothyn my byddyng haue brokyn,
Out of whoo ȝet art not wrokyn.
In helle logge þu xalt be loky[n],
And nevyrmo lacche lyff.

DIABOLUS
I xal þe sey whereffore and why
I dede hem all þis velony:
For I am ful of gret envy,
Of wreth and wyckyd hate
That man xulde leve above þe sky,
Whereas sumtyme dwellyd I;
And now I am cast to helle sty,
Streyte out at hevyn gate.

DEUS
Adam, for þu þat appyl boot
Aȝens my byddyng, well I woot,
Go teyl þi mete with swynk and swoot
Into þi lyvys ende;
Goo nakyd, vngry, and barefoot,
Ete both erbys, gres, and root.
Thy bale hath non other boot.
As wrecch in werlde þu wende.

Womman, þu sowtyst þis synnyng
And bad hym breke myn byddyng.
þerfore þu xalt ben vndyrlyng;
To mannys byddyng bend.

233 lokyn] loky *before* l   243 Ad *canc. in red before s.h.*   253 vndyrlyng] *a letter canc.*

What he byddyth þe, do þu þat thynge,
And bere þi chyldere with gret gronynge,
f. 16r In daungere and in deth-dredynge
Into þi lyvys ende.

Thou wyckyd worm, ful of pryde,
Fowle envye syt be þi syde!
Vpon þi gutt þu xalt glyde,
As werm wyckyd in kende,
Tyl a maydon in medyl-erth be born.
Þu fende, I warn þe beforn,
Thorwe here þi hed xal be to-torn.
On wombe awey þu wende.

DIABOLUS At þi byddyng fowle I falle,
I krepe hom to my stynkyng stalle.
Helle pyt and hevyn halle
Xul do þi byddyng bone.
I falle down here a fowle freke;
For þis falle I gynne to qweke.
With a fart my brech I breke!
My sorwe comyth ful sone.

DEUS For ȝoure synne þat ȝe haue do,
Out of þis blysse sone xal ȝe go,
In erthly labour to levyn in wo,
And sorwe ye xal atast.
For ȝoure synne and mysdoyng
An angell with a swerd brennyng,
Out of þis joye he xal ȝow dyng.
Ȝoure welth awey is past.

Hic recedit Deus, et angelus seraphicus cum gladio flamme[o] verberat Adam et Euam extra paradisum

260 Fowle] o *altered from another letter* 282 s.d. *preceded by rubricated* flammeo] flammea

SERAPHIM ȝe wrecchis vnkend and ryht vnwyse, f. 16^{v}
Out of þis joye hyȝ ȝow in hast!
With flammyng swerd from paradyse
To peyn I bete ȝow, of care to tast.
ȝoure myrth is turnyd to carfull syse,
ȝoure welth with synne awey is wast.
For ȝoure false dede of synful gyse
þis blysse I spere from ȝow ryth fast.
Herein come ȝe no more
Tyl a chylde of a mayd be born
And vpon þe rode rent and torn
To saue all þat ȝe haue forlorn,
ȝoure welth for to restore.

EVA Alas, alas, and weleaway,
þat evyr towchyd I þe tre!
I wende as wrecch in welsom way;
In blake busshys my boure xal be.
In paradys is plenté of pleye,
Fayr frutys ryth gret plenté;
þe ȝatys be schet with Godys keye.
My husbond is lost because of me.
Leve spowse, now þu fonde.
Now stomble we on stalk and ston.
My wyt awey is fro me gon!

A genealogy is written in Textura Quadrata at feet of ff. 16^{v}–18. On f. 16^{v} is written:

Adam genuit < Caym / Abel / Seth) Caym genuit Enoch genuit Iradh genuit

On f. 17:

Maynael genuit Matussahel genuit Lamech.

The main scribe has appended to this in his Anglicana hand:

þat slow Caym. þis Lame[ch] had 2 wyffys, Ada and [*two letters canc.*] Sella. Of Ada com Jabel, fadere of tentys and of herdmen

Remainder of note cropped.

On f. 17^{v}, again in Textura Quadrata:

Seth genuit Enos genuit Caynan genuit Malalchel genuit Jared genuit

On f. 18:

Enok genuit Matussalem genuit Lamech genuit Noe

Wrythe onto my neckebon
With hardnesse of þin honde.

ADAM Wyff, þi wytt is not wurth a rosch.
Leve woman, turne þi thought.
f. 17r I wyl not sle flescly of my flesch,
For of my flesch þi flesch was wrought.
Oure hap was hard, oure wytt was nesch
To paradys whan we were brought.
My wepyng xal be longe fresch,
Schort lykyng xal be longe bought.
No more telle þu þat tale.
For yf I xulde sle my wyff,
I sclow myself withowtyn knyff,
In helle logge to lede my lyff,
With woo in wepyng dale.

But lete vs walke forth into þe londe,
With ryth gret labour oure fode to fynde,
With delvyng and dyggyng with myn hond,
Oure blysse to bale and care to-pynde.
And, wyff, to spynne now must þu fonde,
Oure nakyd bodyes in cloth to wynde
Tyll sum comforth of Godys sonde
With grace releve oure careful mynde.
Now come, go we hens, wyff.
EVA Alas þat ever we wrought þis synne!
Oure bodely sustenauns for to wynne,
Ȝe must delve and I xal spynne,
In care to ledyn oure lyff.

309 *lacks a capitulum and in darker ink* 320 logge] *or* longge; *a stroke over the* o *is higher than usual* 325 *an erasure before* pynde

3
[CAIN AND ABEL]

ABEEL
I wolde fayn knowe how I xuld do
To serve my Lord God to his plesyng.
þerfore, Caym, brother, lete us now go
Vnto oure fadyr withowte lettyng,

Suenge hym in vertu and in norture f. 17v
To com to þe hyȝe joy celestyall;
Remembryng to be clene and pure,
For in mysrewle we myth lythly fall
Aȝens Hevyn Kynge.
Lete us now don oure dyligens
To come to oure faderys presens.
Good brother, passe we hens
To knowe for oure levynge.

CAYM
As to my fadyr lete us now tee
To knowe what xal be his talkyng.
And yet I holde it but vanyté
To go to hym for any spekyng
To lere of his lawe.
For if I haue good anow plenté,
I kan be mery, so moty the.
Thow my fadyr I nevyr se,
I ȝyf not þerof an hawe!

ABEL
Ryth sovereyn fadyr, semely, sad and sure,
Euyr we thank ȝow in hert, body, and thowth,
And alwey shull whyll oure lyf may indure
As inwardly in hert it kan be sought,
Bothe my brother and I.
Fadyr, I falle onto ȝoure kne
To knowe how we xul rewlyd be

[*Play 3*] *No capitulum before* 5 16 yet] yt; *B* þat 19 good] d *written over another letter* *The hand becomes smaller in* 27–33

For godys þat fallyth bothe hym and me;
I wolde fayn wete trewly.

ADAM Sonys, ȝe arn, to spekyn naturaly,
The fyrst frute of kendely engendrure,
f. 18r Befforn whom, saff ȝoure modyr and I,
Were nevyr non of mannys nature.
And ȝit were we al of another portature,
As ȝe haue me oftyn herd seyd sothly.
Wherfore, sonys, yf ȝe wyl lyff sad and sure,
Fyrst I ȝow counseyll most syngulerly
God for to loue and drede.
And suche good as God hath ȝow sent,
The fyrst frute offyr to hym in sacryfice brent,
Hym evyr besechyng with meke entent
In all ȝoure werkys to save and spede.

ABEELL Gramercy, fadyr, for ȝoure good doctrine;
For as ȝe vs techyn, so xal we do.
And as for me, þorwe Goddys grace dyvyne,
I wyl forthwith applye me þerto.
CAYME And þow me be loth, I wyl now also
Onto ȝoure counsell, fadyr, me inclyne.
And ȝitt I say now to ȝow both too,
I had levyr gon hom, well for to dyne!
ADAM Now God graunt good sacryfice to ȝow both too.
He vowchesaff to acceptyn ȝow and all myne,
And ȝeve ȝow now grace to plesyn hym soo
þat ȝe may come to þat blysse þat hymself is inne
With gostly grace;
þat all ȝoure here-levyng
May be to his plesyng,
And at ȝoure hens-partyng
To com to good place.

Below 36 *stands a line written by the main scribe and canc. in red:* As ȝe haue me oftyn seyd sothly, *with* haue *interl. after* ȝe 47 y *canc. before* dyvyne 58–61 *written two lines as one*

Abell dicit:

Almyhtty God and God ful of myth f. 18v
Be whom allþing is made of nowth,
To þe myn hert is redy dyht,
For upon þe is all my thought.

O souereyn Lord reygnyng in eternyté,
With all þe mekenesse þat I kan or may,
This lombe xal I offre it up to the;
Accept it, blyssyd Lord, I þe pray.
My ȝyft is but sympyl, þis is no nay,
But my wyl is good, and evyr xal be;
Þe to servyn and worchepyn both nyht and day.
And þerto þi grace, Lord, grawnt þu me
Throwh þi gret mercy;
Which, in a lombys lyknes,
Þu xalt for mannys wyckydnes
Onys ben offeryd in peynfulnes
And deyn ful dolfoly.

For trewly, Lord, þu art most worthy
Þe best to haue in eche degré.
Both beste and werst, ful certeynly,
All is had þorwe grace of þe.
The best schep, full hertyly,
Amongys my flok þat I kan se,
I tythe it to God of gret mercy,
And bettyr wolde if bettyr myht be.
Evyn here is myn offryng.
I tythe to þe with ryht good wylle
Of þe best þu sentyst me tylle.
Now, gracyous God on hevyn hille,
Accept now my tythyng.

CAYM Amongys all folys þat gon on grownd f. 19r
I holde þat þu be on of þe most,

No capitulum before 66

To tythe þe best þat is most sownd,
And kepe þe werst, þat is nere lost.
But I more wysly xal werke þis stownde
To tythe þe werst—and make no bost—
Off all my cornys þat may be fownde
In all my feldys, both crofte and cost;
I xal lokyn on every syde.
Here I tythe þis vnthende sheff;
Lete God take it or ellys lef.
þow it be to me gret repreff,
I ȝeve no fors þis tyde.

ABELL Now, Caym, brother, þu dost ful ill,
For God þe sent both best and werst.
þerfore þu shewe to hym good wyll
And tythe to God evyr of the best.
CAYM In feyth, þu shewyst now a febyll skyll,
It wolde me hyndyr and do me greff.
What were God þe bettyr, þu sey me tyll,
To ȝevyn hym awey my best sheff
And kepe myself þe wers?
He wyll neyther ete nor drynke,
For he doth neyther swete nor swynke.
þu shewyst a febyl reson, methynke.
What! þu fonnyst as a best, I gesse.

ABELL Ȝit methynkyth my wyt is good
To God euyrmore sum loue to shewe,
f. 19v Off whom we haue oure dayly food;
And ellys we had but lytyl drewe.
CAYM Ȝitt methynkeht þi wytt is wood,
For of þi lore I fynde but fewe.
I wyll neuyr þe more chawnge my mood
For no wordys þat þu dost shewe.
I sey I wyll tythe þe werst.
ABELL Now God þat syt in hefne aboue,
On whom is sett all myn hool loue,
þis wyckyd wyll from þe he showe,
As it plesyth hym best.

The hand is smaller in 118–22 *f. 19v marked 20*

Hic ardent decimum Abel, et Caym quo facto dicit:

CAYM Herke, Abel, brother, what aray is þis?
Thy tythyng brennyth as fyre ful bryght!
It is to me gret wondyr, iwys!
I trow þis is now a straunge syght.
ABELL Goddys wyll, forsothe, it is
þat my tythyng with fyre is lyth;
For of þe best were my tythis,
And of þe werst þu dedyst hym dyght—
Bad thyng þu hym bede.
Of þe best was my tythyng,
And of þe werst was þin offryng.
þerfor God Almyghty, Hevyn Kyng,
Alowyht ryht nowth þi dede.

CAYM What! þu stynkyng losel, and is it so?
Doth God þe love and hatyht me?
þu xalt be ded, I xal þe slo!
þi Lord, þi God, þu xalt nevyr se!
Tythyng more xalt þu nevyr do. f. 20r
With þis chavyl bon I xal sle þe!
þi deth is dyht, þi days be go.
Out of myn handys xalt þu not fle—
With þis strok I þe kylle!
Now þis boy is slayn and dede,
Of hym I xal nevyrmore han drede;
He xal hereafter nevyr ete brede.
With þis gresse I xal hym hylle.

DEUS Caym, come forth and answere me!
Asoyle my qwestyon anon-ryght!
Thy brother Abel, wher is now he?
Ha don and answere me as tyght!
CAYM My brothers kepere ho made me?
Syn whan was I his kepyng-knyght?

130 s.d. *preceded by sign* 155 He] Here, *with* re *erased*

I kannot telle wher þat he be;
To kepe hym was I nevyr dyght.
I knowe not wher he is.
DEUS A, cursyd Caym, þu art vntrewe,
And for þi dede þu xalt sore rewe.
Þi brothers blood, þat þu slewe,
Askyht vengeauns of þi mys.

Thu xalt be cursyd on þe grounde,
Vnprophitable whereso þu wende,
Both veyn, and nowthty, and nothyng sounde;
With what þing þu medele, þu xalt it shende!
CAYM Alas, in whoo now am I wounde,
Acursyd of God as man vnkende!
Of any man yf I be founde,
He xal me slo; I haue no frende!
Alas and weleaway!
f. 20v DEUS Of what man þat þu be sclayn,
He xal haue vij-folde more payn;
Hym were bettyr [nevyr] to be sayn
On lyve be nyth ne day.

CAYM Alas! Alas! Whedyr may I go?
I dare nevyr se man in þe vesage.
I am woundyn as a wrecch in wo
And cursyd of God for my falsage.
Vnprofytabyl and vayn also,
In felde and town, in strete and stage,
I may nevyr make merthis mo.
I wot nevyr whedyr to take passage;
I dare not here abyde.
Now wyl I go wende my way
With sore syeng and welaway,
To loke where þat I best may
From mannys ssyht me hyde.

Introitus Noe

181 never *interl. by another hand in darker ink;* nevyr *supplied* *Remainder of f. 20v (100 mm) blank*

4
[NOAH]

f. 21r
B quire

NOE God of his goodnesse and of grace grounde,
By whoys gloryous power allthyng is wrought,
In whom all vertu plentevously is founde,
Withowtyn whos wyl may be ryth nought,
Thy seruauntys saue, Lord, fro synful sownde
In wyl, in werk, in dede, and in thouht.
Oure welth in woo lete nevyr be fownde;
Vs help, Lord, from synne þat we be in brought,
Lord God ful of myght.
Noe, serys, my name is knowe,
My wyff and my chyldere here on rowe;
To God we pray with hert ful lowe
To plese hym in his syght.

In me, Noe, þe Secunde Age
Indede begynnyth, as I ȝow say:
Afftyr Adam, withoutyn langage,
The Secunde Fadyr am I, in fay.
But men of levyng be so owtrage,
Bothe be nyght and eke be day,
þat lesse þan synne þe soner swage,
God wyl be vengyd on vs sum way,

1 Noe *written in Textura Quadrata*
A genealogy is written in Textura Quadrata at feet of ff. 21r—22v. On f. 21r is written:

Sem
Noe genuit Cham
Japhet

On f. 21v:

Sem genuit Arfaxit genuit Sale genuit Heber genuit Phaleg

On f. 22r:

genuit Reu genuit Sarug genuit Nachor genuit Thare
Abraham
genuit Nacor
Aran

On f. 22v:

Aran genuit Loth

Indede.
Ther may no man go þerowte,
But synne regnyth in every rowte;
In every place rownde abowte
Cursydnes doth sprynge and sprede.

VXOR NOE Allmyghty God of his gret grace
Enspyre men with hertely wyll
For to sese of here trespace,
For synfull levyng oure sowle xal spyll.
f. 21v Synne offendyth God in his face
And agrevyth oure Lorde full ylle.
It causyth to man ryght grett manace
And scrapyth hym out of lyvys bylle,
þat blyssyd book.
What man in synne doth allwey sclepp,
He xal gon to helle ful depp.
Than xal he nevyr aftyr crepp
Out of þat brennyng brook.

I am ȝoure wyff, ȝoure childeryn þese be.
Onto us tweyn it doth longe
Hem to teche in all degré
Synne to forsakyn, and werkys wronge.
Therffore, fere, for loue of me,
Enforme hem wele evyr amonge
Synne to forsake, and vanyté,
And vertu to folwe þat þei fonge,
Oure Lord God to plese.

NOE I warne ȝow, childeryn, on and all,
Drede oure Lord God in hevy[n] hall,
And in no forfete þat we ne fall,
Oure Lord for to dysplese.

SHEM A, dere fadyr, God forbede
þat we xulde do in ony wyse

24 rowte] r *smudged, perhaps altered from another letter* 40 þese ch *canc. in red after* wyff; þese] se *altered from other letters* 44 John *scribbled in left margin by another hand* fere] *an* s *written above the* f 50 hevyn] hevy

Ony werke of synful dede
  Oure Lord God þat xulde agryse.
  My name is Shem, ȝoure son of prise;
I xal werke aftere ȝoure rede.
  And also, wyff, þe weyll awyse
Wykkyd werkys þat þu non brede,
    Nevyr in no degré.

VXOR SEEM
      Forsothe, sere, be Goddys grace,
      I xal me kepe from all trespace f. 22r
      þat xulde offende Goddys face
    Be help of þe Trynyté.

CHAM
I am Cham, ȝoure secunde son,
  And purpose me, be Goddys myght,
Nevyr suche a dede for to don
  þat xuld agreve God in syght.

VXOR CHAM
I pray to God, me grawnt þis bone:
  That he me kepe in such a plyght,
Mornynge, hevenynge, mydday, and none,
  I to affendyn hym day nor nyght.
    Lord God, I þe pray,
      Bothe wakynge and eke in slepe,
      Gracyous God, þu me keppe
      þat I nevyr in daunger crepe
    On dredfull Domysday.

JAPHET
Japhet, þi iij^{de} sone, is my name.
  I pray to God wherso we be
þat he vs borwe fro synfull shame,
  And in vertuous levynge evyrmore kepe me.

VXOR JAPHET
I am ȝoure wyff and pray þe same,
  þat God vs saue on sonde and se;
With no grevauns þat we hym grame,
  He grawnt vs grace synne to fle.
    Lord God, now here oure bone.

57 Shem] *M* Chem *a letter* (S?) *canc. before* ȝoure *several figures scribbled in right margin opposite* 57 63 *some letters scribbled in right margin* 68 *a word or words written by another hand in right margin* 81 *a few letters erased after* vs

NOE
Gracyous God, þat best may,
With herty wyl to the we pray
Þu save us sekyr bothe nyght and day,
Synne þat we noon done.

f. 22^{v} DEUS
Ow! What menyht this myslevyng man
Whiche myn hand made and byldyd in blysse?
Synne so sore grevyht me, ȝa, in certayn,
I wol be vengyd of þis grett mysse!
Myn aungel dere, þu xalt gan
To Noe, þat my servaunt is.
A shypp to make on hond to tan
Þu byd hym swyth for hym and his,
From drynchyng hem to save.
For, as I am God of myght,
I xal dystroye þis werd downryght.
Here synne so sore grevyht me in syght,
Þei xal no mercy haue.

Fecisse hominem nunc penitet me:
Þat I made man sore doth me rewe.
Myn handwerk to sle sore grevyth me,
But þat here synne here deth doth brewe.
Go sey to Noe as I bydde þe:
Hymself, his wyf, his chylderyn trewe,
Tho viij sowlys in shyp to be,
Thei xul not drede þe flodys flowe;
Þe flod xal harme them nowht.
Of all fowlys and bestys thei take a peyre,
In shypp to saue bothe foule and fayere
From all dowtys and gret dyspeyre,
This vengeauns, or it be wrought.

Angelus ad Noe:

Noe, Noe, a shypp loke þu make,
And many a chaumbyr þu xalt haue þerinne.

94 certayn] a *altered from an* e 95 he *canc. before* be 96 gan] a *altered from an* o 108 synne] e *written over another letter* (d?), *with an* e *interlin. above it and a deleting dot below* 112 *a letter canc. before* not *In* 115–21 *the hand is smaller*

Of euery kyndys best a cowpyl þu take
Within þe shyppbord, here lyvys to wynne.
For God is sore grevyd with man for his synne, f. 23r
þat all þis wyde werd xal be dreynt with flood;
Saff þu and þi wyff xal be kept from þis gynne,
And also þi chylderyn with here vertuys good.

NOE How xuld I haue wytt a shypp for to make?
I am of ryght grett age: V C ȝere olde!
It is not for me þis werk to vndyrtake;
For feynnesse of age my leggys gyn folde!
ANGELUS This dede for to do be bothe blythe and bolde.
God xal enforme þe and rewle þe ful ryght.
Of byrd and of beste take, as I þe tolde,
A peyr into þe shypp and God xal þe qwyght.

NOE I am ful redy, as God doth me bydde,
A shypp for to make be myght of his grace.
Alas, þat for synne it xal so be betydde
þat vengeauns of flood xal werke þis manase.
God is sore grevyd with oure grett tresspas,
þat with wylde watyr þe werd xal be dreynt.
A shypp for to make now lete us hens pas,
þat God aȝens us of synne haue no compleynt.

Hic transit Noe cum familia sua pro naui, quo exeunte locum interludii sub intret statim Lameth conductus ab adolescente; et di[*cit*]*:*

LAMETH Gret mornyng I make and gret cause I haue!
Alas, now I se not: for age I am blynde.
Blyndenes doth make me of wytt for to rave;
Whantynge of eyesyght in peyn doth me bynde!

129 feynnesse] feyynnesse, *with a deleting dot under second* y; *Hal* ffeythnnesse
134 d *canc. before* bydde 141 synne] s *has a crossbar almost like that of an* ſ
141 s.d. dicit] di, *remainder cropped*

Whyl I had syht þer myht nevyr man fynde
My pere of archerye in all þis werd aboute.
f. 23v For ȝitt schet I nevyr at hert, are, nere hynde
But yf þat he deyd, of þis no man haue doute.

Lameth þe good archere my name was ovyrall;
For þe best archere myn name dede evyr sprede.
Record of my boy here, wytnes þis he xal:
What merk þat were set me, to deth it xuld blede.

ADOLESCENS It is trewe, maystyr, þat ȝe seyn, indede.
For þat tyme ȝe had ȝoure bowe bent in honde,
If þat ȝoure prycke had be half a myle in brede,
Ȝe wolde þe pryk han hitte if ȝe ny had stonde.

LAMETH I xuld nevyr a faylid what marke þat evyr were sett
Whyl þat I myght loke and had my clere syght.
And ȝitt, as methynkyht, no man xuld shete bett
Than I xuld do now, if myn hand were sett aryght.
Aspye som marke, boy, my bowe xal I bende wyght;
And sett myn hand euyn to shete at som best.
And I dar ley a wagour his deth for to dyght.
Þe marke xal I hitt, my lyff do I hest.

ADOLESCENS Vndyr ȝon grett busche, maystyr, a best do I se.
Take me þin hand swyth and holde it ful stylle.
Now is þin hand evyn as euyr it may be.
Drawe up þin takyll ȝon best for to kylle.

LAMETH My bowe xal I drawe ryght with herty wylle;
This brod arwe I shete, þat best for to sayll.
Now haue at þat busch ȝon best for to spylle.
A sharppe schote I shote; þerof I xal not fayll.

156 dede *canc. in red before* brede

CAYM
Out, out and alas! Myn hert is onsondyr!
With a brod arwe I am ded and sclayn!
I dye here on grounde, myn hert is all to tundyr; f. 24r
With þis brod arwe it is clovyn on twayn!

LAMETH
Herke, boy, cum telle me þe trewth in certeyn,
What man is he þat þis cry doth þus make?

ADOLESCENS
Caym þu hast kyllyd, I telle þe ful pleyn;
With þi sharp shetyng his deth hath he take.

LAMETH
Haue I slayn Cayme? Alas, what haue I done?
Þu stynkynge lurdeyn, what hast þu wrought?
Þu art þe why I scle hym so sone;
Þerfore xal I kyll þe here—þu skapyst nowght!

Hic Lameth cum arcu suo verberat adolescentem ad mortem, dicente adolescente:

ADOLESCENS
Out, out, I deye here! My deth is now sought!
Þis theffe with his bowe hath broke my brayn!
Þer may non helpe be, my dethe is me brought.
Ded here I synke down as man þat is sclayn.

LAMETH
Alas, what xal I do, wrecch wykkyd on woolde?
God wyl be vengyd ful sadly on me:
For deth of Caym I xal haue vij-folde
More peyn þan he had þat Abell dede sle!
These to mennys deth ful sore bought xal be:
Vpon all my blood God wyll venge þis dede.
Wherefore, sore wepyng, hens wyl I fle,
And loke where I may best my hede sone
heyde.

Hic recedat Lameth et statim intrat Noe cum naui cantantes.

NOE
With doolful hert, syenge sad and sore, f. 24v
Grett mornyng I make for this dredful flood!

At the foot of f. 24r the main scribe has written: Noe schyp was in lenght ccc cubytes, In brede fyfty, and þe heyth thretty, þe flod 15 above hyest montayn

Of man and of best is dreynte many a skore;
All þis werd to spyll þese flodys be ful wood.
And all is for synne of mannys wylde mood
þat God hath ordeyned þis dredfull ven-
geaunce.
In þis flood spylt is many a mannys blood.
For synfull levynge of man we haue gret gre-
vauns!

All þis hundryd ȝere ryght here haue I wrought
This schypp for to make as God dede byd me.
Of all maner bestys a copyll is in brought,
Within my shyppborde on lyve for to be.
Ryght longe God hath soferyd amendyng to se;
All þis hundryd ȝere God hath shewyd grace.
Alas, fro gret syn man wyl not fle;
God doth þis vengeauns for oure gret tres-
pase.

VXOR NOE Alas, for gret ruthe of þis gret vengeaunce!
Gret doyl it is to se þis watyr so wyde.
But ȝit thankyd be God of þis ordenaunce,
þat we be now savyd, on lyve to abyde.
SEEM For grett synne of lechory all þis doth betyde.
Alas, þat evyr such synne xulde be wrought!
þis flood is so gret on every a syde
þat all þis wyde werd to care is now brought.

VXOR SEEM Becawse [þe] chylderyn of God, þat weryn good,
Dede forfete ryght sore what tyme þat þei were
Synfully compellyd to Caymys blood,
f. 25r Therfore be we now cast in ryght grett care.
CHAM For synful levynge þis werde doth forfare;
So grevous vengeauns myght nevyr man se.
Ouyr all þis werd wyde þer is no plot bare;
With watyr and with flood God vengyd wyll
be.

210 f *canc. in red before* soferyd 222 þe] of gode *canc. in red before* good

VXOR CHAM Rustynes of synne is cawse of þese wawys.
Alas, in þis flood þis werd xal be lorn!
For offens to God, brekyng his lawys,
On rokkys ryght sharp is many a man torn.

JAPHET So grevous flodys were nevyr ȝett beforn.
Alas, þat lechory þis vengeauns doth gynne!
It were well bettyr euyr to be vnborn
Than for to forfetyn evyrmore in þat synne.

VXOR JAPHET Oure Lord God I thanke of his gret grace,
þat he doth us saue from þis dredful payn.
Hym for to wurchipe in euery stede and place
We beth gretly bownde with myght and with mayn.

NOE Xl^{ti} days and nyghtys hath lasted þis rayn,
And xl^{ti} days þis grett flood begynnyth to slake.
This crowe xal I sende out to seke sum playn;
Good tydyngys to brynge þis massage I make.

Hic emittat coruum et, parum expectans, iterum dicat:

This crowe on sum careyn is fall for to ete;
þerfore a newe masangere I wyll forth now sende.
Fly forth, þu fayr dove, ovyr þese watyrys wete
And aspye afftere sum drye lond oure mornyng to amend.

Hic euolet columba, qua rede[u]nte cum ramo viridi oliue:

Joye now may we make of myrth þat yet were frende. f. 25v
A grett olyve bush þis dowe doth us brynge.
For joye of þis tokyn ryght hertyly we tende
Oure Lord God to worchep: a songe lete vs synge.

249 s.d. redeunte] *D; MS* redeinte *or* redemte 250 myrth] r *smudged* yet] y^{t}
253 *a few letters erased after* lete

Hic decantent hos versus: Mare vidit et fugit, Jordanis conuersus est retrorsum. Non nobis, Domine, non nobis, sed nomini tuo da gloriam. Et sic recedant cum naui.

5
[ABRAHAM AND ISAAC]

Introitus Abrahe et cetera.

[ABRAHAM] Most myghty makere of sunne and of mone,
Kyng of Kyngys and Lord ouyr all,
Allmyghty God in hevyn trone,
I þe honowre and evyrmore xal.
My Lord, my God, to þe I kall;
With herty wyll, Lord, I þe pray,
In synfull lyff lete me nevyr fall,
But lete me leve evyr to þi pay.

Abraham my name is kydde,
And patryarke of age ful olde.
And ȝit be þe grace of God is bredde
In myn olde age a chylde full bolde.
Ysaac, lo, here his name is tolde,
My swete sone þat stondyth me by.
Amongys all chylderyn þat walkyn on wolde
A louelyer chylde is non, trewly.

I thanke God with hert well mylde
Of his gret mercy and of his hey grace,
And pryncepaly for my suete chylde,
þat xal to me do gret solace.
f. 26r Now, suete sone, fayre fare þi face;
Ful hertyly do I love the.
For trewe herty love now in þis place,
My swete childe, com kysse now me.

Play 5 follows immediately upon Play 4. The initial s.d. is on the same line as the final s.d. in Play 4.
1 *s.h. supplied* 20 solace] s *smudged and perhaps written over another letter*

YSAAC At ȝoure byddynge ȝoure mouthe I kys.
With lowly hert I ȝow pray,
Ȝoure fadyrly love lete me nevyr mysse,
But blysse me, ȝoure chylde, both nyght and day.
ABRAHAM Almyghty God þat best may,
His dere blyssyng he graunt þe.
And my blyssyng þu haue allway
In what place þat evyr þu be.

Now, Isaac, my sone so suete,
Almyghty God loke þu honoure,
Wich þat made both drye and wete,
Shynyng sunne and scharpe schoure.
Thu art my suete childe and paramoure;
Ful wele in herte do I þe loue.
Loke þat þin herte in hevyn toure
Be sett, to serve oure Lord God above.

In þi ȝonge lerne God to plese,
And God xal quyte þe weyl þi mede.
Now, suete sone, of wordys these
With all þin hert þu take good hede.
Now fareweyl, sone, God be þin spede,
Evyn here at hom þu me abyde.
I must go walkyn, for I haue nede;
I come aȝen withinne a tyde.

YSAAC I pray to God, Fadyr of Myght, f. 26[v]
Þat he ȝow spede in all ȝoure waye.
From shame and shenshipp day and nyht
God mote ȝow kepe in ȝoure jornay.
ABRAHAM Now fareweyll, sone. I þe pray,
Evyr in þin hert loke God þu wynde.
Hym to serue bothe nyght and day
I pray to God send þe good mynde.

Ther may no man love bettyr his childe
Þan Isaac is lovyd of me.

Almyghty God, mercyful and mylde,
For my swete son I wurchyp þe.
I thank þe, Lord, with hert ful fre
For þis fayr frute þu hast me sent.
Now, gracyous God, wherso he be,
To saue my sone evyrmore be bent.

Dere Lord, I pray to þe also,
Me to saue for þi seruuaunte,
And sende me grace nevyr for to do
Thyng þat xulde be to þ[e] displesaunte.
Bothe for me and for myn infaunte
I pray þe, Lord God, vs to help.
Thy gracyous goodnes þu us grawnt,
And saue þi serwaunt from helle qwelp.

ANGELUS Abraham! How, Abraham!
Lyst and herke weyll onto me.
ABRAHAM Al redy, sere, here I am.
Tell me ȝoure wyll, what þat it be.
f. 27r ANGELUS Almyghty God þus doth bydde þe:
Ysaac þi sone anon þu take,
And loke hym þu slee anoon, lete se;
And sacrafice to God hym make!

Thy wel-belouyd childe þu must now kylle.
To God þu offyr hym, as I say,
Evyn vpon ȝon hey hylle
þat I þe shewe here in þe way.
Tarye not be nyght nor day,
But smertly þi gate þu goo.
Vpon ȝon hille þu knele and pray
To God, and kylle þe childe þer and scloo.

ABRAHAM Now Goddys comaundement must nedys be done—
All his wyl is wourthy to be wrought.

57 *a letter* (s?) *erased before* childe 68 þe] þi 90 his] h *partly effaced by a stain*

But ȝitt þe fadyr to scle þe sone,
Grett care it causyth in my thought!
In byttyr bale now am I brought,
My swete childe with knyf to kylle.
But ȝit my sorwe avaylith ryght nowth,
For nedys I must werke Goddys wylle.

With evy hert I walke and wende,
My childys deth now for to be.
Now must þe fadyr his suete sone schende.
Alas, for ruthe, it is peté!
My swete sone, come hedyr to me.
How, Isaac, my sone dere!
Com to þi fadyr, my childe so fre,
For we must wende togedyr in fere.

ISAAC All redy, fadyr, evyn at ȝoure wyll,
And at ȝoure byddyng I am ȝow by.
With ȝow to walk ovyr dale and hill f. 27v
At ȝoure callyng I am redy.
To þe fadyr evyr most comly
It ovyth þe childe evyr buxom to be.
I wyl obey ful hertyly
To allthyng þat ȝe bydde me.

ABRAHAM Now, son, in þi necke þis fagot þu take,
And þis fyre bere in þinne honde.
For we must now sacrefyse go make,
Evyn aftyr þe wyll of Goddys sonde.
Take þis brennyng bronde,
My swete childe, and lete us go.
Ther may no man þat levyth in londe
Haue more sorwe than I haue wo.

94 s (*?*) *erased before* childe 99 schende] *the* h *partly overlaps the* c And at ȝoure byddyng I am *crossed through in red between* 106 *and* 107 113 necke] *the* k *partially overlaps the* c 115 For] *an* o *interl. over the* o 116 wyll] w *smudged*

YSAAC Fayre fadyr, ȝe go ryght stylle.
I pray ȝow, fadyr, speke onto me.
ABRAHAM Mi gode childe, what is þi wylle?
Telle me thyn hert, I pray to the.
YSAAC Fadyr, fyre and wood here is plenté,
But I kan se no sacryfice.
What ȝe xulde offre fayn wold I se,
þat it were don at þe best avyse.

ABRAHAM God xal þat ordeyn, þat sytt in hevynne,
My swete sone, for þis offryng.
A derere sacryfice may no man nempne
þan þis xal be, my dere derlyng.
YSAAC Lat be, good fadyr, ȝoure sad wepynge;
Ȝoure hevy cher agrevyth me sore.
Tell me, fadyr, ȝoure grett mornyng,
And I xal seke sum help þerfore.

f. 28r ABRAHAM Alas, dere sone, for nedys must me
Evyn here þe kylle, as God hath sent!
Thyn owyn fadyr þi deth must be—
Alas, þat evyr þis bowe was bent!
With þis fyre bryght þu must be brent,
An aungelle seyd to me ryght so.
Alas, my chylde, þu xalt be shent;
þi careful fadyr must be þi fo.

YSAAC Almyghty God of his grett mercye,
Ful hertyly I thanke þe, sertayne.
At Goddys byddyng here for to dye
I obeye me here for to be sclayne.
I pray ȝow, fadyr, be glad and fayne
Trewly to werke Goddys wyll.
Take good comforte to ȝow agayn,
And haue no dowte ȝoure childe to kyll.

131 derere] *second* e *partially written over a second* r 132 *several letters* (de..) *canc. before* derlyng 143 xalt] a *altered from another letter* (u?)

For Godys byddyng, forsothe, it is
þat I of ȝow my deth schulde take.
Aȝens God ȝe don amys
His byddyng yf ȝe xuld forsake.
Ȝowre owyn dampnacyon xulde ȝe bake
If ȝe me kepe from þis r[o]d.
With ȝoure swerd my deth ȝe make,
And werk evyrmore þe wyll of God.

ABRAHAM The wyll of God must nedys be done—
To werke his wyll I seyd nevyr nay.
But ȝit þe fadyr to sle þe sone
My hert doth clynge and cleue as clay!
YSAAC Ȝitt werk Goddys wyll, fadyr, I ȝow pray, f. 28v
And sle me here anoon forthryght.
And turne fro me ȝoure face away,
Myne heed whan þat ȝe xul of smyght.

ABRAHAM Alas, dere childe, I may not chese:
I must nedys my swete sone kylle.
My dere derlyng now must me lese—
Myn owyn sybb blood now xal I spylle!
Ȝitt þis dede or I fulfylle,
My swete sone, þi mouth I kys.
YSAAC Al redy, fadyr, evyn at ȝoure wyll.
I do ȝoure byddyng as reson is.

ABRAHAM Alas, dere sone, here is no grace,
But nedis ded now must þu be.
With þis kerchere I kure þi face;
In þe tyme þat I sle the
Thy lovely vesage wold I not se,
Not for all þis werdlys good.
With þis swerd þat sore grevyht me
My childe I sle and spylle his blood.

153 it *interl. in darker ink* 155 Aȝeng *canc. in red before* Aȝens Aȝens] *a red dot after* A 158 rod] reed 163 ȝit] *an* e *written above* it; sch *canc. before* sle

ANGELUS Abraham, Abraham, þu fadyr fre!
ABRAHAM I am here redy. What is ȝoure wylle?
ANGELUS Extende þin hand in no degré—
I bydde þu hym not kylle!
Here do I se by ryght good skylle
Allmyghty God þat þu dost drede.
For þu sparyst nat þi sone to spylle,
God wyll aqwhyte þe well þi mede.

f. 29r ABRAHAM I thank my God in hevyn above
And hym honowre for þis grett grace.
And þat my Lord me þus doth prove,
I wyll hym wurchep in every place.
My childys lyff is my solace,
I thank myn God evyr for his lyff.
In sacrifice here or I hens pace,
I sle þis shepe with þis same knyff.

Now þis shepe is deed and slayn,
With þis fyre it xal be brent.
Of Isaac my sone I am ful fayn
Þat my swete childe xal not be shent!
This place I name with good entent
Þe Hill of Godys Vesytacyon,
For hedyr God hath to us sent
His comforte aftyr grett trybulacyon.

ANGELUS Herke, Abraham, and take good heyd.
By hymself God hath þus sworn:
For þat þu woldyst a done þis dede,
He wyll þe blysse both evyn and morn.
For þi dere childe þu woldyst haue lorn
At Goddys byddyng, as I the telle,
God hath sent þe word beforn,
Þi seed xal multyplye wherso þu duelle.

192 aqwhyte] q *written below the line* 193 *an* m *with an interl.* e *above it canc. after* God 206 of *interl.*

As sterrys in hevyn byn many and fele,
So xal þi seed encrese and growe.
þu xalt ovyrcome in welth and wele
All þi fomen reknyd be rowe.
As sond in þe se doth ebbe and flowe, f. 29v
Hath cheselys many vnnumerabyll,
So xal þi sede, þu mayst me trowe,
Encres and be evyr prophytabyll.

For to my spech þu dedyst obeye,
Thyn enmyes portys þu shalt possede.
And all men on erthe, as I þe seye,
Thei xal be blyssed in þi sede.
Almyghty God þus þe wyll mede
For þat good wyll þat þu ast done.
þerfore thank God in word and dede,
Both þu þiself and Ysaac þi sone.

ABRAHAM A, my Lord God to wurchep on kne now I fall.
I thank þe, Lord, of þi mercy.
Now, my swete childe, to God þu kall,
And thank we þat Lord now hertyly.
ISAAC With lowly hert to God I crye.
I am his seruuant both day and nyght.
I thank þe, Lord in hevyn so hyȝe,
With hert, with thought, with mayn, with myght.

ABRAHAM Gramercy, Lord and Kyng of Grace!
Gramercy, Lord ouyr lordys all!
Now my joye returnyth his trace.
I thank þe, Lorde in hevyn, þin halle.
ISAAC Ovyr all kyngys crownyd kyng I þe kalle.
At þi byddyng to dye with knyff

f. 29v marked 30 228 by *canc. before* blyssed 233 wurchep] r *malformed, perhaps written over another letter* 244 hevyn] h *blotted and perhaps altered from another letter* halle] h *altered from another letter*

I was ful buxvm evyn as þi thralle.
Lord, now I thank the, þu grauntyst me lyff.

f. 30r ABRAHAM Now we haue wurchepyd oure blyssyd Lorde
On grounde knelyng upon oure kne.
Now lete us tweyn, sone, ben of on acorde,
And goo walke hom into oure countré.
YSAAC Fadyr, as ȝe wyll, so xal it be;
I am redy with ȝow to gon.
I xal ȝow folwe with hert full fre.
And þat ȝe bydde me sone xal be don.

ABRAHAM Now God, allthyng of nowth þat made,
Evyr wurcheppyd he be on watyr and londe.
His grett honowre may nevyrmore fade
In felde nor town, se nor on sonde.
As althyng, Lord, þu hast in honde,
So saue us all wherso we be.
Whethyr we syttyn, walk, or stonde,
Evyr on þin handwerke þu haue pyté.

Explicit

f. 31r

6
[MOSES]

Introitus Moyses

[MOYSES] He þat made allthynge of nought,
Hevyn and erth, both sunne and mone,
Saue all þat his hand hath wrought.
Allmyghty God in hevyn trone,

247 thralle] r *altered from another letter and an* e(?) *interl. above it* *Remainder of f. 30r (84 mm) and all of f. 30v blank*

[*Play 6*] 40 *written in the usual position of foliation and canc.;* 31 *written above and to the left of it*

1 *s.h. supplied*

I am Moyses þat make þis bone.
I pray þe, Lord God, with all my mende,
To us inclyne þi mercy sone.
Þi gracyous lordchep lete us fynde.

The to plesyn in all degré,
Gracyous God and Lord ovyr all,
Þu graunte us grace wherso we be,
And saue us sownd fro synfull fall.
Thy wyll to werke to us, þi thrall,
Enforme and teche us all þi plesans.
In purenesse put us þat nevyr [m]ot fall,
And grounde us in grace from all grevauns.

Hic Moyses videns [rubum] ardentem admirande dicit:

A, mercy, God, what menyth ȝon syte?
A grene busch as fyre doth flame
And kepyth his colowre fayr and bryghte,
Fresch and grene withowtyn blame!
It fyguryth sum thynge of ryght gret fame;
I kannot seyn what it may be.
I wyll go nere, in Goddys name,
And wysely loke þis busch to se.

DEUS Moyses! How, Moyses!
Herke to me anon þis stounde.
MOYSES I am here, Lorde, withowtyn les; f. 31v
Ȝowre gracyous wyll to do I am bounde.
DEUS Thu take þi schon anon ful rownde
Of þi fete in hast, lete se.
Ful holy is þat place and grownde
Þer þu dost stonde, I sey to the.

MOYSES Barfoot now I do me make
And pull of my schon fro my fete.

14 enforme] *or* enferme 16 mot] not 16 s.d. *written slightly larger and more carefully than is usual* rubum] D; *MS* rubrum

Now haue I my shon of take,
What is ȝoure wyll, Lord, fayn wold I wete.

DEUS Com nere, Moyses, with me to mete.
These tabellis I take þe in þin honde;
With my fynger in hem is wrete
All my lawys, þu vndyrstonde.

Loke þat þu preche all abowte;
Hooso wyll haue frenshipp of me,
To my lawys loke þei lowte,
þat þei be kept in all degré.
Go forth and preche anon, let se;
Loke þu not ses nyght nor day.

MOYSES Ȝoure byddyng, Lord, all wrought xal be,
Ȝoure wyll to werk I walk my way.

Custodi precepta Domini Dei tui: Deutronomini vj^to^.

The comaundment of þi Lord God, man, loke þu kepe
Where þat þu walk, wake, or slepe.

Euery man take good hede,
And to my techynge take good intent,
For God hath sent me now indede
Ȝow for to enforme his comaundment.
Ȝow to teche God hath me sent
f. 32r His lawys of lyff þat arn ful wyse.
Them to lerne be dyligent;
Ȝoure soulys may þei saue at þe last asyse.

The preceptys þat taught xal be
Be wretyn in þese tablys tweyn.
In þe fyrst ben wretyn thre
That towch to God, þis is serteyn.
In þe secund tabyl be wretyn ful pleyn
þe tother vij, þat towch mankende.

41 *the ink-colour slightly darker and the hand smaller with this line* 51 *lacks a capitulum*

Herk now well, man, what I xal seyn,
  And prent þise lawys well in þi mende.

1us. Primum mandatum: non habebis deos alienos.

The fyrst comaundement of God, as I ȝow say,
  Of þe fyrst tabyl, forsothe is this:
Þu xalt haue neythyr nyght nore day
  Noon other God but þe Kyng of Blysse.
  Vndyrstonde wele what menyth this,
    Euery man in his degré,
  And sett nevyr ȝoure hert amys
    Vpon þis werdlys vanyté.

For if þu sett þi loue so sore
  Vpon ryches and werdly good,
Þi wurdly rycches þu takyst evyrmore
  Evyn for þi God, as man ovyrwood.
  Amend þe, man, and chaunge þi mood;
    Lese not þi sowle for werdlys welth.
  Only hym loue which bodyly food
    Doth ȝeve all day, and gostly helth.

2. *Secundum mandatum: non [assumes] nomen Dei tui in vanum.* f. 32v

The secund precept of þe fyrst tabyll:
  Þe name of God take nevyr in vayne.
Swere none othis be noon fals fabyll;
  Þe name of God þu nevyr dysteyn.
  Bewhare of othis, for dowte of peyn,
    Amongys felachepp whan þu dost sytt.
  A lytyl othe, þis is serteyn,
    May dampne thy sowle to helle pytt.

66a 1us *and other numbers preceding Latin quotations from the Decalogue are rubricated in left margin* T *written at bottom left corner of f. 32r* 82a assumes] *Hal; MS* assumens

Man, whan þu art sett at þe nale
And hast þi langage as plesyth the,
Loke þin othis be non or smale,
And ȝett alwey loke trewe þei be.
But swere not oftyn, by rede of me.
For yf þu vse oftyntyme to swere,
It may gendyr custom in the.
Beware of custom, for he wyl dere.

3. Tercium mandatum: memento vt sabbatum sanctifice[*s*].

The iijde comaundment of God, as I rede,
Doth bydde the halwe well þin haly day.
Kepe þe well fro synfull dede,
And care not gretly for rych aray.
A ryght pore man, þis is non nay,
Of sympyl astat, in clothis rent,
Maybe bettyr than rych with garmentys gay
Oftyntyme doth kepe þis comaundment.

For rych men do shewe oftyntyme pompe and pride
On haly days, as oftyn is sene.
Whan pore men passe and go besyde,
At wurthy festys riche men woll bene.
f. 33r Thyn haly day þu kepyst not clene
In gloteny to lede þi lyff.
In Goddys hous ȝe xulde, bedene,
Honoure ȝoure God, both mayden and wyff.

4. Quartum mandatum: honora patrem tuum et matrem tuam.

Off þe secunde tabyll þe fyrst comaundment,
And in þe ordyr þe iiijte, I sey in fay,
He byddyth þe euyrmore with hert bent
Both fadyr amd modyr to wurchep alway.
Thow þat þi fadyr be pore of array,
And ȝow neuyr so rych of golde and good,

98a sanctifices] *D; MS* sanctificet

Ȝitt loke þu wurchep hym nyght and day
Of whom þu hast both flesch and blood.

In þis comaundmente includyd is
Thi bodyli fadyr and modyr also.
Includyd also I fynde in þis
Thi gostly fadyr and modyr þerto.
To þi gostly fadyr evyr reuerens do;
þi gostly modyr is Holy Cherch.
These tweyn saue þi sowle fro woo;
Euyr them to wurchep loke þat þu werch.

5. *Quintum mandatum: non occides.*

The fyfft comaundement byddyth all us
Scle no man, no whight þat þu kyll.
Vndyrstonde þis precept þus:
Scle no wyght with wurd nor wyll.
Wykkyd worde werkyht oftyntyme grett ill;
Bewar þerfore of wykkyd langage.
Wyckyd spech many on doth spyll;
Therfore of spech beth not owtrage.

6. *Sextum mandatum: non makaberis.* f. 33^{v}

The sexte comaundement byddith every man
þat no wyght lede no lecherous lay.
Forfett neuyr be no woman
Lesse þan þe lawe alowe þi play.
Trespas nevyr with wyff ne may,
With wedow nor with non othyr wyght.
Kepe þe clene, as I þe say,
To whom þu hast þi trowth plyght.

7. *Septimum mandatum: non furtum facies.*

Do no thefte, no thynge þu stele
þe vij^{te} precept byddyth þe ful sore.

132 kyll] *a final* e *erased?*

Whyll þu arte in welth and wele,
Euyll-gett good loke þu restore.
Off handys and dede be trewe evyrmore.
For yf þin handys lymyd be,
þu art but shent, þi name is lore
In felde and town and in all countré.

8. Octauum mandatum: non loqueris contra proximum tuum falsum testimonium.

The viij^{te} precept þus doth þe bydde:
Fals wyttnes loke non þu bere.
þe trowth nevyrmore loke þat þu hyde,
With fals wyttnes no man þu dere.
Nowther for love, ne dred, ne fere,
Sey non other than trowth is.
Fals wytnes yf þat þu rere,
Aȝens God þu dost grettly amys.

9. Nonum mandatum: non desiderabis vxorem proximi tui, et cetera.

f. 34^{r} The ix^{te} precept of lawe of lyff
Evyn þus doth bydde every man:
Desyre not þi neyborys wyff,
þow she be fayr and whyte as swan
And þi wyff brown; ȝitt natt for-than
þi neyborys wyff þu nevyr rejoyse.
Kepe þe clene as evyr þu can
To þin owyn wyff and þin owyn choyse.

10. Decimum mandatum: non concupisces domum proximi tui, non seruum, non ancillam, non bo[vem], *non asinum, nec omnia que illius sunt, et cetera.*

The x^{de} comaundement of God and last is þis:
Thi neyborys hous desyre þu nowth;
Maydon, nor servaunt, nor nowth of his,
Desyre hem nevyr in wyll nor thowth;

170b bovem] *Hal; MS* bos

Oxe nere asse þat he hath bought,
Nere no thynge þat longyht hym to.
Godys lawe must nedys be wrought;
Desyre no thynge þin neybore fro.

The vj^te comaundement of lechory
Doth exclude þe synfull dede.
But theys tweyn last most streytly,
Both dede and thought þei do forbede.
In wyll nere thought no lechory þu lede:
þi thought and wyll þu must refreyn,
All þi desyre, as I þe rede;
In clennes of lyff þiself restreyn.

Frendys, þese be þe lawys þat ȝe must kepe.
Therfore every man sett well in mende,
Wethyr þat þu do wake or slepe, f. 34^v
These lawys to lerne þu herke ful hynde,
And Godys grace xal be þi frende.
He socowre and saue ȝow in welth fro woo.
Farewell, gode frendys, for hens wyll I wende;
My tale I haue taught ȝow, my wey now I goo.

Explicit Moyses

f. 35^r

7
[JESSE ROOT]

YSAIAS I am þe prophete callyd Isaye,
Replett with Godys grett influens,
And sey pleynly be spyryte of prophecie
þat a clene mayde thourgh meke obedyens
Shall bere a childe which xal do resystens
Ageyn foule Zabulon, þe devyl of helle;
Mannys soule ageyn hym to defens,
Opyn in þe felde þe fend he xal felle.

Remainder of f. 34^v (162 mm) blank, except for the scribbled wethyr þat þu do *after* 194

Wherefore I seye quod virgo concipiet
  Et pariet filium, nomen Emanuel.
Oure lyf for to save he xal suffyr deth,
  And bye us to his blysse, in hevyn for to dwell.
  Of sacerdotale lynage, þe trewth I ȝow tell,
    Flessch and blood to take God wyll be born.
  Joye to man in erth, and in hevyn aungell
    At þe chyldys byrth joye xal make þat morn.

RADIX JESSE Egredietur virga de radice Jesse,
  Et flos de radice eius ascendet:
A blyssyd braunch xal sprynge of me
  That xal be swettere þan bawmys breth.
  Out of þat braunch in Nazareth
    A flowre xal blome of me, Jesse Rote,
  The which by grace xal dystroye deth
    And brynge mankende to blysse most sote.

DAUYD REX I am David of Jesse rote,
  The fresch kyng by naturall successyon.
And of my blood xal sprynge oure bote,
  As God hymself hath mad promyssyon.
f. 35v Of regall lyff xal come such foyson
    þat a clene mayde modyr xal be,
  Ageyns þe devellys fals illusyon
    With regall power to make man fre.

JEREMIAS PROPHETA I am þe prophete Jeremye
  And fullich acorde in all sentence
With Kyng Dauid and with Ysaie,
  Affermynge pleynly beforn þis audyens
  That God, of his high benyvolens,
    Of prest and kynge wyll take lynage,
  And bye us all from oure offens,
    In hevyn to haue his herytage.

Double vertical lines follow seye *in* 9 *and* filium *in* 10 + *drawn in right margin opposite* 23 *and* 40 27 spyr *canc. before* sprynge

SALAMON REX

I am Salamon, þe secunde kynge,
And þat wurthy temple, forsothe, made I,
Which þat is fygure of þat mayde ȝynge
þat xal be modyr of grett Messy.

EZECHIEL PROPHETA

A vysion of þis, ful veryly,
I, Ezechiel, haue had also,
Of a gate þat sperd was, trewly,
And no man but a prince myght þerin go.

ROBOAS REX

The iij^{de} kynge of þe jentyll Jesse,
My name is knowe, Kyng Roboas.
Of oure kynrede ȝitt men xul se
A clene mayde trede down foule Sathanas.

MICHEAS PROPHETA

And I am a prophete calde Mycheas.
I telle ȝow pleynly þat þus it is:
Evyn lyke as Eve modyr of wo was,
So xal a maydyn be modyr of blyss.

ABIAS REX

I that am calde Kynge Abias f. 36^{r}
Conferme for trewe þat ȝe han seyd,
And sey also, as in þis cas,
þat all oure myrth comyth of a mayd.

DANYEL PROPHETA

I, prophete Danyel, am well apayed.
In fygure of þis I saw a tre.
All þe fendys of hell xall ben affrayd
Whan maydenys frute þeron þei se.

ASA REX

I, Kynge Asa, beleve all þis
þat God wyll of a maydyn be born,
And, vs to bryngyn to endles blys,
Ruly on rode be rent and torn.

JONAS PROPHETA

I, Jonas, sey þat on þe iij^{de} morn
Fro deth he xal ryse; þis is a trew tall

44 of *interl.* + *drawn in left margin opposite* 45 *and in right margin opposite* 47 49 jeng *canc. before* jentyll *a circled* l *and the word* Danyel *written in right margin opposite* 59 70 trew] *or* trow tall] *traces of an* e *appear under the second* l

Fyguryd in me, þe which longe beforn
Lay iij days beryed within þe qwall.

JOSOPHAT REX
And I, Josophat, þe vj^te kynge, serteyn,
Of Jesse rote in þe lenyall successyon,
All þat my progenitouris hath befor me seyn
Feythffully beleve withowtyn all dubytacyon.

ABDIAS PROPHETA
I, Abdias prophete, make þis protestacyon:
þat aftyr he is resyn to lyve onys aȝen,
Deth xal be drevyn to endles dampnacyon,
And lyff xal be grawntyd of paradys ful pleyn.

JORAS REX
And I, Joras, also, in þe numbre of sefne
Of Jesse rote kynge, knowlych þat he
Aftyr his resurreccyon returne xal to hefne,
Both God and verry man, ther endles to be.

ABACUCH PROPHETA
I, Abacuch prophete, holde wele with the.
Whan he is resyn he xal up stye,
In hevyn as juge sitt in his se,
Vs for to deme whan we xal dye.

f. 36v OZIAS REX
And I, Ozyas, kynge of hygh degré,
Spronge of Jesse rote, dare well sey this:
Whan he is gon to his dygnyté,
He xal send þe Sprytt to his discyplis.

JOELL PROPHETA
And I, Joel, knowe full trewe þat is.
God bad me wryte in prophesye
He wolde sende down his Sprytt, iwys,
On ȝonge and olde, ful sekyrlye.

JOATHAS REX
My name is knowe, Kyng Joathan,
The ixe kynge spronge of Jesse.
Of my kynrede God wol be man,
Mankend to saue, and þat joyth me.

72 qwall] *traces of an* e *appear under the second* l *Several letters written in a small hand in right margin* 79 *an erasure before* endles 99 gold *with a deleting dot under the* l *canc. in red before* God

AGGEUS PROPHETA

With ȝow I do holde, þat am prophete Aggee.
Com of þe same hygh and holy stok,
God of oure kynrede indede born wyl be,
From þe wulf to saue al shepe of his flok.

ACHAS REX

Off Jesse, Kyng Achas is my name,
þat falsly wurchepyd ydolatrye
Tyl Ysaie putt me in blame
And seyd a mayd xulde bere Messye.

OZYAS PROPHETA

Off þat byrthe wyttnes bere I,
A prophete, Osyas men me calle.
And aftyr þat tale of Isaye,
þat mayd xal bere Emanuelle.

EZECHIAS REX

My name is knowyn, Kyng Ezechyas,
þe xj^te kyng of þis geneologye,
And say, forsothe, as in þis cas,
A mayde be mekenes xal brynge mercye.

SOPHOSAS PROPHETA

I, a prophete callyd Sophonye, f. 37^r
Of þis matyr do bere wyttnes,
And for trowth [d]o sertyfie
þat maydens byrth oure welth xal dresse.

MANASSES REX

Of þis nobyll and wurthy generacyon
The xij^e kyng am I, Manasses,
Wyttnessynge here be trew testyficacyon
þat maydenys childe xal be Prince of Pes.

BARUK PROPHETA

And I, Baruk prophete, conferme wurdys thes:
Lord and Prince of Pes þow þat chylde be,
[To] al his fomen ageyn hym þat pres,
Ryght a grym syre at Domysday xal he be.

AMON REX

Amon Kynge for þe last conclusyon
Althynge befornseyd for trowth do testyfie,
Praynge þat Lord of oure synne remyssyon;
At þat dredful day he us graunt mercye.

104 *a stain over* saue   119 do] to   127 To *supplied*

Thus we all of þis genealogye
   Acordynge in on here in þis place,
Pray þat hey3 Lorde whan þat we xal dye,
   Of his gret goodnesse to grawnt us his grace.

Explicit Jesse

Remainder of f. 37^{r} and foot of f. 37^{v} contain the following genealogy in Textura Quadrata. On f. 37^{r}:

Barpanter Asmaria }	genuit	Joachym
Ysakar Nasaphat }	genuit	Anna
Joachym Anna }	genuit	sponsa Joseph fabro Maria, mater Jesu Christi
Cleophas et Anna }	genuit	sponsa Alpheo ij^{a} Maria, mater Symonem et Judam Jacobum minorem et Joseph Just[um][1]
Salome et Anna }	genuit	sponsa Zebedeo iij^{a} Maria, mater Johannem euangelistam et Jacobum Majorem

Above and at the right of this genealogy on f. 37^{r} is written a note in the same script:

Emeria fuit soror Anne que habebat quondam filiam
Elizabeth que nupta fui[t][2] Zakarie de quo peperit Johanne[m][3]
Baptistem precursorem Domini
Elyud Eminẽ filia beatus Geruasius episcopus

On f. 37^{v} in Textura Quadrata, (lines 1–4) and Fere-Textura (line 5):

	mater Samue vxor Rague }	lis
Quinque sunt Anne	vxor Tob mater beate Mar }	ie
	Anna prophetissa	

Below this genealogy the following note appears in large Fere-Textura in red:

Est Ysakar Anne pater; Melophat sic quoque mater vel Nasaphat[4]

---

[1] Justum] Just (*cropped*).
[2] fuit] fui (*cropped*).
[3] Johannem] Johanne (*cropped*).
[4] *The bottom of the letters in the words* vel Nasaphat *cropped.*

8

f. 37v

[JOACHIM AND ANNA]

CONTEMPLACIO Cryst conserve þis congregacyon
Fro perellys past, present, and future,
And þe personys here pleand, þat þe pronunciacyon
Of here sentens to be seyd mote be sad and sure;
And þat non oblocucyon make þis matere obscure,
But it may profite and plese eche persone present
From þe gynnynge to þe endynge so to endure,
þat Cryst and every creature with þe conceyte be content.

This matere here mad is of þe Modyr of Mercy:
How be Joachym and Anne was here concepcyon
Sythe offred into þe temple, compiled breffly;
Than maryed to Joseph; and so, folwyng, þe Salutacyon,
Metyng with Elyzabeth, and þerwith a conclusyon,
In fewe wurdys talkyd, þat it xulde nat be tedyous
To lernyd nyn to lewd, nyn to no man of reson.
þis is þe processe, now preserve ȝow Jesus.

þerfore of pes I ȝow pray, all þat ben here present,
And tak hed to oure talkyn[g], what we xal say.
I beteche ȝow þat Lorde þat is evyr omnypotent
To governe ȝow in goodnes, as he best may.
In hevyn we may hym se.
Now God þat is Hevyn Kynge
Sende us all hese dere blyssynge,
And to his towre he mote vs brynge.
Amen for charyté.

16 of oure *canc. in red before* now   18 talkyng] talkyn

f. 38^{r} YSAKAR

The prestys of God offre sote ensens
Vnto here God, and þerfore they be holy.
We þat mynistere here in Goddys presens,
In vs xuld be fownd no maner of foly.
Ysakar, prynce of prestys, am I,
þat þis holyest day here haue mynystracyon,
Certyfyenge all tribus in my cure specyaly
þat this is þe hyest fest of oure solennyzacyon.

This we clepe Festum Encenniorum,
þe newe fest, of which iij in þe ȝere we exercyse.
Now all þe kynredys to Jerusalem must cum
Into þe temple of God, here to do sacryfyse.
Tho þat be cursyd my dygnyté is to dysspyse,
And þo þat be blyssyd here holy sacrefyse to take.
We be regal sacerdocium, it perteyneth vs to be wysse
Be fastyng, be prayng, be almes, and at du tyme to wake.

JOACHYM

Now all þis countré of Galylé,
With þis cetye of Nazareth specyal,
þis fest to Jerusalem must go we
To make sacrefyce to God eternal.
My name is Joachym, a man in godys substancyall.
'Joachym' is to say, 'He þat to God is redy'.
So haue I be and evyrmore xal,
For þe dredful domys of God sore drede I.

I am clepyd ryghtful, why wole ȝe se,
For my godys into thre partys I devyde:
On to þe temple and to hem þat þer servyng be;
Anodyr to þe pylgrimys and pore men; þe iij^{de} for hem with me abyde.

26 *a mark stands to the right of the s.h.*
38 dygnyté] *second* y *altered from another letter?*
41 tyme] t *altered from another letter*
53 iij^{de}] ^{de} *in red ink*

So xulde euery curat in þis werde wyde (f. 38v)
Ȝeve a part to his chauncel, iwys,
A part to his parochonerys þat to povert slyde,
The thryd part to kepe for hym and his.

But, blyssyd wyff Anne, sore I drede
In þe temple þis tyme to make sacryfice;
Becawse þat no frute of vs doth procede,
I fere me grettly þe prest wole me dysspice.
Than grett slawndyr in þe tribus of vs xulde aryse.
But þis I avow to God with all þe mekenes I can:
Ȝyff of his mercy he wole a childe us devyse,
We xal offre it up into þe temple to be Goddys man.

ANNA
Ȝoure swemful wurdys make terys trekyl down be my face.
Iwys, swete husbond, þe fawte is in me.
My name is Anne, þat is to sey 'grace';
We wete not how gracyous God wyl to us be.
A woman xulde bere Cryst, þese profecyes haue we;
If God send frute and it be a mayd childe,
With all reuerens I vow to his mageste,
Sche xal be here footmayd to mynyster here most mylde.

JOACHYM
Now lete be it as God wole, þer is no more.
Tweyn turtelys for my sacryfice with me I take.
And I beseche, wyff, and evyr we mete more,
Þat hese grett mercy vs meryer mut make.

ANNA
For dred and for swem of ȝoure wourdys I qwake.
Thryes I kysse ȝow with syghys ful sad,
And to þe mercy of God mekely I ȝow betake.
And þo þat departe in sorwe, God make þer metyng glad.

71 If (?) *canc. before* God, *then written in left margin* 78 Anna *scribbled in right margin* 80 *A letter* (I?) *erased before* mekely mekely] ly *interl. in small script*

SENIOR TRIBUS Worchepful Sere Joachym, be ȝe redy now?
All ȝoure kynrede is come ȝow to exorte
f. 39^{r} þat þei may do sacrifice at þe temple with ȝow,
For ȝe be of grett wurchep, as men ȝow report.
JOACHYM All synfull, seke, and sory God mote comforte.
I wolde I wore as men me name.
Thedyr, in Goddys name, now late us all resorte.
A, Anne, Anne, Anne, God scheeld us fro shame!

ANNE Now am I left alone, sore may I wepe.
A, husbond, ageyn God wel mote ȝow brynge,
And fro shame and sorwe he mote ȝow kepe.
Tyl I se ȝow ageyn I kannot sees of wepynge.
SENIOR Prynce of oure prestys, if it be ȝoure plesynge,
We be com mekely to make oure sacrefice.
YSAKAR God do ȝow mede, bothe elde and ȝynge.
Than devowtly we wyl begynne servyse.

There they xal synge þis sequens: 'Benedicta sit beata Trinitas'. And in þat tyme Ysakar with his ministerys ensensyth þe autere; and þan þei make her offryng, and Isaker seyth:

Comyth up, serys, and offeryth all now,
Ȝe þat to do sacryfice worthy are.
Abyde a qwyle, sere; whedyr wytte þu?
þu and þi wyff arn barrany and bare;
Neyther of ȝow fruteful nevyr ȝett ware.
Whow durste þu amonge fruteful presume and abuse?
It is a tokyn þu art cursyd þare.
Whereffore with grett indygnacyon þin offeryng I refuse!

Et refudit sacrificium Joachim.

Amonge all þis pepyl barreyn be no mo.
Therefore comyth up and offeryth here alle.
þu, Joachym, I charge þe, fast out þe temple þu go.

84 may *interl.* sacrifice] *first* c *altered from another letter* 87 wore] *or* were
97 s.d. *preceded by the rubricated mark* ☞

Et redit flendo

Than with Goddys holy wourde blysse ȝow I shalle.

Ministro cantando:

Adjutorium nostrum in nomine Domini, f. 39v
CHORUS Qui fecit celum et terram.
MINISTER Sit nomen Domini benedictum
CHORUS Ex hoc nunc et usque in seculum.
EPISCOPUS Benedicat vos diuina majestas et vna Deitas,
Pater, et Filius, et Spiritus Sanctus.
CHORUS Amen.

Signando manu cum cruce sole[m]niter, et recedant tribus extra templum.

[YSAKAR] Now of God and man blyssyd be ȝe alle.
Homward aȝen now returne ȝe.
And in þis temple abyde we xalle
To servyn God in Trinyté.

JOACHYM A, mercyfful Lord, what is þis lyff?
What haue I do, Lorde, to haue þis blame?
For hevynes I dare not go hom to my wyff,
And amonge my neyborys I dare not abyde for shame.
A, Anne, Anne, Anne, al oure joye is turnyd to grame!
From ȝoure blyssyd felachepp I am now exilyd.
And ȝe here onys of þis fowle fame,
Sorwe wyl sle ȝow to se me thus revylyd.

109 holy *interl.* 109 s.d. Ministro] *the last few letters barely legible* 110 Adjutorium nostrum *scribbled at right* 114 *several letters* (?et vna) *canc. before* majestas 115 *the rubricated mark* ✠ *precedes* Pater *and follows* Pater *and* Filius 116 s.d. solemniter] solenniter 117 *s.h. supplied* 123 dare *canc. after* For 124 neyborys] *first* y *altered from another letter?*

But s[e]n God soferyth thys, vs must sofron nede.
Now wyl I go to my she[p]herdys and with hem abyde,
And þer evyrmore levyn in sorwe and in drede.
Shame makyth many man his hed for to hyde.
Ha, how do ȝe, felas? In ȝow is lytel pryde.
How fare ȝe and my bestys, þis wete wolde I veryly.

PRIMUS PASTOR
A, welcom hedyr, blyssyd mayster; we pasture hem ful wyde.
They be lusty and fayr, and grettly multyply.

How do ȝe, mayster? Ȝe loke al hevyly.
How doth oure dame at hom? Sytt she and sowyht?

JOACHYM
To here þe speke of here, it sleyth myn hert, veryly.
How I and sche doth, God hymself knowyth.
f. 40r The meke God lyftyth up, þe proude overthrowyht.
Go do what ȝe lyst, se ȝoure bestys not stray.

SECUNDUS PASTOR
Aftere grett sorwe, mayster, ever gret grace growyht.
Sympyl as we kan, we xal for ȝow pray.

TERCIUS PASTOR
Ȝa, to pray for careful, it is grett nede;
We all wul prey for ȝow knelende.
God of his goodnes send ȝow good spede,
And of ȝoure sorwe ȝow sone amende.

JOACHYM
I am nott wurthy, Lord, to loke up to hefne.
My synful steppys an vemynyd þe grounde.
I, lothfolest þat levyth; þu, Lord hyest in þi setys sefne.
What art þu? Lord. What am I? Wrecche, werse þan an hownde.

129 sen] *B; MS* son sofron] r *corrected from another letter?* 130 shepherdys] sherherdys *A rough line drawn into left margin under* 132; Pastores *written by another hand in right margin;* a *written in left margin by another hand opposite* 135; b *written opposite* 139 *and* 141, c *or* cc *opposite* 143, *and* d *opposite* 145 *No capitulum before* 137
139 *The s.h.* ijus Pastor *canc. by red line of the s.h.* Joachym, *which is sloppily interl. above*
140 knowyth] y *altered from another letter* (h*?*) 149 *indistinct notations written in left margin* 150 an vemynyd] *B* Anvemynyd

þu has sent me shame which myn hert doth wounde—
I thank þe more herefore þan for all my prosperité.
þis is a tokyn þu lovyst me, now to the I am bounde;
þu seyst þu art with hem þat in tribulacyon be.

And hoso haue þe, he nedyth not care thanne.
My sorwe is feryng I haue do sum offens.
Punchyth me, Lorde, and spare my blyssyd wyff Anne
þat syttyth and sorwyth ful sore of myn absens.
Ther is not may profyte but prayour to ȝoure presens;
With prayorys prostrat byfore þi person I wepe.
Haue mende on oure avow for ȝoure mech magnyficens,
And my lovyngest wyff Anne, Lord, for þi mercy, kepe.

ANNA A, mercy, Lord! Mercy, mercy, mercy!
We are synfolest it shewyth þat ȝe send us all þis sorwe.
Why do ȝe thus to myn husbond, Lord? Why? Why? Why?
For my barynes? [Ȝe] may amend þis þiself, and þu lyst, tomorwe.
And it plese so þi mercy, þe, my Lord, I take to borwe,
I xal kepe myn avow qwhyl I leve and leste.
I fere me I haue offendyd þe; myn hert is ful of sorwe.
Most mekely I pray þi pety þat þis bale þu wyl breste. f. 40v

158 feryng] r *malformed, perhaps altered from another letter* 168 Ȝe] *M; MS* he
169 þi] i *encircled by a loop*

Here þe aungel descendith þe hefne syngyng, 'Exultet celum laudibus, resultet terra gaudiis, archangelorum gloria sacra canun[*t*] *solemnia'*

JOACHYM Qwhat art þu, in Goddys name, þat makyst me adrad?
It is as lyth abowt me as al þe werd were fere!
ANGELUS I am an aungel of God com to make þe glad.
God is plesyd with þin helmes and hath herd þi prayere;
He seyth þi shame, þi repreff, and þi terys cler.
God is avengere of synne and not nature doth lothe;
Whos wombe þat he sparyth and makyth bar-reyn her
He doth to shewe his myth and his mercy bothe.

Thu seest þat Sara was nynty ȝere bareyn;
Sche had a son, Ysaac, to whom God ȝaff his blyssynge.
Rachel also had þe same peyn;
She had a son, Joseph, þat of Egypt was kynge.
A strongere þan Sampson nevyr was be wryt-ynge,
Nor an holyere þan Samuel, it is seyd thus;
Ȝett here moderys were bareyn bothe in þe gyn-nynge.
Þe concepcyon of all swych, it is ful mervel-yous!

And in þe lyke wyse, Anne, þi blyssyd wyff,
Sche xal bere a childe xal hygth Mary,
Which xal be blyssyd in here body and haue joys fyff,
And ful of þe Holy Goost inspyred syngulyrly.
Sche xal be offryd into þe temple solemply,
Þat of here non evyl fame xuld sprynge thus.

172 s.d. canunt] canun, *remainder cropped* 173 *s.h. written before* 172 s.d. 182 son] so *smudged* 194 of here *interl.*

And as sche xal be bore of a barrany body,
 So of here xal be bore without nature Jesus,

That xal be Savyour vnto al mankende. f. 41r C quire
 In tokyn, whan þu come to Jherusalem, to þe Gyldyn Gate,
þu xalt mete Anne, þi wyff; haue þis in þi mende.
 I xal sey here þe same, here sorwys to rebate.

JOACHYM Of þis imcomparabyl comfort I xal nevyr forgete þe date!
 My sorwe was nevyr so grett, but now my joy is more!
 I xal hom in hast, be it nevyr so late.
 A, Anne, blyssyd be þat body of þe xal be bore!

Now farewel, myn shepherdys, governe ȝow now wysly.

PRIMUS PASTOR Haue ȝe good tydyngys, maystyr? þan be we glad.

JOACHYM Prayse God for me, for I am not wourthy.

SECUNDUS PASTOR In feyth, sere, so we xal with all oure sowlys sad.

TERCIUS PASTOR I holde it helpfful þat on of vs with ȝow be had.

JOACHYM Nay, abyde with ȝoure bestys, sone, in Goddys blyssynge.

PRIMUS PASTOR We xal make us so mery now þis is bestad
 þat a myle on ȝoure wey ȝe xal here us synge.

ANNE Alas, for myn husbond me is ful wo.
 I xal go seke hym whatsoevyr befalle.
I wote not in erth which wey is he go.
 Fadyr of Hefne, for mercy to ȝoure fete I falle.

The paper of quires C, D, and F–M (except for ff. 95–6, and 112) bears a YHS in a Sun watermark. Dots appear in the loops of the capitula preceding 197, 205, 213, 221, 229, and 237   þat xal be s *written as catchword at foot of f. 40v; several rubbed letters appear at the left and right of these words*   211 is *canc. before* þis   bestad] st *partly obscured by a stain*   *A rough line is drawn in right margin opposite* 212   216 Hefne] *final* e *smudged*

ANGELUS
Anne, þin husbond ryght now I was withall,
þe aungel of God þat bar hym good tydynge;
And as I seyd to hym, so to þe sey I xal:
God hath herd þi preyour and þi wepynge.

At þe Goldyn Gate þu xalte mete hym ful mylde,
And in grett gladnes returne to ȝoure hous.
So be proces þu xalt conseyve and bere a childe
f. 41v Whiche xal hyght Mary; and Mary xal bere Jesus,
Which xal be Savyour of all þe werd and us.
Aftere grett sorwe evyr grett gladnes is had.
Now myn inbassett I haue seyd to ȝow thus.
Gooth in oure Lordys name and in God beth glad.

ANNE
Now blyssyd be oure Lorde and all his werkys ay!
All heffne and erthe mut blysse ȝow for this.
I am so joyful I not what I may say;
þer can no tounge telle what joye in me is!
I to bere a childe þat xal bere all mannys blys,
And haue myn hosbonde ageyn! Ho myth haue joys more?
No creature in erth is grauntyd more mercy, iwys.
I xal hyȝe me to þe ȝate to be þer before.

Here goth þe aungel aȝen to hefne.

A, blyssyd be oure Lord, myn husbond I se.
I xalle on myn knes and to hymward crepe.

JOACHYM
A, gracyous wyff Anne, now fruteful xal ȝe be.
For joy of þis metyng in my sowle I wepe.
Haue þis kusse of clennesse and with ȝow it kepe.
In Goddys name, now go we, wyff, hom to oure hous.

ANNE
þer was nevyr joy sank in me so depe.
Now may we sey, husbond, God is to us gracyous,

229 ay] y *malformed*   240 wepy *canc. in red before* metyng   243 nevyr *interl.*

Veryly.

JOACHYM
3a, and if we haue levyd wel herebefore,
I pray þe, Lord, þin ore,
So mote we levyn evyrmore,
And, be þi grace, more holyly.

ANNE
Now homward, husbond, I rede we gon, f. 42r
Ryth hom al to oure place,
To thank God þat sytt in tron,
þat þus hath sent us his grace.

9
[THE PRESENTATION OF MARY IN THE TEMPLE]

CONTEMPLACIO
Sovereynes, ʒe han sen shewyd ʒow before
Of Joachym and Anne here botherys holy metynge.
How oure Lady was conseyvid and how she was bore,
We passe ovyr þat, breffnes of tyme consyderynge;
And how oure Lady in here tendyr age and ʒyng
Into þe temple was offryd, and so forth proced.
þis sentens sayd xal be hire begynnyng.
Now þe Modyr of Mercy in þis be oure sped.

And as a childe of iij ʒere age here she xal appere
To alle pepyl þat ben here present.
And of here grett grace now xal ʒe here,
How she levyd evyr to Goddys entent

245 Veryly *written at right of* 244, *preceded by a capitulum written over some black sign*
250 *No capitulum*

Play 9 follows immediately upon Play 8. Dots appear in the loops of all capitula in this play.
11 here she xal *canc. in red before* now

With grace.
That holy matere we wole declare
Tyl fortene ȝere how sche dyd fare.
Now of ȝoure speche I pray ȝow spare,
All þat ben in þis place.

Here Joachym and Anne, with oure Lady betwen hem beyng al in whyte as a childe of iij ȝere age, presente here into the temple, thus seyng Joachym:

f. 42v JOACHIM
Blyssyd be oure Lord. Fayr frute haue we now.
Anne, wyff, remembyr wole ȝe
þat we made to God an holy avow
þat oure fyrst childe þe servaunt of God xulde be.
The age of Mary, oure dowtere, is ȝerys thre;
þerfore to thre personys and on God lete us here present.
þe ȝonger she be drawyn, þe bettyr semyth me.
And for teryeng of oure avow, of God we myth be shent.

ANNE
It is as ȝe sey, husbond, indede.
Late us take Mary, oure dowtere, us betwen,
And to þe temple with here procede.
Dowtere, þe aungel tolde us ȝe xulde be a qwen!
Wole ȝe go se þat Lord ȝoure husbond xal ben,
And lerne for to love hym and lede with hym ȝoure lyff?
Telle ȝoure fadyr and me her ȝoure answere, let sen.
Wole ȝe be pure maydyn and also Goddys wyff?

MARIA
Fadyr and modyr, if it plesynge to ȝow be,
Ȝe han mad ȝoure avow, so ssothly wole I,

17 a.s. *an* s(*?*) *canc. before* thus here Johym and Anne with *scribbled by another hand in space left at bottom of f. 42r* 18 JOACHIM *written in Textura Quadrata and preceded by a capitulum* 20 þat] t *ill-formed and blotted*

To be Goddys chast seruaunt whil lyff is in me.
But to be Goddys wyff I was nevyr wurthy:
I am þe sympelest þat evyr was born of body.
I haue herd ȝow seyd God xulde haue a modyr swete;
þat I may leve to se hire, God graunt me for his mercy,
And abyl me to ley my handys vndyr hire fayr fete.

Et genuflectet ad Deum.

JOACHYM Iwys, dowtere, it is wel seyd;
Ȝe answere and ȝe were twenty ȝere olde!
ANNE Whith ȝoure speche, Mary, I am wel payd. f. 43^{r}
Can ȝe gon alone? Lett se, beth bolde.
MARIA To go to Goddys hous, wole ȝe now beholde,
I am joyful thedyrward as I may be.
JOACHYM Wyff, I [am] ryght joyful oure dowtere to beholde.
ANNE So am I, wys husbond. Now in Goddys name go we.

JOACHYM Sere prince of prestes, and it plese ȝow,
We þat were barreyn God hath sent a childe.
To offre here to Goddys service we mad oure avow;
Here is þe same mayde, Mary most mylde.
ISAKAR Joachym, I haue good mende how I ȝow revyled.
I am ryght joyful þat God hath ȝove ȝow þis grace.
To be amonge fruteful now be ȝe reconsylid.
Com, swete Mary, com; ȝe haue a gracyous face.

Joachym flectendo ad Deum sic dicens:

40 ȝoure *canc. before* mercy *with two crossed strokes in fainter ink, not in the manner of the main scribe;* his *interl. above in the same ink* 48 am *supplied*

JOACHYM Now Fadyr, and Sone, and Holy Gost,
On God and personys thre,
We offre to þe, Lorde of myghtys most,
Oure dowtere, þi servaunt evyrmore to be.
ANNA Therto most bounde evyrmore be we.
Mary, in þis holy place leve ȝow we xall.
In Goddys name now up go ȝe;
Oure fadyr, oure prest, lo, doth ȝow call.

MARIA Modyr, and it plese ȝow, fyrst wole I take my leve
Of my fadyr and ȝow, my modyr, iwys.
I haue a fadyr in hefne, þis I beleve;
Now, good fadyr, with þat fadyr ȝe me blysse.

f. 43v JOACHYM In nomine Patris, et Filii, et Spiritus Sancti.
MARIA Amen. Now ȝe, good modyr.
ANNE In nomine Patris, et Filii, et Spiritus Sancti.
MARIA Amen.

Now oure Lord thank ȝow for this.
Here is my fadyr and my modyr bothe;
Most mekely I beseche I may ȝow kys.
Now forȝeve me yf evyr I made ȝow wrothe.

Et [*am*]*plexendo osculabit patrem et matrem.*

JOACHYM Nay, dowtere, ȝe offendyd nevyr God nor man.
Lovyd be þat Lord ȝow so doth kepe.
ANNE Swete dowtyr, thynk on ȝoure modyr, An;
Ȝoure swemynge smytyht to myn hert depe.
[MARIA] Fadyr and modyr, I xal pray for ȝow and wepe
To God with al myn hert specyaly.
Blysse me day and nyght, and evyr her ȝe slepe,
Good fadyr and modyr, and beth mery.

73 *written at right of* 72, *divided by a double virgule* 74 *preceded by an unnecessary capitulum; the s.h.* Maria *canc.* 77 s.d. amplexendo] *Hal; MS* explexendo 82 *s.h. supplied by a reviser* 85 beth] th *crossed through in black*

JOACHYM A, ho had evyr suche a chylde?
Nevyr creature ȝit þat evyr was bore!
Sche is so gracyous, she is so mylde—
So xulde childyr to fadyr and modyr evyrmore.
ANNE Than xulde thei be blyssyd and plese God sore.
Husbond, and it plese ȝow, not hens go we xal
Tyl Mary be in þe temple above thore;
I wold not for al erthe se here fal.

EPISCOPUS Come, gode Mary. Come, babe, I þe call.
Þi pas pratyly to þis plas pretende.
Þu xalt be þe dowtere of God eternall
If þe fyftene grees þu may ascende. f. 44r
It is meracle if þu do! Now God þe dyffende.
From Babylony to Hevynly Jherusalem þis is þe way.
Every man þat thynk his lyf to amende,
Þe fyftene psalmys in memorye of þis mayde say.

Maria, et sic deinceps usque ad fine[m] xv^{cim} psalmorum.

MARIA The fyrst degré gostly applyed,
It is holy desyre with God to be.
In trobyl to God I haue cryed,
And in sped þat Lord hath herde me.

Ad Dominum cum tribularer clamaui, et exaudiuit me.

The secunde is stody with meke inquysissyon, veryly,
How I xal haue knowynge of Godys wylle.

94–6 *written in small form* 100 thynk] th *written over an erasure,* k *over another letter* 101 s.d. finem] *M; MS* fine *Latin passages between* 105 *and* 162 *written in Textura Quadrata (but* 129a, 145a, *and* 157a *in Fere-Textura), with initial letters of each line rubricated and, on f. 44r, surmounted by a red dot* 102–69 *lack capitula*

To þe mownteynes of hefne I haue lyfte myn ey,
From qwens xal comyn helpe me tylle.

Leuaui oculos meos in montes, vnde ueniat auxilium mihi.

The thrydde is gladnes in mende in hope to be
That we xall be savyd all thus.
I am glad of these tydyngys ben seyd to me,
Now xal we go into Goddys hous.

Letatus sum in hiis que dicta sunt mihi: in domum Domini ibimus.

The fourte is meke obedyence as is dette
To hym þat is above þe planetys sefne.
To þe I haue myn eyn sette
þat dwellys above þe skyes in hefne.

Ad te leuaui oculos meos, qui habitas in celis.

The fyfte is propyr confessyon,
þat we be nought withowth God thus.
But God in vs haue habytacyon,
Peraventure oure enemyes shulde swelle vs.

f. 44v *Nisi quia Dominus erat in nobis, dicat nunc Israel, nisi quia Dominus erat in nobis. . . .*

The sexte is confidens in Goddys strenght alon,
For of all grace from hym comyth þe strem.
They þat trust in God as þe Mownt Syon,
He xal not be steryd endles þat dwellyth in
Jherusalem.

Qui confidunt in Domino sicut Mons Syon, non commouebitur in eternum, qui habitat in Hierusalem.

125a Hierusalem *preceded by a capitulum*

The sefte is vndowteful hope of immortalyté
  In oure Lordeis grac[e] and mercy.
Whan oure Lord conuertyth oure captiuité,
  Than are we mad as joyful mery.

In conuertendo Dominus captiuitatem Syon, facti sumus sicut consolati.

The eyted is contempt of veynglory in vs
  For hym þat al mankende hath multyplyed.
But yf oure Lord make here oure hous,
  They an laboryd in veyn þat it han edyfied.

Nisi Dominus edificauerit domum, in uanum laborauerù[n]t qui edificant eam.

The nynte is a childely fer indede
  With a longyng love in oure Lorde þat ay is.
Blyssyd arn all they þat God drede,
  Whiche þat gon in his holy weys.

Beati omnes qui timent Dominum, qui ambulant in viis eius.

The tende is myghty soferauns of carnal tempta-
      cyon,
  For þe fleschly syghtys ben fers and fel.
Ofte ȝough is fowth with with suech vexacyon.
  Þu, seynge God, say so, clepyd Israel.

Sepe expugnauerunt me a juuentute mea, dicat nunc Israel.

The elefnte is accusatyff confessyon of iniquité,
  Of which ful noyous is þe noyis.
Fro depnes, Lord, I haue cryed to the;
  Lord, here in sped my sympyl voys.

De profundis clamaui ad te, Domine; Domine, exaudi uocem meam. f. 45r

127 Lordeis grace] *M* Lorde-is grace; *MS* Lorde is as gracy 129 *one or two letters erased after* joyful 133 *one or two letters erased after* it 133a laborauerunt] *M; MS* laborauerut 141 þu] *Hal* Than *The handwriting on f. 45 is quite small*

The twelfte is mekenes þat is fayr and softe
In mannys sowle withinne and withowte.
Lord, myn herte is not heyned on lofte,
Nyn myn eyn be not lokynge abowte.

Domine, non est exaltatum cor meum, neque elati sunt oculi mei.

The threttene is feyth þerwith,
With holy dedys don expresse.
Haue mende, Lorde, of Davyth,
And of all his swettnes.

Memento, Domine, Dauid et omnis mansuetudinis eius.

The fourtene is brothyrly concorde, iwys,
þat norchyth love of creaturys echon.
Se how good and how glad it is
Bretheryn for to dwelle in on.

Ecce quam bonum et quam jocundum habitare fratres in vnum.

The fyftene is gracyous. With on acorde,
Whiche is syne of godly love, semyth me,
Se, now blysse oure Lord,
All þat oure Lordys servauntys be.

Ecce nunc benedicite Dominum, omnes serui Domini.

EPISCOPUS A, gracyous Lord, þis is a mervelyous thynge
þat we se here all in syght:
A babe of thre ȝer age so ȝynge
To come vp þese grecys so vpryght!
It is an hey meracle and, be Goddys myght,
No dowth of, she xal be gracyous.
MARIA Holy fadyr, I beseche ȝow forthryght,
Sey how I xal be rewlyd in Goddys hous.

148 heyned] *or* heyued 162 *no capitulum*

EPISCOPUS Dowtere, God hath ȝovyn vs comaundementys ten, f. 45v
Which, shortely to say, be comprehendyd in tweyn.
And þo must be kept of all Crysten men,
Or ellys here jugement is perpetual peyn.
Ȝe muste love God s[o]vereynly and ȝoure evyn-Crystyn pleyn,
God fyrst for his hyȝ and sovereyn dygnyté;
He lovyd ȝow fyrst, love hym ageyn,
For of love to his owyn lyknes he made the.

Love Fadyr, Sone, and Holy Gost:
Love God þe Fadyr for he gevyth myght;
Love God þe Sone for he gevyth wysdam, þu wost;
Love God þe Holy Gost for he gevyth love and lyght.
Thre personys and on God þus love of ryght
With all þin hert, with all þi sowle, with all þi mende,
And with all þe strenghthis in þe bedyght.
Þan love þin evyn-Crystyn as þiself withowtyn ende.

Thu xalt hate nothynge but þe devyl and synne—
God byddyth the lovyn þi bodyly enmy,
And as for ȝoureself here, þus xal ȝe begynne:
Ȝe must serve and wurchep God here dayly,
For with prayȝer [come] grace and mercy.
Se the haue a resonable tyme to fede,
Thanne to haue a labour bodyly,
Þat þerin be gostly and bodely mede.

Ȝoure abydynge xal be with ȝoure maydenys fyve
Swyche tyme as ȝe wole haue consolacyon.

174 sovereynly] *M; MS* severeynly 183 myght *canc. at end of line and* mende *interl. above it* 190 come] *M; MS* with 191 Se the] *B; MS* sethe

MARIA This lyff me lyketh as my lyve;
Of here namys I beseche ȝow to haue informacyon.

f. 46[r] EPISCOPUS There is þe fyrst, Meditacyon,
Contryssyon, Compassyon, and Clennes,
And þat holy mayde, Fruyssyon.
With these blyssyd maydenes xal be ȝoure besynes.

MARIA Here is an holy felachepp I fele.
I am not wurthy amonge hem to be.
Swete systerys, to ȝow all I knele;
To receyve me I beseche ȝoure charyté.

EPISCOPUS They xal, dowtere; and on þe tothere syde se
Ther ben sefne prestys indede
To schryve, to teche, and to mynystryn to the,
To lerne þe Goddys lawys, and Scrypture to rede.

MARIA Fadyr, knew I here namys, wele were I.

EPISCOPUS Ther is Dyscressyon, Devocyon, Dylexcyon, and Deliberacyon;
They xal tende upon ȝow besyly
With Declaracyon, Determynacyon, Dyvynacyon.
Now go, ȝe maydenys, to ȝoure occupacyon,
And loke ȝe tende þis childe tendyrly.
And ȝe, serys, knelyth and I xal gyve ȝow Goddys benyson
In nomine Patris, et Filii, et Spiritus Sancti.

Et recede[*t*] *cum ministris suis; omnes virgines dicent 'Amen'.*

[MARIA] To ȝow, fadyr and modyr, I me comende.
Blyssyd be þe tyme ȝe me hedyr brought.

205 beseche] sake *canc. in red after* be *and* seche *written following the cancellation;* c *altered by erasure from a* t   217 s.d. recedet] *M; MS* recedent   Amen *not underscored*
218 *s.h. supplied*

JOACHYM Dowtere, þe Fadere of oure Feyth þe mot defende,
As he of his myght made allthynge of nowth.

ANNE Mary, to þi sowle solas he sende,
In whos wysdam all þis werd was wrought.
Go we now hens, husbonde so hende,
For owth of care now are we brought.

Hic Joachim et Anna recedent domum.

MARIA Be þe Holy Gost at hom be ȝe brought. f. 46v

Ad virgines:

Systerys, ȝe may go do what ȝe xall;
To serve God fyrst here is al my thought.
Beforn þis holy awtere on my knes I fall.

Lord, sefne petycyons I beseche ȝow of here:
Fyrst, þat I may kepe þi love and þi lawe.
þe secunde, to lovyn myn evyn-Crystyn as myself dere.
þe thrydde, from all þat þu hatyst me to withdrawe.
The fourte, all vertuys to þi plesauns [to] knawe.
þe fyfte, to obey þe ordenaryes of þe temple echon.
þe sexte, and þat all pepyl may serve þe with awe,
þat in þis holy tempyl fawte be non.

The sefnte, Lord, I haske with grett fere,
þat I may se onys in my lyve
þat lady þat xal Goddys sone bere,
þat I may serve here with my wyttys fyve,

234 to *supplied*

If it plese ȝow; and ellys it is not þerwith to stryve.
With prayers prostrat for þese gracys I wepe.
O my God, devocyon depe in me dryve
Þat myn hert may wake in þe thow my body slepe!

Here þe aungel bryngyth manna in a cowpe of gold lyke to confeccyons, þe hefne syngynge. Þe aungel seyth:

[ANGELUS] Merveyle not, mekest maydon, of my mynystracyon.
I am a good aungel sent of God Allmyght
With aungelys mete for ȝoure sustentacyon,
Ȝe to receyve it for natural myght.
f. 47r We aungellys xul serve ȝow day and nyght.
Now fede ȝow þerwith, in Goddys name.
We xal lerne ȝow þe lyberary of oure Lordys lawe lyght,
For my sawys in ȝow shewyth sygnes of shame.

MARIA To thank oure sover[ey]n Lord not sufficyth my mende.
I xal fede me of þis fode my Lord hath me sent;
All maner of savowrys in þis mete I fynde,
I felt nevyr non so swete ner so redolent.
ANGELUS Eche day þerwith ȝe xal be content;
Aunge[lys] alle howrys xal to ȝow apere.
MARIA Mercy, my Makere, how may þis be ment?
I am þe sympelest creature þat is levynge here.

ANGELUS In ȝoure name, Maria, fyve letterys we han:
M: mayde most mercyfull and mekest in mende.

246 *s.h. supplied* 251 Goddys] o *malformed* 252 þe lyberary *underlined in pencil; a pencilled* × *appears in right margin* 254 sovereyn] soveryen 259 Aungelys] *M; MS* aunge

A: auerte[r] of þe anguysch þat Adam began.
R: regina of regyon, reyneng withowtyn ende.
I: innocent be influens of Jesses kende.
A: aduocat most autentyk, ȝoure [anceter] Anna.
Hefne and helle here kneys down bende
Whan þis holy name of ȝow is seyd, Maria.

MARIA I qwake grettly for dred to here þis comendacyon.
Good swete aungel, why wole ȝe sey thus?
AUNGELL For ȝe xal hereaftere haue a salutacyon
þat xal þis excede, it is seyd amonge vs.
The Deyté þat dede xal determyn and dyscus.
Ȝe xal nevyr, lady, be lefte here alone.
MARIA I crye þe mercy, Lorde, and þin erthe cus, f. 47v
Recomendynge me to þat Godhyd þat is tryne in trone.

Hic osculet terram. Here xal comyn alwey an aungel with dyvers presentys, goynge and comyng, and in þe tyme þei xal synge in hefne þis hympne: 'Jesu Corona Virginum'. And aftyr, þer comyth a minister fro þe busschop with a present and seyth:

MINISTER Prynce of oure prestes, Ysakare be name,
He hath sent ȝow hymself his servyce, indede,
And bad ȝe xulde fede ȝow, spare for no shame;
In þis tyme of mete no lenger ȝe rede.
MARIA Recomende me to my fadyr, sere, and God do hym mede.
These vesselys aȝen sone I xal hym sende.
I xal bere it my systerys—I trowe þei haue more nede;
Goddys foyson is evyr to his servauntys hendyr þan we wende.

264 auerter] auerte 267 anceter] antecer 272 *a letter erased before* haue
282 *Red loop that normally precedes speaker headings is lacking*

Systerys, oure holy fadyr Isakare
Hath sent vs hese servyce here ryght now.
Fede ȝow þerof hertyly, I pray ȝow nat spare.
And if owght beleve, specyaly I pray ȝow
That þe pore men þe relevys þerof haue now.
Fayn, and I myth, I wolde do þe dedys of
mercy.
Pore folk faryn God knowyth how.
On hem evyr I haue grett pety.

[CONTEMPLACIO'S LINK]

CONTEMPLACIO Lo, sofreynes, here ȝe haue seyn
In þe temple of oure Ladyes presentacyon.
She was nevyr occapyed in thyngys veyn,
f. 48r But evyr besy in holy ocupacyon.

And we beseche ȝow of ȝoure pacyens
Þat we pace þese materys so lythly away;
If þei xulde be do with good prevydens,
Eche on wolde suffyce for an hool day.

Now xal we procede to here dissponsacyon,
Which aftere þis was xiiij ȝere.
Tyme sufficyth not to make pawsacyon;
Hath pacyens with vs we besech ȝow her.
And in short spas,
The Parlement of Hefne sone xal ȝe se,
And how Goddys sone com man xal he,
And how þe Salutacyon aftere xal be,
By Goddys holy gras.

298 *and* 302 *lack capitula*
Remainder of f. 48r *blank*

The playnumber 10 *appears in right margin opposite* 301–4

f. 49r
D quire

10
[THE MARRIAGE OF MARY AND JOSEPH]

Tunc venit Abysakar Episcopus

[EPISCOPUS] Listenyth, lordyngys bothe hye and lowe, [A]
And tendyrly takyth heyd onto my sawe.
Beth buxom and benyngne ȝoure busshopp to knowe,
For I am þat lord þat made þis lawe.
With hertys so hende herkyn nowe:
Ȝoure damyselys to weddyng, ȝa, loke þat ȝe drawe,
þat passyn xiiij ȝere, for what þat ȝe owe.
þe lawe of God byddyth þis sawe:
þat at xiiij ȝere of age
Euery damesel, whatso sche be,
To þe encrese of more plenté,
Xulde be browght in good degré
Onto here spowsage.

JOACHYM Herke now, Anne, my jentyl spowse,
How þat þe buschop his lawe hath tolde,
þat what man hath a dowtyr in his house
þat passyth xiiij ȝerys olde,
He muste here brynge, I herde hym rowse,
Into þe tempyl a spowse to wedde.
Wherfor oure dowtyr ryth good and dowse,
Into þe tempyl sche must be ledde,
And þat anoon-ryght sone.
ANNE Sere, I grawnt þat it be so.
Aȝen þe lawe may we not do.
With here togedyr lete us now go,
I hold it ryght weyl done.

S.d. Abysakar] *Hal* ab Ysakar 1 *s.h. supplied letter* (l.?) *canc. before* lowe *Episcopus' speeches are lettered in the left margin. These letters are represented here in the outer margin* 18 rowse] *Hal* kowse

JOACHYM Sere busshopp, here aftyr þin owyn hest
We haue here brought oure dowtyr dere,
Mary, my swete childe; she is ful prest,
Of age she is ful xiiij ȝere.

f. 49v EPISCOPUS Welcome, Joachym, onto myn areste,
[B] Bothe Anne þi wyff and Mary clere.
Now, Mary chylde, to þe lawe þu leste
And chese þe a spowse to be þi fere—
þat lawe þu must fulffylle.

MARIA Aȝens þe lawe wyl I nevyr be,
But mannys felachep xal nevyr folwe me.
I wyl levyn evyr in chastyté
Be þe grace of Goddys wylle.

[C] EPISCOPUS A, fayre mayde, why seyst þu so?
What menyth the for to levyn chast?
Why wylt þu not to weddyng go?
þe cawse þu telle me, and þat in hast!

MARIA My fadyr and my modyr, sertys, also,
Er I was born, ȝe may me trast,
Thei were bothe bareyn, here frute was do;
They come to þe tempyl at þe last
To do here sacryfice.
Bycause they hadde nothyr frute nere chylde,
Reprevyd þei wore of wykkyd and wyllde.
With grett shame þei were revylyd,
Al men dede them dyspyce.

My fadyr and my modyr, thei wepte full sore.
Ful hevy here hertys wern of þis dede.
With wepynge eyn þei preyd, þerfore,
þat God wolde socowre hem and sende hem sede.
Iff God wold graunt hem a childe be bore,
They behest þe chylde here lyff xulde lede

Folio 49v marked 50

In Goddys temple to serve evyrmore,
And wurchep God in loue and drede.
Than God, ful of grace,
He herd here longe prayour, f. 50r
And þan sent hem both seed and flowre.
Whan I was born in here bowre,
To þe temple offryd I was.

Whan þat I was to þe temple brought
And offerde up to God above,
Ther hestyd I, as myn hert thought,
To serve my God with hertyly love.
Clennesse and chastyté myn hert owth
Erthely creature nevyr may shoue.
Such clene lyff xuld ȝe nouht
In no maner wyse reprove.
To þis clennesse I me take.
This is þe cawse, as I ȝow tell,
þat I with man wyll nevyr mell!
In þe servyse of God wyl I evyr dwell—
I wyl nevyr haue other make.

EPISCOPUS A, mercy, God, þese wordys wyse [D]
Of þis fayr mayde clene,
Thei trobyl myn hert in many wyse—
Her wytt is grett, and þat is sene!
In clennes to levyn in Godys servise
No man here blame, non here tene.
And ȝit in lawe þus it lyce,
þat such weddyd xulde bene.
Who xal expownd þis oute?
þe lawe doth after lyff of clennes;
þe lawe doth bydde such maydenes expres
þat to spowsyng they xulde hem dres.
God help us in þis dowhte!

61 *a mark follows this line* 63 flowre] w *written over another letter* 65 *rhyme bracket is rubricated*

f. 48v This ansuere grettly trobelyth me.
To mak a vow, to creaturys it is lefful—
Vovete et reddite in Scripture haue we—
And to observe oure lawe also it is nedful.
In þis to dyscerne, to me it is dredful.
þerfore, to cow[n]cell me in þis cas I calle
þe holde and þe wyse, and swiche as ben spedful.
In þis sey ȝoure avyse, I besech ȝow alle.

MINISTER
To breke oure lawe and custom it wore hard indede;
And on þat other syde, to do aȝen Scrypture.
To ȝeve sentens in þis degré ȝe must take goo[d] hede,
For dowteles þis matere is dyffuse and obscure.
Myn avyse here in þis, I ȝow ensure:
þat we prey all God to haue relacyon;
For be prayour grett knowlech men recure,
And to þis I counsell ȝow to ȝeve assygnacyon.

[E] EPISCOPUS
Trewly ȝoure counsell is ryght good and eylsum,
And as ȝe han seyd, so xal it be.
I charge ȝow, bretheryn and systerys, hedyr ȝe com,
And togedyr to God now pray we
That it may plese his fynyte deyté
Knowleche in þis to sendyn vs.
Mekely eche man falle down on kne
And we xal begynne 'Veni Creator Spiritus.'

Et hic cantent 'Veni Creator'.

This ansuere grettly trobelyth me et cetera ut supra *written at bottom of f. 50r preceded by a reference mark which also appears at top left corner of f. 48r* *The loop of the capitulum before* 92 *is dotted. The same is true of the capitula before* 100, 175, 183, 191, 233, 255, 298, 302, 310, 314, 331, 335, 409, 429, 437, 445, 453, *and* 457
97 cowncell] cowcell 101 aȝen] a *interl. above the line* 102 good] goo
114 *a letter canc. before* falle *The s.d. Et hic cantent 'Veni Creator' is written at right of* 113

And whan 'Veni Creator' is don þe buschop xal [*seyn*]*:*

[EPISCOPUS] Now, Lord God, of lordys wysest of alle, f. 50v
I pray þe, Lorde, knelynge on kne; [F]
With carefull herte I crye and calle,
þis dowteful dowte enforme þu me.
ANGELUS Thy prayour is herd to hyȝ hevyn halle.
God hath me sent here down to the
To telle þe what þat þu do xalle,
And how þu xalt be rewlyd in iche degré.
Take tent and vndyrstond:
This is Goddys owyn byddyng,
þat all kynsmen of Dauyd þe kyng
To þe temple xul brynge here du offryng
With whyte ȝardys in þer honde.

Loke wele what tyme þei offere there
All here ȝardys in þin hand þu take;
Take heed whose ȝerde doth blome and bere,
And he xal be þe maydenys make.
EPISCOPUS I thank þe, Lord, with mylde chere. [G]
Thi wurde xal I werkyn withowtyn wrake.
I xal send for hem bothyn fer and nere;
To werke þi wyl I vndyrtake.
Anon it xal be do.
Herk, masangere, þu wend þi way;
Dauyd kynsmen, as I þe say,
Byd hem come offyr þis same day,
And brynge white ȝardys also.

NUNCIUS Oy! Al maner men, takyth to me tent
That be owgth of kynrede to Dauid þe kyng!
My lord þe busshop hath for ȝow sent,
To þe temple þat ȝe come with ȝoure offryng.

And whan '*Veni Creator*' is don þe buschop xal seyn *is not underlined* seyn] seyng 116 *s.h. supplied* *Below the s.d. is written* Now, Lord God, of lordys whysest of all et cetera. *This line is preceded by the reference mark* †, *which also appears at top of f.* 50r *Several figures are scribbled at the bottom of f.* 48r 131 ȝerde] ȝ *smudged* 141 also *canc. in red before* also

f. 53r
F quire

He chargight þat ȝe hast ȝow, for he is redy bent
Ȝow to receyve at ȝoure comyng.
He byddyth ȝow ferthermore in handys þat ȝe hent
A fayre white ȝerde everych of ȝow ȝe bryng
In hyght.
Tary not, I pray ȝow,
My lord, as I say ȝow,
Now to receyve ȝow
Is full redy dyght.

f. 51r
E quire

JOSEPH In gret labore my lyff I lede,
Myn ocupasyoun lyth in many place.
For febylnesse of age my jorney I may nat spede.
I thank the, gret God, of thi grace.

PRIMUS GENERACIONIS DAUID What chere, Joseph? What ys the case
That ye lye here on this ground?

JOSEPH Age and febylnesse doth me enbrase,
That I may nother well goo ne stond.

SECUNDUS GENERACIO[NIS DAUID] We be commandyd be the beschoppys sond
That euery man of Dauyd kynrede
In the tempyll offyr a wond;
Therfor in this jorney let vs procede.

JOSEPH Me to traveyll yt is no nede.
I prey you, frendys, go forth youre wey.

TERCIUS GENERACION[IS DAUID] Yis, com forth, Joseph, I you rede,
And knowyth what the buschop woll sey.

QUARTUS GENER[ACIONIS DAUID] Ther ys a mayd whos name ys clepyd Mary
Doughter to Joachym as it is told.

A reference mark appears after line 154 *and at the top left corner of f. 51r. F. 51r is written in a different hand, and together with the blank ff. 51v, 52r, and 52v comprises E quire; the watermark is a 'Pot'* 163 GENERACIONIS] Generacio; *letters at the end of this speaker heading and the speaker headings of lines* 169 *and* 171 *are cropped owing to trimming of the folio* 165 to *deleted after* tempyll 167 JOSEPH] Tercius Generationis *canc. and* Joseph *written below* 169 Yis] *Hal* This 171 GENERACIONIS] Gener 172 it is told] I haue herd *altered by adding a* t *to* i *and cancelling* haue herd; is told *written above the cancelled words*

Here to mary thei woll asay
To som man dowty and bold.

JOSEPH Benedicité! I cannot vndyrstande — f. 53^{r} (cont.) F quire
What oure prince of prestys doth men,
þat every man xuld come and brynge with hym a whande.
Abyl to be maryed, þat is not I, so mote I then!
I haue be maydon evyr and evyrmore wele ben,
I chaungyd not ȝet of all my long lyff!
And now to be maryed? Sum man wold wen
It is a straunge thynge an old man to take a ȝonge wyff!

But nevyrþelesse, no doute, of we must forth to towne.
Now, neyborys and kynnysmen, lete us forth go.
I xal take a wand in my hand and cast of my gowne.
Yf I falle þan I xalle gronyn for wo!
Hoso take away my staff I say he were my fo!
Ʒe be men þat may wele ren, go ȝe before.
I am old and also colde, walkyng doth me wo.
þerfore now wol[d]e I, so my staff holde I, þis jurny to wore.

EPISCOPUS Serys, ȝe xal vndyrstande — [H]
þat þis is þe cawse of oure comynge,
And why þat ech of ȝow bryngyth a wande:
For of God we haue knowynge
Here is to be maryde a mayde ȝynge.
All ȝoure roddys ȝe xal brynge vp to me,

174 man] many *A word* (Joseph ?) *scribbled at bottom right of f. 51^{r}* 175 *the text continues on f. 53^{r}* JOSEPH] Primus Generacionis Dauid *canc. and* Joseph *written above* 190 wolde] wole *Pointing after* falle, xalle; away, say; men, ren; old, colde; wolde I, holde I *in* 186, 187, 188, 189, *and* 190 *respectively indicates internal rhyme*

And on hese rodde þat þe Holy Gost is syttynge,
He xal þe husbond of þis may be.

Hic portent virgas

f. 53v JOSEPH
It xal not be [I], I ley a grote!
I xal abyde behynde preuyly.
Now wolde God I were at hom in my cote!
I am aschamyd to be seyn, veryly.

PRIMUS GENERACIONIS DAUID
To wurchep my Lord God hedyr am I come
Here for to offyr my dewe offrynge.
A fayr white ȝarde in hand haue I nome,
My lord, sere busshop, at ȝoure byddynge.

SECUNDUS GENERACIONIS DAUID
Off Dauythis kynred, sertys, am I com.
A fayr white ȝarde in hand now I bryng.
My lord þe busshop, after ȝoure owy[n] dom
þis ȝarde do I offre at ȝoure chargyng
Ryht here.

TERCIUS GENERACIONIS DAUID
And I a ȝarde haue both fayr and whyght;
Here in myn hond it is redy dyght,
And here I offre it forth within syght,
Ryght in good manere.

QUARTUS GENERACIONIS DAUID
I am þe fourte of Dauidis kyn,
And with myn offrynge my God I honoure.
þis fayr whyte ȝarde is offryng myn;
I trost in God of sum socoure.
Com on, Joseph, with offrynge þin,
And brynge up þin as we han oure.
þu taryst ryth longe behynde, certeyn!
Why comyst not forth to Goddys toure?
Com on, man, for shame!

JOSEPH
Com? Ȝa! Ȝa! God help! Full fayn I wolde,
But I am so agyd and so olde

199 I, I] *first* I *supplied by M* 203 my *canc. before* wurchep 204 dw *canc. before* dewe 206 To my woursyp *scribbled in left margin* 209 owyn] owym

Þat both myn leggys gyn to folde—
I am ny almost lame!

EPISCOPUS A, mercy, Lord, I kan no sygne aspy. f. 54r
It is best we go ageyn to prayr. [I]
VOX He brought not up his rodde ȝet, trewly,
To whom þe mayd howyth to be maryed her.

EPISCOPUS Whath! Joseph, why stande ȝe there byhynde?
Iwys, sere, ȝe be to blame!
JOSEPH Sere, I kannot my rodde fynde.
To come þer, in trowth, methynkyht shame.
EPISCOPUS Comyth thens!
JOSEPH Sere, he may euyl go þat is ner lame—
In soth, I com as fast as I may!
EPISCOPUS Offyr up ȝoure rodde, sere, in Goddys name.
Why do ȝe not as men ȝow pray?

JOSEPH Now in þe wurchep of God of hevyn
I offyr þis ȝerde as lely-whyte,
Prayng þat Lord of gracyous stewyn
With hert, with wytt, with mayn, with myght.
And as he made þe sterrys seven,
Þis sympyl offrynge þat is so lyght
To his wurchep he weldygh evyn,
For to his wurchep þis ȝerd is dyght.
Lord God, I þe pray,
To my herte þu take good hede,
And nothynge to my synful dede;
Aftyr my wyl þu qwyte my mede
As plesyth to þi pay.

I may not lyfte myn handys heye!
Lo. Lo. Lo! What se ȝe now?
EPISCOPUS A, Mercy! Mercy! Mercy, Lord, we crye!
Þe blyssyd of God we se art thou.

237 *written in right margin* 240 offyr] holde *or* helde *canc. and* offyr *interl. above*

Et clamant omnes 'Mercy! Mercy!'

f. 54v [EPISCOPUS] A, gracyous God in hevyn trone,
Ryht wundyrful þi werkys be!
Here may we se a merveyl one:
A ded stok beryth fleurys fre!
Joseph, in hert withoutyn mone,
þu mayst be blyth with game and gle.
A mayd to wedde þu must gone
Be þis meracle I do wel se.
Mary is here name.

JOSEPH What! Xuld I wedde? God forbede!
I am an old man, so God me spede!
And with a wyff now to levyn in drede,
It wore neyther sport nere game!

EPISCOPUS Aȝens God, Joseph, þu mayst not stryve.
God wyl þat þu a wyff haue;
þis fayr mayde xal be þi wyve,
She is buxum and whyte as laue.

JOSEPH A! Shuld I haue here? Ȝe lese my lyff!
Alas, dere God, xuld I now rave?
An old man may nevyr thryff
With a ȝonge wyff, so God me saue.
Nay, nay, sere, lett bene!
Xuld I now in age begynne to dote?
If I here chyde she wolde clowte my cote,
Blere myn ey, and pyke out a mote!
And þus oftyntymes it is sene.

EPISCOPUS Joseph, now as I þe saye,
God hath assygnyd here to þe.
f. 55r þat God wol haue do, sey þu not nay—
Oure Lord God wyl þat it [so be].

JOSEPH Aȝens my God not do I may.
Here wardeyn and kepere wyl I evyr be.
But, fayr maydon, I þe pray,
Kepe þe clene as I xal me—

259 *s.h. supplied* 288 so be] be so

I am a man of age!
Therfore, sere busshop, I wyl þat ȝe wete
þat in bedde we xul nevyr mete,
For, iwys, mayden suete,
An old man may not rage.

EPISCOPUS This holyest virgyn xalt þu maryn now.
Ȝoure rodde floreschyth fayrest þat man may se.
þe Holy Gost, we se, syttyht on a bow.
Now ȝelde we all preysyng to þe Trenyté.

Et hic cantent 'Benedicta sit beata Trinitas'

Joseph, wole ȝe haue þis maydon to ȝoure wyff
And here honour and kepe as ȝe howe to do?
JOSEPH Nay, sere, so mote I thryff!
I haue ryght no nede þerto!
EPISCOPUS Joseph, it is Goddys wyl it xuld be so.
Sey aftyr me as it is skyl.
JOSEPH Sere, and to performe his wyl I bow þerto,
For allthynge owyght to ben at his wyl.

[EPISCOPUS] Sey þan after me:

Episcopus et idem Joseph:

'Here I take þe, Mary, to wyff,
To hauyn, to holdyn, as God his wyll with us
wyl make.
And as longe as bethwen us lestyght oure lyff
To loue ȝow as myselff my trewth I ȝow take.'

Nunc ad Mariam sic dicens Episcopus:

[EPISCOPUS] Mary, wole ȝe haue þis man, f. 55v
And hym to kepyn as ȝoure lyff?

301 s.d. *written at right of 300* 310 *s.h. supplied* s.d. *written at right of 309–10*
314 *s.h. supplied*

MARIA In þe tenderest wyse, fadyr, as I kan,
And with all my wyttys fyff.

EPISCOPUS Joseph, with þis ryng now wedde þi wyff,
And be here hand now þu here take.
JOSEPH Sere, with þis rynge I wedde here ryff,
And take here now here for my make.
EPISCOPUS Mary, mayd, withoutyn more stryff,
Onto þi spowse þu hast hym take.
MARIA In chastyté to ledyn my lyff
I xal hym nevyr forsake,
But evyr with hym abyde.
And, jentyll spowse, as ȝe an seyd,
Lete me levyn as a clene mayd;
I xal be trewe, be not dysmayd,
Both terme, tyme, and tyde.

EPISCOPUS Here is þe holyest matremony þat evyr was in þis werd!
þe hyȝ names of oure Lord we wole now syng hy.
We all wole þis solempn dede record
Devowtly: Alma chorus Domini nunc pangat nomina Summi.

Now goth hom all, in Godys name,
Whereas ȝoure wonyng was before.
Maydenys, to lete here go alone it wore shame,
It wold hevy ȝoure hertys sore.
ȝe xal blysse þe tyme þat sche was bore.
Now loke ȝe at hom here brynge.
MARIA To haue ȝoure blyssyng, fadyr, I falle ȝow before.
EPISCOPUS He blysse ȝow þat hath non hendyng
In nomine Patris, et Filii, et Spiritus Sancti.

316 tenderest] *or* tenderist *A superfluous s.h. for Episcopus written at bottom right of f. 55*[r]

Joseph, þiselph art old of age f. 56r
   And þi wyff of age is ȝonge;
And as we redyn in old sage,
   Many man is sclepyr of tonge.
Þerfore, euyl langage for to swage,
   Þat ȝoure good fame may leste longe,
Iij damysellys xul dwelle with ȝow in stage,
   With þi wyff to be evyrmore amonge.
      I xal these iij here take:
         Susanne þe fyrst xal be,
         Rebecca, þe secunde, xal go with the,
         Sephore, þe thrydde; loke þat ȝe thre
      Þis maydon nevyr ȝe forsake.

SUSANNE Sere, I am redy att ȝoure wyll
   With þis maydon for to wende.
REBECCA Ȝoure byddyng, sere, [I] xall fulffyl
   And folwe þis maydon fayr and hende.
SEPHOR To folwe hyre it is good skyl,
   And to ȝoure byddynge wole I bende.
JOSEPH Now, sere buschop, hens go I wyl,
   For now comyth onto my mende
      A matere þat nedful is.
EPISCOPUS Farewel, Joseph and Mary clere,
         I pray God kepe ȝow all in fere
         And sende ȝow grace in good manere
      To serve þe Kynge of Blysse.

MARIA Fadyr and modyr, ȝe knowe þis cas
   How þat it doth now stonde with me:
With myn spowse I must forth passe,
   And wott nevyr whan I xal ȝow se.
Therfore I pray ȝow here in þis plas f. 56v
   Of ȝoure blyssynge, for charyté,
And I xal spede þe betyr and haue more gras
   In what place þat evyr I be.

359 I *supplied* 371 How] *an initial incomplete* W *canc.*

On knes to ȝow I falle.
I pray ȝow, fadyr and modyr dere,
To blysse ȝoure owyn dere dowtere
And pray for me in all manere,
And I for ȝow all.

JOACHYM Almyghty God, he mote þe blysse,
And my blyssynge þu haue also.
In all godnesse God þe wysse
On londe or on watyr, wherevyr þu go.
ANNA Now God þe kepe from every mysse
And saue þe sownd in welth from wo.
I pray þe, dowtyr, þu onys me kys
Or þat þi modyr parte þe fro.
I pray to God þe saue.
I pray þe, Mary, my swete chylde,
Be lowe and buxhum, meke and mylde,
Sad and sobyr, and nothyng wylde,
And Goddys blyssynge þu haue.

JOACHYM F[a]rwel, Joseph, and God ȝow spede
Wherso ȝe be, in halle or boure.
JOSEPH Almyghty God ȝoure weys lede
And saue ȝow sownd from all doloure.
ANNA Goddys grace on ȝow sprede.
Farewel, Mary, my swete flowre.
Fareweyl, Joseph, and God ȝow rede.
Fareweyl, my chylde and my tresowre,
f. 57r Farewel, my dowtere ȝyng.
MARIA Farewel, fadyr and modyr dere,
At ȝow I take my leve ryght here.
God þat sytt in hevyn so clere
Haue ȝow in his kepyng.

JOSEPH Wyff, it is ful necessary þis ȝe knowe,
þat I and my kynrede go hom before.
For in soth we haue non hous of oure owe;
þerfore I xal gon ordeyn and thanne come ȝow fore.

396 Farwel] *MS* Forwel

We ar not ryche of werdly thynge,
  And ȝet of oure sustenauns we xal not mys.
Therfore abydyth here stylle to ȝoure plesynge;
  To worchep ȝoure God is all ȝoure blysse.

He þat is and evyr xal be
  Of hefne and helle ryche kynge
In erth hath chosyn poverté,
  And all ryches and welthis refusynge.

MARIA
  Goth, husbond, in oure Lordys blyssynge;
    He mote ȝow spede in all ȝoure nede.
  And I xal here abyde ȝoure aȝencomynge
    And on my Sawtere-book I xal rede.

Now blyssyd be oure Lord for this.
  Of hefne and erthe and all þat beryth lyff
I am most bound to ȝow, Lord, iwys,
  For now I am bothe mayde and wyff.

Now, Lord God, dysspose me to prayour
  þat I may sey þe holy psalmes of Dauyth,
Wheche book is clepyd þe Sawtere,
  þat I may preyse the, my God, þerwith.
  Of þe vertuys þerof þis is þe pygth; f. 57v
    It makyht sowles fayr þat doth it say;
  Angelys be steryd to help us þerwith;
    It lytenyth therkeness and puttyth develys
        away.

þe song of psalmus is Goddys deté,
  Synne is put awey þerby.
It lernyth a man vertuysful to be,
  It feryth mannys herte gostly.
  Who þat it vsyth custommably,
    It claryfieth þe herte and charyté makyth cowthe.
  He may not faylen of Goddys mercy
    þat hath þe preysenge of God evyr in his mowthe.

413 *and* 425 *lack capitula*

O holy psalmys, O holy book,
Swetter to say than any ony,
þu lernyst hem love Lord þat on þe look,
And makyst hem desyre thyngys celestly.
With these halwyd psalmys, Lord, I pray the specyaly
For all þe creatures qwyke and dede,
þat þu wylt shewe to hem þi mercy,
And to me specyaly þat do it rede.

I haue seyd sum of my Sawtere and here I am
At þis holy psalme indede.
Benedixisti, Domine, terram tuam.
In þis holy labore, Lord, me spede.

JOSEPH Mary, wyff and mayd most gracyous,
Displese ȝow not, I pray ȝow, so long I haue be.
I haue hyryd for us a lytyl praty hous,
And þerin ryght hesely levyn wole we.

Come forth, Mary, and folwe me,
To Nazareth now wele we go.
f. 58r And all þe maydonys bothe fayr and fre,
With my wyff comyth forth also.
Now lystenyth well, wyff, what I tell þe:
I must gon owth hens fer þe fro.
I wyll go laboryn in fer countré,
With trewth to maynteyn oure housholde so—
þis ix monthis þu seyst me nowth.
Kepe þe clene, my jentyl spowse,
And all þin maydenys in þin howse,
þat evyl langage I here not rowse,
For hese love þat all hath wrought.

MARIA I pray to God he spede ȝoure way,
And in sowle-helth he mote ȝow kepe,

Several words scribbled in left margin opposite 449–51 (of þe vyn. R. Wych*?*) *and* 455
450 creatures] *abbreviation for* ys *canc. before* es

And sende ȝow helth bothe nyth and day;
He shylde and saue ȝow from al shenschepe.
Now, Lord of Grace, to þe I pray,
With morny mood on kne I krepe.
Me saue from synne, from tene and tray,
With hert I murne, with eye I wepe,
Lord God of peté.
Whan I sytt in my conclaue
All myn hert on þe I haue.
Gracyous God my maydenhed saue
Euyr clene in chastyté.

11

f. 58v

[THE PARLIAMENT OF HEAVEN; THE SALUTATION AND CONCEPTION]

CONTEMPLACIO Fowre thowsand sex vndryd foure, I telle,
Man for his offens and fowle foly
Hath loyn ȝerys in þe peynes of helle,
And were wurthy to ly þerin endlesly;
But thanne xulde perysche ȝoure grete mercye.
Good Lord, haue on man pyté!
Haue mende of þe prayour seyd by Ysaie,
Lete mercy meke þin hyest mageste.

Wolde God þu woldyst breke þin hefne myghtye
And com down here into erth,
And levyn ȝerys thre and threttye,
Thyn famyt folke with þi fode to fede.
To staunche þi thrysté lete þi syde blede,
For erste wole not be mad redempcyon.
Cum vesyte vs in þis tyme of nede.
Of þi careful creaturys, Lord, haue compassyon!

[*Play 11*] *A rubricated mark written in top margin. Red dots appear in loops of all capitula, except those preceding 213, 245, 253, 277, 285, 297, 305, 313, 317, 321, and 329*

1 ȝere deleted before I   10 to *canc. between* in *and* to   11 levyn] levym, *with deleting dot under the final minim*   13 thrysté] *D* thirsty; *MS* thryste

A, woo to vs wrecchis of wrecchis be,
For God hath haddyd ssorwe to sorwe!
I prey þe, Lord, þi sowlys com se,
How þei ly and sobbe for syknes and sorwe.
With þi blyssyd blood from balys hem borwe,
Thy careful creaturys cryenge in captyvyté.
A, tary not, gracyous Lord, tyl it be tomorwe!
The devyl hath dysceyved hem be his
iniquité.

'A', quod Jeremye, 'who xal gyff wellys to myn
eynes
þat I may wepe bothe day and nyght
To se oure bretheryn in so longe peynes?'
Here myschevys amende may þi mech myght.
As grett as þe se, Lord, was Adamys contrys-
f. 59r syon ryght.
From oure hed is falle þe crowne.
Man is comeryd in synne, I crye to þi syght:
Gracyous Lord, gracyous Lord, gracyous
Lord, come downe!

VIRTUTES Lord, plesyth it þin hyȝ domynacyon
On man þat þu mad to haue pyté.
Patryarchys and prophetys han mad supplycacyon,
Oure offyse is to presente here prayerys to the.
Aungelys, archaungelys, we thre
þat ben in þe fyrst ierarchie,
For man to þin hy mageste
Mercy, mercy, mercy we crye!

2 *rubricated in left margin opposite* 17; *a smaller* 2 *is written in the same ink as that of the rest of this page above and slightly to left of* 17, *and is partially covered by the capitulum* 17 of *canc. by another hand in dark ink and* that *interl. above* 18 haddyd] h *canc. with a heavy vertical stroke in dark ink* 20 for syknes and sorwe *canc. and* bothe eve and morewe *interl. above in black by the hand of the reviser of* 17 (*perhaps Scribe C*) 35 patryarchys] t *written over an* r, h *malformed and possibly altered from another letter* mad] d *altered from another letter* (n?) 36 Sory *canc. in dark brown and red before* prayerys

The aungel, Lord, þu made so gloryous,
Whos synne hath mad hym a devyl in helle,
He mevyd man to be so contraryous.
Man repentyd, and he in his obstynacye doth dwelle.
Hese grett males, good Lord, repelle,
And take man onto þi grace;
Lete þi mercy make hym with aungelys dwelle,
Of Locyfere to restore þe place.

PATER *Propter miseriam inopum*
Et gemitum pauperum *nunc exurgam*

For þe wretchydnes of þe nedy
And þe porys lamentacyon
Now xal I ryse þat am almyghty;
Tyme is come of reconsyliacyon!
My prophetys with prayers haue made supplicacyon, f. 59v
My contryte creaturys crye all for comforte.
All myn aungellys in hefne withowte cessacyon,
They crye þat grace to man myght exorte.

VERITAS Lord, I am þi dowtere Trewth.
þu wylt se I be not lore.
Thyn vnkynde creaturys to save were rewthe:
The offens of man hath grevyd þe sore.
Whan Adam had synnyd þu seydest þore
þat he xulde deye and go to helle.
And now to blysse hym to resstore—
Twey contraryes mow not togedyr dwelle!

Thy trewthe, Lord, xal leste withowtyn ende,
I may in no wyse fro þe go.

42 hadh(?) *canc. in red before* hath 45 grett] *or* grete 48a *written in Textura Quadrata* 49 for þe *written at right by another hand* 63 resstore] *second* s *written over another letter*

þat wretche þat was to þe so vnkende,
He may not haue to meche wo!
He dyspysyd þe and plesyd þi fo.
þu art his creatour and he is þi creature.
þu hast lovyd trewthe, it is seyd, evyrmo;
þerfore in peynes lete hym evyrmore endure.

MISERICORDIA O Fadyr of Mercy and God of Comforte
þat counsell us in eche trybulacyon,
Lete ȝoure dowtere Mercy to ȝow resorte,
And on man þat is myschevyd haue compassyon.
Hym grevyth ful gretly his transgressyon.
All hefne and erthe crye for mercy;
f. 60r Mesemyth þer xuld be non excepcyon,
Ther prayers ben offeryd so specyally.

Threwth sseyth she hath evyr be than;
I graunt it wel: she hath be so.
And þu seyst endlessly þat mercy þu hast kept for man;
Than, mercyabyl Lorde, kepe us bothe to.
Thu seyst, 'Veritas mea et Misericordia mea cum ipso';
Suffyr not þi sowlys than in sorwe to slepe.
þat helle hownde þat hatyth þe, byddyth hym ho;
þi love, man, no lengere lete hym kepe.

JUSTICIA Mercy, me merveylyth what ȝow movyth!
Ʒe know wel I am ȝoure systere Ryghtwysnes.
God is ryghtful and ryghtffulnes lovyth.
Man offendyd hym þat is endles,
Therfore his endles punchement may nevyr se[se].
Also he forsoke his makere þat made hym of clay,

88 *a letter erased before* no 93 sese] *last two letters erased and* es *written over them in darker ink by another hand; final* e, *interl. above the original last letter (evidently by the main scribe), survives*

And þe devyl to his maystyr he ches.
Xulde he be savyd? Nay, nay, nay!

As wyse as is God he wolde a be,
This was þe abhomynabyl presumpcyon.
It is seyd ȝe know wel þis of me,
þat þe ryghtwysnes of God hath no diffynicyon.
Therffore late þis be oure conclusyon:
He þat sore synnyd ly stylle in sorwe.
He may nevyr make aseyth be resoun:
Whoo myght thanne thens hym borwe?

MISERICORDIA Systyr Ryghtwysnes, ȝe are to vengeabyl. f. 60ᵛ
Endles synne God endles may restore.
Above all hese werkys God is mercyabyl.
þow he forsook God be synne, be feyth he forsook hym nevyr þe more.
And þow he presumyd nevyr so sore,
Ȝe must consyder þe frelnes of mankende.
Lerne, and ȝe lyst; þis is Goddys lore:
þe mercy of God is withowtyn ende.

PAX To spare ȝoure speches, systerys, it syt:
It is not onest in Vertuys to ben dyscencyon.
The pes of God ovyrcomyth all wytt.
þow Trewth and Ryght sey grett resoun,
Ȝett Mercy seyth best to my pleson.
For yf mannys sowle xulde abyde in helle,
Betwen God and man evyr xulde be dyvysyon,
And than myght not I, Pes, dwelle.

Therefore mesemyth best ȝe thus acorde;
Than hefne and erthe ȝe xul qweme;
Putt bothe ȝoure sentens in oure Lorde,
And in his hyȝ wysdam lete hym deme.

102 in] *a thin tittle written perhaps accidentally above* n   *f.* 60ᵛ *marked* 60   111 *a word* (...erne*?*) *canc. in red before* Lerne

This is most syttynge me xulde seme,
And lete se how we fowre may all abyde.
Þat mannys sowle it xulde perysche, it wore sweme,
Or þat ony of vs fro othere xulde dyvyde.

VERITAS In trowthe hereto I consente,
I wole prey oure Lorde it may so be.
JUSTICIA I, Ryghtwysnes, am wele contente,
For in hym is very equyté.
f. 61r MISERICORDIA And I, Mercy, fro þis counsel wole not fle
Tyl Wysdam hath seyd I xal ses.
PAX Here is God now, here is Vnyté;
Hefne and erth is plesyd with pes.

FILIUS I thynke þe thoughtys of pes and nowth of wykkydnes.
This I deme, to ses ȝoure contraversy.
If Adam had not deyd, peryschyd had Ryghtwysnes,
And also Trewth had be lost þerby.
Trewth and Ryght wolde chastyse foly.
Ȝiff another deth come not, Mercy xulde perysch;
Þan Pes were exyled fynyaly.
So tweyn dethis must be, ȝow fowre to cherysch.

But he þat xal deye, ȝe must knawe
Þat in hym may ben non iniquyté,
Þat helle may holde hym be no lawe,
But þat he may pas at hese lyberté.
Qwere swyche on his prevyde and se,
And hese deth for mannys deth xal be redempcyon.
All hefne and erth seke now ȝe.
Plesyth it ȝow þis conclusyon.

133 *a capitulum drawn, then surrounded by deleting dots* 141 Trewth] r *written over the contraction for re or an incomplete* h; *B* Terrewth 147 may] a *partially rubbed*

VERITAS I, Trowthe, haue sowte þe erthe withowt and withinne,
And in sothe þer kan non be fownde
þat is of o day byrth withowte synne,
Nor to þat deth wole be bownde.
MISERICORDIA I, Mercy, haue ronne þe hevynly regyon rownde,
And þer is non of þat charyté
þat for man wole suffre a deddly wounde.
I cannott wete how þis xal be.

JUSTICIA Sure I can fynde non sufficyent, f. 61^{v}
For servauntys vnprofytable we be echon.
He[se] love nedyth to be ful ardent
That for man to helle wolde gon.
PAX That god may do is non but on.
þerfore þis is Pesys avyse:
He þat ȝaff þis counsell, lete hym ȝeve þe comforte alon,
For þe conclusyon in hym of all þese lyse.

FILIUS It peyneth me þat man I mad;
þat is to seyn, peyne I must suffre fore.
A counsel of þe Trinité must be had.
Whiche of vs xal man restore?
PATER In ȝoure wysdam, son, man was mad thore,
And in wysdam was his temptacyon.
þerfor, sone, sapyens ȝe must ordeyn herefore,
And se how of man may be salvacyon.

FILIUS Fadyr, he þat xal do þis must be both God and man—
Lete me se how I may were þat wede.

153 withowt] inne and with *canc. in red between* with *and* owt 156 to þat] *H* that to 160 I] I I *From f. 61^{v} to end of play script is larger and lines more widely spaced* 163 Hese] he; *H* The; *a faint* s *added after* He *by another hand* *A word* (han?) *written longitudinally by another hand at left of* 164 166 Pesys *altered by another hand to* be hys 174 *a letter canc. before* was *by a red stroke and a deleting dot*

And syth in my wysdam he began,
I am redy to do þis dede.

SPIRITUS SANCTUS I, the Holy Gost, of ȝow tweyn do procede.
This charge I wole take on me:
I, Love, to ȝoure lover xal ȝow lede.
þis is þe assent of oure Vnyté.

f. 62r MISERICORDIA Now is þe loveday mad of us fowre fynialy,
Now may we leve in pes as we were wonte.
Misericordia et Veritas obviauerunt sibi,
Justicia et Pax osculate sunt.

Et hic osculabunt pariter omnes.

PATER From vs, god aungel Gabryel, þu xalt be sende
Into þe countré of Galylé—
The name of þe cyté Nazareth is kende—
To a mayd, weddyd to a man is she,
Of whom þe name is Joseph, se,
Of þe hous of Davyd bore.
The name of þe mayd fre
Is Mary, þat xal al restore.

FILIUS Say þat she is withowte wo and ful of grace,
And þat I, þe Son of þe Godhed, of here xal be bore.
Hyȝe þe, þu were there apace,
Ellys we xal be there the beffore,
I haue so grett hast to be man thore
In þat mekest and purest virgyne.
Sey here she xal restore
Of ȝow aungellys þe grett ruyne.

f. 62v SPIRITUS SANCTUS And if she aske þe how it myth be,
Telle here I, þe Holy Gost, xal werke al this.

183 procede *canc. in red before* ȝow 190 Galylé] first l *rubbed* 192 weddyd] e *rubbed* 196 restore] *a flourish representing -e appears on* r, *but is evidently rendered redundant by addition of a final* e

Sche xal be savyd thorwe oure Vnyté.
In tokyn, here bareyn cosyn Elyzabeth is
Qwyk with childe in here grett age, iwys.
Sey here to vs is nothynge impossyble.
Here body xal be so fulfylt with blys
þat she xal sone thynke þis sownde credyble.

GABRIEL In thyn hey inbassett, Lord, I xal go;
It xal be do with a thought.
Beholde now, Lord, I go here to;
I take my flyth and byde nowth.

Ave, gracia plena, Dominus tecum.

Heyl, ful of grace, God is with the.
Amonge all women blyssyd art thu.
Here þis name Eva is turnyd Aue;
þat is to say, withowte sorwe ar ȝe now.

Thow sorwe in ȝow hath no place,
ȝett of joy, lady, ȝe nede more.
Therfore I adde and sey 'ful of grace', f. 63r
For so ful of grace was nevyr non bore.
ȝett who hath grace, he nedyth kepyng sore;
Therfore I sey God is with the,
Whiche xal kepe ȝow endlesly thore.
So amonge all women bly[ss]yd are ȝe.

MARIA A, mercy, God, þis is a mervelyous herynge,
In þe aungelys wordys I am trobelyd her.
I thynk, how may be þis gretynge?
Aungelys dayly to me doth aper,
But not in þe lyknes of man þat is my fer.
And also thus hyȝly to comendyd be,

213 *s.h. written in decorative hand with rubricated* G 216a *written in Textura Quadrata* Maria *crossed through in black ink after* Ave tecum] *a cursive* m *interl. above* um 217 *lacks a capitulum* of *canc. in red after* of 228 blyssyd] blyllyd, *with* ll *altered to* ss *in darker ink* 229 herynge] thynge, *with* t *erased,* h *altered to* r, *and* he *interl. above*

And am most vnwurthy, I cannot answere.
Grett shamfastnes and grett dred is in me.

GABRYEL Mary, in þis take ȝe no drede,
For at God grace fownde haue ȝe.
Ȝe xal conceyve in ȝoure wombe indede
A childe, þe sone of þe Trynyté.
f. 63v His name of ȝow Jesu clepyd xal be.
He xal be grett, þe Son of þe Hyest clepyd, of kende.
And of his fadyr, Davyd, þe Lord xal ȝeve hym þe se,
Reynyng in þe hous of Jacob, of which regne xal be non ende.

MARIA Aungel, I sey to ȝow,
In what manere of wyse xal þis be?
For knowyng of man I haue non now:
I haue evyrmore kept and xal my virginyté.
I dowte not þe wordys ȝe han seyd to me,
But I aske how it xal be do.
GABRYEL The Holy Gost xal come fro above to the,
And þe vertu of hym hyest xal schadu þe so.

Therfore þat holy of þe xal be bore,
He xal be clepyd þe Son of God sage.
And se Elyzabeth, ȝoure cosyn thore,
She hath conseyvid a son in hyre age.
This is þe sexte monyth of here passage,
f. 64r Of here þat clepyd was bareyn.
Nothynge is impossyble to Goddys vsage.
They thynkyth longe to here what ȝe wyl seyn.

Here þe aungel makyth a lytyl restynge and Mary beholdyth hym, and þe aungel seyth:

236 Grett] G *partially rubbed* 244 non] n 245 Maria *scribbled at left of s.h.*
251 tyl(*?*) *scribbled by another hand at left of s.h.* 253 gost *deleted after* holy

Mary, come of and haste the,
  And take hede in thyn entent
Whow þe Holy Gost, blyssyd he be,
  Abydyth þin answere and þin assent.
Thorwe wyse werke of dyvinyté,
  The secunde persone, verament,
Is mad man by fraternyté
  Withinne þiself in place present.

Ferthermore, take hede þis space
  Whow all þe blyssyd spyrytys of vertu
þat are in hefne byffore Goddys face,
  And all þe gode levers and trew
That are here in þis erthely place,
  Thyn owyn kynrede, þe sothe ho knew,
And þe chosyn sowlys þis tyme of grace
  þat are in helle and byde rescu,

As Adam, Abraham, and Davyd in fere, f. 64v
  And many othere of good reputacyon,
þat þin answere desyre to here,
  And þin assent to þe Incarnacyon,
In which þu standyst as persevere
  Of all mankende savacyon.
Gyff me myn answere now, lady dere,
  To all these creaturys comfortacyon.

MARIA With all mekenes I clyne to þis acorde,
  Bowynge down my face with all benyngnyté.
Se here þe handmayden of oure Lorde,
  Aftyr þi worde be it don to me.
GABRYEL Gramercy, my lady fre,
    Gramercy of ȝoure answere on hyght.
  Gramercy of ȝoure grett humylyté,
    Gramercy, ȝe lanterne off lyght!

276 rescu *scratched through in different ink, with three dots above and three dots below in this ink;* þer(*?*) rescu *written in a third ink by another scribe* (*the scribe of ff. 95–6 and 112?*)
281 persevere] *second* e *written over a* y   289 my *interl.*   291 of *canc. after* of

Here þe Holy Gost discendit with iij bemys to oure Lady, the Sone of þe Godhed nest with iij bemys to þe Holy Gost, the Fadyr godly with iij bemys to þe Sone. And so entre all thre to here bosom, and Mary seyth:

f. 65r MARIA

A, now I fele in my body be
Parfyte God and parfyte man,
Havyng al schapp of chyldly carnalyté;
Evyn al at onys þus God began,

Nott takynge fyrst o membyr and sythe another,
But parfyte childhod ȝe haue anon.
Of ȝoure handmayden now ȝe haue mad ȝoure modyr
Withowte peyne in flesche and bon.
Thus conceyved nevyr woman non
þat evyr was beynge in þis lyff.
O myn hyest Fadyr in ȝoure tron,
It is worthy ȝoure son—now my son—haue a prerogatyff.

I cannot telle what joy, what blysse,
Now I fele in my body!
Aungel Gabryel, I thank ȝow for thys.
Most mekely recomende me to my Faderys mercy.
To haue be þe modyr of God ful lytyl wend I.
Now myn cosyn Elyzabeth fayn wold I se,
How sche hath conseyvid as ȝe dede specyfy.
Now blyssyd be þe hyȝ Trynyté.

f. 65v GABRYEL

Fareweyl, turtyl, Goddys dowtere dere.
Farewel, Goddys modyr. I þe honowre.
Farewel, Goddys sustyr and his pleynge fere;
Farewel, Goddys chawmere and his bowre.

MARIA

Farewel, Gabryel, specyalé.
Farewel, Goddys masangere expresse.
I thank ȝow for ȝoure traveyl hye;
Gramercy of ȝoure grett goodnes,

entre *written by another hand below* 292 s.d. 293 *lacks a capitulum* 317 Gabryel] ry *smudged; s.h. here and at* 329 *not underscored*

And namely of ȝoure comfortabyl massage,
For I vndyrstande by inspyracyon
þat ȝe knowe by syngulere preuylage
Most of my sonys Incarnacyon.
I pray ȝow, take it into vsage
Be a custom ocupacyon
To vesyte me ofte be mene passage;
Ȝoure presence is my comfortacyon.

GABRIEL At ȝoure wyl, lady, so xal it be,
Ȝe gentyllest of blood and hyest of kynrede
þat reynyth in erth in ony degré,
Be pryncypal incheson of þe Godhede.

I comende me onto ȝow, þu trone of þe Trinyté,
O mekest mayde, now þe modyr of Jesu.
Qwen of Hefne, Lady of Erth, and Empres of
Helle be ȝe; f. 66r
Socour to all synful þat wole to ȝow sew
Thorwe ȝoure body beryth þe babe oure blysse
xal renew.
To ȝow, Modyr of Mercy, most mekely I
recomende.
And as I began I ende, with an Ave new
Enjouyd hefne and erth; with þat I ascende.

Angeli cantando istam sequenciam:
'Aue Maria, gratia plena, Dominus tecum, uirgo se[r]ena'.

12
[JOSEPH'S DOUBT]

f. 67r
G. quire

JOSEPH How, dame, how! Vndo ȝoure dore, vndo!
Are ȝe at hom? Why speke ȝe notht?

From 333 *the writing is smaller* 340 enjouyd] *Hal, H,B,M* enjonyd 340 s.d. serena] *Hal; MS* sesena; And þan Mary seyth *canc. in red and brown. Remainder of f. 66r (138 mm) blank; f. 66v blank, except for* fare well *scribbled by another hand*

[*Play 12*] 1 *s.h. written in Textura Quadrata*

SUSANNA Who is ther? Why cry ȝe so?
  Telle us ȝoure herand; wyl ȝe ought?
JOSEPH Vndo ȝoure dore, I sey ȝow to.
  For to com in is all my thought.
MARIA It is my spowse þat spekyth us to.
  Ondo þe dore, his wyl were wrought.

Wellcome hom, myn husbond dere.
  How haue ȝe ferd in fer countré?
JOSEPH To gete oure levynge, withowtyn dwere,
  I haue sore laboryd for þe and me.

MARIA Husbond, ryght gracyously now come be ȝe.
  It solacyth me sore sothly to se ȝow in syth.
JOSEPH Me merveylyth, wyff, surely! Ȝoure face I cannot se,
  But as þe sonne with his bemys quan he is most bryth.

MARIA Husbond, it is as it plesyth oure Lord, þat grace of hym grew.
  Who þat evyr beholdyth me, veryly,
They xal be grettly steryd to vertu.
  For þis ȝyfte and many moo, good Lord, gramercy.

JOSEPH How hast þu ferde, jentyl mayde,
  Whyl I haue be out of londe?
MARIA Sekyr, sere, beth nowth dysmayde,
  Ryth aftyr þe wyl of Goddys sonde.
JOSEPH That semyth evyl, I am afrayd.
  Þi wombe to hyȝe doth stonde!
I drede me sore I am betrayd,
  Sum other man þe had in honde
f. 67v   Hens sythe þat I went!
      Thy wombe is gret, it gynnyth to ryse.
      Than hast þu begownne a synfull gyse.

how hast *canc. in red between* 12 *and* 13   13 Maria *written in another hand in right margin*   14 ȝw(*?*) *canc. before* ȝow   *The loop of the capitulum before* 17 *is dotted*

Telle me now in what wyse
Thyself þu ast þus schent.

Ow, dame, what þinge menyth this?
With childe þu gynnyst ryth gret to gon.
Sey me, Mary, þis childys fadyr ho is?
I pray þe telle me, and þat anon.
MARIA The Fadyr of Hevyn and ȝe it is—
Other fadyr hath he non.
I dede nevyr forfete with man, iwys.
Wherfore I pray ȝow, amende ȝoure mon.
This childe is Goddys and ȝoure.
JOSEPH Goddys childe! þu lyist, in fay!
God dede nevyr jape so with may!
And I cam nevyr ther, I dare wel say,
Ȝitt so nyh þi boure.

But ȝit I sey, Mary, whoos childe is this?
MARIA Goddys and ȝoure, I sey, iwys.

JOSEPH Ȝa, ȝa, all olde men to me take tent,
And weddyth no wyff in no kynnys wyse
Þat is a ȝonge wench, by myn asent,
For doute and drede and swych servyse.
Alas, alas, my name is shent!
All men may me now dyspyse
And seyn, 'Olde cokwold, þi bowe is bent
Newly now aftyr þe Frensche gyse.'
Alas and welaway! f. 68r
Alas, dame, why dedyst þu so?
For þis synne þat þu hast do
I the forsake and from þe go
For onys, evyr, and ay.

MARIA Alas, gode spowse, why sey ȝe thus?
Alas, dere hosbund, amende ȝoure mod.
It is no man but swete Jesus.
He wyll be clad in flesch and blood
And of ȝoure wyff be born.

47 *lacks a capitulum* 62 Alas] s *interl.* so *canc. before* thus

SEPHOR
Forsothe, þe aungel, þus seyd he,
þat Goddys sone in Trynité
For mannys sake a man wolde be
To save þat is forlorn.

JOSEPH
An aungel! Allas, alas! Fy, for schame!
Ȝe syn now in þat ȝe to say,
To puttyn an aungel in so gret blame!
Alas, alas! Let be! Do way!
It was sum boy began þis game
þat clothyd was clene and gay.
And ȝe ȝeve hym now an aungel name.
Alas, alas, and welaway
þat evyr this game betydde.
A, dame, what thought haddyst þu?
Here may all men þis proverbe trow,
þat many a man doth bete þe bow,
Another man hath þe brydde.

f. 68v MARIA
A, gracyous God in hefne trone,
Comforte my spowse in þis hard cas.
Mercyful God, amend his mone,
As I dede nevyr so gret trespas.

JOSEPH
Lo, lo, serys, what told I ȝow,
þat it was not for my prow
A wyff to take me to—
An þat is wel s[e]ne now!
For Mary, I make God avow,
Is grett with childe, lo.
Alas, why is it so?
To þe busshop I wole it telle
þat he þe lawe may here do,
With stonys here to qwelle.

Nay, nay, ȝet God forbede
þat I xuld do þat ve[n]geabyl dede
But if I wyst wel qwy.

72 to *canc. in red before* to 89 þat it *canc. before* not 91 sene] sone
97 ll *or incomplete* w *canc. before* here 99 vengeabyl] *H; MS* vegeabyl

I knew nevyr with here, so God me spede,
Tokyn of thynge in word nor dede
þat towchyd velany.
Nevyrþeles, what forthy,
þow she be meke and mylde,
Withowth mannys company
She myght not be with childe!

But I ensure, myn was it nevyr!
Thow þat she hath not don here devyr,
Rather than I xuld pleynyn opynly,
Serteynly ȝitt had I levyr
Forsake þe countré forevyr
And nevyr come in here company.
For and men knew þis velany,
In repreff þei wolde me holde.
And ȝett many bettyr than I,
Ȝa, hath ben made cokolde!

Now, alas, whedyr xal I gone? f. 69r
I wot nevyr whedyr nor to what place,
For oftyntyme sorwe comyth sone,
And longe it is or it pace.
No comforte may I haue here.
Iwys, wyff, þu dedyst me wronge!
Alas, I taryed from þe to longe!
All men haue pety [on me] amonge,
For to my sorwe is no chere.

MARIA God, þat in my body art sesyd,
þu knowist myn husbond is dysplesyd
To se me in þis plight.
For vnknowlage he is desesyd,
And þerfore, help þat he were esyd,
þat he myght knowe þe ful perfyght.
For I haue levyr abyde [d]espyt
To kepe þi sone in privité

102 Nevyr þe les *canc. in red before* Tokyn M *and* B *scribbled in bottom margin of f. 68r* 125 on me] *H; MS* onime 133 despyt] *G(see note); MS* respyt

Grauntyd by þe Holy Spyryt,
þan þat it xulde be opynd by me.

DEUS Descende, I sey, myn aungelle,
Onto Joseph for to telle
Such as my wyl is.
Byd hym with Mary abyde and dwelle,
For it is my sone ful snelle
þat she is with, iwys.

ANGELUS Almyghty God of Blys,
I am redy for to wende
Wedyr as þi wyl is,
To go bothe fer and hynde.

Joseph, Joseph, þu wepyst shyrle.
Fro þi wyff why comyst þu owte?

f. 69v JOSEPH Good sere, lete me wepe my fylle;
Go forthe þi wey and lett me nowght.

ANGELUS In þi wepynge þu dost ryght ylle—
Aȝens God þu hast myswrought!
Go chere þi wyff with herty wylle,
And chawnge þi chere, amende þi thought.
Sche is a ful clene may.
I telle þe, God wyl of here be born,
And sche clene mayd as she was beforn,
To saue mankynd, þat is forlorn.
Go chere hyre, þerfore, I say.

JOSEPH A, Lord God, benedicité.
Of þi gret comforte I thank the
þat þu sent me þis space.
I myght wel a wyst, pardé,
So good a creature as she
Wold nevyr a don trespace,
For sche is ful of grace.
I know wel I haue myswrought.
I walk to my pore place
And aske forgyfnes, I haue mysthought.

Now is þe tyme sen at eye
þat þe childe is now to veryfye,
Which xal saue mankende,
As it was spoke be prophesye.
I thank þe, God, þat syttys on hye,
With hert, wyl, and mende,
þat evyr þu woldyst me bynde
To wedde Mary to my wyff,
þi blysful sone so nere to fynde,
In his presens to lede my lyff.

Alas, for joy I qwedyr and qwake.
Alas, what hap now was this?
A mercy, mercy, my jentyl make, f. 70r
Mercy, I haue seyd al amys!
All þat I haue seyd, here I forsake.
Ȝoure swete fete now lete me kys.
MARY Nay, lett be my fete, not þo ȝe take;
My mowthe ȝe may kys, iwys,
And welcom onto me.
JOSEPH Gramercy, myn owyn swete wyff,
Gramercy, myn hert, my love, my lyff.
Xal I nevyrmore make suche stryff
Betwyx me and þe.

A, Mary, Mary, wel þu be,
And blyssyd be þe frewte in the,
Goddys Sone of Myght.
Now, good wyff, ful of pyté,
As be not evyl payd with me
þow þat þu haue good ryght.
As for my wronge in syght
To wyte þe with ony synne,
Had þu not be a vertuous wythe,
God wold not a be þe withinne.

I knowlage I haue don amys.
I was nevyr wurthy, iwys,
For to be þin husbonde.

I xal amende aftere thys,
Ryght as þin owyn wyl is,
To serve þe at foot and honde,
And þi chylde bothe to vndyrstonde,
To wurchep hym with good affeccyon.
And þerfore telle me, and nothynge whonde,
The holy matere of ȝoure concepcyon.

f. 70v MARIA At ȝowre owyn wyll as ȝe bydde me:
Ther cam an aunge[l] hyght Gabryell,
And gret me fayr, and seyd, 'Aue!'
And ferthermore to me gan tell
God xulde be borne of my bodé,
þe fendys powsté for to felle.
þorwe þe Holy Gost, as I wel se,
þus God in me wyl byde and dwelle.

JOSEPH Now I thank God with spech and spelle
þat euyr, Mary, I was weddyd to the.
MARY It was þe werk of God, as I ȝow telle.
Now blyssyd be þat Lord so purveyd for me.

f. 71r

13
[THE VISIT TO ELIZABETH]

MARIA Bvtt, husbond, of oo thynge I pray ȝow most mekely:
I haue knowyng þat oure cosyn Elyzabeth with childe is.
þat it plese ȝow to go to here hastyly,
If owught we myth comforte here, it wore to me blys.

JOSEPH A, Godys sake! Is she with childe? Sche?
Than wole here husbond, Zakarye, be mery.

F. 70v marked 70   214 aungel] aunge   217 xulde] xulde xulde   223 of *interl.*   *Remainder of f. 70v (119mm) blank*

In Montana they dwelle, fer hens, so moty the,
In þe cety of Juda, I knowe it veryly.
It is hens, I trowe, myles two and fyfty—
We are lyke to be wery or we come at þat
same.
I wole with a good wyl, blyssyd wyff Mary;
Now go we forthe, than, in Goddys name.

MARIA [Good] husbond, þow it be to ȝow peyne,
This jurny, I pray ȝow, lete us go fast;
For I am schamfast of þe pepyl to be seyne,
And namely of men þerof I am agast.
Pylgrymagys and helpyngys wolde be go in hast.
Þe more þe body is peynyd þe more is þe mede.
Say ȝe ȝoure devocyonys and I xal myn icast.
Now in þis jurny God mote us spede.

JOSEPH Amen, amen, and evyrmore,
Lo, wyff, lo how starkly I go before.

Et sic transient circa placeam.

CO[N]TEMPLACIO Sovereynes, vndyrstondyth þat Kynge Davyd here f. 71v
Ordeyned foure and twenty prestys of grett
devocyon,
In þe temple of God aftere here l[o]t [to] apere.
Þei wer[e] clepyd *summi sacerdotes* for here mynis-
tracyon.
And on was prynce of prestys, havynge domynacyon;
Amonge whiche was an old prest clepyd Zakarye,
And he had an old woman to his wyff of holy
conversacyon,
Whiche hyth Elizabeth, þat nevyr had childe,
verylye.

8 o *and a minim canc. before* I 11 wyl *canc. before* wole *A dot appears in loop of capitulum preceding* 13, *and also in capitula before* 23, 31, *and* 150 13 Good] *H; MS* Goth 19 icast] *Hal* reast; *B* I cast; *a vertical mark follows* I 22 s.d. transient] i *blotted, perhaps altered from another letter* 23 CONTEMPLACIO] Comtemplacio 25 lot] *B; MS* let to *supplied* 26 were] *D; MS* weryd; *M* weryn 29 wyff *canc. in red before* woman

In hese mynistracyon, the howre of incense,
The aungel Gabryel apperyd hym to.
þat hese wyff xulde conseyve he ȝaff hym intelligence,
[He, seinge] hese vnwurthynes and age, not belevyd so;
The plage of dompnesse hise lippis lappyd, lo.
Thei wenten hom and his wyff was conseyvenge—
This concepcyon Gabryel tolde oure Lady to—
And in soth, sone aftere, þat sage sche was sekynge.

And of here tweyners metyng
Here gynnyth þe proces.
Now God be oure begynnynge,
And of my tonge I wole ses.

JOSEPH A, a, wyff, in feyth I am wery.
Therfore I wole sytt downe and rest me ryght here.
Lo, wyff, here is þe hous of Zakary;
Wole ȝe I clepe Elyzabeth to ȝow to apere?

f. 72^r MARIA Nay, husbond, and it plese ȝow, I xal go ner.
Now þe blyssyd Trynité be in þis hous.
A, cosyn Elizabeth, swete modyr, what cher?
Ȝe grow grett! A, my God, how ȝe be gracyous!

ELIZABETH Anon as I herd of ȝow þis holy gretynge,
Mekest mayden and þe Modyr of God, Mary,
Be ȝoure breth þe Holy Gost vs was inspyrynge;
þat þe childe in my body enjoyd gretly
And turnyd down on his knes to oure God reverently.
Whom ȝe bere in ȝoure body, þis veryly I ken.
Fulfyllyd with þe Holy Gost þus lowde I cry:
Blyssyd be þu amonge all women!

34 He seinge] *M* (*see note*); *MS* Hese juge 35 lippis *interl.*, to(?) *canc. in red before* lo 37 gab *canc. before* tolde

And blyssyd be þe frute off þi wombe also,
þu wurthyest virgyne and wyff þat evyr was wrought.
How is it þat þe Modyr of God me xulde come to,
þat wrecche of all wrecchis, a whyght wers þan nought;
And þu art blyssyd, þat belevyd veryly in þi thought
þat þe wurde of God xulde profyte in the.
But how þis blyssydnes abought was brought,
I cannot thynk nyn say how it myght be.

MARIA To þe preysynge of God, cosyn, this seyd mut be:
Whan I sat in my lytyl hous onto God prayinge,
Gabryel come and seyde to me 'Ave'.
Ther I conceyvyd God at my consentynge,
Parfyte God and parfyte man at onys beynge. f. 72v
Than þe aungel seyd onto me
þat it was sex monethys syn ȝoure conseyvynge;
þis cawsyth my comynge, cosyn, ȝow to comfort and se.

ELIZABETH Blyssyd be ȝe, cosyn, for ȝoure hedyrcomynge.
How I conseyvyd I xal to ȝow say:
þe aungel apperyd þe howre of incensynge
Seynge I xulde conseyve, and hym thought nay!
Sethe for his mystrost he hath be dowm alway.
And þus of my concepcyon I haue tolde ȝow sum.
MARIA For þis holy psalme I begynne here þis day:

Magnificat anima mea Dominum,
Et exultauit spiritus meus in Deo salutari meo.
ELIZABETH Be þe Holy Gost with joye Goddys son is in þe cum,
þat þi spyryte so injouyid þe helth of þi God so.

74 *two letters canc. in red before* cosyn 77 of *interl.* *The Latin verses* 82–124 *written in Textura Quadrata*

MARIA Quia respexit humilitatem ancille sue.
Ecce enim ex hoc beatam me dicent omnes generaciones.
ELIZABETH For he beheld þe lownes of hese handmayde, ȝe.
[L]o, ferforthe for þat, all generacyonys blysse ȝow in pes.

MARIA Quia fecit mihi magna qui potens est,
Et sanctum nomen eius.
ELIZABETH For grett thyngys he made, and also myghtyest,
And ryght holy is þe name of hym in vs.

f. 73r MARIA Et misericordia eius a progenie in progenies
Timentibus eum.
ELIZABETH Ȝa, þe mercy of hym fro þat kynde into þe kynde of pes,
For all þat hym drede now is he cum.

MARIA Fecit potenciam in brachio suo,
Disspersit superbos mente cordis sui.
ELIZABETH The pore in his ryght arme he hath mad so,
þe prowde to dyspeyre [in] þe thought of here hertys only.

MARIA Deposuit potentes de sede,
Et exaltauit humiles.
ELIZABETH The prowde men fro hey setys put he,
And þe lowly vpon heyth in þe sete of pes.

MARIA Esurientes impleuit bonis,
Et diuites dimisit inanes.
ELIZABETH Alle þe pore and þe nedy he fulfyllyth with his goodys,
And þe ryche he fellyth to voydnes.

MARIA Suscepit Israel puerum suum,
Recordatus est misericordie sue.

88 handmayde ȝe] *written as one word, with* de *in darker ink* 89 Lo] So Et *written in bottom margin of f. 72v* 101 in] *H; MS* and

ELIZABETH Israel for his childe vp toke he to cum,
On his mercy to thynk, for hese þat be.

MARIA Sicut locutus est ad patres nostros,
Abraham et semini eius in secula.
ELIZABETH As he spak here to oure forfaderys in clos,
Abraham and to all hese sed of hym in þis werd, sa.

MARIA Gloria Patri, et Filio,
Et Spiritui Sancto.
ELIZABETH Preysyng be to þe Fadyr in hevyn, lo!
þe same to þe Son here be so,
þe Holy Gost also to ken.

MARIA Sicut erat in principio, et nunc, et semper, f. 73v
Et in secula seculorum, amen.
ELIZABETH As it was in þe begynnynge, and now is, and xal be forevyr,
And in þis werd in all good werkys to abydyn then.

MARIA This psalme of prophesye seyd betwen vs tweyn,
In hefne it is wretyn with aungellys hond,
Evyr to be songe and also to be seyn
Euery day amonge us at oure evesong.

But, cosyn Elyzabeth, I xal ȝow here kepe,
And þis thre monethis abyde here now,
Tyl ȝe han childe; to wasche, skore, and swepe,
And in all þat I may to comforte ȝow.
ELIZABETH A, ȝe Modyr of God, ȝe shewe us here how
We xulde be meke þat wrecchis here be.
All hefne and herthe wurchepp ȝow mow,
þat are trone and tabernakyl of þe hyȝ Trinité.

The handwriting is small in 120–2

JOSEPH A, how do ȝe, how do ȝe, fadyr Zacharye?
We falle fast in age, withowte oth.
Why shake ȝe so ȝoure hed? Haue ȝe þe palsye?
Why speke ȝe not, sere? I trowe ȝe are not wroth.
ELIZABETH Nay, wys fadyr Joseph, þerto he were ful loth.
It is þe vesytac[y]on of God; he may not speke, veryly.
Lete us thank God þerfor, both.
He xal remedy it whan it plesyth his mercy.

[CONCLUSION]

JOSEPH Of ȝoure dissese thynkys no greff,
Thank God of al aduersyté;
For he wyl chastyse and repreff
Þo þat he lovyth most hertylé.

Mary, I hold best þat we go hens;
We haue fer hom, withowt fayl.
MARIA Al redy, husbond, without defens,
I wyl werke be ȝoure counsayl.
Cosyn, be ȝoure leve and ȝoure lycens,
For homward now us must travayl.
Of þis refreschynge in ȝoure presens
God ȝeld ȝow, þat most may avayl.

f. 74r ELIZABETH Now, cosynes bothe, God ȝow spede.
And wete ȝow wele withowtyn mo,
Ȝoure presens comfortyth me indede.
And þerfore now am I ryght wo

142 *a letter* (h*?*) *canc. before* Why 144 vesytacyon] vesytacon
The reference mark + *appears at the right of* 146 *and in the bottom margin followed by:*
his mercy
ELIZABETH. Come, I pray ȝow specialy,
Iwys, ȝe are welcome, Mary.
si placet: For þis comfortabelest comynge, good God, gramercy.
CONTEMPLACIO.
147–74 *written two lines as one* 160 wo *canc. before* mo

That ȝe, my frendys and my kynrede,
þus sone now xul parte me fro.
But I pray God he mote ȝow lede
In every place wherso ȝe go.

Here Mary and Elizabet partyn, and Elizabeth goth to Zakarie and seyth:

Good husbond, ryse up I beseke ȝow,
And go we to þe temple now fast
To wurchep God, with þat we mow,
And thank hym bothe, this is my cast,
Of þe tyme þat is comynge now.
For now is cum mercy, and venjauns is past!
God wyl be born for mannys prow
To brynge us to blysse þat evyr xal last.

[ALTERNATE CONCLUSION]

Come, I pray ȝow specialy.
Iwys, ȝe are welcome, Mary.
For þis comfortabelest comynge, good God, gra-
mercy.

CONTEMPLACIO Lystenyth, sovereynys, here is a conclusyon.
How þe Aue was mad here is lernyd vs:
þe aungel seyd, 'Ave, gracia plena. Dominus
tecum,
Benedicta tu in mulieribus'.
Elyzabeth seyd, 'Et benedictus
Fructus uentris tui.' Thus þe Chirch addyd
'Maria' and 'Jesus' her.
Who seyth oure Ladyes Sawtere dayly for a ȝer
þus,
He hath pardon ten thowsand and eyte hun-
dryd ȝer.

165 lede] sp *canc. in red and* l *interl. above*
The Latin verses in 152A–155A; Maria *and* Jesus *in* 155A; *and* Benedictus, Magnificat, *and* Benedictus *in* 171A–172A *written in Textura Quadrata.*

Than ferther to oure matere for to procede,
Mary with Elizabeth abod þer stylle
Iij monthys fully, as we rede,
Thankynge God with hertly wylle.

A, Lord God, what hous was þis on
þat [held] þese childeryn and here moderys to
As Mary and Elizabeth, Jesus and John,
And Joseph and Zakarye also.

And evyr oure Lady abod stylle þus
Tyl Johan was of his modyr born.
And þan Zakarye spak, iwus,
þat had be dowm and his spech lorn.

He and Elizabeth prophesyed as þus:
They mad 'Benedictus' them beforn.
And so 'Magnificat' and 'Benedictus'
Fyrst in þat place þer made worn.

Whan all was don oure Lady fre
Toke here leve than aftere this
At Elizabeth and at Zakarie,
And kyssyd Johan and gan hym blys.

Now most mekely we thank ȝou of ȝoure pacyens
And beseke ȝou of ȝoure good supportacyon.
If here hath be seyd ore don any inconuenyens,
We asygne it to ȝoure good deliberaci[on],
Besekynge to Crystys precyous Passyon
Conserve and rewarde ȝoure hedyrcomynge.
With 'Aue' we begunne and 'Aue' is oure conclusyon:
'Ave Regina Celorum' to our Lady we synge.

158A–185A *written two lines as one* 162A *preceded by a small capitulum*
163A held] *supplied by H* 181A deliberacion] deliberaci, *remainder cropped*

f. 74v

14
[THE TRIAL OF MARY AND JOSEPH]

DEN Avoyd, serys, and lete my lorde þe buschop come
And syt in þe courte, þe lawes for to doo.
And I xal gon in þis place, them for to somowne,
Tho þat ben in my book—þe court ȝe must com too!

I warne ȝow here all abowte
þat I somown ȝow, all þe rowte!
Loke ȝe fayl for no dowte
At þe court to pere.
Both Johan Jurdon and Geffrey Gyle,
Malkyn Mylkedoke and fayr Mabyle,
Stevyn Sturdy and Jak-at-þe-Style,
And Sawdyr Sadelere.

Thom Tynkere and Betrys Belle,
Peyrs Pottere and Whatt-at-þe-Welle,
Symme Smalfeyth and Kate Kelle,
And Bertylmew þe bochere.
Kytt Cakelere and Colett Crane,
Gylle Fetyse and fayr Jane,
Powle Pewterere and Pernel Prane,
And Phelypp þe good flecchere.

Cok Crane and Davy Drydust,
Luce Lyere and Letyce Lytyltrust,
Miles þe myllere and Colle Crakecrust,
Bothe Bette þe bakere and Robyn Rede.
And loke ȝe rynge wele in ȝoure purs,
For ellys ȝoure cawse may spede þe wurs,
þow þat ȝe slynge Goddys curs
Evyn at myn hede!

A cross sign written in top margin of f. 74v 1 DEN *written in Fere-Textura and preceded by a capitulum* 5 *lacks a capitulum* *Playnumber* 14 *written on f. 75r* 24 *the rubricated loop normally reserved for s.h. precedes* and Robyn Rede *and* Fast com away *in* 29

Fast com away,
Bothe Boutyng þe browstere and Sybyly Slynge,
Megge Merywedyr and Sabyn Sprynge,
Tyffany Twynkelere, fayle for nothynge,
The courte xal be þis day!

f. 75r *Hic intrabit page[n]tum de Purgacione Marie et Joseph.*
Hic dicit Primus Detractor:

[PRIMUS DETRACTOR] A, a, serys, God saue ȝow all!
Here is a fayr pepyl, in good fay.
Good serys, telle me what men me calle;
I trowe ȝe kannot be þis day.
Ȝitt I walke wyde and many way,
But ȝet þer I come I do no good:
To reyse slaw[n]dyr is al my lay.
Bakbytere is my brother of blood.

Dede he ought come hedyr in al þis day?
Now wolde God þat he wore here.
And be my trewth I dare wel say
þat yf we tweyn togedyr apere,
More slawndyr we to xal arere
Within an howre thorweouth this town
Than evyr þer was þis thowsand ȝere,
And ellys I shrewe ȝow bothe vp and down!

Now be my trewth I haue a syght
Euyn of my brother, lo! where he is.
Welcom, dere brother, my trowth I plyght!
Ȝowre jentyl mowth let me now kys.
SECUNDUS DETRACTOR Gramercy, brother, so haue I blys!
I am ful glad we met þis day.

30 browstere] b *roughly altered from another letter or letters* 31 spy *canc. in red before* Sprynge *In bottom margin of f. 74v is written in Fere-Textura:* a. 14 kl. Aprilis translacio Sancte Marie Magdalene, et Sancti Joseph sponsi Dei genetricis Marie e.x. kl. Aprilis Adam creatus est *Brief scribblings appear above and below this note*
33 s.d. pagentum] pagetum 34 *s.h. supplied* 40 slawndyr] slawdyr
49 I] *altered from an* s

PRIMUS DETRACTOR
Ryght so am I, brothyr, iwys,
Mech gladdere than I kan say.

But ȝitt, good brother, I ȝow pray,
Telle all þese pepyl what is ȝoure name;
For yf þei knew it, my lyf I lay, f. 75v
They wole ȝow wurchep and speke gret fame.

SECUNDUS DETRACTOR
I am Bakbytere, þat spyllyth all game,
Bothe kyd and knowyn in many a place!

PRIMUS DETRACTOR
Be my trowth, I seyd þe same,
And ȝet sum seyden þu xulde haue evyl grace.

SECUNDUS DETRACT[OR]
Herk, Reysesclaundyr, canst þu owth telle
Of any newe thynge þat wrought was late?

PRIMUS DETRACT[OR]
Within a shorte whyle a thynge befelle,
I trowe þu wylt lawhȝ ryght wel þerate;
For, be trowth, ryght mekyl hate,
If it be wyst, þerof wyl growe.

SECUNDUS DETRACTOR
If I may reyse þerwith debate,
I xal not spare þe seyd to sowe.

PRIMUS DETRACTOR
Syr, in þe tempyl a mayd þer was
Calde Mayd Mary, þe trewth to tell.
Sche semyd so holy withinne þat plas,
Men seyd sche was fedde with holy aungell.
Sche made a vow with man nevyr to melle,
But to leve chast and clene virgine.
Howevyr it be, here wombe doth swelle
And is as gret as þinne or myne!

SECUNDUS DETRACTOR
Ȝa, þat old shrewe Joseph, my trowth I plyght,
Was so anameryd upon þat mayd
Þat of hyre bewté whan he had syght,
He sesyd nat tyll [he] had here asayd!

66 DETRACTOR] Detract, *remainder cropped; also in 68* 74 DETRACTOR] trac *corrected from some earlier spelling* 75 þat *canc. in dark brown and red before* þe 80 il *canc. before* it 85 he *supplied*

f. 76r PRIMUS DETRACTOR
A, nay, nay, wel wers she hath hym payd:
Sum fresch ȝonge galaunt she lovyth wel more
Þat his leggys to here hath leyd!
And þat doth greve þe old man sore.

SECUNDUS DETRACTOR
Be my trewth, al may wel be,
For fresch and fayr she is to syght.
And such a mursel, as semyth me,
Wolde cause a ȝonge man to haue delyght.

PRIMUS DETRACTOR
Such a ȝonge damesel of bewté bryght,
And of schap so comely also,
Of hire tayle ofte-tyme be lyght
And rygh tekyl vndyr þe too.

SECUNDUS DETRACTOR
That olde cokolde was evyl begylyd
To þat fresche wench whan he was wedde.
Now muste he faderyn anothyr mannys chylde,
And with his swynke he xal be fedde.

PRIMUS DETRACTOR
A ȝonge man may do more chere in bedde
To a ȝonge wench þan may an olde.
Þat is þe cawse such lawe is ledde,
Þat many a man is a kokewolde.

Hic sedet Episcopus Abizachar inter duos legis doctores et, audientes hanc defam[*a*]*cionem, vocat ad se detractores dicens:*

EPISCOPUS
Herke, ȝe felawys, why speke ȝe such schame
Of þat good virgyn, fayr Mayd Mary?
Ȝe be acursyd so hire for to defame,
She þat is of lyff so good and holy.
Of hire to speke suche velany
Ȝe make myn hert ful hevy of mood.
f. 76v I charge ȝow sese of ȝoure fals cry,
For sche is sybbe of myn owyn blood.

SECUNDUS DETRACTOR
Syb of þi kyn þow þat she be,
All gret with chylde hire wombe doth swelle!

102 *a capitulum erased in left margin* 105 s.d. defamacionem] *D; MS* defamocionem

Do calle here hedyr, þiself xal se
þat it is trewthe þat I þe telle.

PRIMUS DETRACTOR
Sere, for ȝoure sake I xal kepe cowncelle;
Ȝow for to greve I am ryght loth.
But lest, serys, lyst what seyth þe belle:
Oure fayr mayd now gret with childe goth!

PRIMUS DOCTOR LEGIS
Take good heed, serys, what ȝe doth say,
Avyse ȝow wele what ȝe present.
Ȝyf þis be fownd fals anothyr day,
Ful sore ȝe xal ȝoure tale repent!

SECUNDUS DETRACTOR
Sere, þe mayd forsothe is good and gent,
Bothe comely and gay and a fayr wench;
And feetly with help sche can consent
To set a cokewolde on þe hye benche!

SECUNDUS DOCTOR LEGIS
Ȝe be to besy of ȝoure langage!
I hope to God ȝow fals to preve.
It were gret rewthe she xulde so outrage,
Or with such synne to myscheve.

EPISCOPUS
This evy talys my hert doth greve,
Of hire to here such fowle dalyawnce.
If she be fowndyn in suche repreve,
She xal sore rewe here governawns!

Sym Somnore, in hast wend þu þi way;
Byd Joseph and his wyff be name
At þe coorte to appere þis day, f. 77^{r}
Here hem to pourge of here defame.
Sey þat I here of hem grett schame
And þat doth me gret hevynes.
If þei be clene withowtyn blame,
Byd hem come hedyr and shew wyttnes.

DEN
All redy, sere, I xal hem calle
Here at ȝoure courte for to appere.
And yf I may hem mete withall,
I hope ryght sone þei xal ben here.
Awey, serys, lete me com nere!
A man of wurchep here comyth to place.

Of curtesy, mesemyth, ȝe be to lere;
Do of ȝoure hodys, with an evyl grace.

Do me sum wurchep befor my face,
Or be my trowth I xal ȝow make!
If þat I rolle ȝow up in my race,
For fere I xal do ȝoure ars qwake!
But ȝit sum mede and ȝe me take,
I wyl withdrawe my gret rough toth.
Gold or sylvyr I wyl not forsake,
But [do] evyn as all somnorys doth.

A, Joseph, good day, with þi fayr spowse!
My lorde þe buschop hath for ȝow sent.
It is hym tolde þat in þin house
A cockoldeis bowe is ech nyght bent.
He þat shett þe bolt is lyke to be schent.
Fayre mayde, þat tale ȝe kan best telle.
Now be ȝoure trowth, telle ȝoure entent:
Dede not þe archere plese ȝow ryght well?

f. 77v MARIA Of God in hevyn I take wyttnes,
þat synful werk was nevyr my thought.
I am a mayd ȝit of pure clennes,
Lyke as I was into þis werd brought.
DEN Othyr wyttnes xal non be sought.
þu art with childe eche man may se.
I charge ȝow bothe ȝe tary nought,
But to þe buschop com forth with me.

JOSEPH To þe buschop with ȝow we wende—
Of oure purgacyon hawe we no dowth.
MARIA Almyghty God xal be oure frende
Whan þe trewthe is tryed owth.
DEN Ȝa, on þis wyse excusyth here every scowte
Whan here owyn synne hem doth defame!

161 do *supplied* 171 werk *canc. in red after* my 176 tary] t *written over another letter*

But lowly þan þei gyn to lowth
Whan þei be gylty and fowndyn in blame.

Therfore, com forth, Cokewolde be name!
þe busschop xal ȝoure lyff appose.
Com forth also, ȝe goodly dame,
A clene huswyff, as I suppose!
I xal ȝow tellyn withowtyn glose,
And ȝe were myn, withowtyn lak,
I wolde ech day beschrewe ȝoure nose
And ȝe dede brynge me such a pak!

My lord þe buschop, here haue I brought
þis goodly copyl at ȝoure byddyng;
And as mesemyth as be here fraught,
'Fayr chylde, lullay' sone must she syng.
PRIMUS DETRACTOR To here a credyl and ȝe wolde brynge, f. 78r
Ȝe myght saue mony in here purse.
Becawse she is ȝoure cosyn ȝynge,
I pray ȝow, sere, lete here nevyr fare þe wers.

EPISCOPUS Alas, Mary, what hast þu wrought?
I am aschamyd evyn for þi sake.
How hast þu chaungyd þin holy thought?
Dude old Joseph with strenght þe take?
Or hast þu chosyn another make
By whom þu art þus brought in schame?
Telle me who hath wrought þis wrake.
How has þu lost þin holy name?

MARIA My name, I hope, is saff and sownde.
God to wyttnes, I am a mayd.
Of fleschly lust and gostly wownde
In dede nere thought I nevyr asayd.

PRIMUS DOCTOR LEGIS How xulde þi wombe þus be arayd,
So grettly swollyn as þat it is?
But if sum man þe had ovyrlayd,
þi wombe xulde never be so gret, iwys!

214 DOCTOR] *first* o *altered from another letter*

SECUNDUS DOCTOR LEGIS
Herke þu, Joseph, I am afrayd
þat þu hast wrought þis opyn synne.
þis woman þu hast þus betrayd
With gret flaterynge or sum fals gynne.

SECUNDUS DETRACTOR
Now, be myn trowth, ȝe hytte þe pynne!
With þat purpose, in feyth, I holde.
Telle now how þu þus hire dudyst wynne,
Ore knowlych þiself for a cockewold.

f. 78v **JOSEPH**
Sche is for me a trewe clene mayde,
And I for hire am clene also.
Of fleschly synne I nevyr asayde
Sythyn þat sch[e] was weddyd me to.

EPISCOPUS
Thu xalt not schape from vs ȝitt so;
Fyrst þu xalte tellyn us another lay.
Streyt to þe awter þu xalt go,
þe drynge of vengeawns þer to asay.

Here is þe botel of Goddys vengeauns.
This drynk xal be now þi purgacyon.
þis [hath] suche vertu by Goddys ordenauns
þat what man drynk of þis potacyon
And goth serteyn in processyon
Here in þis place þis awtere abowth,
If he be gylty, sum maculacion
Pleyn in his face xal shewe it owth.

Iff þu be gylty, telle us, lete se.
Ouyr Godys myght be not to bolde!
If þu presume and gylty be,
God þu dost greve many a folde.

JOSEPH
I am not gylty, as I fyrst tolde,
Allmyghty God I take wytnes.

EPISCOPUS
Than þis drynke in hast þu holde,
And on processyon anon þe dresse.

Hic Joseph bibit et sepcies circuiuit altare dicens:

229 sche] sch
238 And] d *interl.*
236 hath *supplied, following* hath *interl. by another hand in black*
244 presue *canc. after* þu

JOSEPH
This drynk I take with meke entent.
As I am gyltles, to God I pray:
Lord, as þu art omnypotente, f. 79r
On me þu shewe þe trowth þis day.

Modo bibit

About þis awtere I take þe way,
O gracyous God, help þi servaunt!
As I am gyltles aȝen ȝon may,
þin hand of mercy þis tyme me graunt.

DEN
This olde shrewe may not wele gon!
Longe he taryeth to go abowth.
Lyfte up þi feet, sett forth þi ton,
Or be my trowth þu getyst a clowte!

SECUNDUS DETRACTOR
Now, sere, evyl thedom com to þi snowte!
What heylyght þi leggys now to be lame?
þu dedyst hem put ryght freschly owte
Whan þu dedyst pley with ȝon ȝonge dame!

PRIMUS DETRACTOR
I pray to God gyf hym myschawns!
Hese leggys here do folde for age.
But with þis damysel whan he dede dawns,
þe olde charle had ryght gret corage!

DEN
The shrewe was þan sett in a dotage
And had good lust þat tyme to pleyn.
Ȝaff sche not ȝow cawdel to potage
Whan ȝe had don, to comforte ȝoure brayn?

JOSEPH
A, gracyous God, help me þis tyde
Ageyn þis pepyl þat me doth fame.
As I nevyrmore dede towch here syde,
þis day help me fro werdly schame.
Abowte þis awtere to kepe my fame,
Vij tymes I haue gon round abowte.
If I be wurthy to suffyr blame, f. 79v
O ryghtful God, my synne shewe owughte.

267 leggys] y *altered from an* e 281 sw *canc. in red before* shewe

EPISCOPUS
Joseph, with hert thank God þi Lorde
Whos hey3 mercy doth the excuse.
For þi purgacyon we xal recorde
With hyre of synne þu dedyst nevyr muse.
But, Mary, þiself mayst not refuse:
All grett with chylde we se þe stonde.
What mystyr man dede þe mysvse?
Why hast þu synnyd ageyn þin husbonde?

MARIA
I trespacyd nevyr with erthely wyght.
þerof I hope þurowe Goddys sonde
Here to be purgyd before 3oure syght
From all synne clene, lyke as myn husbonde.
Take me þe botel out of 3oure honde,
Here xal I drynke beforn 3oure face.
Abowth þis awtere than xal I fonde
Vij tymes to go, by Godys grace.

PRIMUS DOCTOR LEGIS
Se, þis bolde bysmare wolde presume
Ageyn God to preve his myght!
þow Goddys vengeauns hyre xuld consume,
Sche wyl not telle hyre fals delyght.
þu art with chylde we se in syght;
To us þi wombe þe doth accuse!
þer was nevyr woman 3itt in such plyght
þat from mankynde hyre kowde excuse.

PRIMUS DETRACTOR
f. 80r
In feyth, I suppose þat þis woman slepte
Withowtyn all coverte whyll þat it dede snowe;
And a flake þerof into hyre mowthe crepte,
And þerof þe chylde in hyre wombe doth growe.

SECUNDUS DETRACTOR
Than beware, dame, for this is wel iknowe:
Whan it is born, yf þat þe sunne shyne,
It wyl turne to watyr ageyn, as I trowe;
For snow onto watyr doth evyrmore reclyne.

300 presume *canc. in dark brown and red after* xuld *and* consume *interl. above* consume] o *blotted and an* o *interl. above* 313 ren *canc. after* evyrmore

SECUNDUS DOCTOR LEGIS With Goddys hyȝ myght loke þu not jape!
Of þi purgacyon wel þe avyse.
Yf þu be gylty þu mayst not schape;
Beware evyr of God, þat ryghtful justyce!
If God with vengeauns set on þe his syse,
Not only þu but all þi kyn is schamyd.
Bettyr it is to telle þe trewth, devyse,
Than God for to greve and of hym be gramyd.

MARIA I trostyn in his grace, I xal hym nevyr greve;
His servaunt I am in worde, dede, and thought.
A mayd vndefyled I hope he xal me preve.
I pray ȝow, lett me nought.
EPISCOPUS Now, be þat good Lord þat all þis werd hath wrought,
If God on þe shewe ony manyr tokyn,
Purgacyon, I trowe, was nevyr so dere bowth,
If I may on the in any wyse be wrokyn.

Holde here þe botel and take a large draught,
And abowth the awtere go þi processyon.
MARYA To God in þis case my cawse I haue betaught;
Lord, thorwe þin helpe I drynke of þis potacyon.

Hic Beata Uirgo bibit de potacione et postea circuiuit altare dicens:

MARIA God, as I nevyr knew of mannys maculacion, f. 80v
But evyr haue lyued in trew virginité,
Send me þis day þi holy consolacyon
þat all þis fayr peple my clennes may se.

O, gracyous God, as þu hast chose me
For to be þi modyr, of me to be born,
Saue þi tabernacle, þat clene is kepte for þe,
Which now am put at repref and skorn.

316 not] t *squeezed in* *F. 80v marked 80 twice; the first instance is faint and smudged*
A line drawn in pencil under 335

Gabryel me tolde with wordys he[re]beforn
   Þat ȝe of ȝoure goodnes wold become my chylde.
Help now of ȝoure hyȝness my wurchep be not lorn;
   A, dere son, I pray ȝow, help ȝoure modyr mylde.

EPISCOPUS Almyghty God, what may þis mene?
   For all þe drynke of Goddys potacyon,
Þis woman with chylde is fayr and clene,
   Withowtyn fowle spotte or maculacion!
   I cannat, be non ymagynacyon,
      Preve hyre gylty and synful of lyff.
   It shewyth opynly by here purgacyon
      Sche is clene mayde, bothe modyr and wyff!

PRIMUS DETRACTO[R] Be my fadyr sowle, here is gret gyle!
   Because sche is syb of ȝoure kynreed,
Þe drynk is chaungyd by sum fals wyle
   Þat sche no shame xulde haue þis steed!

EPISCOPUS Becawse þu demyst þat we do falshede,
      And for þu dedyst hem fyrst defame,
   Þu xalt ryght here, magré þin heed,
      Beforn all þis pepyl drynk of þe same.

f. 81r PRIMUS DETRACTOR Syr, in good feyth oo draught I pulle,
   If these to drynkerys haue not all spent.

Hic bibit, et scenciens dolorem in capite cadit, et dicit:

Out, out! Alas, what heylith my soulle?
   A, myn heed with fyre methynkyht is brent!
   Mercy, good Mary, I do me repent
      Of my cursyd and fals langage!

342 herebeforn] *D; MS* he beforn 354 DETRACTOR] Detracto, *remainder cropped* 363 s.d. scenciens] scencienes cadit] i *altered from a* y, *or vice versa* *A heavy black line drawn over original line between* 367 *and* 368

MARIA Now god Lord in hevyn omnypotent,
Of his grett mercy ȝoure seknes aswage.

EPISCOPUS We all on knes fall here on grownd,
þu, Goddys handemayd, prayng for grace.
All cursyd langage and schame onsownd,
Good Mary, forȝeve us here in þis place.
MARIA Now God forȝeve ȝow all ȝowre trespace,
And also forȝeve ȝow all defamacyon
þat ȝe haue sayd, both more and lesse,
To myn hynderawnce and maculacion.

EPISCOPUS Now, blyssyd virgyne, we thank ȝow alle
Of ȝoure good hert and gret pacyens.
We wyl go with ȝow hom to ȝoure halle
To do ȝow servys with hyȝ reverens.
MARIA I thank ȝow hertyly of ȝoure benevolens.
Onto ȝoure owyn hous I pray ȝow ȝe goo,
And take þis pepyl hom with ȝow hens;
I am not dysposyd to passyn hens froo.

EPISCOPUS Than farewel, mayden and pure virgyne,
Farewel, trewe handmayd of God in blys!
We all to ȝow lowly inclyne
And take oure leve of ȝow as wurthy is.
MARIA Allmyghty God ȝoure weys wysse, f. 81v
For þat hyȝ Lord is most of myght.
He mote ȝow spede þat ȝe not mys
In hevyn of hym to haue a syght.

JOSEPH Honouryd in hevyn be þat hyȝ Lorde
Whos endles grace is so habundaunt
þat he doth shewe þe trewe recorde
Of iche wyhgt þat is his trewe servaunt.
That Lord to wurchepe with hert plesaunt
We bothe be bownd ryght on þis place,

372 onsownd] w *written over one or two letters* 386 *lacks a capitulum*
390 wysse] wys se, *perhaps adapted from* wys

Which oure purgacyon us dyde graunt
And prevyd us pure by hieȝ grace.

MARIA Forsothe, good spowse, I thank hym hyȝly
Of his good grace for oure purgacyon.
Oure clennesse is knowyn ful opynly
Be vertu of his grett consolacyon.

f. 82r

15
[THE NATIVITY]

JOSEPH Lord, what travayl to man is wrought!
Rest in þis werd behovyth hym non.
Octauyan, oure emperour, sadly hath besought;
Oure trybute hym to bere folk must forth ichon;
It is cryed in every bourgh and cety be name.
I þat am a pore tymbre-wryth
Born of þe blood of Dauyd,
þe emperorys comawndement I must
holde with,
And ellys I were to blame.

Now, my wyff, Mary, what sey ȝe to this?
For sekyr, nedys I must forth wende
Onto þe cyté of Bedleem fer hens, iwys.
þus to labore I muste my body bende.
MARIA Myn husbond and my spowse, with ȝow wyl I
wende;
A syght of þat cyté fayn wolde I se.
If I myght of myn alye ony þer fynde,
It wold be grett joye onto me.

401 p..r *canc. in red before* pure *Remainder of f. 81r (97 mm) blank, except for a cross sign and the words* E explicit cum gaudio, Amen, *written by another hand in black and ringed by flourished circles*

[*Play 15*] 1 *s.h. written in Textura Quadrata and preceded by a capitulum* 6 *and* 7 *written as one line, with a point after* wryth 7 *Two letters* (b..) *canc. in red before* blood

JOSEPH My spowse, ȝe be with childe, I fere ȝow to kary,
For mesemyth it were werkys wylde.
But ȝow to plese ryght fayn wold I.
Ȝitt women ben ethe to greve whan þei be with childe.

Now latt us forth wende as fast as we may,
And almyghty God spede us in oure jurnay.

MARIA A, my swete husbond, wolde ȝe telle to me
What tre is ȝon standynge vpon ȝon hylle?
JOSEPH Forsothe, Mary, it is clepyd a chery tre;
In tyme of ȝere ȝe myght fede ȝow þeron ȝoure fylle.

MARIA Turne ageyn, husbond, and beholde ȝon tre,
How þat it blomyght now so swetly.
JOSEPH Cum on, Mary, þat we worn at ȝon cyté, f. 82v
Or ellys we may be blamyd, I telle ȝow lythly.

MARIA Now, my spowse, I pray ȝow to behold
How þe cheryes growyn vpon ȝon tre.
For to haue þerof ryght fayn I wold,
And it plesyd ȝow to labore so mech for me.

JOSEPH Ȝoure desyre to fulfylle I xal assay, sekyrly.
Ow! To plucke ȝow of these cheries, it is a werk wylde!
For þe tre is so hyȝ it wol not be lyghtly—
Þerfore lete hym pluk ȝow cheryes begatt ȝow with childe!

MARIA Now, good Lord, I pray the, graunt me þis boun,
To haue of þese cheries and it be ȝoure wylle.
Now I thank it God, þis tre bowyth to me down!
I may now gaderyn anowe and etyn my fylle.

No capitulum before 22

JOSEPH
Ow! I know weyl I haue offendyd my God in Trinyté
Spekyng to my spowse these vnkynde wurdys.
For now I beleve wel it may non other be
But þat my spowse beryght þe Kyngys Son of Blys;
He help us now at oure nede.
Of þe kynrede of Jesse worthely were ȝe bore,
Kyngys and patryarkys ȝow beffore.
All þese wurthy of ȝoure kynred wore,
As clerkys in story rede.

MARIA
Now gramercy, husbond, for ȝoure report.
In oure weys wysely late us forth wende.
þe Fadyr allmyghty, he be oure comfort,
þe Holy Gost gloryous, he be oure frende.

f. 83[r] JOSEPH
Heyl, wurchepful sere, and good day!
A ceteceyn of þis cyté ȝe seme to be.
Of herborwe for [my] spowse and me I ȝow pray;
For trewly þis woman is ful weré,
And fayn at reste, sere, wold she be.
We wolde fulffylle þe byddynge of oure emperour
For to pay trybute as ryght is oure.
And to kepe ourseselfe from dolowre,
We are come to þis cyté

CIUES
Sere, ostage in þis town know I non
þin wyff and þu in for to slepe;
This ceté is besett with pepyl every won,
And ȝett þei ly withowte, ful every strete.

Withinne no wall, man, comyst þu nowth
Be þu onys withinne þe cyté gate.
Onethys in þe strete a place may be sowth
þeron to rest withowte debate.

59 my *supplied by H*

JOSEPH
Nay, sere, debate, þat wyl I nowth—
All such thyngys passyn my powere.
But ȝitt my care and all my thought
Is for Mary, my derlynge dere.

A, swete wyff, what xal we do?
Wher xal we logge þis nyght?
Onto þe Fadyr of Heffne pray we so,
Vs to kepe from every wykkyd whyt.

CIUES
Good man, o word I wyl þe sey,
If þu wylt do by þe counsel of me:
Ȝondyr is an hous of haras þat stant be þe wey;
Amonge þe bestys herboryd may ȝe be.

MARIA
Now þe Fadyr of Hefne, he mut ȝow ȝelde. f. 83v
His sone in my wombe, forsothe, he is.
He kepe þe and þi good be fryth and felde.
Go we hens, husbond, for now tyme it is.

But herk now, good husbond, a newe relacyon,
Which in myself I know ryght well:
Cryst, in me hath take incarnacyon,
Sone wele be borne, þe trowth I fele.

In þis pore logge my chawmere I take,
Here for to abyde þe blyssyd byrth
Of hym þat all þis werd dude make.
Betwyn myn sydys I fele he styrth.

JOSEPH
God be þin help, spowse, it swemyth me sore,
Þus febyly loggyd and in so pore degré.
Goddys sone amonge bestys for to be bore—
His woundyr werkys fulfyllyd must be—

In an hous þat is desolat, withowty[n] any wall;
Fyer nor wood non here is.

90 *No capitulum.* ral *canc. before* relacyon 102 withowtyn] withowty

MARIA Joseph, myn husbond, abydyn here I xal,
For here wyl be born þe Kyngys Sone of Blys.

JOSEPH Now, jentyll wyff, be of good myrth,
And if ȝe wyl owght haue, telle me what ȝe thynk.
I xal not spare for schep nor derth.
Now telle me ȝoure lust of mete and drynk.

MARIA For mete and drynk lust I ryght nowth—
Allmyghty God my fode xal be.
Now þat I am in chawmere brought,
I hope ryght well my chylde to se.
f. 84r Therfore, husbond, of ȝoure honesté,
Avoyd ȝow hens out of þis place,
And I alone with humylité
Here xal abyde Goddys hyȝ grace.

JOSEPH All redy, wyff, ȝow for to plese
I wyl go hens out of ȝoure way,
And seke sum mydwyuys ȝow for to ese
Whan þat ȝe trauayle of childe þis day.
Farewell, trewe wyff and also clene may,
God be ȝoure comforte in Trinyté.
MARIA To God in hevyn for ȝow I pray,
He ȝow preserve wherso ȝe be.

Hic dum Joseph est absens parit Maria Filium Vnigenitum.

JOSEPH Now God, of whom comyth all releffe,
And as all grace in þe is grownde,
So saue my wyff from hurt and greffe
Tyl I sum mydwyuys for here haue fownde.
Travelynge women in care be bownde
With grete throwys whan þei do grone;
God helpe my wyff þat sche not swownde.
I am ful sory sche is alone!

108 derke *canc. before* derth

It is not conuenyent a man to be
þer women gon in travalynge.
Wherfore sum mydwyff fayn wold I se,
My wyff to helpe þat is so ȝenge.

ZELOMY Why makyst þu, man, suche mornyng? f. 84v
Tell me sumdele of ȝoure gret mone.
JOSEPH My wyf is now in gret longynge,
Trauelyng of chylde, and is alone.
For Godys loue, þat sytt in trone,
As ȝe mydwyuys þat kan ȝoure good,
Help my ȝonge spowse in hast anone.
I drede me sore of þat fayr food!

SALOMÉ Be of good chere and of glad mood,
We ij mydwyuys with þe wyll go.
þer was nevyr woman in such plyght stood
But we were redy here help to do.

My name is Salomee, all men me knowe
For a mydwyff of wurthy fame.
Whan women travayl, grace doth growe;
þeras I come I had nevyr shame.
ZELOMYE And I am Zelomye, men knowe my name,
We tweyn with the wyl go togedyr
And help þi wyff fro hurt and grame.
Com forth, Joseph, go we streyth thedyr.

JOSEPH I thank ȝow, damys, ȝe comforte my lyff.
Streyte to my spowse walke we þe way.
In þis pore logge lyght Mary my wyff.
Hyre for to comforte, gode frendys, asay.
SALOMÉ We dare not entre þis logge, in fay—
þer is þerin so gret bryghtnes!
Mone be nyght nor sunne be day
Shone nevyr so clere in þer lyghtnesse! f. 85r

138 *some scribbles above s.h.* 146 *No capitulum* 148 s *canc. before* in

ZELOMYE Into þis hous dare I not gon;
þe woundyrfful lyght doth me affray.
JOSEPH Than wyl myself gon in alon
And chere my wyff if þat I may.
All heyl, maydon and wyff, I say!
How dost þu fare? Telle me þi chere.
The for to comforte in gesyn þis day,
Tweyn gode mydwyuis I haue brought here.

The for to helpe, þat art in harde bonde,
Zelomye and Salomee be com with me.
For dowte of drede withowte þei do stond,
And dare not come in for lyght þat they se.

Hic Maria subridendo dicat:

MARIA The myght of þe Godhede in his magesté
Wyl not be hyd now at þis whyle.
The chylde þat is born wyl preue his modyr fre,
A very clene mayde, and þerfore I smyle.

JOSEPH Why do ȝe lawghe, wyff? Ȝe be to blame!
I pray ȝow, spowse, do no more so!
In happ þe mydwyuys wyl take it to grame,
And at ȝoure nede helpe wele non do.
Iff ȝe haue nede of mydwyuys, lo,
Perauenture thei wyl gon hens.
þerfor be sad, and ȝe may so,
And wynnyth all þe mydwyuis good diligens.

f. 85v MARIA Husbond, I pray ȝow, dysplese ȝow nowth,
þow þat I lawghe and gret joye haue.
Here is þe chylde þis werde hath wrought,
Born now of me, þat allthynge xal saue.
JOSEPH I aske ȝow grace, for I dyde raue!
O gracyous childe, I aske mercy.

177 s.d. *The redundant s.h.* Maria *after* dicat *deleted* 182 lawghe] lawghte, *with deleting dots under* te, *and* e *interl. above* 185 Zellony *written by another hand in right margin*

As þu art Lord and I but knaue,
Forȝeue me now my gret foly.

Alas, mydwyuis, what haue I seyd?
I pray ȝow com to us more nere,
For here I fynde my wyff a mayd
And in here arme a chylde hath here—
Bothe mayd and modyr sch[e] is in fere!
þat God wole haue may nevyrmore fayle.
Modyr on erth was nevyr non clere
Withowth sche had in byrth travayle.

ZELOMY In byrth trauayle muste sche nedys haue,
Or ellys no chylde of here is born.
JOSEPH I pray ȝow, dame, and ȝe vowchsaue,
Com se þe chylde my wyff beforn.

SALOMÉ Grete God be in þis place.
Swete systyr, how fare ȝe?
MARIA I thank þe Fadyr of his hyȝ grace;
His owyn son and my chylde here ȝe may se.

ZELOMYE All heyl, Mary, and ryght good morn.
Who was mydwyfe of þis fayr chylde?
MARIA He þat nothynge wyl haue forlorn
Sent me þis babe, and I mayd mylde.

ZELOMYE With honde lete me now towch and fele f. 86r
Yf ȝe haue nede of medycyn. H quire
I xal ȝow comforte and helpe ryght wele
As other women yf ȝe haue pyn.
MARIA Of þis fayr byrth þat here is myn
Peyne nere grevynge fele I ryght non.
I am clene mayde and pure virgyn;
Tast with ȝoure hand ȝoureself alon.

Hic palpat Zelomye Beatam Virginem dicens:

202 sche] sch 210 *No capitulum* 225 ll *or an incomplete* w *canc. after* with

ZELOMY
O myghtfull God, haue mercy on me!
  A merveyle þat nevyr was herd beforn
Here opynly I fele and se:
  A fayr chylde of a maydon is born,

And nedyth no waschynge as other don:
  Ful clene and pure forsoth is he,
Withoutyn spott or ony polucyon,
  His modyr nott hurte of virgynité!

Coom nere, gode systyr Salomé.
  Beholde þe brestys of þis clene mayd,
Ful of fayr mylke how þat þei be,
  And hyre chylde clene, as I fyrst sayd.
  As other ben nowth fowle arayd,
    But clene and pure bothe modyr and chylde.
  Of þis matyr I am dysmayd,
    To se them both thus vndefyled!

SALOMÉ
It is not trewe, it may nevyr be!
  þat bothe be clene I cannot beleve!
A mayd mylke haue nevyr man dyde se,
  Ne woman bere chylde withowte grett greve.
f. 86v I xal nevyr trowe it but I it preve!
    With hand towchynge but I assay,
  In my conscience it may nevyr cleue
    þat sche hath chylde and is a may.

MARIA
Ȝow for to putt clene out of dowth,
  Towch with ȝoure hand and wele asay.
Wysely ransake and trye þe trewthe owth
  Whethyr I be fowlyd or a clene may.

Hic tangit Salomee Mari[*am*] *et, cum arescerit manus eius, vlulando et quasi flendo dicit:*

230 *No capitulum* 240 dyf *canc. before* dysmayd 244 *The contraction for* ys *appended to* mayd, *and* haue *crossed through, both in black* 246 *preceded by an unnecessary capitulum* 253 ransak *written faintly by another hand in right margin* 253 s.d. Mariam] *D; MS* Marie vlulando] *second* l *written over an erasure?*

SALOMEE
Alas, alas, and weleawaye!
For my grett dowth and fals beleve
Myne hand is ded and drye as claye—
My fals vntrost hath wrought myscheve!

Alas þe tyme þat I was born,
Thus to offende aȝens Goddys myght!
Myn handys power is now all lorn,
Styff as a stykke, and may nowth plyght.
For I dede tempte þis mayde so bryght
And helde aȝens here pure clennes,
In grett myscheff now am I pyght.
Alas, alas for my lewdnes!

O Lord of Myght, þu knowyst þe trowth,
þat I haue evyr had dred of þe.
On every power whyght evyr I haue rowthe,
And ȝove hem almes for loue of þe.
Bothe wyff and wedowe þat askyght, for the,
And frendles chylderyn þat haddyn grett
nede,
I dude them cure, and all for the, f. 87r
And toke no rewarde of them, nor mede.

Now as a wrecch for fals beleve
þat I shewyd in temptynge þis mayde,
My hand is ded and doth me greve.
Alas, þat evyr I here assayde!

ANGELUS
Woman, þi sorwe to haue delayde,
Wurchep þat childe þat þer is born;
Towch þe clothis þer he is leyde,
For he xal saue all þat is lorn.

SALOMEE
O gloryous chylde and Kynge of Blysse,
I aske ȝow mercy for my trespace.

254 *preceded by a capitulum* *A blot obscures* as *in* 261 *and* dede *in* 262 278 *In* ANGELUS *and all subsequent speaker headings in this play, the initial letter is marked with a red stroke* 279 sc *canc. before* childe 280 leyde] *an* a *written over* -e- *in black*

I knowlege my synne, I demyd amys.
O blyssyd babe, grawnt me sum grace!
Of ȝow, mayde, also here in þis place
I aske mercy knelynge on kne.
Moste holy mayde, grawnt me solace,
Sum wurde of comforte sey now to me.

MARIA As Goddys aungel to ȝow dede telle,
My chylde is medycyn for every sor.
Towch his clothis be my cowncelle,
Ȝowre hand ful sone he wyl restor.

Hic Salomee tangit fimbriam Christi dicens:

SALOMEE A, now blyssyd be þis chylde euyrmore!
Þe Sone of God, forsothe he is,
Hath helyd myn hand þat was forlore
Thorwe fals beleve and demynge amys!

f. 87v In every place I xal telle þis:
Of a clene mayde þat God is born,
And in oure lyknes God now clad is,
Mankend to saue þat was forlorn;
His modyr a mayde as sche was beforn,
Natt fowle polutyd as other women be,
But fayr and fresch as rose on thorn,
Lely-wyte, clene with pure virginyté.

Of þis blyssyd babe my leve now do I take,
And also of ȝow, hyȝ Modyr of Blysse.
Of þis grett meracle more knowlege to make,
I xal go telle it in iche place, iwys.
MARIA Farewel, good dame, and God ȝoure wey wysse.
In all ȝoure jurnay God be ȝoure spede!
And of his hyȝ mercy þat Lord so ȝow blysse
þat ȝe nevyr offende more in word, thought,
nore dede.

300 in *obscured by a blot which partially covers* Mankend *in* 301 *and* modyr *in* 302

ZELOMY And I also do take my leve here
Of all þis blyssyd good company,
Praynge ȝoure grace bothe fere and nere
On us to spede ȝoure endles mercy.
JOSEPH The blyssyng of þat Lord þat is most myghty
Mote sprede on ȝow in every place;
Of all ȝoure enmyes to haue þe victory,
God þat best may, grawnt ȝow his grace.
AMEN

16
[THE SHEPHERDS]

f. 88^{v}

Angelus ad pastores dicit 'Gloria in excelsis Deo'.

ANGELUS Joye to God þat sytt in hevyn,
And pes to man on erthe grownde.
A chylde is born benethe þe levyn,
Thurwe hym many folke xul be vnbownde!
Sacramentys þer xul be vij
Wonnyn þo[r]we þat childys wounde.
Therfore I synge a joyful stevene.
þe flowre of frenchep now is founde,
God þat wonyght on hyȝ!
He is gloryed mannys gost to wynne,
He hath sent salue to mannys synne;
Pes is comyn to mannys kynne
Thorwe Goddys sleytys slyȝ.

314 call *written by another hand in left margin* 318 *preceded by a capitulum* *Remainder of f. 87^{v} (39 mm) and f. 88^{r} blank*

[*Play 16*] First s.d. Gloria in excelsis Deo *crossed through in fainter ink* 6 þorwe] þowe *crossed through in darker ink; another word. interl. above by another hand, altered to* thorogh(*?*) 9 hyȝ] *an* e *added in black by a reviser, apparently Scribe C* 13 sleytys *partially erased* slyȝ *obscured by* hye *written over it in black, and followed by* wysdam I saye, *written by the reviser in black. Interl. above* sleytys slyȝ *are two partially erased words* (.....heye*?*) *also in black*

PRIMUS PASTOR
Maunfras, Maunfras, felawe myne,
I saw a gret lyght with shene shyne!
Ʒit saw I nevyr so selkowth syne
Shapyn vpon þe skyes.
It is bryghtere þan þe sunnebem,
It comyth ryght ouyr all þis rem,
Evyn above Bedleem.
I saw it brenne thryes.

SECUNDUS PASTOR
Thu art my brother, Boosras.
I haue beholdyn þe same pas!
I trowe it is tokenynge of gras
f. 89r þat shynynge shewyght beforn.
Balaam spak in prophesye
A lyght xuld shyne vpon þe skye
Whan a sone of a mayd Marye
In Bedleem were iborn.

TERCIUS PASTOR
Thow I make lyty[l] noyse,
I am an herde þat hattyht Moyse.
I herde carpynge of a croyse
Of Moyses in his lawe.
Of a mayd a barne born,
On a tre he xulde be torn;
Delyver folkys þat arn forlorn,
The chylde xulde be slawe.

14 breme (*?*) *written in right margin by another hand* 15 shene *canc. in black and* bryght *interl. above by the reviser* 16 selkowth *almost entirely erased and* mervelus *written above by the reviser;* a *interl. by the reviser before* syne 24 *a miswritten letter canc. before* tokenynge 28 sone *canc. in faint black ink and* chyld *interl. above by C* 30 lytyl] lyty; *the reviser has added an* l *to* lyty *and the words* of this 31 *The reviser has interl.* man þat *after* herde, *canc.* Moyse, *and interl.* sayyng *above; he has added* amys *after the line* 32 *The reviser has canc.* carpynge *and interl.* spekyng *above; he has canc.* croyse *and interl.* chyld of blys *above* 34 *The reviser has canc.* barne *and interl.* child *above; he has canc.* born *and written* xuld be borne *at the right. The revised passage reads:*

Thow I make lytyl noyse of this
I am an herde man þat hattyht sayyng amys
I herde spekyng of a chyld of blys
Of Moyses in his lawe
Of a mayd a child xuld be borne. . . .

PRIMUS PASTOR
Balaam spak in prophecie
Out of Jacob xuld shyne a skye.
Many folke he xulde bye
With his bryght blood.
Be þat bryght blod þat he xulde blede
He xal us brynge fro þe develys drede,
As a duke most dowty in dede,
Thorwe his deth on rode.

SECUNDUS PASTOR
Amos spak with mylde meth,
A frute swettere than bawmys breth,
His deth xulde slen oure sowlys deth
And drawe us all from helle.
Therfore such lyght goth beforn
In tokyn þat þe childe is born (f. 89v)
Whiche xal saue þat is forlorn,
As prophetys gonne spelle.

TERCIUS PASTOR
Danyel þe prophete þus gan speke:
'Wyse God, from woo us wreke,
þi bryght hevyn þu to-breke
And medele þe with a mayde'.
This prophecye is now spad:
Cryst in oure kende is clad.
þerfore mankend may be glad,
As prophetys beforn han seyd.

'Gloria in Excelsis Deo' cantent.

PRIMUS PASTOR
Ey! Ey! þis was a wondyr note (A (on f. 90r))
þat was now songyn above þe sky.
I haue þat voys ful wele I wote,
þei songe 'Gle, glo, glory'.

SECUNDUS PASTOR
Nay, so moty the, so was it nowth.
I haue þat songe ful wele invm.

The two stanzas following 61 s.d. *are marked* B, *the subsequent three stanzas are marked* A; *the stanzas marked* B *are here* 74–89 s.d.; *those marked* A *are* 62–73. *Stanza beginning at* 90 *is marked* C 62 *preceded by a small incomplete capitulum* 67 invm] v *altered from another letter* (o?)

In my wyt weyl it is wrought,
It was 'Gle, glo, glas, glum'.

TERCIUS PASTOR
The songe methought it was 'Glory'.
And aftyrwarde he seyd us to,
þer is a chylde born xal be a prynce myghty.
For to seke þat chylde I rede we go.

B (f. 89v cont.) PRIMUS PASTOR
The prophecye of Boosdras is spedly sped,
Now leyke we hens as þat lyght us lede.
Myght we se onys þat bryght on bed,
Oure bale it wolde vnbynde.
We xulde shodyr for no shoure.
Buske we us hens to Bedleem boure
To se þat fayr fresch flowre,
The mayde mylde in mynde.

SECUNDUS PASTOR
Lete us folwe with all oure myght.
With songe and myrth we xul us dyght,
And wurchep with joye þat wurthy wyght
þat Lord is of mankynne.
Lete us go forthe fast on hye
f. 90r And honowre þat babe wurthylye,
With merthe, songe, and melodye.
Haue do! þis songe begynne.

Tunc pastores cantabunt 'Stella celi extirpauit', quo facto ibunt ad querendum Christum.

C PRIMUS PASTOR
Heyle, floure of flourys, fayrest ifownde!
Heyle, perle peerles, prime rose of prise!
Heyl, blome on bedde, we xul be vnbownde
With þi blody woundys and werkys full wyse!
Heyl, God grettest, I grete þe on grownde!
þe gredy devyl xal grone grysly as a gryse

72 xal] xal *canc. before* xal   77 bale *canc. and* sorow *interl. above by the reviser*   78 shodyr] *B* shadyr; o *malformed and obscured by a stroke with which the reviser has canc.* shodyr; *he has interl.* not let *above*   79 *The reviser has canc.* Buske *and written* Go *at left*   86 *a superfluous stroke appears over an erasure before* forthe   94 on grownde] ongrownde

Whan þu wynnyst þis worlde with þi wyde
wounde
And puttyst man to paradys with plenty of prys.
To loue þe is my delyte.
Heyl, floure fayr and fre, f. 90v
Lyght from þe Trynyté!
Heyl, blyssyd mote þu be!
Heyl, mayde fayrest in syght!

[SECUNDUS] PASTOR
Heyl, floure ovyr flourys fowndyn in fryght!
Heyl, Cryst, kynde in oure kyth!
Heyl, werker of wele to wonyn us wyth!
Heyl, wynnere, iwys!
Heyl, formere and frende!
Heyl, fellere of þe fende!
Heyl, clad in oure kende!
Heyl, Prince of Paradys!

TERCIUS PASTOR
Heyl, lord ouyr lordys, þat lyggyst ful lowe!
Heyl, kynge ovyr kyngys, þi kynrede to knowe!
Heyl, comely knyth, þe deuyl to ouyrthrowe!
Heyl, flowre of alle!
Heyl, werkere to wynne
Bodyes bowndyn in synne!
Heyl, in a bestys bynne,
Bestad in a stalle!

JOSEPH
Herdys on hylle,
Beth not stylle,
But seyth ȝoure wylle
To many a man:
How God is born
þis mery morn;
þat is forlorn
Fyndyn he can.

F. 90v marked 90 103 SECUNDUS] ij floury s] l *altered from another letter* 118 bestad] d *altered from another letter* (l.?) 119–34 *written two lines as one, divided by two brown virgules and one red, a pattern that also appears after* 120, 128, 132; *virgules following* 124 *lack rubrication* 122 a man] aman

PRIMUS PASTOR

We xull telle
Be dale and hylle
How Harwere of Helle
   Was born þis nyght,
Myrthis to melle
And fendys to quelle
Þat were so felle
   Aȝens his ryght.

f. 91r **SECUNDUS PASTOR**

Farewel, babe and barne of blys!
Farewel, Lord þat lovely is!
Þe to wurchep þi feet I kys,
   On knes to þe I falle.
      The to wurchepe I falle on kne.
      All þis werd may joye of þe,
      Now farewel, Lorde of grett pousté!
   Ȝa, farewel, kynge of alle!

TERCIUS PASTOR

Thow I be þe last þat take my leve,
Ȝit, fayre mullynge, take it nat at no greve.
Now, fayre babe, wele mut þu cheve;
   Fayr chylde, now haue good day!
      Fareweyl, myn owyn dere derlyng!
      Iwys, þu art a ryght fayr thyng.
      Farewel, my Lorde and my swetyng!
   Farewel, born in pore aray!

MARIA

Now, ȝe herdmen, wel mote ȝe be.
   For ȝoure omage and ȝoure syngynge,

148 a ryght] aryght   *Remainder of f. 91r (85 mm) blank. F. 91v blank, except for several scribblings and the following names and motto, all in later hands:*

William Dere
Polerd
Wylliam Dere
John Hasycham
John Taylphott of Parish
Bedonson wee that will not
when we paie when we would
we shall saie (find?) nay
(?) Evosund
John

My sone xal aqwyte ȝow in hefne se
And ȝeue ȝow all ryght good hendynge.
Amen

[*There is no Play 17*]

18
[THE MAGI]

f. 92^{r}

HERODE[S REX] As a lord in ryalté, in non regyon so ryche,
And rulere of all remys, I ryde in ryal aray!
Ther is no lord of lond in lordchep to me lyche,
Non lofflyere, non lofsummere, evyrlestyng is
my lay!

Of bewté and of boldnes I bere evermore þe belle.
Of mayn and of myght I mastyr every man!
I dynge with my dowtynes þe devyl down to helle,
For bothe of hevyn and of herth I am kynge,
sertayn!

I am þe comelyeste kynge clad in gleterynge golde,
Ʒa, and þe semelyeste syre þat may bestryde a
stede!
I welde att my wyll all wyghtys upon molde,
Ʒa, and wurthely I am wrappyd in a wurthy
wede.

Ʒe knyghtys so comely, bothe curteys and kene,
To my paleys wyl I passe full prest, I ȝow plyth.
Ʒe dukys so dowty, folwe me bedene.
Onto my ryal paleys þe wey lyth ful ryght.

[*Play 18*] *The right margins of ff. 92 and 93 drastically cropped; the s.h. on f. 92*^{r} *and part of the playnumber partially cut away*
1 HERODES REX] Herode, *remainder cropped* regyon *interl.* 4 lofflyere] ff *adapted from another letter* 5 *no capitulum* *The capitulum for the fourth stanza mistakenly drawn opposite* 12

Wyghtly fro my stede I skyppe down in hast,
To myn hey3 hallys I haste me in my way.
Ȝe mynstrell, of myrth blowe up a good blast
Whyll I go to chawmere and chaunge myn array.

PRIMUS REX Heyl be ȝe, kyngys tweyne,
Ferre rydyng out of ȝoure regne!
Methynkyth be ȝoure presentys seyne
Ȝe sekyn oure Sauyour.
Fro Saba haue I folwyd ferre
The glemynge of ȝon gay sterre.
A chyldys blood xal bye vs dere
Þat þer is born in bestys boure.

My name is Kynge Baltazare.
f. 92v Of prophetys speche I am ware.
Therfore a ferre wey I fare,
A maydenys childe to seche.
For he made man of þe moolde,
And is kynge of hevyn holde.
I wyl hym offere þe rede golde,
As reson wyl me teche.

SECUNDUS REX Melchizar, þat my name is kydde.
In hote loue myn herte is hydde
To þe blosme upon his bedde,
Born by bestys bynne.
In Tarys I am kynge with crowne
By bankys and brymmys browne.
I haue trauaylid by many a towne
My lordys love to wynne.

I seke hym with ensens sote.
Of all prestys he xal be rote.
His bryght blood xal be oure bote,

17 Wyghtly] *second* y *written over another letter* (*perh.* j) 18 me] m *adapted from another letter?* 20 *an incomplete letter canc. before* chawmere 21 *a letter or notation cropped after* Rex 27 *a letter erased after* bye 47 be] *an* n *erased after the* e

To brynge us out of bende.
  The childe xal be chosyn a preste,
  In all vertuys fownden meste.
  Beforn his faderys fayr breste
Ensens he xal up sende.

TERCIUS REX In Ypotan and Archage
I am kynge knowyn in kage.
To seke a childe of semlant sage
  I haue faryn ryght ferre.
    Jasper is my name knowyn
    In many countrés þat are myn owyn.
    Thorwe byttyr blastys þat gyn blowyn
  I stryke aftere þe sterre.

I brynge myrre to my present, f. 93[r]
A byttyr lycour verament.
For he xal tholyn byttyr dent
  In a maydonys flesch is clad.
On byttyr tre he xal be bent,
Man and God omnypotent;
With byttyr betynge his flesch be rent
  Tyl all his blood be bledde.

HER[ODES REX] Now I regne .... kynge arayd ful rych,
  Rollyd in rynggys and robys of array.
Dukys with dentys I dryve into þe dych,
  My dedys be ful dowty demyd be day!
I xall marryn þo men þat r....yn on myche,
  And þerinne sette here sacrementys sottys ....
      say!

63 tholyn *obliterated and obscured by hole in leaf; the reviser, possibly C, has written* suffyr *over it* 69 HERODES REX] Her, *remainder cropped;* as(?) *and* þi (*or* þat) *erased after* regne *and* lyk a *written over it by the reviser* 73 *the reviser has canc.* men *and interl.* herytykys *above; a word or words* (ra....yn) *erased after* þat *and* beleuyn *written over it by the reviser* a myche *altered by the reviser to* amysse 74 þerinne] -ne *erased* here] *an initial* t *added in black* sottys *altered by the reviser to* sallsse (*for* fallsse)*; the subsequent words* (wole asay?) *partially erased and* þey are I *written over them by the reviser*

þer is no lorde in þis werde þat lokygh me lyche.
For to lame l....... of þe lesse lay
I am jolyere than þe jay,
Stronge thevys to steke,
þat wele oure lawys breke.
On þo wrecchis I wyll be wreke,
And hont hem vndyr ha[y].

In kyrtyl of cammaka kynge am I cladde,
Cruel and curryd in myn crowne knowe!
I sytt in ondyr Sesar in my se...e sadde.
Sorwyn to sottys, such seed wyll I sowe!
Boys now blaberyn, bostynge of a baron bad,
In bed[de] is born be bestys, suche bost is blowe.
f. 93v I xal prune þat pap-hawk and preuyn hym as a pad,
Scheldys and shaftys sh.....h... sowe!
My knyghtys xaln rydyn on rowe,
Knave chylderyn for to qwelle!
Be Mahound, dyngne duke of helle,
Sowre deth his lyff xall selle
Such thrett wolde me throwe!

Styward bolde,
Walke þu on wolde
And wysely beholde

75 werde] *the reviser has added an* l *before the* r lyche *altered to* lyke *by the reviser, who also has added* iwysse 76 *a word* (*?*lovers *?*levers) *following* lame *mostly erased and altered to* herytykkys *by the reviser* 81 hay] *B; MS* ha, *remainder cropped*
Thus revised, 73–6 *would read:*

I xall marryn þo herytykys þat beleuyn amysse,
And þerin sette there sacrementys, fallsse þey are I say!
þer is no lorde in þis we[rl]d þat lokygh me lyke, iwysse,
For to lame herytykkys of þe lesse lay. . . .

84 in ondyr *altered to* herevndyr se...e] *the word partially erased and altered to* sette *by the reviser* 85 seed] *the second* e *ill-formed* 87 bedde] *B; the final letters erased and the word altered to* Bedlem *by the reviser* 88 prune *altered to* pryke *and* pap-hawk *altered to* paddoke *by the reviser* 89 *The words between* and *and* sowe *mostly erased and altered by the reviser to* sperys schall I ther 90 xaln *altered to* xalle *and* a *interl. after* on *by the reviser* 91 b *or* k *canc. by the main scribe before* chylderyn 94 *The reviser has appended* -ys *to* thrett *and has interl.* ouyr before *throwe* 95–150 *written two lines as one, divided by two brown virgules and one red. F93v lacks capitula, which were evidently cropped with the left margin* 95 Styward *canc. by the reviser, whose substituted word* (...or) *has been mostly cut away with the left margin* 96 *The reviser has canc.* on wolde *and written at right* ouyr mowlde

All abowte.
Iff anythynge
Shuld greve þe kynge,
Brynge me tydynge
If þer be ony dowte.

SENESCALLUS Lord kynge in crowne,
I go fro towne.
By bankys browne
I wyll abyde,
And with erys lyste
Est and west
Iff any geste
On grownde gynnyth glyde.

Tunc ibit Senescallus et obuiabit tribus regibus, et dicit eis:

Kyngys iij
Vndyr þis tre,
In þis countré
Why wyll ȝe abyde?
Herowde is kynge
Of þis wonynge.
Onto his dwellynge
Now xul ȝe glyde.

PRIMUS REX Now lede us alle
To þe kyngys halle.
How it befalle,
We pray to the,
Wyttys to wete
He may us pete
In flesshe be glete
Godys frute fre.

SENESCALLUS Folwyth in stownde
Vpon þis grownde.
To þe castel rownde

100 þe *altered to* þat(*?*) *in black* 110 s.d. *a notation interl. above the s.d. by the reviser has been partially cut away with the left margin;* [H]erodys nupre *remains*

I xal ȝow tech,
Where kynge gynny[th] wyde
Vp in þis tyde
In pompe and pryde
His myght gynnyth reche.

Sere kyng in trone,
Here comyth anone
f. 94r By strete and stone
Kyngys thre.
They bere present.
What thei haue ment,
Ne whedyr they arn bent
I cannot se.

HERODES REX I xal hem craue
What they haue.
Iff they raue
Or waxyn wood,
I xal hem reve,
Here wyttys deve,
Here hedys cleve,
And schedyn here blood!

PRIMUS REX Heyl be þu, kynge in kage ful hye!
Heyl, we nyghe þin halle ryght nye.
Knowyst þu ought þat chylde slye?
He is born hereabowth.
He is born of a mayd ȝynge,
He xal be kynge ouyr every kynge.
We go to seke þat louely thynge,
To hym fayn wolde I lowth.

SECUNDUS REX Balaam spak in prophecye
A sterre xulde ful louelye
Lythtyn upon mayd Marye,
Comyn of Jacobys kynne.

131 where] h *interl.* gynnyth] gynny; gynny *canc. and* wonyt *interl. above by the reviser*
155 a mayd] amayd 160 a sterre] asterre

þe childe is born and lyth hereby,
Blomyd in a maidenys body.
A sterre hath strekyn upon þe sky
And ledde us fayr be fenne.

TERCIUS REX The sterre hath ledde us out of þe est
To seke a baron born best.
He xal be kynge of myghtys mest,
As prophecy gynnyth spelle.
We be kyngys in wey wery.
Syr kynge, for þi curtesy,
Telle us to þat childe so louely;
In what town gynnyth he dwelle?

HERODES REX ȝe thre kyngys rekenyd be rowe, f. 94[v]
Ley now downe ȝoure wurdys lowe.
Such a carpynge is vnknowe,
Onrekenyd in my regne!
I am a kynge of hyȝ degré,
þer xal non ben above me!
I haue florens and fryhthis fre,
Parkys and powndys pleyne.

But goth to fynde þat ȝe sech;
And yf ȝe knowe such a lech
And ȝe hym fynde, I ȝow besech,
Comyth aȝen be me.
And I xal be both blyth and bowne
þat all worchep to hym be done;
With reuerens I xal seke hym sone
And honour hym on kne.

And þerfore, kyngys, I ȝow pray,
Whan ȝe haue don ȝoure jurnay,
Come aȝen þis same way,
þe trewth to me to telle.

164 maidenys] *the* d *partially written over the* i 165 A sterre] Asterre 172 kynge] k *malformed;* g *written over another letter* (k?) 175 REX] -x *partially cropped with the right margin* 187 do *canc. before* bowne

Come and telle me as ȝe spede,
And I xal qwyte ryght wel ȝoure mede,
With gold, and tresour, and rych wede,
With furrys rych and wurth pelle.

PRIMUS REX
Kynge, haue good day!
I go my way
To seche
Lord of Myght;
He xal be ryght
Oure leche.

SECUNDUS REX
Kynge ful sterne,
Be felde and ferne
I goo
To sekyn a kynge,
He takyth wonynge
In woo.

TERCIUS REX
If we hym fynde
Oure kynge ful kynde
Be a may,
From kynge and qwen
We comyn aȝen
Þis day.

HERODES REX
A, fy, fy on talys þat I haue ben tolde
Here beforn my cruel kne!
How xulde a barn wax so bolde
Be bestys yf he born be?
f. 95r He is yong and I am old,
An hardy kyng of hye degré.
This daye tho kynggys xal be kold
If þey cum ageyne be me!
My goddys I xall vp reyse!
A derke devyll with falsnese, I saye,

119–216 *written three lines as one, divided by virgules as before* 212 kynde] y *altered from an* e, *or vice versa* 217 transient *written by another hand at right in black* *Ff. 95–6 written by Scribe C on 'Hand' paper, a different kind from that of the rest of the play. They are not rubricated, and some of the writing on ff. 95r and 96r has been cut away with the right margins* 223 xal be] xalbe

Shall cast a myst in þe kynggys eye;
Be bankys and be dalys drey,
Þat be derk þei xall cum this weyys.

PRIMUS [REX] Go we to sek owr Lord and our lech,
Yon stere will us tech þe weyis full sone.
To saue vs from myschyff God I here besech,
Onto his joyis þat we may rech;
I pray hem of this bone.

Tunc ibunt reges cum muneribus ad Jesum, et Primus Rex dicit:

Heyle be þou, kyng cold clade!
Heyll, with maydynnys mylk fade!
Heyll, I cum to þe with gold glade.
As wese wrytyng bere it record,
Gold is þe rycheste metall,
And to weryng most ryall.
Gold I gyff þe in this hall
And know þe for my Lorde.

SECUNDUS R[EX] Lorde, I knele vpon my kne,
Sote encence I offere to the.
Thow xalte be þe fyrst of hyȝ degré,
Non so mekell of myght!
In Goddys howse, as men xall se,
Thow xalt honour þe Trynité;
Iij personys in oon Gode free,
And all oo Lord of Myght.

TERCIUS R[EX] Lord, I knele downe be thy bede, f. 95[v]
In maydyns fleshe þou arte hede.
Thy name xal be wyde rede,
And kyng ouyr all kynggys.
Byttyr myre to þe I brynge,
For byttyr dentys on þe þei xall dyng;
And byttyr deth xall be þy endyng,
And þerfor I make mornyng.

228 *a miswritten letter canc. after* and 230 REX *supplied, the original cropped* 239 þe *interl.* 243 REX] R, *remainder cropped* knele *canc. before* kne 245 dr *canc. before* degré 251 REX] R, *remainder cropped* 258 mornyng] *a final* ys *erased*

MARIA

Kynggys kynde,
Frome þe fende
God yow defende.
Homwarde ȝe wende,
And to your placys ȝe lende
þat ȝe xulde tende.

PRIMUS REX

Now haue we þe place fownde,
To Herode go we this stownde.
With owr wordys we were bownde
That we xulde cum ageyne.
Go we apace and sey owr spech,
For we haue fownde oure Lord and lech.
All þe truth we wyll hem tech,
How þe kyng is borne of a quene.

SECUNDUS REX

Myn hede is hevy as lympe of leede,
But yf I slepe I am adrede
My witt xall fare þe warse.
I wax hevy in lyme and fla[n]ke,
Downe I ley me vpon this banke,
Vnder this bryght sterre, iwys.

TERCIUS REX

Broþer, I must lye þe bye,
I will go neuyr ouyr þis stye
Tyll I haue a slepe.
The yong kyng and his moþyr Mary
Save vs all frome euery velany.
Now Cryst vs save and kepe.

f. 96r PRIMUS REX

Such hevynese haue vs cawght,
I must drynk with yow a drawght,
To slepe a lytyll whyle.
I am hevy heed and footte,
I xulde stumbyll at resch and root
And I xuld goo a myle.

273 is *interl.* 276 flanke] flamke 283 all *interl.* Such hevynese haue vs cawght *written above* 285, *but evidently too far to left, and so canc. and rewritten* 287 wyll *canc. before* whyle

Hic dormiunt reges, et venit angelus et dicit eis:

ANGE[LUS] Ȝe kynggys on this hill,
Werk ȝe not aftyr Herodys wyll.
For yf ȝe do he wyll yow kyll
þis day or nyght.
My Lorde yow sent this tydyng
To rest yow, kynggys in rych clothyng.
And whan ȝe rysyn and goo to your dwellyng,
Tak home þe wey full ryght.

Whether þat ȝe be wakyn or slepe,
My Lorde God xall yow keppe.
In goode tyme ȝe dede down drepe
To take yowr rest.
Herowdys, to þe devyl he tryste f. 97r
To marre ȝow in a myrke myste.
My Lord God is ful of lyste
To glathe ȝow for his geste.

And þerfore, kyngys, whan ȝe ryse,
Wendyth forth be weys wyse
þer ȝoure hall be sett in syse
In dyverse londe.
Fadyr of God in allthynge
Hath ȝow grawntyd his swete blyssynge.
He xal ȝow saue from all shendynge
With his ryght honde.

Tunc surgant reges, et dicat Primus Rex:

[PRIMUS REX] A bryght sterre ledde us into Bedleem;
A bryghtere thynge I saw in drem,

291 ANGELUS] Ange, *remainder cropped* 293 For *written in left margin and followed by a virgule* 296 To *written in left margin and followed by a virgule* 299 be *interl.* slepyne *canc. before* slepe Herode to be devyll he tryst *written below* 302 *on f. 96r as catchword. Some letters and* Loke ferþ *written at right below* 302. *Remainder of f. 96r (78 mm) and all of f. 96v blank. With f. 97r the main hand resumes* 303 *a letter erased before* tryste 304 a myrke *altered by the reviser to* a thyrke 309 *a hole after* hall 311 þe *written at the left by the reviser* 314 s.d. *a red loop of the sort that normally precedes a s.h. appears before* Primus 315 *s.h. supplied*

Bryghtere than þe sunnebeem—
An aungell I saw ryght here.
þe fayre floure þat here gan falle,
From Herowdys Kynge he gan vs kalle.
He taught us hom tyll oure halle
A wey by another mere.

SECUNDUS REX
I sawghe a syght,
Myn hert is lyght
To wendyn home.
God, ful of myght,
Hath us dyght
Fro develys dome.

TERCIUS REX
Oure God I blysse.
He sent us, iwys,
His aungel bryght.
Now we wake
þe wey to take
Home full ryght.

f. 97v

19
[THE PURIFICATION]

SYMEON JUSTUS
I haue be prest in Jherusalem here
And tawth Goddys lawe many a ȝere,
Desyrynge in all my mende
þat þe tyme we[re] neyhand nere
In which Goddys son xul apere
In erthe to take mankende,
Or I deyd þat I myght fynde
My Savyour with myn ey to se.

323–34 *written three lines as one, divided as before* 331 bl *canc. before* bryght 332 be *interl. by the reviser before* wake 333 to *canc. and* whe *interl. above by the reviser* *Remainder of f. 97r (67 mm) blank.*

[*Play 19*] *A cross sign appears at top left of f. 97v. A dot appears in loop of capitulum for stanza 1* 1 *s.h. in Textura Quadrata* 4 were] *B; MS* we

But þat it is so longe behynde,
It is grett dyscomforte onto me.

For I wax olde and wante my myght
And begynne to fayle my syght,
þe more I sorwe þis tyde,
Save only, as I telle ȝow ryght,
God of his grace hath me hyght
þat blysful byrth to byde.
Wherfore now here besyde
To sancta sanctorum wyl I go,
To pray God to be my gyde,
To comfort me aftyr my wo.

Here Symeon knelyth and seyth:

A, gode God in Trinité,
Whow longe xal I abyde the
Tyl þat þu þi son doth sende,
þat I in erth myght hym se?
Good Lord, consydyr to me—
I drawe fast to an ende—
þat, or my strenthis fro me wende,
Gode Lorde, send dow[n] þi son,
þat I with my ful mende
Myght wurchepp hym if I con;

Bothe with my fete and hondys to f. 98r
To go to hym and handele also,
My eyn to se hym, in certayn,
My tonge for to speke hym to,
And all my lemys to werke and do,
In his servyse to be bayn,
Send forth þi son, my Lord sovereyn,
Hastely, anon, withowte teryenge;
For fro þis world I wolde be fayn—
It is contrary to my levynge.

23 þu *deleted after* son 28 down] *D; MS* dow 30 Angelus *written in left margin by another hand* 33 se hym in certayn *and several other words on ff. 98r and 98v discoloured by stains*

ANGELUS Symeon, leff þi careful stevene,
For þi prayer is herd in hevene.
To Jherusalem fast now wynne,
And þer xalt se ful evene
He þat is Goddys son for to nemene
In þe templ[e] þer þu dwellyst inne.
The dyrknes of orygynal synne
He xal make lyght and clarefye.
And now þe dede xal begynne
Whiche hath be spokyn be prophecye.

SYMEON A, I thank þe, Lord of Grace,
þat hath grauntyd me tyme and space
To lyve and byde thys!
And I wyl walk now to þe place
Where I may se þi sonys face,
Which is my joye and blys.
I was nevyr lyghtere, iwys,
To walke nevyr herebeforn!
For a mery tyme now is
Whan God, my Lord, is born!

ANNA PROPHETESSA Al heyl, Symeon, what tydyngys with ȝow?
Why make ȝe al þis myrth now?
Telle me whedyr ȝe fare.
SYMEON Anne Prophetes, and ȝe wyst whov,
So xulde ȝe, I make avow,
And all maner men þat are.
For Goddys son, as I declare,
Is born to bye mankende!
f. 98v Oure Savyour is come to sesyn oure care,
þerfore haue I grett merth to wende.

And þat is þe cawse I hast me
Onto þe temple hym to se.
And þerfore lett me not, good frende.

41 cum do *written at right in black, remainder cropped* 46 temple] templ 73 t *or a cross sign deleted by stroke and deleting dot before* And

ANNA Now blyssyd be God in Trinyté
Syn þat tyme is come to be!
And with ȝow wyl I wende
To se my Savyour ende,
And wurchepp hym also
With all my wytt and my ful mende.
As I am bound now wyl I do.

Et tunc ibunt ambo ad templum et prophetissa.

SYMEON In þe temple of God, who vndyrstod,
þis day xal be offeryd with mylde mood
Which þat is kynge of alle,
þat xal be skorgyd and shedde his blood
And aftyr dyen on þe rood
Withowtyn cawse to calle;
For whos Passyon þer xal beffalle
Swych a sorwe bothe sharpe and smerte,
þat as a swerd perce it xalle
Ȝevene thorwe his moderys herte.

ANNA PROP[HETISSA] Ȝa, þat xal be, as I wel fende,
For redempcyon of all mankende,
þat blysse for to restore
Whiche hath be lost fro oute of mende,
As be oure fadyr of oure owyn kende,
Adam, and Eue beffore.

MARIA Joseph, my husbond, withowtyn mys,
Ȝe wote þat fourty days nere is
Sythe my sonys byrth ful ryght.
Wherfore we must to þe temple, iwys, f. 99r
þer for to offre oure sone of blys
Up to his fadyr in hyght.
And I in Goddys syght
Puryfyed for to be,

81 *a miswritten letter canc. before* vndyrstod 91 PROPHETISSA] Prop, *remainder cropped* fende *altered to* fynde *by another hand* 97 *s.h. obscured by a blot* 103–6 *written two lines as one, divided by double virgules*

In clene sowle with al my myght,
In presence of þe Trinyté.

JOSEPH To be purefyed haue ȝe no nede,
Ne þi son to be offryd, so God me spede.
For fyrst þu art ful clene,
Vndefowlyd in thought and dede;
And anothyr, þi son, withowtyn drede,
Is God and man to mene.
Wherefore it nedyd not to bene,
But to kepe þe lawe on Moyses wyse.
Whereffore we xal take us betwene
Dowys and turtelys for sacrefyce.

Et ibunt ad templum.

SYMEON All heyl, my kyndely comfortour!
ANNA PROPHETISSA All heyl, mankyndys creatoure!
SYMEON All heyl, þu God of Myght!
ANNA PROPHETISSA All heyl, mankyndys Savyour!
SYMEON All heyl, bothe kynge and emperour!
ANNA PROPHETISSA All heyl, as it is ryght.
SYMEON All heyl also, Mary bryght!
ANNA PROPHETISSA All heyl, salver of seknes!
SYMEON All heyl, lanterne of lyght!
ANNA PROPHETISSA All heyl, þu modyr of mekenes!

MARIA Symeon, I vndyrstand and se
Þat bothyn of my sone and me
Ȝe haue knowynge clere.
And also in ȝoure compané
My sone desyryth for to be,
And þerffore haue hym here.

118 creatoure] a *altered from another letter*

Et accipiet Jhesum.

SYMEON Welcome, prynce withowte pere! f. 99v
Welcome, Goddys owyn sone!
Welcome, my Lord so dere,
Welcome with me to wone.

Suscepimus Deus misericordiam tuam.

Lord God in mageste,
We haue receyvyd þis day of þe
In myddys of þi temple here
Thy grett mercy, as we may se.
Therfore þi name of grett degré
Be wurchepyd in all manere
Over all þis werde, bothe fer and nere,
Ȝevyn onto þe [vterest] ende.
For now is man owt of daungere,
And rest and pes to all mankende.

Nunc dimittis seruum tuum, Domine, et cetera.

The psalme songyn every vers, and þerqwyl Symeon pleyth with þe child; and qwhan þe psalme is endyd he seyth:

Now lete me dye, Lorde, and hens pace,
For I, þi servaunt in þis place
Haue sen my Sauyour dere,
Whiche þu hast ordeyned beforn þe face
Of al mankynde þis tyme of grace
Opynly to appere.
Þi lyth is shynand clere
To all mankyndys savacyon.
Mary, take ȝoure childe now here,
And kepe wel þis, manis savacyon.

136a *and* 146a *written in Textura Quadrata* 144 vterest] vnterest

f. 100r ANNA PROPHETISSA
Ne I rowth nere to dye also,
For more than fowre skore ȝere and to
þis tyme hath bede to se.
And sythe þat it is come þerto,
What Goddys wyl is with me to do,
Ryght evyn so mot it be.

JOSEPH
Take here these candelys thre,
Mary, Symeon, and Anne.
And I xal take þe fowrte to me
To offre oure childe up thanne.

MARIA
Hyest fadyr, God of powere,
Ȝoure owyn dere son I offre ȝow here.
As I to ȝoure lawe am sworn,
Receyve þi childe in glad manere.
For he is þe fyrst, þis childe so dere,
þat of his modyr is born.
But þow I offre hym ȝow beforn,
Good Lord, ȝit ȝyf me hym aȝen,
For my comforte were fully lorn
If we xuld longe asondyr ben.

Mari leyth þe childe on þe autere.

JOSEPH
Sere prest of þe temple, now
Haue he[re] fyff pens vnto ȝow,
Oure childe aȝen to take.
It is þe lawe, as ȝe woot how.

CAPELLANUS
Joseph, ȝe an do ryght anow
As for ȝoure childys sake.
But othere offerynge ȝett must ȝe make.
And þerfore take ȝoure sone, Mary.
In meche joye ȝe may awake
Whylys he is in ȝoure company.

f. 100v MARIA
Therto I am ful glad and fayn
For to receyve my childe agayn,

To all mankyndys *canc. in red below* 157   162 ȝ *canc. before* evyn   177 now] o *smudged and* o *interl. above*   178 here] *B; MS* he   *F. 100v marked* 100   *Loop of capitulum preceding* 187 *dotted*

Ellys were I to blame;
And afterewarde for to be bayn
To offre to God, in ful certayn,
As in my sonys name
With fowlys bothe wylde and tame.
For in Goddys servyse I xal nevyr irke.
JOSEPH Lo, Mary, haue here tho same
To do þi dewtys of Holy Kyrke.

And þer Mary offeryth fowlys onto þe autere and seyth:

MARIA Allmyghtyfful Fadyr, mercyful Kynge,
Receyvyth now þis lytyl offrynge,
For it is þe fyrst in degré
Þat ȝoure lytyl childe so ȝynge
Presentyth today be my shewyng
To ȝoure hyȝ magesté.
Of his sympyl poverté,
Be his devocyon and my good wylle,
Vpon ȝoure awtere receyve of me
Ȝoure sonys offrynge, as it is skylle.
1468

20

f. 101r

[THE SLAUGHTER OF THE INNOCENTS; THE DEATH OF HEROD]

Tunc, respiciens, Senescallus vadyt ad Herodem dicens:

SENESCALLUS Lord, I haue walkyd be dale and hylle
And wayted as it is ȝoure wyll.
The kyngys iij stelyn awey full styll
Thorwe Bedleem londe.
They wyl nevyr, so moty the,

194 servyse *interl.* 202 *a letter* (ȝ?) *canc. in brown and red before* To 204 *some letters written by another hand in right margin* 206 1468 *written at right and looped in red like a s.h.* *The remainder of f.* 100v (64 *mm*) *blank, except for a cross sign*

[*Play* 20] *A rubricated* 1 *erased before the playnumber* 20

Com in þe lond of Galylé
For to se ȝoure fay[r] ceté
Ne dedys of ȝoure honde.

HERODES REX I ryde on my rowel, ryche in my regne!
Rybbys ful reed with rape xal I rende!
Popetys and pap-hawkys I xal puttyn in peyne,
With my spere prevyn, pychyn, and to-pende!
The gomys with gold crownys ne gete nevyr [geyn]!
To seke þo sottys sondys xal I sende.
Do howlott howtyn, Hoberd and Heyn!
Whan here barnys blede vndyr credyl bende,
Sharply I xal hem shende!
The knaue childeryn þat be
In all Israel countré,
Thei xul haue blody ble
For on I calde vnkende!

It is tolde in Grw
His name xulde be Jesu
Ifownde.
To haue hym ȝe gon;
Hewe þe flesch with þe bon,
And gyf hym wownde!

Now, kene knyghtys, kythe ȝoure craftys,
And kyllyth knaue chylderyn and castyth hem in clay!
Shewyth on ȝoure shulderys scheldys and schaftys,
Shapyht amonge schelchownys a shyrlyng shray!

7 fayr] *B; MS* fay 9 *name-loop omitted from s.h.* 13 gomys *altered in black to* gollys *or* gowys, ne *canc. and* þei *interl. after* gete *in black by a reviser* geyn] ageyn 22–7 *written three lines as one, divided by two brown virgules and one red* 25 *an incomplete letter canc. before* ȝe 28 kythe *canc. and* scharpe *interl. above*, craftys *canc. and* knyvys *interl. above by Scribe C* 31 schelchownys] *altered to* schelchowthys *by the reviser* a shyrlyng] ashyrlyng shar *canc. before* shray

Doth rowncys rennyn with rakynge raftys
Tyl rybbys be to-rent with a reed ray!
Lete no barne beleve onbete baftys
Tyl a beggere blede be bestys baye!
Mahound þat best may. f. 101ᵛ
I warne ȝow, my knyghtys,
A barn is born, I plyghtys,
Wolde clymbyn kynge and knytys
And lett my lordly lay.

Knyghtys wyse,
Chosyn ful chyse,
Aryse, aryse,
And take ȝoure tolle!
And every page
Of ij ȝere age,
Or evyr ȝe swage,
Sleyth ilke a fool!

On of hem alle
Was born in stalle.
Folys hym calle
Kynge in crowne!
With byttyr galle
He xall down falle!
My myght in halle
Xal nevyr go down!

PRIMUS MILES I xall sle scharlys
And qwenys with therlys;
Here knaue gerlys
I xal steke!

32 rowncys *canc. and* your speris *interl. above by the reviser* rennyn] rennyne *with deleting dot under final* e rakynge *canc. and* longe (*?*) *interl. above by the reviser* 34 barne *canc. and* chyld *interl. above by the reviser* 37–72 *written two lines as one, divided as before* 39 cly *and some miswritten letters canc. in red before* clymbyn ky *canc. before* knytys 42 cos *or* cof *canc. in red before* chosyn 48 fool] *or* foal 51 Angelus *written in left margin in another hand*

Forth wyl I spede
To don hem blede.
Thow gerlys grede
We xul be wreke!

SECUNDUS MILES
For swerdys sharpe
As an harpe
Quenys xul karpe
And of sorwe synge!
Barnys ȝonge,
They xul be stunge;
Thurwe levyr and lunge
We xal hem stynge!

ANGELUS
Awake, Joseph, and take þi wyff,
Thy chylde also, ryd belyff.
For Kynge Herowde with sharpe knyff
His knyghtys he doth sende.
The Fadyr of Hevyn hath to þe sent
Into Egypte þat þu be bent,
For cruel knyghtys þi childe haue ment
With swerd to sle and shende.

JOSEPH
Awake, good wyff, out of ȝoure slepe,
And of ȝoure childe takyght good kepe
Whyl I ȝoure clothis ley on hepe
And trus hem on þe asse.
Kynge Herowde þe chylde wyl scloo,
Þerfore to Egypte muste we goo—
An aungel of God seyd me soo.
And þerfore lete us passe.

f. 102[r] *Tunc ibunt milites ad pueros occidendos, et dicat Prima Femina:*

PRIMA FEMINA
Longe lullynge haue I lorn!
Alas! Qwhy was my baron born?
With swappynge swerde now is he shorn,
Þe heed ryght fro þe nekke!

70 stunge] g *miswritten or adapted from another letter*

Shanke and shulderyn is al to-torn!
Sorwyn I se behyndyn and beforn,
Both mydnyth, mydday, and at morn—
   Of my lyff I ne recke!

SECUNDA FEMINA
Serteynly I sey þe same:
Gon is all my good game!
My lytyll childe lyth all lame
   Þat lullyd on my pappys.
      My fourty wekys gronynge
      Hath sent me sefne ȝere sorwynge.
      Mykyl is my mornynge
   And ryght hard arne myn happys.

PRIMUS MILES
Lorde in trone,
Makyght no mone.
Qwenys gyn grone
   In werdl aboute.
      Upon my spere
      A gerle I bere,
      I dare well swere.
   Lett moderys howte!

SECUNDUS MILES
Lord, we han spad
As ȝe bad:
Barnis ben blad
   And lyne in dych!
      Flesch and veyn
      Han tholyd peyn.
      And ȝe xul reyne
   Euyrmore rych!

HERODES REX
Ȝe xul haue stedys
To ȝoure medys,
Londys and ledys,
   Fryth and fe!

105–28 *written two lines as one, divided by virgules as above*   108 go hom wardys *written in right margin in another hand, perhaps by C*

Wele haue ȝe wrought,
My fo is sought,
To deth is he brought!
Now come up to me.

In sete now am I sett as kynge of myghtys most.
All þis werd for þer loue to me xul þei lowt,
Both of hevyn, and of erth, and of helle cost!
For dygne of my dygnyté þei haue of me dowt!
f. 102v þer is no lord lyke on lyve to me wurth a toost,
Nother kyng nor kayser in all þis worlde abought!
If any brybour do bragge or blowe aȝens my bost,
I xal rappe þo rebawdys and rake þem on rought
With my bryght bronde!
þer xal be neythe[r] kayser nere kynge
But þat I xal hem down dynge,
Lesse þan he at my byddynge
Be buxum to myn honde!

Now, my jentyll and curteys knyghtys, herke to me þis stownde:
Good tyme sone, methynkygh, at dyner þat we were.
Smertly, þerfore, sett a tabyll anon here ful sownde,
Couerid with a coryous cloth and with rych wurthy fare—
Servyse for þe lovelyest lorde þat levynge is on grownde.
Beste metys and wurthyest wynes loke þat ȝe non spare,
þow þat a lytel pynt xulde coste a thowsand pownde!
Bryngе alwey of þe beste, for coste take ȝe no care.

130 lowt *partially obscured by a blot* 131 hevyn *canc. in red before* helle cost 135 or bragger *canc. in red before* do 138 neyther] neythey 148 thowsand] Ml

Anon þat it be done!
SENESCALLUS My lorde, þe tabyl is redy dyght.
Here is watyr, now wasch forthryght.
Now blowe up, mynstrall, with all ȝoure
myght!
Þe servyse comyth in sone.

HERODES REX Now am I sett at mete
And wurthely servyd at my degré.
Com forth, knyghtys, sytt down and ete
And be as mery as ȝe kan be.
PRIMUS MILES Lord, at ȝowre byddynge we take oure sete,
With herty wyl obey we the.
Þer is no lorde of myght so grett
Thorwe all þis werde in no countré,
In wurchepp to abyde. f. 103r J quire
HERODES I was nevyr meryer herebeforn
Sythe þat I was fyrst born
Than I am now ryght in þis morn—
In joy I gynne to glyde!

MORS Ow! I herde a page make preysyng of pride!
All prynces he passyth, he wenyth, of powsté.
He wenyth to be þe wurthyest of all þis werde
wyde,
Kynge ovyr all kyngys þat page wenyth to be!
He sent into Bedlem to seke on every syde,
Cryst for to qwelle yf þei myght hym se.
But of his wykkyd wyl, lurdeyn, ȝitt he lyede!
Goddys sone doth lyve! Þer is no lord but he.
Ouyr all lordys he is kynge.
I am Deth, Goddys masangere.
Allmyghty God hath sent me here
Ȝon lordeyn to sle, withowtyn dwere,
For his wykkyd werkynge.

155 REX] x *partially cropped* 179 *a letter* (w*?*) *canc. in red before* Ȝon

I am sent fro God; Deth is my name.
Allthynge þat is on grownd I welde at my wylle:
Both man, and beste, and byrdys wylde and tame,
Whan þat I come them to, with deth I do them kylle.
Erbe, gres, and tres stronge, take hem all in-same;
Ȝa, þe grete myghty okys with my dent I spylle.
What man þat I wrastele with, he xal ryght sone haue schame—
I ȝeve hym such a trepett he xal evyrmore ly stylle.
For Deth kan no sporte.
Wher I smyte þer is no grace,
For aftere my strook man hath no space
To make amendys for his trespace
But God hym graunt comforte.

f. 103v Ow! Se how prowdely ȝon kaytyff sytt at mete!
Of deth hath he no dowte: he wenyth to leve evyrmore!
To hym wyl I go and ȝeve hym such an hete
Þat all þe lechis of þe londe his lyf xul nevyr restore.
Aȝens my dredful dentys it vaylyth nevyr to plete!
Or I hym part fro I xal hym make ful pore.
All þe blood of his body I xal hym owt swete,
For now I go to sle hym with strokys sad and sore,
Þis tyde.
Bothe hym and his knyghtys all,
I xal hem make to me but thrall.
With my spere sle hem I xall
And so cast down his pride!

HERODES REX Now, kende knyghtys, be mery and glad,
With all good diligens shewe now sum myrth!

186 des *or* def *canc. before* dent 194 kaytyff] t *adapted from another letter*
201 strokys] r *smudged* 202 *preceded by a capitulum*

For, be gracyous Mahound, more myrth nevyr I had,
Ne nevyr more joye was inne from tyme of my byrth!
For now my fo is ded and prendyd as a padde.
Aboue me is no kynge on grownd nere on gerth.
Merthis, þerfore, make ȝe, and be ryght nothynge sadde.
Spare nother mete nor drynke, and spare for no dyrthe
Of wyne nor of brede.
For now am I a kynge alone,
So wurthy as I may þer be none!
Þerfore, knyghtys, be mery echone,
For now my fo is dede.

PRIMUS MILES Whan þe boys sprawlyd at my sperys hende,
By Sathanas oure syre, it was a goodly syght!
A good game it was þat boy for to shende
Þat wolde a bene oure kynge and put ȝow from ȝoure ryght.

SECUNDUS MILES Now trewly, my lorde þe kynge, we had ben vnhende, f. 104r
And nevyr non of us able for to be a knyght,
If þat any of us to hem had ben a frende
And a savyd any lyff aȝen þi mekyl myght,
From deth hem to flytt.

HERODES REX Amongys all þat grett rowthte,
He is ded, I haue no dowte.
Þerfore, menstrell, rownd abowte,
Blowe up a mery fytt!

Hic, dum buccinant, Mors interficiat Herodem et duos milites subito, et Diabolus recipiat eos

DIABOLUS All oure! All oure! Þis catel is myn!
I xall hem brynge onto my celle.

212 gerth] e *adapted from an* r *by another hand, possibly Scribe C*
224 vnhende] hende *canc. and* kende *interl. above*
234 d *canc. before* celle

I xal hem teche pleys fyn,
And shewe such myrthe as is in helle!
It were more bettyr amongys swyn
Þat evyrmore stynkyn, þerbe to dwelle,
For in oure logge is so gret peyn
Þat non erthely tonge can telle!
With ȝow I go my way.
I xal ȝow bere forth with me
And shewe ȝow sportys of oure gle.
Of oure myrthis now xal ȝe se
And evyr synge 'Welaway!'

MORS Off Kynge Herowde all men beware,
Þat hath rejoycyd in pompe and pryde.
For all his boste of blysse ful bare,
He lyth now ded here on his syde.
For whan I come I cannot spare;
Fro me no whyht may hym hyde.
Now is he ded and cast in care
In helle pytt evyr to abyde—
His lordchep is al lorn.
f. 104v Now is he as pore as I,
Wormys mete is his body.
His sowle in helle ful peynfully
Of develis is al to-torn.

All men dwellyng upon þe grownde,
Beware of me, be myn councel;
For feynt felachep in me is fownde—
I kan no curtesy, as I ȝow tel!
For, be a man nevyr so sownde,
Of helth in herte nevyr so wel,
I come sodeynly within a stownde.
Me withstande may no castel!
My jurnay wyl I spede.
Of my comyng no man is ware,
For whan men make most mery fare,

255–8 *written two lines as one, divided by brown virgules* 269 me *canc. before* mery

þan sodeynly I cast hem in care,
And sle þem evyn in dede!

Thow I be nakyd and pore of array
And wurmys knawe me al abowte,
3it loke ȝe drede me nyth and day;
For whan Deth comyth ȝe stande in dowte!
Evyn lyke to me, as I ȝow say,
Shull all ȝe be here in þis rowte,
Whan I ȝow chalange at my day,
I xal ȝow make ryght lowe to lowth
And nakyd for to be.
Amongys wormys, as I ȝow telle,
Vndyr þe erth xul ȝe dwelle,
And thei xul etyn both flesch and felle,
As þei haue don me.

21

f. 106^{r}

[CHRIST AND THE DOCTORS]

Modo de doctoribus disputantibus cum Jesu in templo

PRIMUS DOCTOR Scripture sacre esse dinoscimur doctos,
We to bere þe belle of all maner clergyse.
SECUNDUS DOCTOR Velud rosa omnium florum flos,
Lyke onto us was nevyr clerke so wyse.
PRIMUS DOCTOR Loke what scyens ȝe kan devyse
Of redynge, wrytynge, and trewe ortografye,
Amongys all clerkys we bere þe prysse
Of gramer, cadens, and of prosodye.

SECUNDUS DOCTOR No clerke abyl to bere oure book
Of versyfyeng nor of other scyens.

274 d *canc. before* nyth *Remainder of f. 104*^{v} *(56 mm) blank. F. 105 blank except for* all men dwellyng upon the *written near the top of f. 105*^{r} *in another hand and a scribbled word on f. 105*^{v}

[*Play 21*] *Initial Latin line looped and underscored in red*
7 all] ll *altered from another letter; a letter (i?) interl. above* a

Of swete musyke whoso wyll look,
Seke no ferther but to oure presens.
Of dyaletyk we haue þe hyȝ excellence,
Of sophestrye, logyk, and phylosophye.
Ageyn oure argemente is no recystence
In metaphesyk ne astronomye.

PRIMUS DOCTOR
Of calculacyon and negremauncye,
Also of augrym and of asmatryk,
O lynyacyon þat longyth to jematrye,
Of dyetis and domys þat longyth to phesyk.
In all þis scyens is non us lyke
In Caton, Gryscysme, nor Doctrynal.
And for endytynge with retoryke,
þe hyest degré is oure be call.

SECUNDUS DOCTOR
In grett canon and in cevyle lawe,
Also in scyens of polycye,
f. 106v Is non to us wurthe an hawe.
Of all cunnynge we bere þe maystrye.
Therfore in þis temple we sytt on hye
And of most wurchep kepe þe souereynté.
þer is on erthe no man so wurthye
þe hyȝ stat to holdyn as we tweyn be.

JESUS
Omnis sciencia a Domino Deo est:
Al wytt and wysdam, of God it is lent.
Of all ȝoure lernynge withinne ȝoure brest
Thank hyghly þat Lord þat hath ȝow sent.
Thorwe bost and pryde ȝoure soulys may be shent.
Of wytt and wysdome ȝe haue not so mech
But God may make at hese entente
Of all ȝoure connynge many man ȝow lech.

15 argern *canc. in red before* argemente 16 metaphesyk] a *written over an erased letter* (r*?*) 23 retor, *with* o *interl., canc. in red before* retoryke 24 be call *canc. and* over all *interl. above in black by a reviser* 34 sent *canc. before* lent

PRIMUS DOCTOR
Goo hom, lytyl babe, and sytt on þi moderys lappe!
And put a mokador aforn þi brest,
And pray þi modyr to fede þe with þe pappe.
Of þe for to lerne we desyre not to lest.

SECUNDUS DOCTOR
Go to þi dyner, for þat behovyth the best!
Whan þu art athreste, þan take þe a sowke.
Aftyr, go to cradyl, þerin to take þi rest,
For þat canst þu do bettyr þan for to loke on book.

JESUS
Stondynge þat ȝe be so wytty and wyse,
Can ȝe owth tellyn how þis werde was wrought?
How longe xal it laste can ȝe devyse
With all þe cunnynge þat ȝe han sought?

PRIMUS DOCTOR
Nay, all erthely clerkys þat telle can nought:
It passyth oure wytt þat for to contryve.
It is not possyble abought to be brought: f. 107r
Þe worldys endyng no man kan dysscryve.

JESUS
How it was wrought and how longe it xal endure,
Þat I telle be good delyberacyon.
Not only þerof but of every creature,
How it is wrought I knowe þe plasmacyon.

SECUNDUS DOCTOR
Of þi wurdys I haue skorne and derys[y]on.
How schulde a chylde þat nevyr lettyr dude lere
Com to þe wytt of so hyȝ cognysion
Of þe grete werkys þat so wundyrfull were?

JESUS
Allthynge is brought to informacyon
Be thre personys, oo God in Trynité.
And on of þo thre hath take incarnacyon,
Bothe flesch and blood, of a mayd fre.

42 mokador] *second* o *malformed* 44 to] t *altered from another letter* lyest *canc. in red before* lest 56 worldys] l *adapted from an incomplete* d 58 can *interl. after* I *by another hand* 61 derysyon] deryson 62 dude *altered to* dyde *in darker ink by another hand* 64 wundyrfull] *second* u *adapted from another letter* (o?)

And be þat myght of þo personys thre
Hevyn, and erth, and allthynge is wrought.
And as it plesyth þat hyȝ mageste,
Allthynge xal leste, and lenger nowght.

PRIMUS DOCTOR
I grawnt weyl allthynge þat God dyde make,
And withowtyn hym nothynge may be.
But o thynge þu seydyst and þat I forsake:
þat oo God alone was personys thre.
Ryght onpossyble þat is to me:
That on is thre I kannot thynke.
If þu canst preve it, anon lett se,
For in oure hertys it may nevyr synke.

f. 107^{v} JESUS
In þe sunne consydyr ȝe thyngys thre:
The splendure, þe hete, and þe lyght.
As þo thre partys but oo sunne be,
Ryght so thre personys be oo God of Myght.

SECUNDUS DOCTOR
In very feyth, þis reson is ryght!
But ȝitt, fayr babe, oo thynge we pray ȝow:
What do all þo thre personys hyght?
Vs to enforme ȝe sey to me now.

JESUS
The fyrst is calde þe Fadyr of Myght,
þe secunde þe Sone of Wysdam and Wytt,
þe Holy Gost þe iij^{de}, of grace he is lyght;
And in oo substauns all these iij be knyt.

PRIMUS DOCTOR
Another questyon I aske ȝow ȝitt:
Ȝe seyd on of þese iij toke flesch and blood,
And sche a clene mayde—I kannot beleue it!
Clene mayde and modyr nevyr ȝit in oo persone stood.

JESUS
Lyke as þe sunne doth perysch þe glas,
þe glas not hurte of his nature,
Ryght so þe Godhede entryd has
þe Virgynes wombe, and sche mayd pure.

80 f *canc. before* synke 82 and þe] e *malformed and to the right* 93 ȝitt *canc. before* I 97 perysch *canc. and* pers *interl. above in black by another hand*

That maydonys childe xal do grett cure,
Convicte þe devyl in þe opyn felde,
And with his bolde berst fecch hom his crea-
ture.
Mankende to saue, his brest xal be þe shelde.

SECUNDUS DOCTOR
This childys doctryne doth passe oure wytt!
Sum aungel of hevyn I trowe þat he be.
But, blyssyd babe, of oo dowte ȝitt f. 108r
We pray ȝow enforme us for charyté:
Which toke flesch of þe personys thre
Ageyn þe fende to holde such batayle?

JESUS
The secunde persone, forsothe, is he
Xal fray þe fende withowte fayle.

PRIMUS DOCTOR
Why rather he than any of þat tother?
The fyrst or þe thyrde, why come they nowth?

JESUS
This is þe cawse why, sertys, and non other:
Ageyn þe secunde þe trespas was wrought.
Whan þe serpent Adam to synne browth,
He temptyd hym nowght be þe Faderys
myght;
Of þe Gostys goodnes spak he ryght nowght;
But in connynge he temptyd hym ryght.

Myght is þe Faderys owyn propyrté,
To þe Gost aproperyd is goodnes.
In none of these tweyn temptyd he,
Mankende to synne whan he dede dresse.
To þe Sone connynge doth longe expres;
Therwith þe serpent dyd Adam asay.
'Ete of þis appyl', he seyd no lesse,
'And þu xalt haue connynge as God verray'.

Þus þe secunde person attrybute
Was only towchyd be temptacyon.

103 bolde *canc. and* bluddy *interl. above in black by another hand* 113 tother] *an* o *written over* to *in slightly darker ink* 122 aproperyd] *B* apperyd

Wherfore hymself wyl holde þe sewte
And kepe his propyrté fro maculacion.

f. 108v SECUNDUS DOCTOR
This is an hevynly declaracyon:
Oure naturall wytt it doth excede.
So ȝonge a childe of such informacyon,
In al þis werld nevyr er non ȝede.

PRIMUS DOCTOR
We be not worthy to kepe þis sete
Whyll þat oure mayster is in presens.
þe maystry of us þis childe doth gete;
We must hym wurchep with hyȝ reverens.
Come forth, swete babe of grett excellens,
þe whysest clerke þat evyr ȝett was born.
To ȝow we ȝeve þe hyȝ resydens,
Vs more to teche as ȝe haue done beforn.

Hic adducunt Jesum inter ipsos et in scanno altiori ipsum sedere faciunt, ipsis in inferioribus scannis sedentibus, et ait ij[us] *doctor:*

SECUNDUS DOCTOR
So ȝonge a chylde suche clergye to reche,
And so sadly to sey it, we woundyr sore
Who was ȝoure mayster, who dede ȝow teche?
Of what man had ȝe þis wurthy lore?

JESUS
My wytt and my lernynge is no ȝonge store:
Or þis worde was wrought allþinge dede I knowe.
Fyrst, or ȝe wore borne, ȝerys many score
Thorwe þe myght of my fadyr my wytt in me dede flowe.

PRIMUS DOCTOR
Or þat we weryn born? Nay, þat may nat be!
þe ȝongest of us tweyn is iij score ȝere of age.
And þiselfe art but a chylde, al men may wel se;
Late camst out of cradyl, as it semyth be þi vesage.

134 *a letter canc. before* naturall 139 w *canc. before* doth 142 bar *canc. before* born 150 knowe] *the* o *bites the* w 152 dede flawe *or* dede flowe *canc. in red and* dede flowe *interl. above*

JESUS
I am of dobyl byrth and of dobyl lenage:
  Fyrst be my fadyr I am without gynnynge.
And lyke as he is hendeles in his hyȝ stage, f. 109r
  So xal I also neuyrmor haue endynge.

For be my fadyr, Kynge Celestyall
  Without begynnyng, I am endles.
But be my modyr, þat is carnall,
  I am but xij ȝere of age, þat is expres.
  My body of ȝoughȝ doth shewe wyttnes,
    Which of my modyr here I dude take.
  But [be] myn hyȝ godhede, þis is no lesse,
    Allthynge in þis worlde, forsothe, dude I make.

SECUNDUS DOCTOR
Be ȝoure fadyr, þat endles is,
  Who is ȝoure modyr? Telle us we pray.

JESUS
Be my fadyr, þe hyȝ Kynge of Blys,
  A modyrles chylde I am, veray.

PRIMUS DOCTOR
  Who was ȝoure fadyr, to us than say.
    Be ȝoure modyr a woman þat was?

JESUS
  I am fadyrles. As for þat may,
    Of fleschly luste she dude nevyr trespas.

SECUNDUS DOCTOR
Telle us, I pray ȝow, what is ȝoure name?
  What hyght ȝoure modyr, telle us also.

JESU
Jesu of Nazareth, I am þe same,
  Born of a clene mayd, prophetys seyd so.
  Ysaye seyd þus: Ecce virgo,
    A mayd xal conceyve in clennes a chylde,
  Ȝitt ageyn nature and al kende, loo,
    From all wem of synne pure and vndefylde.

Mary, þe chylde of Joachym and Anne, f. 109v
  Ys þat clene mayd, and here childe am I.

g *written in black by another hand in upper right corner of f. 109r* 165 ȝoughȝ] h *adapted from another letter?* 167 be *supplied* 174 w *canc. before* modyr 183 al kende] alkende

þe frute of here wombe xal saue euery manne
From þe grett dowte of þe fyndys tormentry.

PRIMUS DOCTOR
All þe clerkys of þis worlde, trewly,
Cannot brynge this to declaracyon
Lesse þan þei haue of God Almyghty
Sum influens of informacyon.

SECUNDUS DOCTOR
No[w], jentyl Jesu, we ȝow pray,
Whyl þat we stodye, a whyle to dwelle,
In cas mo dowtys þat we fynde may,
þe trewth of hem ȝe may us telle.

JESU
Goo take ȝoure stodye and avyse ȝow well,
And all ȝoure leysere I xal abyde.
If any dowtys to me ȝe mell,
þe trewth þerof I xall vnhyde.

MARIA
Alas, alas, myn hert is wo!
My blyssyd babe awey is went.
I wott nevyr whedyr þat he is go.
Alas, for sorwe myn hert is rent!
Jentyl husbond, haue [ȝou] hym sent
Out on herrande to any place?
But yf ȝe knowe were [he] ys bent,
Myn hert for woo asondyr wyl race.

JOSEPH
On my massage I hym not sent,
Forsothe, good wyff, in no degré.
How longe is it þat he hens went?
What tyme dude ȝe ȝoure childe last se?

f. 110r MARIA
Trewly, gode spowse, not þese days thre.
þerfore myn herte is cast in care.
Hym for to seke wherso he be,
In hast, good husbonde, lete us forth fare.

JOSEPH
Than to Hierusalem lete us streyte wende,
For kynred gladly togedyr wole gon.

193 Now] No 205 ȝou *supplied, following a reviser, who interl.* you *before* hym 207 he] *B; MS* her 210 god *canc. in red before* good 217 Hierusalem] i *written over an* e

I hope he [is] þer with sum good frende;
þer he hath cosynys ryght many on.
MARIA I am aferde þat he hath fon
For his grett wyttys and werkys good.
Lyke hym of wytt forsoth is non;
Euery childe with hym is wroth and wood.

Alas, my babe, my blys, my blood,
Whedyr art þu þus gon fro me?
My sowle, my swetyng, my frute, myn food,
Send me ssum wurd where þat þu be.
Telle me, good serys, for charyté,
Jesu, my childe, þat babe of blysse,
Amonge þis compayné dude ȝe hym se?
For Godys hyȝ loue, telle where he is.

PRIMUS DOCTOR Of oo qwestyon I am bethought,
All of ȝoure modyr, þat blyssyd may:
In what governauns is she brought?
How is sche rewlyd be nyght and day?
JESU An old man, Joseph, as I ȝow say,
Here weddyd be meracle onto his wyff,
Here for to fede and kepe alway,
And bothyn in clennesse be maydonys o lyff.

SECUNDUS DOCTOR What nede was it here to be wedde (f. 110v)
Onto a man of so grett age
Lesse þan þei myght bothe a go to bedde
And kept þe lawe of maryage?
JESUS To blynde þe devyl of his knowlache,
And my byrth from hym to hyde;
þat holy wedlok was grett stopage
þe devyl in dowte to do abyde.

Also whan sche xulde to Egypte gon
And fle from Herowde for dowte of me,

219 is *supplied, following a reviser, who interl.* is *in black after* he 232 hyȝ *canc. in black* *F. 110r marked* 110 Jesus adhuc *written at right below* 248 *with red s.h. loop and underlining, and a brown line across the page below* 248. . *This s.h. crossed through in red, the line in brown* 250 I *canc. before* And

Becawse she xulde nat go alon,
Joseph was ordeyned here make to be,
My fadyr, of his hyȝ magesté,
Here for to comforte in þe way.
These be þe cawsys, as ȝe may se,
Why Joseph weddyd þat holy may.

MARIA A, dere childe, dere chylde, why hast þu þus done?
For þe we haue had grett sorwe and care.
Thy fadyr and I thre days haue gone
Wyde þe to seke, of blysse ful bare.
JESUS Why haue ȝe sought me with evy fare?
Wete ȝe not wele þat I muste ben
Amonge hem þat is my faderys ware,
His gostly catel for to ovyrsen?

MARIA Ȝoure faderys wyl must nedys be wrought,
It is most wurthy þat it so be.
Ȝitt on ȝoure modyr haue ȝe sum thought,
And be nevyrmore so longe fro me.
f. 111r As to my thynkynge, these days thre
Þat ȝe absente haue ben away
Be more lengere in þer degré
Þan all þe space of xij ȝere day.

JESUS Now for to plese my modyr mylde
I xal ȝow folwe with obedyence.
I am ȝoure sone and subjecte childe,
And owe to do ȝow hyȝ reverence.
Home with ȝow I wyl go hens,
Of ȝow clerkys my leve I take.
Euery childe xulde with good dyligens,
His modyr to plese, his owyn wyl forsake.

PRIMUS DOCTOR O blyssyd Jesu, with ȝow we wende,
Of ȝow to haue more informacyon.

260 blysse *canc. and* comfort *carelessly interl. above by another hand* 261 evy] he *written over* e *in black by another hand* 262 ben] e *malformed, perhaps carelessly doubled; a final* e *dotted for deletion* 280 to *interl. in black by another hand after* wyl

Ful blyssyd is ȝoure modyr hende,
Of whom ȝe toke ȝoure incarnacyon.
We pray ȝow, Jesu, of consolacyon
At oure most nede of ȝow to haue.
All þat hath herd þis consummacyon
Of þis pagent, ȝoure grace þem saue.
Amen

[22]
[THE BAPTISM]

f. 112^r

JOHANNES Ecce vox clamantes in deserto.
I am þe voys of wyldirnese
Þat her spekyth and prechy[t]h yow to.
Loke ȝe forsake all wrecchidnesse;
Forsake all synne þat werkyth woo,
And turne to vertu and holynese.
Beth clene of levyng in your sowle also.
Than xall ȝe be savyd from peynfulnese
Of fyere brynnyng in hell.
If þat ȝe forsak synne,
Hevyn blysse xall ȝe wyne.
Drede ȝe not þe devyllys gynne,
With angellys xall yow dwell.

Penitenciam nunc agite
Appropinquabit regnum celorum:
For your trespas penaunce do ȝe
And ȝe xall wyn hevyn Dei Deorum.
In hevyn blyse ye xall wyn to be
Among þe blyssyd company omnium supernorum,

287 Amen *and scribbles written at right by another hand* *Remainder of f. 111^r (64 mm) blank, except for* Amen *written in black by another hand below the* Amen *of the main scribe; a black* o *appears lower on the page. F. 111^v blank except for two inscriptions:* hic incipyt Johannes Baptysta, *written by Scribe C; and* Tho: Kinge the yownger / Hath demised, *written by a seventeenth-century hand*

[*Play 22*] *The interpolated f. 112 was written by Scribe C on paper different from that in the rest of the play. It is unwatermarked and unrubricated*
1 *s.h. stands at top of page* 3 prechyth] prechych 6 to *interl.*

þeras is all merth, joye, and glee
Inter agmina angelorum,
In blyse to abyde.
Baptyme I cowncell yow for to take
And do penaunce for your synnys sake.
And for your offens amendys ȝe make,
Your synnys for to hyde.

I gyff baptym in watyr puere
þat is callyd Flom Jordon.
My baptym is but sygnyfure
Of his baptym þat his lyke hath non.
f. 112v He is a lord of gret valour;
I am not worthy to onbokyll his schon.
For he xall baptyze, as seyth Scryptour,
þat comyth of hem all euerychone,
In þe Holy Goost.
He may dampne and he may save,
All goodnese of hem we haue.
þer may no man his werkys deprave,
For he is Lord of myghtys most.

Hic accedit Jesus ad Johannem, quem intuens Johannes dicat, digito demonstrans Jesum:

Ecce Agnus Dei qui tollit peccata mundi.

Beholde, þe Lombe of God is this
þat comyth now here beforne,
þe wich xall wasch þe worldys mys
And save all þat that was forlorne.
This same lombe, forsoth, it is
þat of a mayd full clene was borne.
Shamfull deth þis lambe, iwys,
Xall suffer for us, and be all to-torne

23 take *canc. before* for vt *written near bottom at right on f. 112r* 32 v *canc. before* onbokyll 33 scrypture *canc. before* seyth 38 no *interl.* 39 s.d. quem] quê 47 lambe] b *altered from another letter* (p?)

And rent on a roode.
He xall suffer for mannys sake
Lytyll rest and moch gret sorow and wrake:
Hys bake xall be bowndyn to a stake
And betyn owt all his bloode.

JESUS Johan Baptyste, myn owyn good frende f. 113r
þat feythffully doth prech my wylle,
I the thanke with all my mende
For þat good servyse þu dost me tylle.
Thy desyre is synne to shende,
All synful lyff þu woldyst spylle.
Thyn entente hath a good hende;
þe lawe of God þu dost fulffylle
þis tyde.
Baptym to take I come to the,
And conferme þat sacrement þat nowe xal be.
In Flom Jordon þu baptyze me,
In watyr þat is wyde.

JOHANNES My Lorde God, þis behovyth me nought,
With myn hondys to baptyze the.
I xulde rather of the haue sought
Holy baptym þan þu of me.
JESUS Suffyr now, Johan, my wyl were wrought;
All ryghtffullnes þus fulfyll we.
Me to baptyze take þu no dowth;
þe vertu of mekenes here tawth xal be,
Euery man to lere
And take ensawmple here by me,
How mekely þat I come to þe.
Baptym confermyd now xal be;
Me to baptyze take þu no dwere.

With f. 113r the main hand resumes 54 *the s.h. is from f. 112v, written by Scribe C* 59 synful lyff] *written as one word* 72 ryghtffullnes] (*?*) ffl *canc. in red between* ryght *and* ffullnes 79 dwere *canc. and* fere *written against it in black by another hand, perhaps Scribe C*

JOHANNES All men may take exaunple, lo,
Of lowly mekenes evyn ryght here
Be oure Lorde God þat comyth me to,
Hese pore servaunt and his su..tere.
f. 113v Euery man lere to werke ryght so,
Bothe kynge, and caysere, and grett empere;
Be meke and lowe þe pore man to,
And put out pryde in all manere—
God doth here þe same.
To þi byddynge, my Lord so dere,
I me obey with gladsum chere,
And baptyze the with watyr clere.
Euyr halwyd be þi name.

Spiritus Sanctus hic descendat super ipsum, et Deus, Pater Celestis, dicet in celo:

[DEUS] This is my wel-belovyd chylde,
Ouyr whom my Spryte doth ouyrsprede,
Clene, and pure and vndefylyd
Of body, of sowle, for thought, for dede.
That he is buxhum, meke, and mylde
I am wel plesyd, withowtyn drede,
Wysly to wysse ȝow from weys wylde.
To lysten his lore all men I rede,
And ȝoure erys to herke.
Take good heed what he doth preche
And folwyth þe lawys þat he doth teche.
For he xal be ȝoure altheris leche,
To saue ȝow from deuelys derke.

JOHANNES BAP[TYST] Here I se with opyn syght
The Sone of God þat þu erte:
The Holy Goost ouyr the doth lyght,
þi faderys voys I here ful smerte.
The childe of God, as I þe plyght,
þat þu be, whilys I am qwerte,

83 su..tere] *a letter* (w?) *erased after the* u   84 man *interl.*   92 s.d. *a capitulum stands before* Pater   93 *s.h. supplied*   96 of *canc. in red before* dede *and* for *interl. above by main scribe*   106 BAPTYST] Bap, *remainder cropped*   107 erte] *first* e *written over an erased* a?

I xall wyttnes to every whyght f. 114r
And teche it trewly with all myn hert.
To sese, it were grett synne.
For Goddys sone I wurchypp the,
From hevyn þin hyȝ mageste.
Thu comyst hedyr from dygnité,
Mannys sowle to wynne.

JESUS Johan Baptyste, þu be wyttnes,
The trewth loke þat þu nat hyde.
For now I passe forth into wyldernes,
The Holy Gost xal be my gyde.

Hic Jesus transit in desertum dicens et cetera:

In whylsum place of desertnes
Xl^{ti} days, a terme ful wyde,
And fourty nyghtys, both more and lesse,
Withowtyn bodyly fode þer to abyde—
For man þus do I swynke.
Into deserte I passe my way
For mannys sake, as I ȝow say.
Xl^{ti} nyghtys and xl^{ti} day
I xal nowther ete nor drynke.

JOHAN BAPTYST In place where I passe wyttnes I bere,
The trewth xal I telle wheresoevyr I go:
þat Cryst, þe Sone of God, is become oure fere,
Clad in oure clothynge to sofer for us wo.
I baptyzid with myn owyn handys Cryst Jesu ryght here.
And now he is to wyldyrnes, penawns þer to do,
Informyng so all us, þat lord þat hath no pere,
To do for oure trespace penawnce here also.
Of penawnce do I preche. f. 114v
In wyttnes ryght be this

124 terme *has been rubbed or smudged and touched up in black, apparently without revision of the word; the same has occurred in several other words in the subsequent six lines*

Þat what man for his mys
Doth penawns here, iwys,
His sowle he doth wel leche.

All men on ground þat be ȝitt on lyue,
For ȝoure grett offens loke ȝe be repentaunt.
Of all ȝoure venym synne, I rede þat ȝe ȝow shryve,
For God is ful redy mercy for to graunt.
Be contryte for ȝoure trespas and penauns do belyve;
Reconsyle ȝoureself and be to God plesaunt.
With contryscyon, schryffte, and penauns, þe devil may ȝe dryve;
Fer fro ȝoure felachep he xal not be erraunt,
Ȝow for to meve.
Do penauns and synne forsake,
Shryfte of mowth loke þat ȝe make;
And þan þe fende in helle so blake,
He xal ȝow nevyrmore greve.

A tre þat is bareyn and wyl bere no frute,
Þe ownere wyl hewe it down and cast it on þe fyre.
Ryght so it be [be] man þat folwyth þe fowle sute
Of þe devyl of helle, and werkyth his desyre.
God wyl be vengyd on man þat is both dum and mute,
Þat wyl nevyr be shrevyn, but evyrmore doth delyre.
Clothe the in clennes, with vertu be indute,
And God with his grace he wyl þe sone inspyre
To amendynge of þi mys.
Schryfte of mowthe may best þe saue,
Penauns for synne what man wyl haue,
f. 115r Whan þat his body is leyd in grave,
His sowle xal go to blys.

151 conty, *with* r *written over the* y, *canc. in red before* contryscyon 154 per *canc. in red before* penauns 156 fende] *a tittle placed over first* e *and* d *adapted from* ll (*originally* felle) 160 be *supplied* 165 grace] r *written over another letter* 170 xal go *partially obscured by a stain, as is* good *in* 171

Corne þat is good, men kepe it ful clene;
Chaff þat is sympyl is sett wul nere at nought.
So good men of levynge to God chosyn bene
Whan synful men be lyke chaff, and to helle xul be brought.
Good penauns ȝow to preche ful hertyly do I mene,
Shryfft and satysfaccyon evyrmore to haue in thought.
What man in good penauns and schryfte of mowth be sene,
Of God he is wel-belovyd, þat all þis worlde hath wrought,
And allþinge of nowth dede make.
Now haue I tawght ȝow good penauns.
God graunt ȝow grace at his plesauns
To haue of synne delyverauns,
For now my leve I take.

23 [THE PARLIAMENT OF HELL; THE TEMPTATION]

f. 116^{r}

SATHAN Now Belyard and Belzabub, ȝe derwurthy devel of helle,
And wysest of councel amongys all þe rowte,
Herke now what I sey, a tale I xall ȝow telle
Þat trobelyth sore my stomak; þerof I haue grett dowte.
BELYALL Syr Sathanas, oure souereyn syre, with þe wol we dwelle.
All redy at þi byddynge, to þe do we lowte.
If þu haue any nede of oure wyse counselle,
Telle us now þi qwestyon all out and oute;
Sey al þi dowt beden[e].

183 *a letter scribbled in lighter ink at right; some scribbles below* *Remainder of f. 115*^{r} *(110 mm) and f. 115*^{v} *blank*

[*Play 23*] 2 of councel *obscured by a blot* 9 bedene] beden, *remainder cropped*

BELSABUB
Ʒa, sere, telle us þi dowte by and by,
And we xul telle þe so sekyrly
Þat þu xalt knowe verryly
What þi dowte doth mene.

SATHAN
The dowte þat I haue, it is of Cryst, iwys.
Born he was in Bedleem, as it is seyd,
And many a man wenyth þat Goddys sone he is,
Born of a woman, and she a clene mayd.
And all þat evyr he prechyth, it is of hevyn blys.
He wyl lese oure lawe, I am ryght sore afrayd!
Fayn wolde I knowe who were fadyr his,
For of þis grett dowte I am sore dysmayd,
Indede.
If þat he be Goddys childe
And born of a mayd mylde,
Than be we rygh sore begylde,
And short xal ben oure spede!

Therfore, serys, sumwhat þat ʒe shewe
In þis grett dowth what is best to do.
If he be Goddys sone, he wyl brede a shrewe
And werke us mech wrake, both wrech and woo!
Sorwe and care he wyl sone strewe;
f. 116v All oure gode days þan xulde sone be goo.
And all oure lore and all oure lawe he wyl down hewe,
And þan be we all lorn, if þat it be soo—
He wyll don vs all tene!
He wyll be lorde ouyr hevyn and helle,
And feche awey all oure catelle.
Þerfore shewe now sum good counselle,
What comfort may best bene.

BELYALL
The best wytt þat I kan say,
Hym to tempte, forsoth, it is.

17 a woman] awoman clene] l *altered from another letter* (h?) 26 *a word canc. in red before* oure 33 *a word* (lore?) *canc. in red before* lore down *obscured by a blot* 34 ll (?) *after* be *erased, canc. in red, and deleted by dots placed below* 35 wyll] ll *written in black over an erasure*

With sotyl whylys, if þat þu may,
Asay to make hym to don amys.
If þat he synne, þis is no nay,
He may nat be Kynge of Blys.
Hym to tempte go walke þi way,
For best counsell I trowe be this.
Go forth now and assay.

BELSABUB The best wytt I hold it be
Hym to tempte in synnys thre,
The whiche mankendeis frelté
Doth falle sonest alway.

SATHAN So afftyr ȝoure wytt now wyll I werke;
I wyll no lengere now here abyde.
Be he nevyr so wyse a clerke,
I xal apposyn hym withinne a tyde.

BELSABUB Now, louely Lucyfer in helle so derke,
Kynge and lorde of synne and pryde,
With sum myst his wyttys to merke,
He send þe grace to be þi gyde,
And evyrmore be þi spede.

BELYALL All þe deuelys þat ben in helle f. 117r
Shul pray to Mahound, as I þe telle,
þat þu mayst spede þis jurney well,
And comforte the in þis dede.

JESUS Xl^{ti} days and xl^{ti} nyght
Now haue I fastyd for mannys sake.
A more grett hungyr had neuyr no wyght
Than I myself begynne to take.
For hungyr in peyn stronge am I pyght,
And bred haue I non myn hungyr for to slake.
A lytel of a loof relese myn hungyr myght,
But mursele haue I non my comforte for to make.
This suffyr I, man, for the.
For þi glotenye and metys wronge
I suffyr for þe þis hungyr stronge.
I am afferde it wyl be longe
Or þu do þus for me.

65 caas *canc. before* dede 68 A more] Amore

SATHAN

The Sone of God if þat þu be,
Be þe grett myght of þi Godhede,
Turne these flyntys, anon lett se,
From arde stonys to tendyr brede!
More bettyr it is, as I telle the,
Wysely to werke aftyr my reed
And shewe þi myght of grett majesté,
Than thorwe grett hungyr for to be dede.
These stonys now bred þu make.
Goddys sone if þat þu be,
Make these stonys bred, lett se;
þan mayste þu ete ryght good plenté,
Thyn hungyr for to slake.

f. 117v JESUS

Nott only be bred mannys lyff ȝitt stood,
But in þe wurde of God, as I þe say.
To mannys sowle is neuyr mete so good
As is þe wurd of God, þat prechid is alway.
Bred materyal doth norch blood,
But to mannys sowle, þis is no nay,
Nevyrmore may be a betyr food
þan þe wurd of God, þat lestyth ay.
To here Goddys wurde, þerfore, man, loue.
Thi body doth loue materal brede;
Withoute þe wurde of God þi soule is but
dede.
To loue prechynge, þerfore, I rede,
If þu wylt duellyn in blysse above.

SATHAN

For no grett hungyr þat I kan se
In glotony þu wylt not synne.
Now to þe temple com forth with me,
And þer xal I shewe þe a praty gynne.
Vp to þis pynnacle now go we,
I xal þe sett on þe hyȝest pynne.
Ther I preue what þat þu be.
Or þat we tweyn part atwynne,
I xal knowe what myght þu haue.

An obliterated capitulum stands at left of 100–2

Hic ascendit Deus pinnaculum templi dum diabolus dicit quod sequitur:

Whan þu art sett upon þe pynnacle,
þu xalt þer pleyn a qweynt steracle,
Or ellys shewe a grett meracle;
Thysself from hurte þu saue.

Hic Satanas ponit Jesum super pinnaculum dicens:

Now if þu be Goddys Ssone of Myght,
Ryght down to þe erth anon þu falle, f. 118r
And saue þisylf in every plyght
From harm, and hurte, and scappys alle.
For it is wretyn [þat] aungelys bryght
þat ben in hevyn, þi faderys halle,
The to kepe both day and nyght
Xul be ful redy as þi thralle,
Hurt þat þu non haue.
þat þu stomele not ageyn þe ston
And hurt þi fote as þu dost gon,
Aungell be redy all everychon
In weys þe to saue.

JESUS It is wretyn in holy book,
þi Lorde God þu xalt not tempte.
Allthynge must obeye to Goddys look:
Out of his myght is non exempt.
Out of þi cursydnes and cruel crook
By Godys grace man xal be redempt,
Whan þu to helle, þi brennynge brook,
To endles peyne xal evyr be dempt,
Therin alwey to abyde.
Thi Lorde God þu tempt no more!
It is nott syttenge to þi lore.
I bydde þe sese anon, þerfore,
And tempte God in no tyde.

117 Thysself] *a dot stands at left of first* s (*for deletion?*) 122 wretyn] n *in darker ink* þat] with 125 thralle] tharalle, *with deleting dot under the first* a 134 *some letters canc. before* is 137 brennynge] re *written over another letter* (e.?)

SATHAN Ow! In gloteny nor in veynglory it doth ryght nott avayl!
Cryst for to tempt it profyteth me ryght nought.
I must now begynne to haue a newe travayl:
In covetyse to tempt hym it comyth now in my thought.
f. 118v For if I went þus away and shrynkyd as a snayle,
Lorn were þe labore all þat I haue wrought.
þerfore in covetyse oure syre I xal asayle,
And assay into þat synne yf he may be brought
Anon forthryght.
Syr, ȝitt onys I pray to the,
To þis hyȝ hyl com forth with me.
I xal þe shewe many a ceté
And many a wurthy syght.

Tunc Jesus transit cum diabolo super montem, et diabolus dicit:

Into þe northe loke forth evyn pleyn;
The Towre of Babolony þer mayst þu se.
The ceté of Jerusalem stondyth þer ageyn,
And evyn fast þerby stondyth Galylé;
Nazareth, Naverne, and þe kyngdom of Spayn;
Zabulon and Neptalym, þat is a rych countré;
Bothe Zebee and Salmana þu mayst se, serteyn;
Itayl and Archage, þat wurthy remys be;
Bothe Januense and Jurye;
Rome doth stonde before þe ryght;
The temple of Salamon, as sylver bryght,
And here mayst þu se opynly with syght
Both Fraunce and Normandye.

Turne þe now on þis syde and se here Lumbardye;
Of spycery þer growyth many an C balys.
Archas, and Aragon, and grett Almonye,
Parys, and Portyngale, and þe town of Galys;

146 trar *canc. before* travayl

Pownteys, and Poperynge, and also Pycardye,
Erlonde, Scottlonde, and þe londe of Walys;
Grete pylis and castellys þu mayst se with eye, f. 119r
Ʒa, and all þe wyd werde, withoute mo talys.
All þis longygh to me.
If þu wylt knele down to þe grownde
And wurchepp me now in þis stownde,
All þis world þat is so rownd,
I xal it gyve to the.

JESUS Go abak, þu fowle Sathanas!
In Holy Scrypture wretyn it is,
Thi Lorde God to wurchipp in every plas
As for his thrall, and þu servaunt his.

SATHAN Out! Out! Harrow! Alas! Alas!
I woundyr sore what is he this?
I cannot brynge hym to no trespas,
Nere be no synne to don amys.
He byddyth me gon abakke!
What þat he is I kannot se;
Whethyr God or man, what þat he be
I kannot telle in no degré.
For sorwe I lete a crakke.

Hic uenient angeli cantantes et ministrantes ei, 'Gloria tibi Domine' dicens.

JESUS Now all mankende exaunple take
By these grete werkys þat þu dost se,
How þat þe devyll of helle so blake
In synne was besy to tempte me.
For all hise maystryes þat he dyd make,
He is ouyrcom and now doth fle.
All þis I suffyr for mannys sake,
To teche þe how þu xalt rewle the
Whan þe devylle dothe the assayle. f. 119v
Loke þu concente nevyr to synne

180 stownde] e *blotted* 181 world] l *altered from a* d*?* 185 Lorde] or *smudged* 189 *some letters canc. in red before* no 195 s.d. dicens *enclosed in red speaker's loop*

For no sleytys ne for no gynne.
And þan þe victory xalt þu wynne;
þe devyl xal lesyn all his travayl.

To suffyr temptacyon, it is grett peyn.
If þu withstonde it, þu wynnyst grett mede.
Of God þe more grace þu hast, serteyn,
If þu withsett þe devyl in his dede.
Thow þat þe fende tempt þe ageyn,
Of his power take þu no drede,
For God hath the ȝovyn both myght and mayn
Hym for to withsytt evyr at nede—
þu hast more myght than he!
Whan þe devyl doth tempte the thoo,
Shewe þi myght aȝens þi foo.
Whan þi sowle partyth the froo,
In blysse þan xal it be.
Amen

f. 121r

24
[THE WOMAN TAKEN IN ADULTERY]

Hic de muliere in adulterio deprehensa:

JESUS Nolo mortem peccatoris.
Man, for þi synne take repentaunce.
If þu amende þat is amys,
Than hevyn xal be þin herytaunce.
Thow þu haue don aȝens God grevauns,
ȝett mercy to haske loke þu be bolde.

Remainder of f. 119v (90 mm) blank except for scribblings in lighter ink and a cipher in black (see above p. xxv)

F. 120r blank except for scribbled numbers and lines; f. 120v blank

[*Play 24*] gyn at Nolo morte[m] *written by main scribe in top margin*
1 Nolo *preceded by a capitulum*

His mercy doth passe in trewe balauns
All cruel jugement be many folde.

Thow þat ȝoure synnys be nevyr so grett,
For hem be sad and aske mercy.
Sone of my fadyr grace ȝe may gett
With þe leste teer wepynge owte of ȝoure ey.
My fadyr me sent the, man, to bye;
All þi raunsom mysylfe must pay;
For loue of þe mysylfe wyl dye.
Iff þu aske mercy, I sey nevyr nay.

Into þe erth from hevyn above
þi sorwe to sese and joy to restore,
Man, I cam down all for þi loue.
Loue me ageyn—I aske no more.
þow þu myshappe and synne ful sore,
Ȝit turne aȝen and mercy craue.
It is þi fawte and þu be lore;
Haske þu mercy and þu xalt haue.

Vppon þi neybore be not vengabyl,
Ageyn þe lawe if he offende.
Lyke as he is, þu art vnstabyl—
Thyn owyn frelté evyr þu attende.
Euyrmore þi neybore helpe to amende, f. 121^{v}
Evyn as þu woldyst he xulde þe.
Ageyn hym wrath if þu accende,
The same in happ wyll falle on the.

Eche man to othyr be mercyable,
And mercy he xal haue at nede.
What man of mercy is not tretable,
Whan he askyth mercy, he xal not spede.
Mercy to graunt I com, indede.
Whoso aske mercy, he xal haue grace.
Lett no man dowte for his mysdede,
But evyr aske mercy whyl he hath space.

F. 121^{v} marked 120

SCRIBA
Alas, alas, oure lawe is lorn!
A fals ypocryte, Jesu be name,
Þat of a sheppherdis dowtyr was born,
Wyl breke oure lawe and make it lame!
He wyl us werke ryght mekyl shame,
His fals purpos if he upholde.
All oure lawys he doth defame—
Þat stynkynge beggere is woundyr bolde!

PHARISEUS
Sere scrybe, in feyth þat ypocryte
Wyl turne þis londe al to his lore.
Þerfore I councell hym to indyte,
And chastyse hym ryght wel þerfore.

SCRIBA
On hym beleve many a score,
In his prechynge he is so gay.
Ech man hym folwygh evyr more and more—
Aȝens þat he seyth no man seyth nay.

f. 122r K quire

PHARISEUS
A fals qwarel if we cowde feyne,
Þat ypocrite to puttyn in blame,
All his prechynge xulde sone disteyne,
And than his wurchepp xuld turne to shame.
With sum falshede to spyllyn his name
Lett us assay his lore to spylle.
Þe pepyl with hym yff we cowde grame,
Than xulde we sone haue al oure wyll.

ACCUSATOR
Herke, Sere Pharysew and Sere Scrybe,
A ryght good sporte I kan ȝow telle.
I vndyrtake þat ryght a good brybe
We all xul haue to kepe councell.
A fayre ȝonge qwene hereby doth dwelle,
Both fresch and gay upon to loke.
And a tall man with here doth melle;
The wey into hyre chawmere ryght evyn he toke.

Lett us thre now go streyte thedyr,
The wey ful evyn I xall ȝow lede.
And we xul take them both togedyr
Whyll þat þei do þat synful dede.

SCRIBA

Art þu sekyr þat we xal spede?
Shall we hym fynde whan we cum there?

ACCUSATOR

Be my trowth, I haue no drede,
þe hare fro þe forme we xal arere!

PHARISEUS

We xal haue game and þis be trewe!
Lete vs thre werke by on assent.
We wyl here brynge evyn beforn Jesu
And of here lyff þe truth present,
How in advowtrye hyre lyff is lent. f. 122v
Than hym beforn whan she is browth,
We xul hym aske þe trew jugement,
What lawfull deth to here is wrouth.

Of grace and mercy hevyr he doth preche,
And þat no man xulde be vengeable.
Ageyn þe woman if he sey wrech,
Than of his prechynge he is vnstable.
And if we fynde hym varyable
Of his prechynge þat he hath tawth,
Than haue we cawse bothe juste and able
For a fals man þat he be cawth.

SCRIBA

Now be grete God, ȝe sey ful well!
If we hym fyndyn in varyaunce,
We haue good reson, as ȝe do tell,
Hym for to brynge to foule myschauns.
If he holde stylle his dalyauns,
And preche of mercy, hire for to saue,
Than haue we mater of gret substauns
Hym for to kylle and putt in graue.

Grett reson why I xal ȝow telle:
For Moyses doth bydde in oure lawe
That euery advowterere we xuld qwelle,
And ȝitt with stonys thei xulde be slawe.

92 vnstable *altered to* vnstabyl, *or vice versa* 97 Now be *obscured by a blot* 98 we *obscured by the blot*

Ageyn Moyses if þat he drawe,
þat synful woman with grace to helpe,
He xal nevyr skape out of oure awe,
But he xal dye lyke a dogge whelpe!

f. 123[r] ACCUSATOR Ȝe tary ovyrlonge, serys, I sey ȝow;
They wyl sone parte, as þat I gesse.
þerfore, if ȝe wyl haue ȝoure pray now,
Lete us go take them in here whantownnesse.
PHARISEUS Goo þu beforn, þe wey to dresse;
We xal þe folwe within short whyle.
Iff þat we may þat quene dystresse,
I hope we xal Jesu begyle.

SCRIBA Breke up þe dore and go we inne!
Sett to þe shuldyr with all þi myght.
We xal hem take evyn in here synne—
Here owyn trespas shal þem indite.

Hic juuenis quidam extra currit in deploydo, calligis non ligatis et braccas in manu tenens; et dicit accusator:

ACCUSATOR Stow þat harlot, sum erthely wyght,
That in advowtrye here is fownde!
JUUENIS Ȝiff any man stow me þis nyth,
I xal hym ȝeve a dedly wownde!

I[f] any man my wey doth stoppe,
Or we departe, ded xal [he] be.
I xal þis daggare put in his croppe—
I xal hem kylle or he xal me.
PHARISEUS Grett Goddys curse mut go with the!
With suche a shrewe wyll I not melle.
JUUEN[I]S That same blyssynge I ȝyff ȝow thre
And qwheth ȝow alle to þe devyl of helle!

122 *an incomplete* s *precedes* shuldyr 124 s.d. in deploydo] indeploydo
129 If] *B; MS* I 130 he] *Bev; MS* I 135 JUUENIS] Juuenes

In feyth, I was so sore affrayd
Of ȝone thre shrewys, þe sothe to say, f. 123^{v}
My breche be nott ȝett well upteyd,
I had such hast to renne away.
Thei xal nevyr cacche me in such affray.
I am full glad þat I am gon!
Adewe, adewe, a xx^{ti} devyl way,
And Goddys curse haue ȝe everychon!

SCRIBA Come forth, þu stotte, com forth, þu scowte!
Com forth, þu bysmare and brothel bolde!
Com forth, þu hore and stynkynge bych clowte!
How longe hast þu such harlotry holde?
PHARISEUS Com forth, þu quene, com forth, þu scolde!
Com forth, þu sloveyn, com forth, þu slutte!
We xal the teche with carys colde
A lytyl bettyr to kepe þi kutte.

MULYER A, mercy, mercy, serys, I ȝow pray!
For Goddys love haue mercy on me.
Of my myslevynge me not bewray;
Haue mercy on me, for charyté!
ACCUSATOR Aske us no mercy; it xal not be.
We xul so ordeyn for þi lott
þat þu xalt dye for þin advowtrye!
þerfore, com forth, þu stynkynge stott!

MULIER Serys, my wurchepp if ȝe wyl saue
And helpe I haue non opyn shame,
Bothe gold and sylvyr ȝe xul haue,
So þat in clennes ȝe kepe my name.
SCRIBA Mede for to take, we were to blame f. 124^{r} L quire
To save suche stottys. It xal not be!
We xal brynge the to suche a game
þat all advowtererys xul lern be the.

137 *lacks a capitulum* 141 affray] *Bev* a fray 145 scowte] scowtte, *with deleting dot under the first* t

MULIER
Stondynge ȝe wyl not graunt me grace,
But for my synne þat I xal dye,
I pray ȝow kylle me here in þis place
And lete not þe pepyl upon me crye.
If I be sclaundryd opynly,
To all my frendys it xul be shame.
I pray ȝow, kylle me here in þis place
Lete not þe pepyl know my defame.

PHARISEUS
Fy on þe, scowte, þe devyl þe qwelle!
Ageyn þe lawe xul we þe kyll?
Fyrst xal hange þe þe devyl of helle
Or we such folyes xulde fulfyll.
Thow it lyke þe nevyr so ill,
Befforn þe prophete þu xalt haue lawe.
Lyke as Moyses doth charge u[s] tyll,
With grett stonys þu xalt be slawe.

ACCUSATOR
Com forth apase, þu stynkynge scowte,
Before þe prophete þu were þis day,
Or I xal ȝeve þe such a clowte
þat þu xalt fall down evyn in þe way.

SCRIBA
Now, be grett God, and I þe pay,
Such a buffett I xal þe take
þat all þe teth, I dare wel say,
Withinne þin heed for who xul shake.

f. 124v PHARISEUS
Herke, sere prophete, we all ȝow pray
To gyff trewe dom and just sentence
Vpon þis woman, which þis same day
In synfull advowtery hath don offense.

Hic Jesus, dum isti accusant mulierem, continue debet digito suo scribere in terra.

ACCUSATOR
Se, we haue brought here to ȝoure presens
Becawse ȝe ben a wyse prophete,
þat ȝe xal telle be consyens
What deth to hyre ȝe thynke most mete.

183 us] *B; MS* ut   191 teth (*?*) *canc. in red before* teth

SCRIBA
In Moyses lawe ryght þus we fynde,
þat such fals louers xul be slayn;
Streyte to a stake we xul hem bynde
And with grett stonys brest out þer brayn.
Of ȝoure concyens telle us þe playn,
With þis woman what xal be wrought?
Shall we lete here go qwyte agayn,
Or to hire deth xal she be brought?

Jesus nichil respondit, sed semper scrybyt in terra.

[MULIER]
Now, holy prophete, be mercyable!
Vpon me, wrecch, take no vengeaunce.
For my synnys abhomynable
In hert I haue grett repentaunce.
I am wel wurthy to haue myschaunce,
Both bodyly deth and werdly shame.
But, gracyous prophete, of socurraunce
þis tyme pray ȝow, for Goddys name.

PHARISEUS
Ageyn þe lawe þu dedyst offens; f. 125r
þerfore of grace speke þu no more.
As Moyses gevyth in lawe sentens,
þu xalt be stonyd to deth þerfore.

ACCUSATOR
Ha don, sere prophete, telle us ȝoure lore.
Xul we þis woman with stonys kyll,
Or to hire hous hire home restore?
In þis mater tell us ȝoure wyll.

SCRIBA
In a colde stodye methynkyth ȝe sytt.
Good sere, awake! Telle us ȝoure thought.
Xal she be stonyd—telle us ȝoure wytt—
Or in what rewle xal sche be brought?

JESUS
Loke which of ȝow þat nevyr synne wrought,
But is of lyff clennere þan she,
Cast at here stonys and spare here nowght,
Clene out of synne if þat ȝe be.

209 Mulier *written in left margin by another scribe* s.h. *supplied* 216 d *canc. in brown and red before* Goddys 218 speke] ke *interl.* 228 sche] e *blotted*

Hic Jesus, iterum se inclinans, scribet in terra; et omnes accusatores, quasi confusi, separatim in tribus locis se desiungent.

PHARISEUS Alas, alas, I am ashamyd!
I am afferde þat I xal deye!
All myn synnys evyn propyrly namyd
Ȝon prophyte dede wryte befor myn eye.
Iff þat my felawys þat dude aspye,
They wyll telle it bothe fer and wyde.
My synfull levynge if þei outcrye,
I wot nevyr wher myn heed to hyde.

ACCUSATOR Alas, for sorwe myn herte doth blede!
All my synnys ȝon man dude wryte.
f. 125v If þat my felawys to them toke hede,
I kannot me from deth acquyte.
I wolde I wore hyd sumwhere out of syght
þat men xuld me nowhere se ne knowe.
Iff I be take, I am afflyght
In mekyl shame I xal be throwe.

SCRIBA Alas þe tyme þat þis betyd!
Ryght byttyr care doth me enbrace.
All my synnys be now vnhyd,
Ȝon man befor me hem all doth trace.
If I were onys out of þis place,
To suffyr deth gret and vengeauns able,
I wyl nevyr come befor his face,
þow I xuld dye in a stable.

MULIER Thow I be wurthy for my trespas
To suffyr deth abhomynable,
Ȝitt, holy prophete, of ȝoure hyȝ grace,
In ȝoure jugement be mercyable!
I wyl nevyrmore be so vnstable.
O holy prophete, graunt me mercy.

234 afferde] fed *canc. in red after* a 254 *two virgules follow* gret vengeauns able] *Bev* vengeaunsable 257 Thow] h *smudged* s (*?*) *canc. in red before* my

Of myn synnys vnresonable
With all myn hert I am sory.

JESUS Where be þi fomen þat dude þe accuse?
Why haue thei lefte us to alone?
MULIER Bycawse they cowde nat hemself excuse,
With shame they fled hens euyrychone.
But, gracyous prophete, lyst to my mone; f. 126r
Of my sorwe take compassyon. M quire
Now all myn enmyes hens be gone,
Sey me sum wurde of consolacyon.

JESUS For þe synnys þat þu hast wrought
Hath any man condempnyd the?
MULIER Nay, forsoth, þat hath þer nought,
But in ȝoure grace I putt me.
JESUS For me þu xalt nat condempnyd be;
Go hom ageyn and walk at large.
Loke þat þu leve in honesté,
And wyl no more to synne, I þe charge.

MULIER I thanke ȝow hyȝly, holy prophete,
Of þis grett grace ȝe haue me graunt.
All my lewde lyff I xal doun lete
And fonde to be Goddys trewe servaunt.
JESUS What man of synne be repentaunt,
Of God if he wyl mercy craue,
God of mercy is so habundawnt,
þat, what man haske it, he xal it haue.

Whan man is contrite and hath wonne grace,
God wele not kepe olde wreth in mynde;
But bettyr loue to hem he has,
Very contryte whan he them fynde.
Now God þat dyed for all mankende
Saue all þese pepyl both nyght and day.

285 *s.h. canc. in black and* Doctor *written below possibly by the hand that wrote* Mulier *on f. 124v*

And of oure synnys he us vnbynde,
Hyȝe Lorde of Hevyn þat best may.
Amen

f. 127v

25
[THE RAISING OF LAZARUS]

Hic incipit de suscitacione Lazari:

LAZARUS God, þat allthynge dede make of nowth
And puttyst eche creature to his fenaunce,
Saue thyn handwerke þat þu hast wrought,
As þu art Lord of hyȝ substauns.
O gracyous God, at þi plesauns,
Of my dysese now comforte me,
Which þurowe syknes hath such penawnce
Onethys for heedache may I now se.

Systyr Martha, and Mawdelyn eke,
With hast helpe me in bedde to dresse.
For trewly I am so woundyrly seke
I may nevyr schape þis grett seknes—
My deth is com now, I gesse.
Help into chawmere þat I be led.
My grett desesse I hope xal lesse
If I were leyd upon a bed.

MARTHA Lazarus, brother, be of good cher;
I hope ȝoure syknes ryght wel xal slake.
Vpon þis bed rest ȝow rygh her,
And a good slep assay to take.

MAGDALYN Now, jentyl brothyr, for Goddys sake,
Lyfte up ȝowre herte and be not feynt.
An hevy housholde with vs ȝe make
If dedly syknes haue ȝow ateynt.

Ff. 126v and 127r blank except for scribbling.

[*Play 25*] 12 schape] h *altered from another letter* (a?)

LAZARUS Forsothe, dere systeryn, I may not slepe;
My syknes so sore doth evyr encrese.
Of me I pray ȝow, take ryght good kepe
Tyll þat my peyne begynne relese.
MARTHA God graunt grace þat it may sese. f. 128r
Of syknes God make ȝow sownde,
Or ellys oure joy wyll sone dyscres,
In so grett peynes if ȝe ly bownde.

MAGDALYN A, brothir, brothir, lyfte up ȝoure herte!
Ȝoure hevy cher doth us grevaunce.
If deth from us ȝow xulde departe,
Than were we brought in comberaunce.
Ȝe be oure brothyr, syb of alyaunce;
If ȝe wore deed þan had we none.
Ȝe do us brynge in distemperaunce
Whan ȝe us telle ȝe xal hens gone.

PRIMUS CONSOLATOR Dame Martha and Magdalyne,
How faryth ȝoure brothire? Lete us hym se.
MARTHA He is ryght seke and hath grett pyne—
I am aferde deed he xal be.
MAGDALYN A man may haue ryght grett peté,
The fervent hete of hym to fele.
SECUNDUS CONSOLATOR Take ȝe no thought in no degré;
I hope þat he xal fare ful wele.

MARTHA He may nat leve, his colowre doth chaunge.
Com to his bed, ȝe xal hym se.
MAGDALYN Iff he longe leve it wyl be straunge,
But as God wole, so mut it be.
Chere hym, gode frendys, for charyté.
Comforte of hym we kan non gete.
Alas, alas! What eylight me? f. 128v
Myne herte for wo is wundyr grete!

26 encrese] *final* e, *after round* s, *appears an afterthought; also in* relese *in* 28
F. 128r lacks rubrication around speaker headings

TERCIUS CONSOLATOR
Al heyl, Syr Lazarus! How do ȝe fare?
How do ȝe fele ȝow in ȝoure herte?

LAZARUS
I am with syknes all woundyn in care
And loke whan deth me xulde departe.

QUARTUS CONSOLATOR ET NUNCIUS
Ȝe xal haue hele and leve in qwart
If ȝe wol take to ȝow good chere.

LAZARUS
Whan deth on me hath shet his dart,
I xal haue hele and ly on bere.

PRIMUS CONSOLATOR
Be of good comforte and thynke not so,
Put out of herte þat idyl thought.
Ȝoure owyn mysdemynge may werke ȝow wo
And cause ȝow sonere to deth be brought.

SECUNDUS CONSOLATOR
With gret syknes þow ȝe be sought,
Vpon ȝouresylf haue no mystruste.
If þat ȝe haue, I wundyr ryght nought
Þow ȝe be deed and cast in duste.

TERCIUS CONSOLATOR
Many on hath had ryght grett syknesse
And aftyr hath had his hele agayn.
And many a man, þis is no lesse,
With his wantruste hymsylf hath slayn.
Ȝe be a man of ryght sad brayn.
Þow þat ȝoure syknes greve ȝow ryght ill,
Pluk up ȝoure herte with myght and mayn,
And chere ȝouresylf with all ȝoure wyll!

f. 129r LAZARUS
Ageyn my syknes þer is non ese
But Jesu Cryst, my maystyr dere.
If þat he wyst of my dyssese,
Ryght sone, I trust, he wolde ben here.

QUARTUS CONSOLATOR
I xal go to hym, withoutyn dwere,
And of ȝoure syknes telle hym, serteyn.
Loke þat ȝe be of ryght good chere
Whyll þat I go and com ageyn.

63 deth] et *blotted, perhaps altered from other letters* 72 cast] c *malformed* 74 agayn] *altered from* ageyn 76 slayn] *altered from* sleyn hath *written by another hand below* 80

MARTHA
Now, jentyl frend, telle hym ryght thus:
He þat he lovyth hath grett syknes.
Hedyr to come and comforte us,
Say þat we prayd hym of his goodnes.

MAGDALYN
Recomende us onto his hyȝnes,
And telle hym all oure hertys wo.
But he comforte oure hevynes,
Oure werdly joy awey wyl go.

QUARTUS CONSOLATOR ET NUNCIUS
The trewth, forsoth, all every dele
As ȝe haue told, so xal I say.
Go to ȝoure brothyr and cheryse hym wele,
For I walke forth streyte in my way.

MARTHA
What chere, good brothyr? Telle me I pray,
What wele ȝe ete? What wele ȝe drynk?
Loke what is plesynge to ȝoure pay;
Ȝe xal haue what ȝe wole thynke.

LAZARUS
My wynde is stoppyd! Gon is my breth,
And deth is come to make myn ende.
To God in hevyn my sowle I qweth.
Farwell, systeryn, for hens I wende.

Hic Lazarus moritur, et cetera.

MAGDALYN
Alas, for wo myn here I rende! f. 129v
Myn owyn dere brothyr lyth here now ded!
Now haue we lost a trusty frende,
Þe sybbest blood of oure kynreed.

MARTHA
Alas, alas, and weleway!
Now be we tweyn bothe brotherles.
For who my hert is colde as clay!
A, hoo xal comforte oure carefulnes?
Ther had nevyr woman more doolfulnes.
A, systyr Magdalyn, what is ȝoure reed?

96 werdly] s (?) *obliterated after* y here goth he his way *written at right of 100 by another scribe that B identifies as Scribe C* 102 *In the second* wele, l *malformed, perhaps written over an erasure* 106 *One or two letters canc. before* come 118 Mad (?) *canc. in red before* Magdalyn

What whith may helpe oure hevynes
Now þat oure brother is gon and deed?

MAGDALYN
Alas, dere systyr, I cannot telle.
þe best comforte þat I can sey,
But sum man do us sle and qwelle,
Lete us ly down by hym and dey.
Alas, why went he alone awey?
If we had deyd with hym also,
Than had oure care all turnyd to pley
Ther now all joye is turnyd to woo.

PRIMUS CONSOLATOR
Be of good comforte and thank God of al,
For deth is dew to every man.
What tyme þat deth on us xal fal
Non erthely wyght þe oure telle can.

MARTHA
We all xul dye, þat is sertan.
But ȝit þe blood of kynde nature,
Whan deth þe brothyr awey hath tan,
Must nedys murne þat sepulture.

f. 130r SECUNDUS CONSOLATOR
Good frendys, I pray ȝow, holde ȝoure pes.
All ȝoure wepynge may not amende itt.
Of ȝoure sorwynge, þerfore, now ses,
And helpe he were buryed in a cley pitt.

MAGDALYN
Alas, þat wurde myn herte doth slytt,
þat he must now in cley be graue.
I wolde sum man my throte wulde kytt
þat I with hym myght lyne in caue.

TERCIUS CONSOLATOR
Bothe heed and foot now he is wounde
In a chete bothe fayr and clene.
Lete us bere hym streyte to þat grounde
Where þat ȝe thynke his graue xal bene.

MARTHA
We be full lothe þat pytt to sen.
But stondynge it may no bettyr be,

122 sey] say, *with deleting dot under* a *and* e *interl. above* 133 sertan] a *altered from an* e 146 chete] s *written before* c *in darker ink*

The coors take up ȝow thre betwen.
With carefull herte ȝow folwe xal we.

Hic portauit corpus ad sepelliendum.

MAGDALEYN Alas, comforte, I se non othyr,
But all of sorwe, and care, and woo!
We dulfull women must burry oure brothir—
Alas, þat deth me wyl not slo!
If I to pitt with hym myght go,
Þerin evyrmore with hym to abyde,
Than were my care all went me fro,
Þer now grett sorwe doth wounde me wyde.

PRIMUS CONSOLATOR This coors we burry here in þis pytte;
Allmyghty God þe sowle mut haue.
And with þis ston þis graue we shytte,
Fro ravenous bestys þe body to saue.
MAGDALYN He is now brought into his cave. f. 130v
Myn hert for wo þis syght doth kylle!
Lete us sytt down here by þe grave,
Or we go hens wepe all oure fylle.

MARTHA Vs for to wepe no man may lett,
Beforn oure face to se þis syght.
Alas, qwy doth deth us not fett,
Vs for to brynge to þis same plyght?
SECUNDUS CONSOLATOR Arys! For shame, ȝe do not ryght!
Streyth from þis grave ȝe xul go hens.
Þus for to grugge ageyns Godys myght,
Aȝens hyȝ God ȝe do offens.

MAGDALEN Syth I must nedys with ȝow hens gon,
My brotherys graue lete me fyrst kys.
Alas, no whith may helpe my mon.
Farewel, my brothyr. Farewel, my blys.

153 MAGDALEYN] g *altered from a* d 164 ravenous] *altered from* rauenous
165 cave] v *has a rough flourish, as if altered from a* u 173 f *canc. in red before* shame

TERCIUS CONSOLATOR
Hom to ȝoure place we xal ȝow wysse.
For Goddys loue, be of good chere.
Indede, ȝe do ryght sore amys,
So sore to wepe as ȝe do here.

MARTHA
Lete us go hom than to oure place.
We pray ȝow all with us to abyde,
Vs to comforte with sum solace
Tyl þat oure sorwe doth slake and sclyde.

PRIMUS CONSOLATOR
Ȝow for to comforte at every tyde
We xall dwelle here bothe nyght and day.
And God, þat made þis werd so wyde,
Be ȝowre comforte, þat best may.

Hic iiij^{us} Consolator et Nuncius loquitur Jesu, dicens:

f. 131^{r} QUARTUS CONSOLATOR
Heyl, holy prophete, Jesu be name!
Martha and Mawdelyn, þo systeryn too,
Recomende hem to ȝoure hyȝ fame,
And bad me sey to ȝow þus, loo:
How þat Lazare, qwhich þat ȝe lovyd so,
With grett syknes is sore dyssesyd.
To hym they prayd ȝow þat ȝe wolde goo,
If þat ȝoure hyȝnes þerwith were plesyd.

JESUS
Dedly syknes Lazare hath non,
But for to shewe Goddys grete glorye,
For þat syknes is ordeynyd alon
þe Sone of God to gloryfie.

NUNCIUS
They be in dowte þat he xal deye—
Grett syknes hym sore doth holde.
For veruent hete his blood doth dreye;
His colore chaungyth, as they me tolde.

JESUS
Goo hom ageyn and telle hem thus:
I xal come to hem whan þat I may.

NUNC[IU]S
At ȝoure comaundement, O prophete Jesus,
I xal hem telle as ȝe do say.

207 drre, *with deleting dot under the first* r, *canc. before* dreye   211 NUNCIUS] *four minims follow* c

JESUS
Come forth, bretheryn, walke we oure way,
Into Jurye go we anon.
I cam not there ful many a day;
þerfore thedyr now wyl I gon.

OMNES DISCIPULI
The Jewys ageyn the were grym and grylle.
Whan þu wore there they wolde þe a slayn!
With stonys they sowte þe for to kyll, f. 131ᵛ
And wylt þu now go thedyr ageyn?

JESUS
Xij owrys þe day hath, in certeyn,
In them to walke bothe clere and bryght.
He xal not stomble ageyn hyll nor pleyn
þat goth þe wey whyl it is daylyght.

But if men walke whan it is nyght,
Sone they offende in þat dyrknes.
Becawse they may haue no cler syght,
They hurte there fete ofte in such myrkenes.
But as for this, ȝitt nevyrþelesse,
The cawse þerfore I thedyr wyl wende
Is for to reyse from bedde expresse
Lazare, þat slepyth, oure althere frende.

OMNES DISCIPULI
Of his syknes he xal be save.
If þat he slepe, good sygne it is.

JESUS
Lazare is deed and leyd in grave;
Of his slepynge ȝe deme amys.
I was not there, ȝe knew weyl this.
To strengthe ȝoure feyth I am ful glad.
þerfore I telle ȝow þe trewthe, iwys:
Oure frende is deed and vndyr erth clad.

THOMAS
Than goo we all ryght evyn streyth thedyr,
Thereas oure frende Lazare is deed,
And lete us deye with hym togedyr,
þeras he lyth, in þe same stede.

F. 131ᵛ marked 130 222 walke] l *adapted from* r *over a deleting dot* *The ink is darker and the lines slightly less regular from* 225 233 DISCIPULI] p *adapted from an* l syknes] k *altered from another letter* 237 *an incomplete* w (*?*) *canc. before* knew weyl] e *interl.*

f. 132r JESUS

The for to deye haue þu no drede.
The wey streyth thedyr in hast we take.
Be þe grett myght of myn Godhede,
Oute of his slepe he xal awake.

NUNCIUS

All heyl, Martha and Mawdelyn eke,
To Jesu I haue ȝoure massage seyd.
I tolde hym how þat ȝoure brothyr was seke
And with grett peyn in his bed leyd.
He bad ȝe xulde not be dysmayde:
All his syknes he xal askape.
He wyll byn here within a brayde;
As he me tolde, he comyth in rape.

MAWDELYN

That holy prophete doth come to late:
Oure brothyr is beryed iij days or this.
A grett [ston] stoppyth þe pyttys gate
Thereas oure brothere beryde is.

NUNCIUS

Is Lazare deed? Now God his sowle blys.
Ȝit loke ȝe take non hevynes.
So longe to wepe ȝe don amys;
It may not helpe ȝoure sorynes.

MARTHA

Out of myn herte all care to lete,
All sorwe and wo to caste away,
I xal go forth in þe strete
To mete with Jesu if þat I may.

SECUNDUS CONSOLATOR

God be ȝoure spede bothe evyr and ay,
For with ȝoure sustyr we wyl abyde.
Here to comforte we xal asay,
And all here care to caste asyde.

f. 132v TERCIUS CONSOLATOR

Mary Mawdelyn, be of good herte,
And wel bethynke ȝow in ȝoure mynde,
Eche creature hens must depart:
Þer is no man but hens must wende.

250 seyd] sayd, *with deleting dot under* a *and* e *interl. above* 257 MAWDELYN] w *adapted from another letter* (d*?*) 259 ston *supplied, following a reviser* (*C?*), *who interl.* stone *in black*

Deth to no wyht can be a frende.
Allþinge to erth he wyl down cast.
Whan þat God wol, allthynge hath ende;
Lengere than hym lyst, nothynge may last.

MAGDALYN I thanke ȝow, frendys, for ȝoure good chere.
Myn hed doth ake as it xulde brest.
I pray ȝow, therfore, while ȝe ben here,
A lytil whyle þat I may rest.

QUARTUS CONSOLATOR NUNC[IUS] Þat Lord þat made bothe est and west
Graunt ȝow good grace suche rest to take
Þat onto hym xulde plese most best,
As he þis worlde of nought dyd make.

MARTHA A, gracyous Lord, had ȝe ben here,
My brother Lazare þis tyme had lyved.
But iiij days gon upon a bere
We dede hym berye whan he was ded.
Ȝitt now I knowe, withowtyn drede,
What thynge of God þat þu do craue,
Þu xalt spede of þe hyȝ Godhede:
Whatso þu aske, þu xalt it haue.

JESUS Thy brothyr Lazare aȝen xal ryse,
A levynge man aȝen to be.

MARTHA I woot wel þat at þe grett last syse
He xal aryse, and also we.

JESUS Resurreccyon þu mast me se, f. 133r
And hendeles lyff I am also.
What man þat deyth and levyth in me,
From deth to lyve he xal ageyn go.

Eche man in me þat feythful is,
And ledyth his lyff aftere my lore,
Of hendeles lyff may he nevyr mys:
Euere he xal leve, and deye nevyrmore.

283 wyl *canc. in red before* while 285 NUNCIUS] Nunc, *remainder cropped* 290 lyved] y *below the line and above an erased letter* (e?) 292 *several letters* (was?) *canc. in red before* was 300 *a red virgule after* aryse

The body and sowle I xal restore
To endeles joye. Dost þu trowe this?
MARTHA I hope in the, O Cryst, ful sore.
þu art þe Sone of God in blys.

Thy fadyr is God, of lyff endeles;
þiself is sone of lyff and gras.
To sese these wordlys wrecchydnes,
From hefne to erth þu toke þe pas.
JESUS Of hevynly myght ryght grett solas
To all þis world me xul sone se.
Go calle þi systyr into þis plas:
Byd Mary Mawdelyn come hedyr to me.

MARTHA At þi byddyng I xal here calle,
In hast we were here ʒow beforn.
MAWDELYN Alas, my mowth is bytter as galle.
Grett sorwyn my herte on tweyn hath scorn!
Now þat my brothyr from syth is lorn,
þer may no myrth my care releve.
Alas þe tyme þat I was born!
þe swerde of sorwe myn hert doth cleve.

f. 133v PRIMUS CONSOLATOR For his dere loue þat all hath wrought,
Ses sum tyme of ʒoure wepynge;
And put allthynge out of thought
Into þis care þat ʒow doth brynge.
SECUNDUS CONSOLATOR ʒe do ʒoureself ryght grett hyndrynge,
And short ʒoure lyff or ʒe be ware.
For Goddys loue, ses of ʒoure sorwynge,
And with good wysdam refreyn ʒoure care.

MARTHA Sustyr Magdalen, com out of halle.
Oure maystyr is com, as I ʒow say.
He sent me hedyr ʒow for to calle.
Come forth in hast, as I ʒow pray.

311 *two brown virgules and one red after* the 326 *two letters* (l *and* e*?*) *canc. before* releve

MAGDALEN
Ha! Where hath he ben many a longe day?
Alas, why cam he no sonere hedyr?
In hast I folwe ȝow anon þe way.
Methynkyth longe or I come thedyr.

TERCIUS CONSOLATOR
Herke, gode frendys, I ȝow pray,
Aftyr þis woman in hast we wende!
I am aferde, ryght in good fay,
Hereself for sorwe þat she wyl shende.

NUNCIUS
Here brothyr so sore is in hire mende
She may not ete, drynke, nor slepe.
Streyte to his graue she goth on ende,
As a mad woman þer for to wepe.

MAGDALEN
A, souereyn Lord and maystyr dere,
Had ȝe with us ben in presens,
Than had my brother on lyue ben here, f. 134r
Nat ded but qwyk, þat now is hens.
Ageyn deth is no resystens.
Alas, myn hert is woundyrly wo
Whan þat I thynke of his absens
þat ȝe ȝoureself in herte lovyd so.

PRIMUS CONSOLATOR
Whan we haue mynde of his sore deth,
He was to us so jentyl and good,
þat mend of hym oure hertys sleth.
þe losse of hym doth marre oure mood.

SECUNDUS CONSOLATOR
Be bettyr neybore nevyr man stood,
To euery man he was ryght hende.
Vs he dede refresch with drynk and food,
Now he is gon, gon is oure frende.

JESUS
Ȝowre grett wepynge doth me constreyne
For my good frend to wepe also.
I cannot me for wo restreyn,
But I must wepe lyke as ȝe do.

362 jentyl] j *altered to* g *in darker ink; duct of this* g *is unlike the main scribe's*
365 ȝ *canc. in red before s.h.* 368 *virgule after the first* gon 370 ll *or incomplete* w *canc. before* to

Hic Jesus fingit se lacrimari.

TERCIUS CONSOLATOR
Beholde þis prophete, how he doth wepe, lo!
He louyd Lazare ryght woundyrly sore.
He wolde not ellys for hym þus wepe so,
But if þat his loue on hym were þe more.

NUNCIUS
A straw for þi tale! What nedyth hym to wepe?
A man born blynde dede he nat ȝeue syght?
f. 134v Myght he nat thanne his frende on lyve kepe
Be the uertu of þat same hyȝ myght?

JESUS
Where is he put? Telle me anon-ryght.
Brynge me þe weye streyth to his grave.

MARTHA
Lord, at ȝoure wylle we xal brynge ȝow tyght,
Evyn to þat place þer he doth lyne in caue.

MAGDALYN
Whan þat we had þe massangere sent,
Or he had fullych half a myle gon,
Deyd my brother and up we hym hent;
Here in þis graue we beryed hym anon.

JESUS
Þe myght of þe Godhed xal glathe ȝow every-
chon,
Suche syght xal ȝe se hens or ȝe wende.
Sett to ȝoure handys, take of þe ston.
A syght lete me haue of Lazare my frende.

MARTHA
He stynkygh ryght fowle longe tyme or this.
Iiij days gon, forsothe, he was dede.
Lete hym ly stylle ryght evyn as he is.
Þe stynke of his careyn myght hurte us, I drede.

JESUS
As I haue þe tolde, syght of þe Godhede
Thyself xuldyst haue, feythful if þu be.
Take of þe ston, do aftyr my rede.
Þe glorye of þe Godhede anon ȝe xal se.

378 dede *altered to* dyde *by another hand* 379 nat] *or* not 387 Deyd] e *altered to* y *in black* 389 glathe] dd *written over* the *in black by another hand* 394 *incomplete* w *or* ll *canc. before* he 396 hurf *canc. before* hurte

PRIMUS CONSOLATOR
Ȝoure byddynge xal be don anon ful swyfte.
Sett to ȝoure handys and helpe, echon.
I pray ȝow, serys, help me to lyfte;
I may not reyse it myself alon.

SECUNDUS CONSOLATOR
In feyth, it is an hevy ston, f. 135r
Ryth sad of weyth and hevy of peys.

TERCIUS CONSOLATOR
Thow it were twyes so evy as on,
Vndyr vs foure we xal it reyse.

NUNCIUS
Now is þe ston take from þe caue.
Here may men se a rewly sygth
Of þis ded body þat lyth here graue,
Wrappyd in a petéfful plyght.

Jesus, eleuatis ad celum oculis, dicit:

JESUS
I thanke þe, fadyr, of þin hyȝ myght,
þat þu hast herd my prayour þis day.
I know ful wel bothe day and nyght
Euyr þu dost graunt þat I do say,

But for þis pepyl þat stondyth about
And beleue not þe power of þe and me,
Them for to brynge clene out of dowt,
This day oure myght thei all xul se.

Hic Jesus clamat voce magna dicens:

Lazare, Lazare, my frende so fre,
From þat depe pitt come out anon!
Be þe grett myght of þe hyȝ magesté,
Alyve þu xalt on erth ageyn gon.

401 anon] an, *with tittle above* n *and deleting dot below it, and* non, *written in left margin by main scribe* swyfte] s *written over another letter* 404 self] l *altered from an* f 407 evy] *altered by a reviser to* hevy *through addition of* h *in black* on] o *written over a letter, deleting dot placed beneath it, and an* o *interl. above* 410 rewly] y *written over an* e 411 in *interl. in black by a reviser after* here 412 s.d. I thanke þe, fadyr *canc. in red and s.d. written at right* 417 pepyl] second p *adapted from a* y 420 thei] *a black* y *written over* i *by a reviser*

LAZARUS At ȝoure comaundement I ryse up ful ryght.
Hevyn, helle, and erth ȝoure byddyng must obeye.
For ȝe be God and man, and Lord of most myght.
Of lyff and of deth ȝe haue both lok and keye.

Hic resurget Lazarus ligatis manibus et pedibus ad modum sepult[*i*], *et dicit Jesus:*

f. 135v JESUS Goo forthe, bretheryn, and Lazare ȝe vntey,
And all his bondys, losyth hem asundyr.
Late hym walke hom with ȝow in þe wey.
Ageyn Godys myght þis meracle is no wundyr.

PETRUS At ȝoure byddynge his bondys we vnbynde.
Allthynge muste lowte ȝoure mageste.
Be þis grett meracle opynly we fynde
Very God and man in trewth þat ȝe be.

JOHANNES þat þu art very God, every man may se
Be this meracle so grett and so meruayll!
Allthynge vndyr hevyn must nedys obeye þe.
Whan aȝens þe þowh Deth be, he may not preuayll.

OMNES CONSOLATORES We all with o voys for God do þe knowe,
And for oure Sauyour we do þe reverens.
All oure hool loue now in þe doth growe,
O sovereyn Lord of most excellens.
Helpe vs of ȝoure grace whan þat we go hens,
For aȝens deth us helpyht not to stryve.
But aȝen ȝoure myght is no resistens:
Oure deth ȝe may aslake and kepe vs stylle on lyve.

JESUS Now I haue shewyd in opyn syght
Of my Godhed þe gret glorye.

428 s.d. sepulti] sepult' 429 breryn *canc. in red before* bretheryn 433 his] h *written over an erasure* 434 *A reviser has interl.* vnto *in black after* lowte 448 ust (?) *canc. before* vs

Toward my Passyon I wyl me dyght:
The tyme is nere þat I must deye,
For all mankynde his sowle to bye.
A crowne of thorn xal perchyn myn brayn,
And on þe Mont of Caluarye,
Vpon a cros I xal be slayn.

[PASSION PLAY 1]

26

f. 136^{r}
N quire

[PROLOGUES OF SATAN AND JOHN THE BAPTIST; THE CONSPIRACY; THE ENTRY INTO JERUSALEM]

DEMON I am ȝoure lord, Lucifer, þat out of helle cam,
Prince of þis Werd and gret Duke of Helle!
Wherefore my name is clepyd Sere Satan,
Whech aperyth among ȝow a matere to spelle.

I am norsshere of synne to þe confusyon of man,
To bryng hym to my dongeon, þer in fyre to dwelle.
Hosoevyr serve me, so reward hym I kan
Þat he xal syng 'wellaway' evyr in peynes felle.

Lo, þus bountevous a lord þan now am I
To reward so synners, as my kend is:
Whoso wole folwe my lore and serve me dayly,
Of sorwe and peyne anow he xal nevyr mys.

Remainder of f. 135^{v} *(35 mm) blank except for some scribbling*

[*Play 26*] *The main scribe's writing in the Passion Plays is comparatively untidy and irregular, with graphemic distinctions from his work elsewhere in the codex. Initial letters of lines are slashed in red more consistently, though less carefully, than earlier in the codex. The paper of quires N and P–R bears a Bull's Head watermark*

10 reward] d *altered from another letter*

For I began in hefne synne for to sowe
Among all þe angellys þat weryn þere so bryth;
And þerfore was I cast out into helle ful lowe,
Notwithstandyng I was þe fayrest and berere of lyth.

Ȝet I drowe in my tayle of þo angelys bryth
With me into helle—takyth good hed what I say—
I lefte but tweyn aȝens on to abyde þere in lyth;
But þe iij^{de} part come with me, þis may not be seyd nay.

Takyth hed to ȝoure prince, þan, my pepyl euerychon,
And seyth what maystryes in hefne I gan þer do play.
To gete a thowsand sowlys in an houre, methynkyth it but skorn
Syth I wan Adam and Eve on þe fyrst day.

But now mervelous mendys rennyn in myn rememberawns
Of on Cryst, wiche is clepyd Joseph and Maryes sone.
Thryes I tempte hym be ryth sotylle instawnce,
Aftyr he fast fourty days ageyns sensual myth or reson,
For of þe stonys to a mad bred; but sone I had conclusyon; f. 136^{v}
Þan upon a pynnacle, but angelys were to hym assystent—
His answerys were mervelous, I knew not his intencyon;
And at þe last to veynglory, but nevyr I had myn intent.

13 Wylliam Dere *written at the right by another hand* 23 *a letter canc. before* methynkyth

And now hath he xij dysypulys to his attendauns.
To eche town and cety he sendyth hem as bedellys,
In dyverce place to make for hym puruyauns.
The pepyl of hese werkys ful grettly merveyllys:
To þe crokyd, blynd and dowm, his werkys provaylys;
Lazare, þat foure days lay ded, his lyff recuryd;
And where I purpose me to tempt, anon he me asaylys;
Mawdelyn playn remyssyon also he hath ensuryd.

Goddys son he pretendyth, and to be born of a mayde,
And seyth he xal dey for mannys saluacyon.
Þan xal þe trewth be tryed, and no ferdere be delayd,
Whan þe soule fro þe body xal make separacyon.
And as for hem þat be vndre my grett domynacyon,
He xal fayle of hese intent and purpose also,
Be þis tyxt of holde remembryd to myn intencyon:
Quia in inferno nulla est redempcio.

But whan þe tyme xal neyth of his persecucyon,
I xal arere new engynes of malycyous conspiracy!
Plenté of reprevys I xal provide to his confusyon.
Þus xal I false þe wordys þat his pepyl doth testefy.
His discipulis xal forsake hym and here maystyr denye;
Innovmberabyl xal hese woundys be, of woful grevauns;
A tretowre xal countyrfe his deth to fortyfye.
Þe rebukys þat he gyf me xal turne to his displesauns.

Some of hese dyscypulys xal be chef of þis ordenawns. f. 137r
Þat xal fortefye þis term, þat 'in trost is treson'.

52 testefy] *a tittle above* y 58 trost] r *written over an* o

þus xal I venge be sotylté al my malycyous grevauns,
For nothyng may excede my prudens and dyscrecyon.

Gyff me ȝoure love, grawnt me myn affeccyon,
And I wyl vnclose þe tresour of lovys alyawns,
And gyff ȝow ȝoure desyrys afftere ȝoure intencyon;
No poverté xal aproche ȝow fro plentevous abundauns.

Byholde þe dyvercyté of my dysgysyd varyauns,
Eche thyng sett of dewe naterall dysposycyon,
And eche parte acordynge to his resemblauns,
Fro þe sool of þe foot to þe hyest asencyon:

Off fyne cordewan a goodly peyre of long-pekyd schon;
Hosyn enclosyd of þe most costyous cloth of crenseyn
(þus a bey to a jentylman to make comparycyon),
With two doseyn poyntys of cheverelle, þe aglottys of syluer feyn;

A shert of feyn Holond (but care not for þe payment!),
A stomachere of clere Reynes, þe best may be bowth
(þow poverté be chef, lete pride þer be present,
And all þo þat repreff pride, þu sette hem at nowth);

Cadace, wolle, or flokkys, where it may be sowth,
To stuffe withal þi dobbelet and make þe of proporcyon
Two smale legges and a gret body (þow it ryme nowth,
Ȝet loke þat þu desyre to an þe newe faccyon);

A gowne of thre ȝerdys (loke þu make comparison
Vnto all degrees dayly þat passe þin astat);

68 Fro] r *altered from an* o 69 fyne] y *altered from another letter* (o*?*)
72 syluer] s *written over a* y 73 cloth *canc. in red after* Holond

A purse withoutyn mony, a daggere for devoscyon
(And þere repref is of synne, loke þu make debat);

With syde lokkys I schrewe þin here, to þi colere hangyng down, f. 137v
To herborwe qweke bestys þat tekele men onyth;
An hey smal bonet for curying of þe crowne.
And all beggerys and pore pepyll, haue hem in dyspyte.
Onto þe grete othys and lycherye gyf þi delyte.
To maynteyn þin astate lete brybory be present.
And yf þe lawe repreve þe, say þu wylt fyth
And gadere þe a felachep after þin entent.

Loke þu sett not be precept nor be comawndement:
Both sevyle and canoun sett þu at nowth.
Lette no membre of God but with othys be rent—
Lo, þus þis werd at þis tyme to myn intent is browth.
I, Sathan, with my felawus þis werd hath sowth,
And now we han it at houre plesawns.
For synne is not shamfast, but boldnes hath bowth
Þat xal cause hem in helle to han inerytawns.

A beggerys dowtere to make gret purvyauns
To cownterfete a jentylwoman, dysgeysyd as she can.
And yf mony lakke, þis is þe newe chevesauns:
With here prevy plesawns to gett it of sum man;
Here colere splayed and furryd with ermyn, Calabere, or satan,
A seyn to selle lechory to hem þat wyl bey;

85 ouyr þin eyn and þin herys *interl. by the main scribe after* lokkys, *perhaps as alternate reading* 88 in *altered from* on, *or vice versa* 91 ll *canc. before* repreve 101 *the notation that normally precedes a s.d. canc. in red at left;* A beggerys *underscored in red, most of which is erased* 103 *a letter* (w?) *canc. before* newe chevesauns *partially obscured by blot*

And þei þat wyl not by it, yet inow xal þei han,
And telle hem it is for love—she may it not deney.

I haue browth ȝow newe namys, and wyl ȝe se why?
For synne is so plesaunt to ech mannys intent.
Ʒe xal kalle pride 'onesté', and 'naterall kend' lechory,
f. 138r
And covetyse 'wysdam' there tresure is present;

Wreth, 'manhod', and envye callyd 'chastement'
(Seyse nere sessyon, lete perjory be chef);
Glotenye, 'rest' (let abstynawnce beyn absent).
And he þat wole exorte þe to vertu, put hem to repreff!

To rehers al my servauntys, my matere is to breff,
But all þese xal eneryth þe dyvicyon eternal.
Þow Cryst by his sotylté many materys meef,
In evyrlastynge peyne with me dwellyn þei xal.

Remembre, oure seruauntys whoys sowlys ben mortall,
For I must remeffe for more materys to provyde,
I am with ȝow at all tymes whan ȝe to councel me call;
But for a short tyme myself I devoyde.

JOHANNES BAPTIS[TA]
I, Johan Baptyst, to ȝow þus prophesye:
Þat on xal come aftyr me and not tary longe,
In many folde more strengere þan I,
Of whose shon I am not worthy to lose þe thonge.
Wherefore I councel þe ȝe reforme all wronge
In ȝoure concyens of þe mortall dedys sevyn.
And for to do penawns loke þat ȝe fonge;
For now xal come þe kyngdham of hevyn.

Þe weys of oure Lord cast ȝow to aray,
And þerin to walk, loke ȝe be applyande.

124 a *written over another letter* 125 BAPTISTA] Baptis, *remainder cropped*

And make his pathys as ryth as ȝe may,
Kepyng ryth forth, and be not declinande
Neyther to fele on ryth nor on lefte hande, f. 138v
But in þe myddys purpose ȝow to holde.
For þat in all wyse is most plesande,
As ȝe xal here whan I have tolde.

Of þis wey for to make moralysacyon,
Be þe ryth syde ȝe xal vndyrstonde 'mercy';
And on þe lefte syde lykkenyd 'dysperacyon';
And þe patthe betwyn bothyn þat may not wry
Schal be 'hope and drede', to walk in perfectly,
Declynyng not to fele for no maner nede.
Grete cawsys I xal shove ȝow why
þat ȝe xal sewe þe patthe of hope and drede.

On þe mercy of God to meche ȝe xal not holde,
As in þis wyse, behold what I mene:
For to do synne, be þu no more bolde
In trost þat God wole mercyful bene.
And yf be sensualyté, as it is ofte sene,
Synnyst dedly, þu xalt not þerfore dyspeyre;
But þerfore do penawns and confesse þe clene,
And of hevyn þu mayst trost to ben eyre.

þe pathe þat lyth to þis blyssyd enherytawns
Is hope and drede, copelyd be conjunccyon.
Betwyx þese tweyn may be no dysseuerawns,
For hope withoutyn drede is maner of presump-
cyon;
And drede withowtyn hope is maner of dysperacyon. f. 139r
So these tweyn must be knyt be on acorde.
How ȝe xal aray þe wey I haue made
declar[acyon],
Also þe ryth patthis aȝens þe comyng of oure
Lord.

137 syde *canc. in red before* hande Be þe ryth syde lyknyd dysperacyon *and* And þe patthe betwyn bothyn *written as two lines below* 141 *and canc. in red* 148 sewe] *or* sowe 150 behold] *or* beheld 163 declaracyon] declararacyon

Here xal Annas shewyn hymself in his stage beseyn aftyr a busshop of þe hoold lawe in a skarlet gowne, and ouyr þat a blew tabbard furryd with whyte, and a mytere on his hed after þe hoold lawe; ij doctorys stondyng by hym in furryd hodys, and on beforn hem with his staff of astat, and eche of hem on here hedys a furryd cappe with a gret knop in þe crowne; and on stondyng beforn as a Sarazyn, þe wich xal be his masangere, Annas þus seyng:

ANNAS
As a prelat am I properyd to provyde pes,
  And of Jewys jewge, þe lawe to fortefye.
I, Annas, be my powere xal comawnde, dowteles:
  Þe lawys of Moyses no man xal denye!
  Hoo excede my comawndement, anon ȝe certefye;
    Yf any eretyk here reyn, to me ȝe compleyn.
  For in me lyth þe powere all trewthis to trye,
    And pryncypaly oure lawys—þo must I sus-
      teyn.

Ȝef I may aspey þe contrary, no wheyle xal þei
      reyn,
  But anon to me be browth and stonde present
Before here jewge, wich xal not feyn,
  But aftere here trespace gef hem jugement.
  Now, serys, for a prose, heryth myn intent:
    There is on Jesus of Nazareth þat oure lawys
      doth excede.
  Yf he procede thus, we xal us all repent,
    For oure lawys he dystroyt dayly with his
      dede.

f. 139v
Therefore be ȝoure cowncel we must take hede
  What is be[st] to provyde or do in þis case.
For yf we let hym þus go and ferdere prosede,
  Ageyn Sesare and oure lawe we do trespace.

PRIMUS DOCTOR
Serys, þis is myn avyse þat ȝe xal do:
  Send to Cayphas for cowncel, knowe his intent.

173 contrary] *second* r *partially crossed through in black and altered to an* l
176 to *deleted before* gef 182 best] *B; MS* be 185 Annas *written below s.h. here and at* 189. *B attributes this and names written below s.h. in 225 and 233 to Scribe C*

For yf Jesu proce[de], and þus forth go,
  Oure lawys xal be dystroyd, thes se we present.

SECUNDUS DOCTOR
Sere, remembre þe gret charge þat on ȝow is leyd,
  þe lawe to ke[pe], which may not fayle.
Yf any defawth prevyd of ȝow be seyd,
  þe Jewys with trewth wyl ȝow asayl.
  Tak hed whath cownsayl may best provayl.
    After Rewfyn and Leyon I rede þat ȝe sende—
  They arn temperal jewgys þat knowyth þe perayl—
    With ȝoure cosyn Cayphas þis matere to amende.

ANNAS
Now surely þis cowncel revyfe myn herte!
  Ȝoure cowncel is best, as I can se.
Arfexe, in hast loke þat þu styrte,
  And pray Cayphas my cosyn come speke with me.

To Rewfyn and Leon þu go also,
  And pray hem þei speke with me in hast.
For a pryncipal matere þat haue to do,
  Wich must be knowe or þis day be past.

ARFEXE
My souereyn, at ȝoure intent I xal gon
  In al þe hast þat I kan hy
Onto Cayphas, Rewfyn, and Lyon,
  And charge ȝoure intent þat þei xal ply.

Here goth þe masangere forth; and in þe menetyme Cayphas shewyth himself in his skafhald arayd lych to Annas, savyng his tabbard xal be red furryd with white; ij doctorys with hym arayd with pellys aftyr þe old gyse and furryd cappys on here hedys; Cayphas þus seyng: f. 140r

187 procede] *B; MS* proce 190 kepe] *B; MS* ke fayle] fay *adapted from other letters* 194 *with* rede, *the ink is generally darker* 195 perayl] *B* parayl 207 Cayphas] *an interl. letter erased over* s

CAYPHAS
As a primat most preudent, I present here sensyble
Buschopys of þe lawe with al þe cyrcumstawns.
I, Cayphas, am jewge with powerys possyble
To distroye all errouris þat in oure lawys make varyawns.
All thyngys I convey be reson and temperawnce,
And all materis possyble to me ben palpable.
Of þe lawe of Moyses I haue a chef governawns;
To seuere ryth and wrong in me is termynable.

But þer is on Cryst þat [in] oure lawys is varyable;
He perverte þe pepyl with his prechyng ill.
We must seke a mene onto hym reprevable,
For yf he procede, oure lawys he wyl spyll!

We must take good cowncel in þis case
Of þe wysest of þe lawe þat kan þe trewthe telle,
Of þe jewgys of Pharasy and of my cosyn Annas.
For yf he procede, be prossesse oure lawys he wyl felle.

PRIMUS DOCT[OR]
Myn lord, plesyt ȝow to pardon me for to say
þe blame in ȝow is, as we fynde,
To lete Cryst contenue þus day be day,
With his fals wichcraft þe pepyl to blynde.
f. 140v He werkyth fals meraclis ageyns all kende,
And makyth oure pepyl to leve hem in.
It is ȝoure part to take hym and do hym bynde,
And gyf hym jugement for his gret syn.

SECUNDUS DOCTOR
Forsothe, sere, of trewth this is þe case:
Onto oure lawe ȝe don oppressyon
þat ȝe let Cryst from ȝou pace
And wyl not don on hym correxion.

216 deuere *canc. in red before* seuere 217 in *supplied; Bev* 222 ll *or incomplete* w *canc. before* lawe 224 ll *or incomplete* w *canc. before second* he 225 DOCTOR] Doct, *remainder cropped* Cayfas *written by another hand below s.h.* 226 haue fow (?) *canc. in red before* fynde 229 all kende *canc. in black and red before* ageyns 230 l *canc. before* to 233 Cayphas *written by another hand below s.h.*

Let Annas knowe ȝoure intencyon,
With prestys and jewgys of þe lawe;
And do Cryst forsake his fals oppynyon—
Or into a preson lete hem be thrawe!

CAYPHAS Wel, serys, ȝe xal se withinne short whyle,
I xal correcte hym for his trespas.
He xal no lenger oure pepyl begyle;
Out of myn dawngere he xal not pas!

Here comyth þe masangere to Cayphas; and in þe menetyme Rewfyn and Lyon schewyn hem in þe place in ray tabardys furryd, and ray hodys abouth here neckys furryd; þe masangere seyng:

MASANGERE Myn reverent souereyn, and it do ȝow plese,
Sere Annas, my lord, hath to ȝou sent.
He prayt ȝou þat ȝe xal not sese
Tyl þat ȝe ben with hym present.

CAYPHAS Sere, telle myn cosyn I xal not fayl.
It was my purpose hym for to se
For serteyn materys þat wyl provayle,
þow he had notwth a sent to me.

MASAGER I recomende me to ȝoure hey degré. f. 141r
On more massagys I must wende.
CAYPHAS Farewel, sere, and wel ȝe be.
Gret wel my cosyn and my fre[n]de.

Here þe masager metyth with þe jewgys, sayng:

MASAGER Heyl, jewgys of Jewry, of reson most prudent!
Of my massage to ȝou I make relacyon:
My lord, Sere Annas, hath for ȝou sent,
To se his presens withowth delacyon.

240 h *canc. in brown and red before* be thrawe] a *altered from an* o? þow *or* yow *written by another hand under* 252 256 frende] frede

REWFYN Sere, we are redy at his comawndement
To se Sere Annas in his place.
It was oure purpose and oure intent
To a be with hym withinne short space.

LEYON We are ful glad his presence to se;
Sere, telle hym we xal come in hast:
No delacyon þerin xal be,
But to his presens hye us fast.

MASAGER I xal telle my lord, seris, as ȝe say,
Ȝe wyl fulfylle al his plesawns.
REWFYN Sere, telle hym we xal make no delay,
But come in hast at his instawns.

Here þe masangere comyth to Annas, þus seyng:

MASAN[GER] My lord, and it plese ȝou to haue intellygens,
Ser Cayphas comyth to ȝou in hast.
Rewfyn and Lyon wyl se ȝoure presens,
And se ȝow here or þis day be past.

f. 141v ANNAS Sere, I kan þe thank of þi dyligens.
Now ageyn my cosyn I wole walk.
Serys, folwyth me onto his presens,
For of these materys we must talk.

Here Annas goth down to mete with Cayphas, and in þe menetyme þus seyng:

CAYPHAS Now onto Annas let us wende,
Ech of vs to knowe otherys intent.
Many materys I haue in mende,
Þe wich to hym I xal present.

PRIMUS DOCTOR C[AYPHAS]. Sere, of all othere thyng, remembre þis case:
Loke þat Jesus be put to schame.

265 LEYON] e *and* o *written over other letters* 266 hym] y *smudged* 273 MASANGER] Masan, *remainder cropped* *F. 141v marked* 140 282 vs] v *altered from another letter* 285 CAYPHAS] C 287 CAYPHAS] C

SECUNDUS DOCTOR C[AYPHAS] When we come present beforn Annas,
Whe xal rehers all his gret blame.

Here þe buschopys with here clerkys and þe Pharaseus mett [at] þe mydplace, and þer xal be a lytil oratory with stolys and cusshonys, clenly beseyn lych as it were a cownsel hous; Annas þus seyng:

ANNAS Welcome, Sere Cayphas and ȝe jewgys alle!
Now xal ȝe knowe all myn entent:
A wondyr case, serys, here is befalle
On wich we must gyf jewgement—
Lyst þat we aftere þe case repent—
Of on Cryst, þat Goddys sone som doth hym calle.
He shewyth meraclys and sythe present
Þat he is prynce of pryncys alle.

The pepyl so fast to hym doth falle,
Be prevy menys as we aspye,
Ȝyf he procede, son sen ȝe xalle
Þat oure lawys he wyl dystrye.

It is oure part þ[i]s to deny. f. 142r
What is ȝoure cowncell in þis cas?
CAYPHAS Be reson þe trewth here may we try.
I cannot dem hym withouth trespace
Because he seyth in every a place
Þat he [is] Kyng of Jewys in every degré.
Þerfore he is fals, knowe wel þe case:
Sesar is kyng, and non but he!

REWFYN He is an eretyk and a tretour bolde
To Sesare and to oure lawe, sertayn,
Bothe in word and in werke, and ȝe beholde;
He is worthy to dey with mekyl peyn!

288 s.d. at] *B; MS* and beseyn] *a mark like a tittle above first* e 289 jewgys] g *interl.* 292 alle *canc. in red after* jewgement þat oure lawys *written in black by another hand below* 300 301 þis] þus, *with* u *rubbed* (*as a correction?*) 306 is *supplied; D* 309 eretyk] t *smudged and perhaps written over another letter*

LEON

þe cawse þat we been here present:
To fortefye þe lawe; and, trewth to say,
Jesus ful nere oure lawys hath shent—
þerfore he is worthy for to day!

PRIMUS DOCTOR AN[NAS]

Serys, ȝe þat ben rewelerys of þe lawe,
On Jesu ȝe must gyf jugement.
Let hym fyrst ben hangyn and drawe,
And þanne his body in fyre be brent.

SECUNDUS DOCTOR AN[NAS]

Now xal ȝe here þe intent of me:
Take Jesu, þat werke us all gret schame,
Put hym to deth! Let hym not fle,
For than þe comownys, þei wyl ȝow blame.

f. 142v PRIMUS DOCTOR CAYP[HAS]

He werke with wechecrafte in eche place,
And drawyth þe pepyl to hese intent.
Bewhare, ȝe jewgys, let hym not passe;
þan, be my trowthe, ȝe xal repent.

SECUNDUS DOCTOR CAYPHAS

Serys, takyth hede onto þis case,
And in ȝoure jewgement be not slawe.
þer was nevyr man dyd so gret trespace
As Jesu hath don ageyn oure lawe.

ANNAS

Now, bretheryn, þan wyl ȝe here myn intent?
These ix days let us abyde.
We may not gyf so hasty jugement,
But eche man inqwere on his syde:
Send spyes abouth þe countré wyde
To se, and recorde, and testymonye.
And þan hese werkys he xal not hyde,
Nor haue no power hem to denye.

317 ANNAS] An, *remainder cropped* 321 ANNAS] An, *remainder cropped* 324 comownys] *a letter* (w?) *erased and crossed through in red after first* o 325 CAYPHAS] Cayp, *remainder cropped* wechecrafte] f *or* s *canc. in red after* weche 328 repent] pe *canc. in red and marked with deleting dots after* re 329 CAYPHAS] p *written over another letter* (h?)

CAYPHAS This cowncell acordyth to my reson.
ANNAS And we all to þe same.

JESUS Frendys, beholde þe tyme of mercy, f. 143r
The whiche is come now, withowt dowth.
Mannys sowle in blys now xal edyfy,
And þe Prynce of þe Werd is cast owth.

Go to ȝon castel þat standyth ȝow ageyn,
Sum of myn dyscyplis—go forth, ȝe to.
þere xul ȝe fyndyn bestys tweyn:
An asse tyed and here fole also.
Vnlosne þat asse and brynge it to me pleyn.
Iff any ma[n] aske why þat ȝe do so,
Sey þat I haue nede to þis best, certeyn,
And he xal not lett ȝow ȝoure weys for to go.
þat best brynge ȝe to me.
PRIMUS APOSTOLUS Holy prophete, we gon oure way;
We wyl not ȝoure wourd delay.
Also sone as þat we may,
We xal it brynge to the.

Here þei fecch þe asse with þe fole, and þe burgeys seyth:

BURGENSIS Herke, ȝe men, who ȝaff ȝow leve
Thus þis best for to take away?

A s.d. and 6-line passage canc. below 342; *the passage bracketed and the s.d. crossed through in red, a brown* x *over the whole,* vacat *written at left. The canc. material reads:*
Here enteryth þe apostyl Petyr, and Johan þe Euangelyst with hym, Petyr seyng:
O ȝe pepyl despeyryng be glad,
A gret cause ȝe haue, and ȝe kan se:
þe Lord of allþing of nowth mad
Is comyng ȝoure comfort to be.
All ȝoure langorys salvyn xal he,
Ȝoure helthe is more þan kan wete

F. 143 is an interpolation in N quire. The hand, though still that of the main scribe, resembles the hand of quires A—M. The leaf is unwatermarked, but is different from the rest of the quire

352 man] *D; MS* mas   360 ȝow] o *altered from another letter and an* o *interl. above*

361 ff. (?) *canc. before* best   away] *second* a *malformed, perhaps altered from another letter*

But only for pore men to releve
This asse is ordayned, as I ȝow say.

PHILIPPUS
Good sere, take this at no greff.
Oure maystyr us sent hedyr þis day.
He hath grett nede, withowt repreff;
þerfore not lett us, I þe pray,
þis best for to lede.

f. 143v BURGENSIS
Sethyn þat it is so þat he hath ȝow sent,
Werkyth his wyll and his intent:
Take þe beste, as ȝe be bent,
And evyr wel mote ȝe spede.

JACOBUS MINOR
This best is brought ryght now here, lo,
Holy prophete, at þin owyn wylle.
And with þis cloth anon also,
þis bestys bak we xal sone hylle.

PHILIPPUS
Now mayst þu ryde whedyr þu wylt go,
Thyn holy purpos to fulfylle.
Thy best ful redy is dyth þe to;
Bothe meke and tame, þe best is stylle.
And we be redy also,
Iff it be plesynge to þi ssyght,
The to helpe anon forthryght,
Vpon þis best þat þu were dyght,
þi jurney for to do.

Here Cryst rydyth out of þe place and he wyl, and Petyr and Johan abydyn stylle; and at þe last, whan þei haue don þer prechyng, þei mete with Jesu.

PETRUS
O ȝe pepyl dyspeyryng, be glad!
A grett cawse ȝe haue, and ȝe kan se:
The Lord, þat allthynge of nought mad,
Is comynge ȝoure comfort to be.
All ȝoure langoris salvyn xal he;
Ȝoure helthe is more than ȝe kan wete.

362 *a letter canc. in black and red after* for 363 asse] assa, *with deleting dot under second* a *and* -e *interl. above* Thus this best to take *canc. in brown and red below* 364 367 y *canc. before* I 377 whedyr] h *altered from another letter* (e.?) 386 dyspeyryng] *third* y *written over an* e

He xal cawse þe blynde þat þei xal se, f. 144^{r}
þe def to here, þe dome for to speke.

þei þat be crokyd, he xal cause hem to goo,
In þe wey þat Johan Baptyst of prophecyed.
Sweche a leche kam ȝow nevyr non too.
Wherfore, what he comawndyth, loke [b]e applyed!
þat som of ȝow be blynd, it may not be denyid,
For hym þat is ȝoure makere, with ȝoure gostly ey ȝe xal not knowe.
Of his comaundementys in ȝow gret necglygens is aspyed;
Wherefore def fro gostly heryng clepe ȝow I howe.

And some of ȝow may not go, ȝe be so crokyd,
For of good werkyng in ȝow is lytyl habundawns.
Tweyn fete heuery man xuld haue, and it were lokyd,
Wyche xuld bere þe body gostly, most of substawns:
Fyrst is to love God above all other plesawns;
þe secunde is to love þi neybore as þin owyn persone.
And yf þese tweyn be kepte in perseverawns,
Into þe celestyal habytacyon ȝe arn habyl to gone.

Many of ȝow be dome. Why? For ȝe wole not redresse
Be mowthe ȝoure Dedys Mortal, but þerin don perdure.
Of þe wych but ȝe haue contrycyon and ȝow confesse,
ȝe may not inheryte hevyn, þis I ȝow ensure.
And of all þese maladyes ȝe may haue gostly cure,
For þe hevynly leche is comyng ȝow for to vicyte.

F. 144^{r} marks the return to the paper and scribal characteristics of N quire 397 be] *D; MS* ȝe 398 it *written over an erasure in darker ink* dey *canc. in red after* not *and* be *interl. above* denyid] id *an addition* 404 Tweyn] *a* y *erased after* y

And as for payment, he wole shewe ȝow no red[d]ure,
For with þe love of ȝowre hertys he wole be aqwhyte.

f. 144v **JOHANNES APOSTOLUS**

Onto my brotherys forseyd rehersall
þat ȝe xuld ȝeve þe more veray confydens,
I come with hym as testymonyall,
For to conferme and fortefye his sentens.
þis lord xal come without resystens;
Onto þe cetyward he is now comyng.
Wherefore dresse ȝow with all dew dylygens
To honowre hym as ȝoure makere and kyng.

And to fulfylle þe prophetys prophesé,
Vpon an asse he wole hedyr ryde,
Shewyng ȝow exawmple of humylyté,
Devoydyng þe abhomynable synne of pryde,
Whech hath ny conqweryd all þe werd wyde,
Grettest cause of all ȝoure trybulacyon.
Vse it hoso wole, for it is þe best gyde
þat ȝe may haue to þe place of dampnacyon.

Now, brothyr in God, syth we have intellygens
þat oure Lord is ny come to þis ceté,
To attend upon his precyous presens
It syttyth to us, as semyth me.
Wherfore to mete whit hym now go we.
I wold fore nothyng we where to late.
To þe cetéward fast drawyth he;
Mesemyth he is ny at þe [g]ate.

Here spekyth þe iiij ceteseynys, þe fyrst þus seyng:

f. 145r **PRIMUS CIUES DE JERUSALEM**

Neyborys, gret joye in oure herte we may make
þat þis hefly kyng wole vycyte þis cyté!

416 reddure] redrure *Redundant s.h.* Apostolus Johannes *written by main scribe in top margin of F. 144v* 439 where] h *written over an* e 441 gate] g *altered from another letter by another hand in darker ink* here enterith (?) þe fyrst prophete *written in bottom margin of f. 144v by another hand in dark ink* 1640 (*or* 16 *and* 40) *written and canc. in light brown ink at top right of f. 145r* 443 hefly] f *written over another letter*

SECUNDUS CIUES Yf oure eerly kyng swech a jorné xuld take,
To don hym honour and worchepe besy xuld we be.

TERCIUS CIUES Meche more, þan, to þe hevynly kyng bownd are we
For to do þat xuld be to his persone reuerens.

QUARTUS CI[UES] Late vs þan welcome hym with flowrys and brawnchis of þe tre,
For he wole take þat to plesawns becawse of redolens.

Here þe iiij ceteseynys makyn hem redy for to mete with oure Lord, goyng barfot and barelegged and in here shyrtys, savyng þei xal have here gownys cast abouth them. And qwan þei seen oure Lord þei xal sprede þer clothis beforn hym, and he xal lyth and go þerupon. And þei xal falle downe upon þer knes all atonys, þe fyrst þus seyng:

PRIMUS CIUES Now blyssyd he be þat in oure Lordys name
To us in any wyse wole resorte.
And we beleve veryly þat þu dost þe same,
For be þi mercy xal spryng mannys comforte.

Here Cryst passyth forth. Þer metyth with hym a serteyn of chylderyn with flowrys, and cast beforn hym. And they synggyn 'Gloria laus', and beforn on seyt:

Thow sone of Davyd, þu be oure supporte
At oure last day whan we xal dye!
Wherefore we alle atonys to þe exorte,
Cryeng mercy! Mercy! Mercye!

JESU Frendys, beholde þe tyme of mercy, f. 145v
Þe wich is come now withowtyn dowth.
Mannys sowle in blysse now xal edyfy,
And þe Prynce of þe Werd is cast owth.
As I haue prechyd in placys abowth,
And shewyd experyence to man and wyf,

448 CIUES] Ci, *remainder cropped* 453 s.d. seyt] *final* -h *perhaps cropped* chylderyn] c *written over another letter* here entreth þe parte off þe ijde prophete *written in black in bottom margin of f. 145r by the hand of the marginal notation on f. 144v* *Redundant s.h.* Jesu *written in top margin of f. 145v*

Into þis werd Goddys sone hath sowth
For veray loue man to revyfe.

The trewthe of trewthis xal now be tryede,
And a perfyth of corde betwyx God and man,
Wich trewth xal nevyr be dyvide—
Confusyon onto þe fynd Sathan.

PRIMUS PAUPER HOMO
þu sone of Davyd, on vs haue mercyȩ,
As we must stedfast belevyn in þe.
þi goodnesse, Lord, lete us be nye,
Whech lyth blynd here and may not se.

SECUNDUS PAUPER HOMO
Lord, lete þi mercy to us be sewre,
And restore to us oure bodyly syth!
We know þu may us wel recure
With þe lest poynt of þi gret myth.

JESU
Ȝowre beleve hath mad ȝou for to se
And delyveryd ȝou fro all mortal peyn.
Blyssyd be all þo þat beleve on me
And se me not with here bodyly eyn.

Here Cryst blyssyth here eyn and þei may se, þe fryst seyng:

f. 146r PRIMUS PAUPER HOMO
Gromercy, Lord, of þi gret grace!
I þat was blynd now may se.

SECUNDUS PAUPER HOMO
Here I forsake al my trespace
And stedfastly wyl belevyn on þe.

27
[THE LAST SUPPER; THE CONSPIRACY WITH JUDAS]

Here Cryst procedyth on fote with his dyscipulys aftyr hym, Cryst wepyng upon þe cyté, sayng þus:

468 Wich] W *altered from another letter* (A?) 470 Davyd] a *interl.* 482 *lacks a capitulum* Gromercy] G *unusually large*

Play 27 carries on directly from Play 26. A large black cross sign written in left margin opposite the first s.d.

JESU

O Jherusalem, woful is þe ordenawnce
Of þe day of þi gret persecucyon!
þu xalt be dystroy with woful grevans,
And þi ryalté browth to trew confusyon.
ȝe þat in þe ceté han habytacyon,
þei xal course þe tyme þat þei were born,
So gret advercyté and trybulacyon
Xal falle on hem both evyn and morwyn.

þei þat han most chylderyn sonest xal wayle
And seyn, 'Alas, what may þis meen?'
Both mete and drynk sodeynly xal fayle—
þe vengeance of God þer xal be seen.
þe tyme is comyng hes woo xal ben,
þe day of trobyl and gret grevauns.
Bothe templys and towrys, they xal down cleen.
O ceté, ful woful is þin ordenawns!

PETRUS

Lord, where wolte þu kepe þi Maundé?
I pray þe, now lete us haue knowyng,
þat we may make redy for þe,
þe to serve withowte latyng;

JOHANNES

To provyde, Lord, for þi comyng f. 146ᵛ
With all þe obedyens we kan atende,
And make redy for þe in althyng,
Into what place þu wy[lt] us send.

JESU

Serys, goth to Syon and ȝe xal mete
A pore man in sympyl aray
Beryng watyr in þe strete.
Telle hym I xal come þat way.
Onto hym mekely loke þat ȝe say
þat hese hous I wele come tylle.
He wele not onys to ȝow sey nay,
But sofre to haue all ȝoure wylle.

PETRUS

At þi wyl, Lord, it xal be don;
To seke þat place we xal us hye,

20 withowte] *second* w *written over a letter* 24 wylt] wytl, *but* t *is faint and* l *malformed*

JOHANNES In all þe hast þat we may go[n],
  þin comaw[n]dement nevyr to denye.

Here Petyr and Johan gon forth, metyng with Symon leprows beryng a kan with watyr, Petyr þus seyng:

PETRUS Good man, þe prophete, oure Lord, Jesus,
  þis nyth wyl rest wythin þin halle.
On massage to þe he hath sent vs:
  þat for his sopere ordeyn þu xalle.
JOHANNES 3a, for hym and his dyscipulys alle
    Ordeyn þu for his Maundé
  A paschall lomb, whatso befalle,
    For he wyl kepe his Pasch with the.

f. 147r SYMON What, wyl my Lord vesyte my plase?
  Blyssyd be þe tyme of his comyng!
I xal ordeyn withinne short space
  For my good Lordys welcomyng.
  Serys, walkyth in at þe begynnyng
    And se what vetaylys þat I xal take.
  I am so glad of þis tydyng,
    I wot nevyr what joye þat I may make.

Here þe dyscypulys gon in with Symon to se þe ordenawns; and Cryst comyng thedyrward, þus seyng:

JESUS þis path is calsydon be goostly ordenawns,
  Wech xal conuey us wher we xal be.
I knowe ful redy is þe purvyaunce
  Of my frendys þat lovyn me.
  Contewnyng in pees, now procede we;
    For mannys love þis wey I take.
  With gostly ey I veryly se
    þat man for man an hende must make.

Here þe dyscipulys com ageyn to Cryst, Petyr þus seyng:

35 gon] go 36 comawndement] *Bev; MS* comawdement 40 xalle] e *malformed, perhaps written over a letter*

PETRUS All redy, Lord, is oure ordenawns,
As I hope to ȝow plesyng xal be.
Seymon hath don at ȝoure instawns,
He is ful glad ȝoure presens to se.

JOHANNES Allthyng we haue, Lord, at oure plesyng
þat longyth to ȝoure Mawndé, with ful glad chere.
Whan he herd telle of ȝoure comyng,
Gret joye in hym þan dyd appere.

Here comyth Symon owt of his hous to welcome Cryst. f. 147v

SYMON Gracyous Lord, welcome þu be!
Reverens be to þe, both God and man,
My poer hous þat þu wylt se,
Weche am þi servaunt as I kan.

JESU There joye of all joyis to þe is sewre
(Symon, I knowe þi trewe intent),
þe blysse of hefne þu xalt recure;
þis rewarde I xal þe grawnt present.

Here Cryst enteryth into þe hous with his disciplis and ete þe paschal lomb; and in þe menetyme þe cownsel hous befornseyd xal sodeynly onclose schewyng þe buschopys, prestys and jewgys syttyng in here astat lych as it were a convocacyon; Annas seyng þus:

ANNAS Behold, it is nowth, al þat we do!
In alle houre materys we prophete nowth.
Wole ȝe se wech peusawns of pepyl drawyth hym to
For þe mervaylys þat he hath wrowth?

Some othyr sotylté must be sowth,
For in no wyse we may not þus hym leve.
Than to a schrewde conclusyon we xal be browth,
For þe Romaynes þan wyl us myscheve,

81 wrowth *canc. in red before* sowth

And take oure astat and put us to repreve,
And convey all þe pepyl at here owyn request.
And þus all þe pepyl in hym xal beleve.
Þerfore I pray ȝow, cosyn, say what is þe best.

f. 148r CAYPHAS Attende now, serys, to þat I xal seye:
Onto us all it is most expedyent
Þat o man for þe pepyl xuld deye
Þan all þe pepyl xuld perysch and be shent.

Þerfor, late us werk wysely þat we us not repent.
We must nedys put on hym som fals dede.
I sey for me, I had levyr he were brent
Þan he xuld us alle þus ouyrlede.
Þerfore every man on his party help at þis nede,
And cowntyrfete all þe sotyltés þat ȝe kan.
Now late se ho kan ȝeve best rede
To ordeyn sum dystruccyon for þis man.

GAMALYEL Late us no lenger make delacyon,
But do Jesu be takyn in hondys fast,
And all here folwerys to here confusyon,
And into a preson do hem be cast.
Ley on hem yron þat wol last,
For he hath wrouth aȝens þe ryth.
And sythyn aftyr we xal in hast
Jewge hym to deth with gret dyspyth!

REWFYN For he hath trespacyd aȝens oure lawe,
Mesemyth þis were best jewgement:
With wyld hors lete hym be drawe,
And afftyr in fyre he xal be brent!

LEYON Serys, o thyng myself herd hym sey,
Þat he was Kyng of Jewys alle.
Þat is anow to do hym dey,
For treson to Sezar we must it calle.

Scribblings and John *written in bottom margin of f. 147v* 89 *lacks a capitulum*
115 *Several words erased in right margin*

He seyd also to personys þat I know f. 148v
þat he xuld and myth, serteyn,
þe gret tempyl mythtyly ovyrthrow,
And þe thrydde day reysyn't ageyn!

Seche materys þe pepyl doth cons[treyn]
To ȝeve credens to his werkys alle.
In hefne, he seyth, xal be his reyn;
Bothe God and man he doth hym calle!

REWFYN And all þis day we xuld contryve
What shameful deth Jesu xuld haue.
We may not do hym to meche myscheve
þe worchep of oure lawe to save.

LEYON Vpon a jebet lete hym hongyn be!
þis jugement, mesemyth, it is reson
þat all þe countré may hym se
And beware be his gret treson.

REWFYN Ʒet o thyng, serys: ȝe must aspye
And make a ryth sotyl ordenawns
Be what menys ȝe may come hym bye,
For he hath many folwerys at his instawns.

ANNAS Serys, þerof we must have avysement
And ben acordyd or þan we go.
How we xal han hym at oure entent,
Som wey we xal fynd þerto.

MARIA MAGDALEN As a cursyd creature closyd all in care, f. 149r
And as a wyckyd wrecche all wrappyd in wo, O quire

121 constreyn] *B; MS* conseyve 123 xal] x *written over an erasure* (?) 130 is i *canc. before* it is *Below* 140 *the s.h.* Jesus *canc. in red. Alongside this the s.d.* Here Judas Caryoth comyth into þe place *canc. in faint brown ink, and in similar ink* now cownterfetyd *is written, but canc. in red. Above this,* myn hert is ryth *canc. in brown. The s.h.* Mawdelyn *written below the canc.* Jesus, *and in the same ink is the catchword* as a cursyd. *Ff. 149–51, comprising O quire, all appear to be Bunch of Grapes paper (f. 151 bears this mark). The hand, though still that of the main scribe, resembles that of quires A–M, rather than N quire* 141 *a capitulum precedes the s.h.*

Of blysse was nevyr no berde so bare,
As I mysylf þat here now go.
Alas! Alas! I xal forfare
For þe grete synnys þat I haue do,
Lesse than my Lord God sumdel spare,
And his grett mercy receyve me to.
Mary Mavdelyn is my name.
Now wyl I go to Cryst Jesu,
For he is lord of all vertu,
And for sum grace I thynke to sew;
For of myself I haue grett shame.

A mercy, Lord, and salve my synne!
Maydenys floure, þu wasch me fre.
Þer was nevyr woman of mannys kynne
So ful of synne in no countré.
I haue be fowlyd be fryth and fenne
And sowght synne in many a ceté.
But þu me borwe, Lord, I xal brenne,
With blake fendys ay bowne to be!
Wherefore, Kynge of Grace,
With þis oynement þat is so sote,
Lete me anoynte þin holy fote,
And for my balys þus wyn sum bote
And mercy, Lord, for my trespace.

JESUS Woman, for þi wepynge wylle,
Sum socowre God xal þe sende.
Þe to saue I haue grett skylle,
For sorwefful hert may synne amende.
All þi prayour I xal fulfylle;
To þi good hert I wul attende
And saue þe fro þi synne so hylle,
And fro vij develys I xal þe fende.
Fendys, fleth ȝoure weye!
Wyckyd spyritys, I ȝow conjowre,

144 *a letter canc. in red before* I   164 anoynte] noyy *canc. after* a   171 *a stroke canc. in red before* I   173 hende *canc. in red before* hylle   174 xal] x *written over a letter*

Fleth out of hire bodyly bowre!
In my grace she xal evyr flowre
Tyl deth doth here to deye.

MARIA MAGDALENE
I thanke þe, Lorde, of this grett grace. f. 149^{v}
Now þese vij fendys be fro me flytt,
I xal nevyr forffett nor do trespace
In wurd, nor dede, ne wyl, nor wytt.
Now I am brought from þe fendys brace,
In þi grett mercy closyd and shytt,
I xal nevyr returne to synful trace
Þat xulde me dampne to helle pytt.
I wurchep the on knes bare.
Blyssyd be þe tyme þat I hedyr sowth,
And þis oynement þat I hedyr brought.
For now myn hert is clensyd from thought
Þat fyrst was combryd with care.

JUDAS
Lord, methynkyth þu dost ryght ylle
To lete þis oynement so spylle!
To selle it, yt were more skylle,
And bye mete to poer men.
The box was worth of good moné
iij C pens fayr and fre!
Þis myght a bowht mete plenté
To fede oure power ken.

JESUS
Pore men xul abyde—
Ageyn þe woman þu spekyst wronge—
And I passe forth in a tyde.
Off mercy is here mornyng songe.

Here Cryst restyth and etyth a lytyl, and seyth syttyng to his disciplis and Mary Mawdelyn:

JESUS
Myn herte is ryght sory, and no wondyr is: f. 150^{r}
Too deth I xal go, and nevyr dyd trespas.

178 x *canc. before* she 183 *more than usual space left after this line,* 187, 195, *and elsewhere* 204 s.d. gohth here outh *canc. in black and red after* Mawdelyn; *the next s.h. written not in lower right margin, as usual, but on f.* 150^{r} 206 Too] Thoo, *with deleting dot under* h

But ȝitt most grevyth myn hert evyr of this:
On of my bretheryn xal werke þis manas.
On of ȝow here syttynge my treson xal tras—
On of ȝow is besy my deth here to dyth.
And ȝitt was I nevyr in no synful plas
Wherefore my deth xuld so shamfully be pyght.

PETRUS My dere Lord, I pray the þe trewth for to telle,
Whiche of vs ys he þat treson xal do?
Whatt traytour is he þat his Lord þat wold selle?
Expresse his name, Lord, þat xal werke þis woo.

JOHANNES If þat þer be on þat wolde selle so,
Good mayster, telle us now opynly his name.
What traytour is hym þat from þe þat wolde go
And with fals treson fulfylle his grett shame?

ANDREAS It is ryght dredfull such tresson to thynke,
And wel more dredfful to werk þat bad dede!
For þat fals treson to helle he xal synke,
In endles peynes grett myscheff to lede.

JACOBUS MAJOR It is not I, Lord! For dowte I haue drede.
þis synne to fulfylle cam nevyr in my mende.
Iff þat I solde þe, thy blood for to blede,
In doyng þat treson my sowle xulde I shende!

f. 150v MATHEUS Alas, my dere Lord, what man is so wood
For gold or for sylvyr hymself so to spylle?
He þat þe doth selle for gold or for other good,
With his grett covetyse hymself he doth kylle.

BARTHOLOMEUS What man soevyr he be of so wyckyd wylle,
Dere Lord, among vs tell vs his name all owt.
He þat to hym tendyth þis dede to fulffille,
For his grett treson, his sowle stondyth in
dowt.

PHILIPPUS Golde, sylver, and tresoour sone doth passe away,
But withowtyn ende evyr doth laste þi grace.

207 grevyth] g *written over an erasure and touched up in darker ink* 211 sy.. *canc. in red before* synful

A, Lord, who is that wyll chaffare þe for monay?
For he þat sellyth his Lord, to grett is þe trespace!

JACOBUS MINOR That traytour þat doth þis orryble manace,
Bothe body and sowle I holde he be lorn,
Dampnyd to helle pytt fer from þi face,
Amonge all fowle fyndys to be rent and torn.

SYMON To bad a marchawnt, þat traytour he is,
And for þat monye he may mornyng make.
Alas, what cawsyth hym to selle þe Kyng of Blys?
For his fals wynnynge þe devyl hym xal take.

THOMAS For his fals treson þe fendys so blake
Xal bere his sowle depe down into helle pytt.
Resste xal he non haue, but evyrmore wake
Brennyng in hoot fyre, in preson evyr shytt.

THADEUS I woundyr ryght sore who þat he xuld be
Amongys vs all bretheryn þat xuld do þis synne.
Alas, he is lorn, þer may no grace be; f. 151r
In depe helle donjeon his sowle he doth pynne.

JESUS In my dysche he etyht þis treson xal begynne,
Wo xal betydyn hym for his werke of dred.
He may be ryght sory swych ryches to wynne,
A[n]d whysshe hymself vnborn for þat synful ded.

JUDAS The trewth wolde I knowe as leff as ȝe,
And þerfore, good ssere, þe trewth þu me telle.
Whiche of vs all here þat traytour may be?
Am I þat person þat þe now xal selle?

JESUS So seyst þiselff, take hed att þi spelle.
Þu askyst me now here if þu xalt do þat treson;
Remembyr þiself, avyse þe ryght welle;
Þu art of grett age and wotysst what is reson.

240 *a letter canc. in red before* trespace 246 moy (*?*) *canc. in red before* monye 247 þ *canc. before* to *Lines on f. 151r are widely spaced* 260 And] Ad

Here Judas rysyth prevely and goth in þe place and seyt 'Now cownter . . .':

f. 152r P quire JUDAS
Now cowntyrfetyd I haue a prevy treson,
My maysterys power for to felle:
I, Judas, xal asay be some encheson
Onto þe Jewys hym for to selle.
Som mony for hym ȝet wold I telle.
Be prevy menys I xal asay;
Myn intent I xal fulfylle.
No lenger I wole make delay.

Þe princys of prestys now be present,
Vnto hem now my way I take.
I wyl go tellyn hem myn entent—
I trow ful mery I xal hem make.
Mony I wyl non forsake,
And þei profyr to my plesyng;
For covetyse I wyl with hem wake,
And onto my maystyr I xal hem bryng.

Heyl, prynsesse and prestys þat ben present!
New tydyngys to ȝow I come to telle.
Ȝyf ȝe wole folwe myn intent,
My maystyr, Jesu, I wele ȝow selle,
Hese intent and purpose for to felle.
For I wole no lenger folwyn his lawe.
Lat sen what mony þat I xal telle,
And late Jesu my maystyr ben hangyn and drawe.

GAMALYE[L]
Now welcome, Judas, oure owyn frende!
Take hym in, serys, be þe honde.
We xal þe both geve and lende,
And in every qwarel by þe stonde.

Remainder of f. 151r (58 mm) blank except for some scribbled letters. F. 151v blank except for the scribbled name John Holand (*or* Holond) *and three black stains in the shape of attenuated triangles. F. 151v marked* 150 *In P quire the paper is again that of N quire, and the scribal features once more resemble those of N quire* 271 I (*?*) *canc. in dark brown and red before* encheson 274 prevy] y *altered from another letter* 291 what] w *written over another letter* 293 GAMALYEL] Gamalye, *remainder cropped* *Scribblings written vertically in left margin of f. 152r, including the name* hollond

REWFYN Judas, what xal we for þi mayster pay? f. 152v
þi sylver is redy and we acorde.
þe payment xal haue no delay,
But be leyde down here at a worde.

JUDAS Late þe mony here down by layde,
And I xal telle ȝow as I kan.
In old termys I haue herd seyde
þat 'mony makyth schapman'.

REWFYN Here is thretty platys of sylver bryth
Fast knyth withinne þis glove.
And we may have þi mayster þis nyth,
þis xalt þu haue, and all oure love.

JUDAS Ʒe are resonable chapmen to bye and selle.
þis bargany with ȝow now xal I make.
Smyth up! Ʒe xal haue al ȝoure wylle,
For mony wyl I non forsake.

LEYON Now þis bargany is mad ful and fast,
Noyther part may it forsake.
But, Judas, þu must telle us in hast
Be what menys we xal hym take.

REWFYN Ʒa, þer be many þat hym nevyr sowe
Weche we wyl sende to hym in fere.
þerfor be a tokyn we must hym knowe
þat must be prevy betwyx us here.

LEYON Ʒa, beware of þat for ony thynge.
For o dyscypil is lyche þi maystyr in al parayl,
And ȝe go lyche in all clothyng; f. 153r
So myth we of oure purpose fayl.

JUDAS As for þat, serys, haue ȝe no dowth;
I xal ordeyn so ȝe xal not mysse.
Whan þat ȝe cvm hym all abowth,
Take þe man þat I xal kysse.

327 cvm] v *written over another letter* (*?*)

I must go to my maystyr ageyn.
  Dowth not, serys; þis matere is sure inow.

GAMALYEL Farewel, Judas, oure frend, serteyn.
  þi labour we xal ryth wel alow.

JUDAS Now wyl I sotely go seke my maystyr ageyn,
  And make good face as I nowth knew.
I haue hym solde to wo and peyn;
  I trowe ful sore he xal it rew.

Here Judas goth in sotylly wheras he cam fro.

ANNAS Lo, serys, a part we haue of oure entent
  For to take Jesu! Now we must provyde
A sotyl meny to be present
  þat dare fyth and wele abyde.

GAMALYE[L] Ordeyn eche man on his party
  Cressetys, lanternys, and torchys lyth;
And þis nyth to be þer redy
  With exys, gleyvis, and swerdys bryth.

CAYPHAS No lenger þan make we teryeng,
  But eche man to his place hym dyth.
And ordeyn preuely for þis thyng,
  þat it be don þis same nyth.

f. 153^{v} *Here the buschopys partyn in þe place, and eche of hem takyn here leve be contenawns, resortyng eche man to his place with here meny, to make redy to take Cryst. And þan xal þe place þer Cryst is in sodeynly vnclose rownd abowtyn shewyng Cryst syttyng at þe table and hese dyscypulis ech in ere degré; Cryst þus seyng:*

JESU Brederyn, þis lambe þat was set us beforn
  þat we alle haue etyn in þis nyth,

341 GAMALYEL] Gamalye, *remainder cropped* man] a *malformed, possibly written over another letter* 342 bryth *canc. in red before* lyth 344 gleyvis] le *written over other letters* John hollond *and some scribbled letters written vertically in left margin of f. 153^{v}* *The first line of* 348 s.d. *contains unusually tall ascenders* xal *deleted before* sodeynly

It was comawndyd be my fadyr to Moyses and Aaron
Whan þei weryn with þe Chylderyn of Israel in
Egythp.

And as we with swete bredys haue it ete,
And also with þe byttyr sokelyng,
And as we take þe hed with þe fete,
So dede þei in all maner thyng.

And as we stodyn so dede þei stond;
And here reynes þei gyrdyn, veryly,
With schon on here fete and stavys in here hond;
And as we ete it, so dede þei, hastyly.
þis fygure xal sesse; anothyr xal folwe þerby,
Weche xal be of my body, þat am ȝoure hed,
Weche xal be shewyd to ȝow be a mystery
Of my flesch and blood in forme of bred.

And with fervent desyre of hertys affeccyon
I have enterly desyryd to kepe my Mawndé
Among ȝow or þan I suffre my Passyon.
For of þis no more togedyr suppe xal we.
And as þe paschal lomb etyn haue we f. 154r
In þe eld lawe was vsyd for a sacryfyce, Q quire
So þe newe lomb þat xal be sacryd be me
Xal be vsyd for a sacryfyce most of price.

Here xal Jesus take an oblé in his hand lokyng vpward into hefne, to þe Fadyr þus seyng:

Wherefore to þe, Fadyr of Hefne þat art eternall,
Thankyng and honor I ȝeld onto þe,
To whom be þe Godhed I am eqwall,
But be my manhod I am of lesse degré.
Wherefore I as man worchep þe Deyté,
Thankyng þe, fadyr, þat þu wylt shew þis
mystery;

353 *letter(s) erased before* bredys *More blank space than usual is left at bottom of f. 153v* 369 *contains unusually tall ascenders*

And þus þurwe þi myth, fadyr, and blyssyng of me,
Of þis þat was bred is mad my body.

Here xal he spekyn ageyn to his dyscipulys, þus seyng:

Bretheryn, be þe [vertu] of þese wordys þat [re]hercyd be,
þis þat shewyth as bred to ȝoure apparens
Is mad þe very flesche and blod of me,
To þe weche þei þat wole be savyd must ȝeve credens.

And as in þe olde lawe it was comawndyd and precepte
To ete þis lomb to þe dystruccyon of Pharao vnkende,
So to dystroy ȝoure gostly enmye þis xal be kepte
For ȝoure paschal lombe into þe werdys ende.

For þis is þe very lombe withowte spot of synne
Of weche Johan þe Baptyst dede prophesy
Whan þis prophesye he dede begynne,
Seyng, 'Ecce Agnus Dey'.

And how ȝe xal ete þis lombe I xal ȝeve infformacyon
In þe same forme as þe eld lawe doth specyfye,
As I shewe be gostly interpretacyon;
þerfore to þat I xal sey, ȝoure wyttys loke ȝe replye.

f. 154v With no byttyr bred þis bred ete xal be:
þat is to say, with no byttyrnesse of hate and envye,
But with þe suete bred of loue and charyté,
Weche fortefyet þe soule gretlye.

381 *written in right margin and partially cropped, and written again in red at foot of f. 154r, whence emendations are taken. A red marginal mark appears at left of* 381 *and before the rubricated version of this line at bottom of page* vertu *supplied* rehercyd] hercyd 382 apparens] apperens, *with deleting dot under the first* e *and* a *interl. above* 387 gostly] *an imperfect letter after* g xal] x *blotted* 396 wyttys] *B* wyllys; tt *blotted* ȝe *canc. before* loke *Vertical scribblings and drawings appear in left margin of f. 154v Capitals in initial words of stanzas are unusually large and heavily rubricated on f. 154v and on subsequent pages* 397 ȝe *canc. before* be

And it schuld ben etyn with þe byttyr sokelyng:
  þat is to mene, ȝyf a man be of synful dysposysyon,
Hath led his lyff here with myslevyng,
  þerfore in his hert he xal haue byttyr contrycyon.

Also, þe hed with þe feet ete xal ȝe:
  Be þe hed ȝe xal vndyrstand my Godhed,
And be þe feet ȝe xal take myn humanyté.
  þese tweyn ȝe xal receyve togedyr, indede.

This immaculat lombe þat I xal ȝow ȝeve
  Is not only þe Godhed alone,
But bothe God and man, þus must ȝe beleve;
  þus þe hed with þe feet ȝe xal receyve echon.

Of þis lombe vnete yf owth belevyth, iwys,
  Yt xuld be cast in þe clere fyre and brent;
Weche is to mene, yf þu vndyrstande nowth al þis,
  Put þi feyth in God and þan þu xalt not be shent.

The gyrdyl þat was comawndyd here reynes to sprede
  Xal be þe gyrdyl of clennes and chastyté.
þat is to sayn, to be contynent in word, thought, and dede,
  And all leccherous levyng cast ȝow for to fle.

And þe schon þat xal be ȝoure feet vpon
  Is not ellys but exawnpyl of vertuis levyng
Of ȝoure form-faderys ȝou beforn;
  With þese schon my steppys ȝe xal be sewyng.

And þe staf þat in ȝoure handys ȝe xal holde f. 155r
  Is not ellys but þe exawmplys to other men teche;
Hold fast ȝoure stauys in ȝoure handys and beth bolde
  To every creature myn precepttys for to preche.

402 *a word* (?m..n....e) *canc. in red before* man 426 *a stroke canc. before* not

Also, ȝe must ete þis paschall lombe hastyly,
  Of weche sentens þis is þe very entent:
At every oure and tyme ȝe xal be redy
  For to fulfylle my cowmawndement.

For þow ȝe leve þis day, ȝe are not sure
  Whedyr ȝe xal leve tomorwe or nowth.
Þerfor hastyly every oure do ȝoure besy cure
  To kepe my preceptys, and þan þar ȝe not dowth.

Now haue I lernyd ȝow how ȝe xal ete
  Ȝoure paschal lombe, þat is my precyous body.
Now I wyl fede ȝow all with awngellys mete;
  Wherfore to reseyve it, come forth seryattly.

PETRUS Lord, for to receyve þis gostly sustenawns
  In dewe forme, it excedyth myn intellygens.
For no man of hymself may have substawns
  To receyve it with to meche reverens.

For with more delycyous mete, Lord, þu may us not fede
  Þan with þin owyn precyous body.
Wherfore what I haue trespacyd in word, thought, or dede,
  With byttyr contrycyon, Lord, I haske þe mercy.

Whan oure Lord ȝyvyth his body to his dyscypulys, he xal sey to eche of hem, except to Judas:

f. 155v [JESUS] This is my body, flesch and blode,
Þat for þe xal dey upon þe rode.

And whan Judas comyth last, oure Lord xal sey to hym:

440 s (?) *canc. before* come   sey *canc. before* seryattly   hollond *and* hary *written vertically in left margin of f. 155r, the former in the hand of earlier marginalia in this play*
449 *s.h. supplied*

Judas, art þu avysyd what þu xalt take?
JUDAS Lord, þi body I wyl not forsake.

And sythyn oure Lord xal sey onto Judas:

JESU Myn body to þe I wole not denye,
Sythyn þu wylt presume þerupon.
Yt xal be þi dampnacyon, verylye—
I ȝeve þe warnyng now beforn.

And aftyr þat Judas hath reseyvyd, he xal syt þer he was, Cryst seyng:

On of ȝow hath betrayd me
Þat at my borde with me hath ete.
Bettyr it hadde hym for to a be
Bothe vnborn and vnbegete.

Than eche dyscypyl xal loke on other, and Petyr xal sey:

PETRUS Lord, it is not I.

And so all xul seyn tyl þei comyn at Judas, wech xal sey:

JUDAS Is it owth I, Lord?

Þan Jesus xal sey:

JESU Judas, þu seyst þat word.

Me þu ast solde, þat was þi frend;
Þat þu hast begonne, brenge to an ende.

Þan Judas xal gon ageyn to þe Jewys. And, yf men wolne, xal mete with hym and sey þis spech folwyng—or levyn't whether þei wyl—þe devyl þus seyng:

DEMON A, a, Judas, derlyng myn, f. 156r R quire
Þu art þe best to me þat evyr was bore!

461 s.d. Judas, wech] *a blot obscures* s *and* w 462 *and* 464 *lack capitula* *F. 155r is a comparatively short page, with considerable blank space left below* 465 s.d. *Redundant s.h.* Demon *written at top right of f. 156r*

þu xalt be crownyd in helle peyn,
　And þerof þu xalt be sekyr for evyrmore.

Thow hast solde þi maystyr and etyn hym also!
　I wolde þu kowdyst bryngyn hym to helle every del;
But ȝet I fere he xuld do þer sum sorwe and wo
　þat all helle xal crye out on me þat sel.

Sped up þi matere þat þu hast begonne:
　I xal to helle for þe to mak redy.
Anon þu xalt come wher þu xalt wonne;
　In fyre and stynk þu xalt sytt me by.

JESU Now þe Sone of God claryfyed is,
　And God in hym is claryfyed also.
I am sory þat Judas hath lost his blysse,
　Weche xal turne hym to sorwe and wo.

But now in þe memory of my Passyon,
　To ben partabyl with me in my reyn above,
Ȝe xal drynk myn blood with gret devocyon,
　Wheche xal be xad for mannys love.

Takyth þese chalys of þe newe testament,
　And kepyth þis evyr in ȝoure mende.
As oftyn as ȝe do þis with trewe intent,
　It xal defende ȝow fro þe fende.

Than xal þe dysciplys com and take þe blod, Jesus seyng:

f. 156v þis is my blood þat for mannys synne
Outh of myn herte it xal renne.

And þe dyscipulys xul sett þem aȝen þer þei wore, and Jesus xal seyn:

Takyth hed now, bretheryn, what I haue do:
　With my flesch and blood I haue ȝow fed.

490 *lacks a capitulum*

For mannys love I may do no mo
  þan for love of man to be ded.

Werfore, Petyr, and ȝe everychon,
  Ȝyf ȝe loue me, fede my schep,
þat for fawth of techyng þei go not wrong;
  But evyr to hem takyth good kep.

Ȝevyth hem my body, as I haue to ȝow,
  Qweche xal be sacryd be my worde.
And evyr I xal þus abyde with ȝow
  Into þe ende of þe werde.

Hoso etyth my body and drynkyth my blood,
  Hol God and man he xal me take.
It xal hym defende from þe deuyl wood,
  And at his deth I xal hym nowth forsake.

And hoso not ete my body nor drynke my blood,
  Lyf in hym is nevyr a dele.
Kepe wel þis in mende for ȝoure good,
  And every man save hymself wele.

Here Jesus takyth a basyn with watyr and towaly gyrt abowtyn hym and fallyth beforn Petyr on his o kne.

JESUS Another exawmpyl I xal ȝow shewe f. 157r
  How ȝe xal leve in charyté.
Syt here down at wordys fewe,
  And qwat I do ȝe sofre me.

Here he takyth þe basyn and þe towaly and doth as þe roberych seyth beforn.

PETRUS Lord, what wylt þu with me do?
  þis servyce of þe I wyl forsake.
To wassche my feet, þu xal not so—
  I am not worthy it of þe to take.

504 drynkyth] r *written over a* y   *a s.h.* (Petrus?) *erased below* 511 s.d. *and* Jesus *written at top of f. 157r*   514 fe (?) *canc. before* wordys

JESU Petyr, and þu forsake my servyce all
þe weche to ȝow þat I xal do,
No part with me haue þu xal,
And nevyr com my blysse onto.

PETRU[S] þat part, Lord, we wyl not forgo;
We xal abey his comawndement.
Wasche hed and hond, we pray þe so;
We wyl don after þin entent.

Here Jesus wasshyth his dyscipulys feet by and by, and whypyth he[m], and kyssyth hem mekely, and sythy[n] settyth hym down, þus seyng:

JES[U] Frendys, þis wasshyng xal now prevayll.
Ȝoure lord and mayster ȝe do me calle,
And so I am, withowtyn fayl;
Ȝet I haue wasschyd ȝow alle.
f. 157v A memory of þis haue ȝe xall
þat eche of ȝow xal do to othyr.
With vmbyl hert submyt egal,
As eche of ȝow were otherys brother.

Nothyng, serys, so wele plesyth me,
Nor no lyf þat man may lede,
As þei þat levyn in charyté;
In efne I xal reward here mede.
þe day is come, I must procede
For to fulfylle þe prophecy.
þis nyth for me ȝe xal han drede
Whan novmbyr of pepyl xal on me cry.

For þe prophetys spoke of me,
And seydyn of deth þat I xuld take;
Fro whech deth I wole not fle,
But for mannys synne amendys make.

524 *no capitulum* PETRUS] Petru, *remainder cropped* 527 s.d. hem] hen, *remainder cropped* sythyn] sythym 528 JESU] Jes, *most of remainder cropped*

This nyth fro ȝow be led I xal,
And ȝe for fer fro me xal fle,
Not onys dur speke whan I ȝow call,
And some of ȝow forsake me.

For ȝow xal I dey and ryse ageyn.
Vn þe thrydde day ȝe xal me se
Beforn ȝow all walkyng playn
In þe lond of Galylé.

PETRUS Lord, I wyl þe nevyr forsake,
Nor for no perellys fro þe fle!
I wyl rather my deth take f. 158r
þan onys, Lord, forsake þe.

JESU Petyr, yn ferthere þan þu doyst knowe
As for þat promese loke þu not make.
For or þe cok hath twyes crowe,
Thryes þu xal me forsake.

But, all my frendys þat arn me dere,
Late us go; þe tyme drawyth ny.
We may no lengere abydyn here,
For I must walke to Betany.

þe tyme is come, þe day drawyth nere;
Onto my deth I must in hast.
Now, Petyr, make all þi felawys chere;
My flesch for fere is qwakyng fast.

28
[THE BETRAYAL]

Here Jesus goth to Betany-ward, and his dyscipulys folwyng with sad contenawns, Jesus seyng:

560 yn] *Hal* thou doyst] o *written over a letter?* 570 all] hall, *with deleting dot under* h 571 qwakyng] q *malformed, perhaps altered from another letter*

Play 28 follows immediately upon Play 27

Now, my dere frendys and bretheryn echon,
   Remembyr þe wordys þat I xal sey.
Þe tyme is come þat I must gon
   For to fulfylle þe prophesey

Þat is seyd of me, þat I xal dey,
   Þe fendys power fro ȝow to flem;
Weche deth I wole not deney
   Mannys sowle, my spovse, for to redem.

Þe oyle of mercy is grawntyd playn
   Be þis jorné þat I xal take.
Be my fadyr I am sent, sertayn,
   Betwyx God and man an ende to make.

f. 158v Man for my brother may I not forsake,
   Nor shewe hym vnkendenesse be no wey.
In peynys for hym my body schal schake,
   And for love of man, man xal dey.

Here Jesus and his discipulys go toward þe Mount of Olyvet; and whan he comyth a lytyl þerbesyde in a place lych to a park, he byddyt his dyscipulys abyde hym þer, and seyth to Petyr or he goth:

Petyr, with þi felawys here xalt þu abyde
   And weche tyl I come ageyn.
I must make my prayere here ȝou besyde.
   My flesch qwakyth sore for fere and peyn.
PETRUS   Lord, þi request doth me constreyn;
      In þis place I xal abyde stylle,
   Not remeve tyl þat þu comyst ageyn,
      In comfermyng, Lord, of þi wylle.

Here Jesu goth to Olyvet and settyth hym down on his knes, and prayth to his fadyr, þus seyng:

JESU   O fadyr, fadyr! For my sake
   Þis gret Passyon þu take fro me,

8 spovse] v *altered from a* u

Wech arn ordeyned þat I xal take
Ȝyf mannys sowle savyd may be.
And ȝyf it behove, fadyr, for me
To save mannys sowle þat xuld spylle,
I am redy in eche degré
þe vyl of þe for to fulfylle.

Here Jesus goth to his dyscipulis and fyndyth hem sclepyng, Jesus þus seyng to Petyr:

Petyr, Petyr, þu slepyst fast! f. 159r
Awake þi felawys and sclepe no more.
Of my deth ȝe are not agast—
Ȝe take ȝoure rest and I peyn sore.

Here Cryst goth ageyn þe second tyme to Olyvet, and seyth knelyng:

Fadyr in hevyn, I beseche þe,
Remeve my peynes be þi gret grace,
And lete me fro þis deth fle,
As I dede nevyr no trespace.
The watyr and blood owth of my face
Dystyllyth for peynes þat I xal take.
My flesche qwakyth in ferful case
As þow þe joyntys asondre xuld schake.

Here Jesus goth aȝen to his discipulis and fyndyth hem asclepe; Jesus þus seyng, latyng hem lyne:

Fadyr, þe thrydde tyme I come ageyn
Fulleche myn erdon for to spede:
Delyuere me, fadyr, fro þis peyn,
Weche is reducyd with ful gret drede.
Onto þi sone, fadyr, take hede;
þu wotyst I dede nevyr dede but good.
It is not for me, þis peyn I lede,
But for man I swete bothe watyr and blode.

38 þi *canc. before* my 48 s *canc. before* drede

Here an aungel descendyth to Jesus and bryngyth to hym a chalys with an host þerin.

f. 159v ANGELUS Heyl, bothe God and man indede,
The Fadyr hath sent þe þis present.
He bad þat þu xuldyst not drede,
But fulfylle his intent.
As þe Parlement of Hefne hath ment
þat mannys sowle xal now redemyd be,
From hefne to herd, Lord, þu wore sent—
þat dede appendyth onto the.

þis chalys ys þi blood, þis bred is þi body,
For mannys synne evyr offeryd xal be.
To þe Fadyr of Heffne þat is almythty
þi dyscipulis and all presthood xal offere fore the.

Here þe aungel ascendyth aȝen sodeynly.

JESU Fadyr, þi wyl fulfyllyd xal be;
It is nowth to say aȝens þe case.
I xal fulfylle þe prophesye
And sofre deth for mannys trespace.

Here goth Cryst ageyn to his dyscipulys and fyndyth hem sclepyng stylle.

Awake, Petyr, þi rest is ful long!
Of sclep þu wylt make no delay.
Judas is redy with pepyl strong,
And doth his part me to betray.
Ryse up, serys, I ȝou pray,
Onclose ȝoure eyne for my sake.
We xal walke into þe way
And sen hem come þat xul me take.

f. 160r Petyr, whan þu seyst I am forsake
Amonge myn frendys, and stond alone,

53 *s.h. written at top of f. 159v rather than bottom of f. 159r* 61 blood] l *written over an* o
71 pepyl] *second* p *malformed, possibly adapted from another letter*

All þe cher þat þu kanst make
  Geve to þi bretheryn everychone.

Here Jesus with his dyscipulis goth into þe place; and þer xal come in a x personys weyl beseen in white arneys and breganderys, and some dysgysed in odyr garmentys, with swerdys, gleyvys, and other straunge wepoun, as cressettys, with feyr, and lanternys, and torchis lyth; and Judas formest of al, conveyng hem to Jesu be contenawns; Jesus þus s[*eyng*]*:*

Serys, in ȝoure way ȝe haue gret hast
  To seke hym þat wyl not fle.
Of ȝow I am ryth nowth agast.
  Telle me, serys, whom seke ȝe?

LEYON Whom we seke here I telle þe now:
  A tretour, is worthy to suffer deth.
We knowe he is here among ȝow;
  His name is Jesus of Nazareth.

JESU Serys, I am here, þat wyl not fle.
  Do to me all þat ȝe kan.
Forsothe, I telle ȝow I am he,
  Jesus of Nazareth, þat same man.

Here all þe Jewys falle sodeynly to þe erde whan þei here Cryst speke; and quan [*he*] *byddyth hem rysyn, þei rysyn aȝen, Cryst þus seyng:*

Aryse, serys, whom seke ȝe? Fast haue ȝe gon.
  Is howth ȝoure comyng hedyr for me?
I stond beforn ȝow here echon
  þat ȝe may me bothe knowe and se.

RUFYNE Jesus of Nazareth we seke, f. 160v
  And we myth hym here aspye.
JESU I told ȝow now with wordys meke
  Beforn ȝou all þat it was I.

80 s.d. seyng] s, *remainder cropped* 81 What *canc. in red before* Serys
92 s.d. he *supplied* 97 And we *canc. in red after* seke

JUDAS Welcome, Jesu, my maystyr dere,
I haue þe sowth in many a place.
I am ful glad I fynd þe here,
For I wyst nevyr wher þu wace.

Here Judas kyssyth Jesus; and anoon all þe Jewys come abowth hym and ley handys on hym and pullyn hym as þei were wode, and makyn on hym a gret cry all atonys. And aftyr þis Petyr seyth:

PETRUS I drawe my swerd now þis sel.
Xal I smyte, maystyr? Fayn wolde I wete.

And forthwith he smytyth of Malchus here, and he cryeth, 'Help! Myn here, myn here!' And Cryst blyssyth it and 'tys hol.

JESUS Put þi swerd in þe shede fayr and wel,
For he þat smyth with swerd with swerd xal be smete.

A, Judas, þis treson cowntyrfetyd hast þu,
And þat þu xalt ful sore repent!
þu haddyst bettyr a ben vnborn now;
þi body and sowle þu hast shent.

GAMALYEL Lo, Jesus, þu mayst not þe cace refuse:
Bothe treson and eresye in þe is fownde.
Stody now fast on þin excuse
Whylys þat þu gost in cordys bownde.
þu kallyst þe kyng of þis werd rownde;
Now lete me se þi gret powere,
And saue þiself here hool and sownde,
And brynge þe out of þis dawngere.

f. 161r LEYON Bryng forth þis tretoure, spare hym nowth!
Onto Cayphas, þi jewge, we xal þe lede.
In many a place we haue þe sowth,
And to þi werkys take good hede.

104 wher] h *interl.* 106 s.d. Petyr put þi s *canc. in red before* And forthwith . . . 107 *s.h. written above* 106 s.d. 111 be *deleted after* haddyst 122 lede] *final* e *written over a* d

RUFYNE Come on, Jesus, and folwe me!
I am ful glad þat I þe haue.
þu xalt ben hangyn upon a tre;
A melyon of gold xal þe not save!

LEYON Lete me leyn hand on hym in heye!
Onto his deth I xal hym bryng.
Shewe forth þi wychecrafte and nygramansye;
What helpyth þe now al þi fals werkyng?

JESU Frendys, take hede. Ȝe don vnryth
So vnkendely with cordys to bynd me here,
And þus to falle on me be nyth,
As thow I were a thevys fere.
Many tyme beforn ȝow I dede apere—
Withinne þe temple sen me ȝe have—
þe lawys of God to teche and lere
To hem þat wele here sowlys sawe.

Why dede ȝe not me dysprave,
And herd me preche bothe lowd and lowe?
But now as woodmen ȝe gynne to rave
And do thyng þat ȝe notwth knove.

GAMALY[EL] Serys, I charge ȝow, not o word more þis nyth,
But onto Cayphas in hast loke ȝe hym lede.
Have hym forth with gret dyspyte, f. 161v
And to his wordys take ȝe non hede.

Here þe Jewys lede Cryst outh of þe place with gret cry and noyse, some drawyng Cryst forward, and some bakward, and so ledyng forth with here weponys alofte and lytys brennyng. And in þe menetyme, Marye Magdalene xal rennyn to oure Lady and telle here of oure Lordys takyng, þus seyng:

MARIA MAGDELENE O inmaculate modyr, of all women most meke.
O devowtest, in holy medytacyon evyr abydyng.

128 M *canc. in brown and red before* A save] v *malformed, perhaps written over another letter* 131 Shewe] w *ill-formed, possibly altered from a* v 138 þe] þis, *with deleting dots under* is, *and* e *interl. above* þ 145 GAMALYEL] Gamaly, *remainder cropped* *f. 161*v *marked* 160

þe cawse, lady, þat I to ȝoure person seke
Is to wetyn yf ȝe heryn ony tydyng

Of ȝoure swete sone and my reverent Lord, Jèsu,
þat was ȝoure dayly solas, ȝoure gostly consolacyon.

MARYA I wold ȝe xuld telle me, Mawdelyn, and ȝe knew;
For to here of hym̄, it is all myn affeccyon.

MARIA MAGDALENE I wold fayn telle, lady, and I myth for wepyng.
Forsothe, lady, to þe Jewys he is solde!
With cordys þei haue hym bownde, and haue hym in kepyng.
þei hym bety[n] spetously and haue hym fast in holde.

MARIA UIRGO A! A! A! How myn hert is colde.
A, hert hard as ston, how mayst þu lest
Whan þese sorweful tydyngys are þe told?
So wold to God, hert, þat þu mytyst brest!

A, Jesu, Jesu, Jesu, Jesu!
Why xuld ȝe sofere þis trybulacyon and advercyté?
How may thei fynd in here hertys ȝow to pursewe
þat nevyr trespacyd in no maner degré?
For nevyr thyng but þat was good thowth ȝe;
f. 162r Wherefore þan xuld ȝe sofer þis gret peyn?
I suppoce veryly it is for þe tresspace of me.
And I wyst þat, myn hert xuld cleve on tweyn.

For þese langowrys may I [not] susteyn,
þe swerd of sorwe hath so thyrlyd my meende!
Alas, what may I do? Alas, what may I seyn?
þese prongys, myn herte asondyr þei do rende.

O Fadyr of Hefne, wher ben al þi behestys
þat þu promysy[d] me whan a modyr þu me made?

160 betyn] bety spetously] sl *written over an erasure* holde] d *blotted, possibly written over another letter* 173 not *supplied following B* 178 promysyd] promysyst

Þi blyssyd sone I bare betwyx tweyn bestys,
And now þe bryth colour of his face doth fade.

A, good Fadyr, why woldyst þat þin owyn dere sone xal sofre al þis?
And dede he nevyr aȝens þi precept, but evyr was obedyent;
And to every creature most petyful, most jentyl and benyng, iwys;
And now for all þese kendnessys is most shameful schent.

Why wolt þu, gracyous Fadyr, þat it xal be so?
May man not ellys be savyd be non other kende?
Ȝet, Lord Fadyr, þan þat xal comforte myn wo
Whan man is savyd be my chylde and browth to a good ende.

Now, dere sone, syn þu hast evyr be so ful of mercy
Þat wylt not spare þiself for þe love þu hast to man,
On all mankend now have þu pety—
And also thynk on þi modyr, þat hevy woman.

f. 163r

[THE PROCESSION OF SAINTS]

PRIMUS DOCTOR
O thou altitude of al gostly ryches!
O þu incomperhensibele of grete excyllence!
O þu luminarye of pure lyghtnes,
Shete oute þi bemys ontyl þis audyens.

SECUNDUS DOCTOR
O fily altissimi clepyd by eternalyté,
Hele þis congregacyon with þe salve of þi Passyon.

184 now *deleted after* is 187 myn *interl.* *Remainder of f. 162*r *(56 mm) and all of f. 162*v *blank*

*[Procession of Saints] Ff. 163*r *and 163*v *are short pages, written by the main scribe, but rubricated differently from preceding matter. The initial letter of each stanza is large and rubricated, there are no capitula, and rhyme-brackets are rubricated* 1 PRIMUS] 1; *also in 9 and 17* 5 SECUNDUS] 2; *also in 13 and 21*

And we prey þe, Spiritus Paraclyte,
With þe fyre of þi love to slake all detraccyon.

PRIMUS DOCTOR
To þe pepyl not lernyd I stonde as a techer,
Of þis processyon to ȝeve informacyon;
And to them þat be lernyd as a gostly precher,
That in my rehersayl they may haue delectacyon.

SECUNDUS
Welcome of þe apostelys þe gloryous qwere:
Fyrst Petyr, ȝoure prynce, and eke ȝoure presydent;
And Andrewe, ȝoure half-brother, togedyr in fere,
That fyrst folwyd Cryst be on assent.

PRIMUS
O ȝe tweyn luminaryes, Jamys and Jhon,
Contynualy brennyng as bryght as þe sonnbem,
With þe chene of charyté bothe knyt in on,
And offeryd of ȝoure modyr to Cryst in Jherusalem.

f. 163v SECUNDUS
Welcome, Phelypp, þat conuertyd Samaryan,
And conuertyd þe tresorere of þe Qwene Cavdas
With Jamys þe Lesser, þat apud Jherosolyman
Was mad fyrst patryarke by þe ordenauns of Cephas.

PRIMUS
Heyl, Mathew the Apostel and also Evangelyst,
That was clepyd to þe flok of gostly conuersacyon
From thyrknes of concyens þat ȝe were in fest,
With Bertylmew, þat fled all carnall temptacyon.

SECUNDUS
Heyl, Symeon Zelotes, þus be ȝoure name,
And Judas, þat bothe wel lovyd oure Lord.
Thereffore ȝe haue bothe joye and game
Wher nevyr is sstryff, but good acorde.

PRIMUS
Heyl, Poul, grett doctour of þe feyth,
And vessel chosyn be trewe eleccyon.

18 Contynualy] nu *obscured by stain* 19 l *canc. before* chene 24 *a red* l *and* Petyr *interl. above* Cephas 29 SECUNDUS] *the* -us *sign in paler ink here and at* 33 *and* 37

Heyl, Thomas, of whom þe gospel seyth
In Crystys wounde was ȝoure refeccyon.

SECUNDUS Heyl, Johan Baptyst, most sovereyn creature
That evyr was born be naturall conseyvyng,
And hyest of prophetys, as wytnessyth Scrypture;
Heyl, [v]oys þat in desert was allwey cryeng.

[PASSION PLAY 2]

29

f. 165^{r}

[HEROD; THE TRIAL BEFORE ANNAS AND CAYPHAS]

What tyme þat processyon is enteryd into þe place and þe Herowdys takyn his schaffalde, and Pylat, and Annas and Cayphas here schaffaldys also, þan [*xal*] *come þer an exposytour in doctorys wede, þus seyng:*

CONTEMPLACIO Sofreynes and frendys, ȝe mut alle be gret with gode!
Grace, love, and charyté evyr be ȝou among.
Þe maydenys sone preserve ȝou þat for man deyd on rode;
He þat is o God in personys thre defende ȝou fro ȝoure fon.

Be þe leue and soferauns of allmythty God,
We intendyn to procede þe matere þat we lefte þe last ȝere.

40 voys] *B; MS* joys *Below* 40 *stands the roughly-drawn s.h.* Primus *in faint ink similar to contraction marks noted above*

[*Play* 29] *The paper of S and T quires bears a Two Crossed Keys watermark. S quire begins on f. 164. F. 164^{r} shows signs of wear; it is blank except for: the quire-mark in black and two quire-marks below (by the main scribe?); the inscription* Ego R. H. Dunelmensis possideo, *with the motto* οὐ κτηόις ἀλλὰ χρησις *in brown ink;* 2 *at the top left;* In nomine Dei Amen *in black by another hand in the top margin; and a stain in the shape of an attenuated triangle. F. 164^{v} blank, except for scribbling, including* Wylliam, *possibly by the hand that wrote* William Dere *on f. 91^{v}. The play-number* 29 *is the only such number written atop the page rather than in the right margin* Initial s.d.] xal *supplied* 3 rode *obscured by blot, as is* fon *in* 4 6 intendyn] d *altered from a* t

Wherefore we beseche ȝow þat ȝoure wyllys be good
To kepe þe Passyon in ȝoure mende, þat xal be shewyd here.

The last ȝere we shewyd here how oure Lord for love of man
Cam to þe cety of Jherusalem mekely his deth to take;
And how he made his Mawndé, his body ȝevyng þan
To his apostelys, evyr with us to abydyn for mannys sake.

In þat Mawndé he was betrayd of Judas, þat hym solde
To þe Jewys for xxx^{ti} platys, to delyvyr hym þat nyth.
With swerdys and gleyvys [to] Jesu they come with þe tretour bolde,
And toke hym amongys his apostelys about mydnyth.

Now wold we procede how he was browth þan
Beforn Annas and Cayphas, and syth beforn Pylate,
And so forth in his Passyon, how mekely he toke it for man;
Besekyng ȝou for mede of ȝoure soulys to take good hede þeratte.

Here þe Herowndys xal shewe hymself and speke:

HEROWDYS Now sees of ȝoure talkyng and gevyth lordly
f. 165^{v} audyence!
Not o word, I charge ȝou þat ben here present;
Noon so hardy to presume in my hey presence
To onlose hese lyppys ageyn myn intent!
I am Herowde, of Jewys kyng most reverent,
þe lawys of Mahownde my powere xal fortefye;

8 shewyd] w *malformed, perhaps written over another letter* 9 lass *canc. in dark brown and red before* last 11 Mawndé] n *miswritten* 13 y *canc. before* Mawndé 15 to] *B; MS* toke 17 *an erasure* (h*?*) *before* how *Redundant s.h.* Herodes Rex *written in large Textura Quadrata in top margin of f. 165*^{v} *and preceded by a capitulum*

Reverens to þat lord of grace moost excyllent,
For by his powere allþinge doth multyplye.

Ȝef ony Crystyn be so hardy his feyth to denye,
Or onys to erre ageyns his lawe,
On gebettys with cheynes I xal hangyn hym heye,
And with wylde hors þo traytorys xal I drawe!
To kylle a thowsand Crystyn I gyf not an hawe!
To se hem hangyn or brent to me is very plesauns;
To dryvyn hem into doongenys, dragonys to knawe,
And to rend here flesche and bonys onto here sustenauns!

Johan þe Baptyst crystenyd Cryst, and so he dede many on;
þerfore myself dede hym brynge o dawe.
It is I þat dede hym kylle, I telle ȝou everychon,
For and he had go forth, he xuld a dystroyd oure lawe.

Whereas Crystyn apperyth, to me is gret grevauns;
It peynyth myn hert of tho tretowrys to here
For þe lawys of Mahownde I have in governawns,
þe which I wele kepe—þat lord hath no pere;
For he is god most prudent. f. 166r
Now I charge ȝou, my lordys þat ben here,
Yf any Crystyn doggys here doth apere,
Bryng þo tretorys to my hey powere,
And þei xal haue sone jewgement!

PRIMUS MILES My sovereyn lord, heyest of excillens,
In ȝou all jewgement is termynabyle.
All Crystyn doggys þat do not here dyligens,
Ȝe put hem to peynes þat ben inportable.

27 Reverens] Reve *obscured by stain* 41 *lacks a capitulum* 43 lawys] aw *written over a letter* (e.?) 47 here] r *written over a* d

SECUNDUS MILES
Noþing in ȝou may be more comendable
As to dysstroye þo traytorys þat erre
Ageyn oure lawys, þat ben most profytable.
Be rythwysnesse þat lawe ȝe must proferre.

REX HEROW[DE]
Now be gloryous Mahownd, my sovereyn savyour,
These promessys I make as I am trewe knyth:
þoo þat excede his lawys be ony errour,
To þe most xamefullest deth I xal hem dyth!
But o thyng is sore in my gret delyte:
þere is on Jesus of Nazareth, as men me tellyth.
Of þat man I desyre to han a sythte,
For with many gret wondrys oure lawe he fellyth.

The Son of God hymself he callyth,
And Kyng of Jewys he seyth is he;
f. 166ᵛ And many woundrys of hym befallyth.
My hert desyryth hym for to se.
Serys, yf þat he come in þis cowntré,
With oure jurresdyccyon loke ȝe aspye,
And anon þat he be brouth onto me;
And þe trewth myself þan xal trye.

PRIMUS MILES
Tomorwe my jorné I xal begynne,
To seke Jesus with my dew dilygens.
Ȝyf he come ȝoure provynce withinne,
He xal not askape ȝoure hey presens.

SECUNDUS MILES
Myn sovereyn, þis is my owncel þat ȝe xal take:
A man þat is bothe wyse and stronge
Thurwe all Galylé a serge to make
Yf Jesu be enteryd ȝoure pepyl among.
Correcte hese dedys þat be do wronge,
For his body is vndyr ȝoure baylé—
As men talkyn hem among
þat he was born in Galylé.

58 HEROWDE] Herow, *remainder cropped* 79 man] ma *only partially inked*
80 Thurwe] hu *blotted*

REX Thanne of þese materys, serys, take hede.
For a whyle I wele me rest.
Appetyde requyryth me so, indede,
And fesyk tellyth me it is þe best.

Here xal a massanger com into þe place rennyng and criyng, 'Tydyngys! Tydyngys!', and so rownd abowth þe place, 'Jesus of Nazareth is take! Jesus of Nazareth is take!', and forthwith heylyng þe prynces, þus seyng:

MASSANGER All heyle, my lordys, princys of prestys! f. 167r
Sere Cayphas and Sere Annas, lordys of þe lawe,
Tydyngys I brynge ȝou, reseyve þem in ȝoure brestys:
Jesus of Nazareth is take! þerof ȝe may be fawe.

He xal be browth hedyr to ȝou anon,
I telle ȝou trewly, with a gret rowth.
Whan he was take, I was hem among,
And [þat I was] ner to kachyd a clowte:

Malcus bar a lanterne and put hym in pres;
Anoon he had a towche, and of went his ere!
Jesus had his dyscyple put up his swerd and ces,
And sett Malcus ere ageyn as hool as it was ere.

So moty the, methowut it was a strawnge syth.
Whan we cam fyrst to hym he cam vs ageyn
And haskyd whom we sowth þat tyme of nyth.
We seyd, 'Jesus of Nazareth; we wolde haue
hym fayn',

And he seyd, 'It is I þat am here in ȝoure syth'.
With þat word we ovyrthrowyn bakward everychon,
And some on here bakkys lyeng upryth;
But standyng upon fote manly þer was not on.

Cryst stod on his fete, as meke as a lom,
And we loyn stylle lyche ded men tyl he bad us ryse.

97 þat I was] þer was I

Whan we were up, fast handys we leyd hym upon;
But ȝet methought I was not plesyd with þe newe gyse.

Therfore takyth now ȝoure cowncel and avyse ȝou ryth weyl,
f. 167v And beth ryth ware þat he make ȝou not amat.
For, be my thryfte, I dare sweryn at þis seyl,
Ȝe xal fynde hym a strawnge watt.

Here bryng þei Jesus beforn Annas and C[*ayphas*], *and on xal seyn þus:*

Lo, lo, lordys, here is þe man
þat ȝe sent vs fore.

ANNAS þerfore we cone ȝou thanke than,
And reward ȝe xal haue þe more.

Jesus, þu are welcome hedyr to oure presens.
Ful oftyntymes we han þe besyly do sowth.
We payd to þi dyscyple for þe thretty pens,
And as an ox or an hors we trewly þe bowth.

þerfore now art oure as þu standyst us before.
Sey why þu ast trobelyd us and subuertyd oure lawe.
þu hast ofte concludyd us, and so þu hast do more;
Wherefore it were ful nedful to bryng þe a dawe.

CAYPHAS What arn þi dysciplys þat folwyn þe aboute?
And what is þi doctryne þat þu dost preche?
Telle me now somewhath and bryng us out of doute
þat we may to othere men þi prechyng forth teche.

JES[US] Al tymes þat I haue prechyd, opyn it was don
In þe synagog or in þe temple, where þat all Jewys com.
Aske hem what I haue seyd, and also what I haue don;
þei con telle þe my wordys, aske hem everychon.

117 s.d. Cayphas] C 125 ox *written over other letters* (?) 131 doctryne] *or* dottryne 134 JESUS] Jes, *remainder obscured by stain*

PRIMUS JUDEUS
What, þu fela, to whom spekyst þu? f. 168r
Xalt þu so speke to a buschop?
þu xalt haue on þe cheke, I make avow,
And ȝet þerto a knok!

Here he xal smyte Jesus on þe cheke.

JESUS
Yf I haue seyd amys,
þerof wytnesse þu mayst bere.
And yf I haue seyd but weyl in þis,
þu dost amys me to dere.

ANNAS
Serys, takyth hed now to þis man,
þat he dystroye not oure lawe.
And brynge ȝe wytnesse aȝens hym þat ȝe can,
So þat he may be browt of dawe.

PRIMUS DOCTOR
Sere, þis I herd hym with his owyn mowth seyn:
'Brekyth down þis temple without delay,
And I xal settyn't up ageyn
As hool as it was be þe thrydde day'.

SECUNDUS DOCTOR
Ȝa, ser, and I herd hym seyn also
þat he was þe Sone of God.
And ȝet many a fole wenyth so!
I durst leyn þeron myn hod.

TERCIUS DOCTOR
Ȝa, ȝa! And I herd hym preche meche þing
And aȝens oure lawe every del,
Of wheche it were longe to make rekenyng
To tellyn all at þis seel.

CAYPHAS
What seyst now, Jesus? Whi answeryst not? f. 168v
Heryst not what is seyd aȝens þe?
Spek, man, spek! Spek, þu fop!
Hast þu scorn to speke to me?

157 hod] hed, *with* e *lightly slashed and* o *interl. above*

Heryst not in how many thyngys þei þe acuse?

Now I charge þe and conjure be þe sonne and þe mone
þat þu telle us and þu be Goddys sone.

JESUS Goddys sone I am, I sey not nay to þe;
And þat ȝe all xal se at Domysday,
Whan þe Sone xal come in gret powere and mageste
And deme þe qweke and dede, as I þe say.

CAYPHAS A! Out! Out! Allas, what is þis?
Heryth ȝe not how he blasfemyth God?
What nedyth us to haue more wytness?
Here ȝe han herd all his owyn word.

Thynk ȝe not he is worthy to dey?

Et clamabunt omnes:

[OMNES] Ȝys, ȝys, ȝys! All we seye he is worthy to dey! Ȝa, ȝa, ȝ[a]!

ANNAS Takyth hym to ȝow and betyth hym somdel
For hese blasfemyng at þis sel!

Here þei xal bete Jesus about þe hed and þe body, and spyttyn in his face, and pullyn hym down, and settyn hym on a stol, and castyn a cloth ouyr his face; and þe fyrst xal seyn:

PRIMUS JUDEUS A, felawys, beware what ȝe do to þis man,
For he prophecye weyl kan.

SECUNDUS JUDEUS þat xal be asayd be þis batte.

166 *is extra-metrical and lacks a capitulum and rhyme-brackets* 167 *small capitula before this and other couplets on ff. 168*v, *169, 169*r, *171*r, *177–79, and 183*v *are rubricated, a scheme found elsewhere in this MS only in Play 41. Small capitula are otherwise in darker ink and precede stage directions* 178 *s.h. supplied* ȝa] ȝ, *remainder cropped*

Et percuciet super caput.

What, þu Jesus, ho ȝaff þe þat?

TERCIUS JUDEUS
Whar, whar! Now wole I f. 169r
Wetyn how he can prophecy—
Ho was þat?

QUARTUS JUDEUS
A, and now wole I a newe game begynne
þat we mon pley at, all þat arn hereinne:

Whele and pylle, whele and pylle,
Comyth to halle hoso wylle—
Ho was þat?

Here xal þe woman come to [*þe*] *Jewys and seyn:*

PRIMA ANCILLA
What, serys, how take ȝe on with þis man?
Se ȝe not on of hese dysciplys, how he beheldyth ȝou þan?

Here xal þe tother woman seyn to Petyr:

SECUNDA ANCILLA
A, good man, mesemyth be þe
þat þu on of hese dysciplys xulde be.

PETRUS
A, woman, I sey nevyr er þis man
Syn þat þis werd fyrst began.

Et cantabit gallus.

PRIMA ANCILLA
What? þu mayst not sey nay—þu art on of hese men!
Be þi face wel we may þe ken.

PETRUS
Woman, þu seyst amys of me;
I knowe hym not, so mote I the.

183 s.d. *not underscored* 192 s.d. þe *supplied* 195 s.d. ANCILLA] ANCILLE 201 amys] y *written over another letter?*

PRIMUS JUDEUS
A, fela myn, wel met,
For my cosynys ere þu of smet.

Whan we þi maystyr in þe ȝerd toke,
þan all þi felawys hym forsoke;

And now þu mayst not hym forsake,
For þu art of Galylé, I vndyrtake.

PETRUS
Sere, I knowe hym not, be hym þat made me!
   And ȝe wole me beleve for an oth,
f. 169v
I take record of all þis compayné
   þat I sey to ȝow is soth.

Et cantabit gallus. And þan Jesus xal lokyn on Petyr, and Petyr xal wepyn; and þan he xal gon out and seyn:

A, weelaway! Weelaway! Fals hert, why whylt þu
      not brest,
   Syn þi maystyr so cowardly þu hast forsake?
Alas, qwher xal I now on erthe rest
   Tyl he of his mercy to grace wole me take?

I haue forsake my maystyr and my Lord, Jesu,
   Thre tymes, as he tolde me þat I xuld do þe same.
Wherfore I may not haue sorwe anow—
   I, synful creature, am so mech to blame!

Whan I herd þe cok crowyn, he kest on me a loke
   As who seyth, 'Bethynke þe what I seyd before'.
Alas þe tyme þat I evyr hym forsoke!
   And so wyl I thynkyn from hens evyrmore.

217 Lord] d *written over another letter*

30
[THE DEATH OF JUDAS; THE TRIALS BEFORE PILATE AND HEROD]

CAYPHAS Massangere! Massangere!
MASSANGERE Here, lord, here!

CAYPHAS Massanger, to Pylat in hast þu xalt gon,
And sey hym we comawnde us in word and in dede;
And prey hym þat he be at þe mot-halle anoon,
For we han a gret matere þat he must nedys spede.

In hast now go þi way,
And loke þu tery nowth.
MASSANGER It xal be do, lord, be þis day;
I am as whyt as thought.

Here Pylat syttyth in his skaffald, and þe massanger knelyth to hym, þus seyng: f. 170^{r}

Al heyl, Sere Pylat, þat semly is to se,
Prynce of al þis Juré and kepere of þe lawe!
My lord, Busshop Cayphas, comawndyd hym to þe,
And prayd the to be at þe mot-halle by þe day dawe.

PYLAT Go þi way, praty masanger, and comawnde me
also.
I xal be þere in hast, and so þu mayst say.
Be þe oure of prime I xal comyn hem to;
I tery no lenger, no make no delay.

Here þe massanger comyth aȝen and bryngyth an ansuere, þus seyng:

MASSANGER Al heyl, myn lordys, and buschoppys, and princys of
þe lawe!
Ser Pylat comawndyth hym to ȝou and bad me
to ȝou say

Play 30 follows immediately upon Play 29
6 a] *written in black, perhaps over another letter* 18 and *canc. after* lenger
18 s.d. comyth] com^{t} bryngyth] bryng^{t} ansuere] u *malformed, possibly altered from another letter*

He wole be at þe mot-halle in hast sone after þe day dawe;
He wold ȝe xuld be þer be prime withouth lenger delay.

CAYPHAS Now weyl mote þu fare,my good page.
Take þu þis for þi massage.

Here enteryth Judas onto þe Juwys, þus seyng:

JUDAS I, Judas, haue synnyd, and treson haue don,
For I haue betrayd þis rythful blood.
Here is ȝoure mony aȝen, all and som.
For sorwe and thowth I am wax wood!

ANNAS What is þat to us? Avyse þe now,
þu dedyst with us counawnt make:
þu seldyst hym us as hors or kow,
þerfore þin owyn dedys þu must take.

þan Judas castyth down þe mony, and goth and hangyth hymself.

f. 170v CAYPHAS Now, serys, þe nyth is passyd, þe day is come;
It were tyme þis man had his jewgement.
And Pylat abydyth in þe mot-halle alone
Tyl we xuld þis man present.

And þerfore go we now forth with hym in hast.

PRIMUS JUDEUS It xal be don, and þat in short spas.

SECUNDUS JUDEUS Ȝa, but loke yf he be bownd ryth wel and fast.

TERCIUS JUDEUS He is saff anow. Go we ryth a good pas.

Here þei ledyn Jesu abowt þe place tyl þei come to þe halle.

24 s.d. Juwys] w *malformed* 31 seldyst] *B* soldyst 33 *s.h. at top right of f. 170r*

CAYPHAS
Sere Pylat, takyht hede to þis thyng:
Jesus we han beforn þe browth,
Wheche oure lawe doth down bryng,
And mekyl schame he hath us wrowth.

ANNAS
From þis cetye into þe lond of Galylé
He hath browth oure lawys neyr into confusyon,
With hese craftys wrowth be nygramancye
Shewyth to þe pepyl be fals symulacyon.

PRIMUS DOCTOR
ʒa! ʒet, sere, another, and werst of alle,
Aʒens Sesare, oure emperour þat is so fre:
Kyng of Jewys he doth hym calle,
So oure emperourys power nowth xulde be.

SECUNDUS DOCTOR
Sere Pylat, we kannot telle half þe blame
þat Jesus in oure countré hath wrowth.
þerfore we charge þe in þe emperorys name
þat he to þe deth in hast be browth.

PYLAT
What seyst to these compleyntys, Jesu? f. 171r
These pepyl hath þe sore acusyd
Because þu bryngyst up lawys newe
þat in oure days were not vsyd.

JESUS
Of here acusyng me rowth nowth,
So þat þei hurt not here soulys, ne non mo.
I haue nowth ʒet founde þat I haue sowth;
For my faderys wyl, forth must I go.

PYLAT
Jesus, be þis þan I trowe þu art a kyng.
And þe Sone of God þu art also,
Lord of erth and of allþing.
Telle me þe trowth if it be so.

JESUS
In hefne is knowyn my faderys intent,
And in þis werlde I was born.

45 ceyt *canc. in dark and red ink before* cetye 59 ll *or incomplete* w *canc. before* newe

Be my fadyr I was hedyr sent
   For to seke þat was forlorn.

Alle þat me heryn and in me belevyn
   And kepyn here feyth stedfastly,
Þow þei weryn dede, I xal þem recuryn,
   And xal þem bryng to blysse endlesly.

PILATE Lo, serys, now ȝe an erde þis man, how thynk ȝe?
   Thynke ȝe not all, be ȝoure reson,
But as he seyth it may wel be,
   And þat xulde be, be þis incheson?

I fynde in hym non obecyon
   Of errour nor treson, ne of no maner gylt.
f. 171v The lawe wole in no conclusyon
   Withowte defawth he xuld be spylt.

PRIMUS DOCTOR Sere Pylat, þe lawe restyth in þe,
   And we knowe veryly his gret trespas.
To þe emperour þis mater told xal be,
   Yf þu lete Jesus þus from þe pas.

PYLAT Serys, þan telle me o thyng:
What xal be his acusyng?

ANNAS Sere, we telle þe al togedyr,
For his evyl werkys we browth hym hedyr;

And yf he had not an evyl-doere be,
We xuld not a browth hym to þe.

PYLAT Takyth hym þan aftyr ȝoure sawe,
And demyth hym aftyr ȝoure lawe.

CAYPHAS It is not lefful to vs, ȝe seyn,
No maner man for to slen.

77 erde] *first* e *blotted*   97 we *canc. and* ȝe *interl. above*

þe cawse why we bryng hym to þe,
þat he xuld not oure kyng be.

Weyl þu knowyst, kyng we have non
But oure emperour alon.

PYLAT Jesu, þu art Kyng of Juré?
JESUS So þu seyst now to me.

PYLAT Tel me þan,
Where is þi kyngham?

JESUS My kingham is not in þis werld,
I telle þe at o word.

Yf my kyngham here had be,
I xuld not a be delyveryd to þe.

PYLAT Serys, avyse ȝow as ȝe kan; f. 172r
I can fynde no defawth in þis man.

ANNAS Sere, here is a gret record; take hed þerto!
And knowyng gret myschef in þis man
(And not only in o day or to—
It is many ȝerys syn he began),
We kan telle þe tyme, where and whan,
þat many a thowsand turnyd hath he,
As all þis pepyll record weyl kan,
From hens into þe lond of Galylé.

Et clamabunt, 'Ȝa! Ȝa! Ȝa!'

PILAT Serys, of o thyng than gyf me relacyon:
If Jesus were outborn in þe lond of Galelye.
For we han no poer ne no jurediccyon
Of no man of þat contré.
Therfore þe trewth ȝe telle me
And another wey I xal provyde.

105–10 *written two lines as one, divided by red virgules* 106 is *interl.*

If Jesus were born in þat countré,
þe jugement of Herowdys he must abyde.

CAYPHAS
Sere, as I am to þe lawe trewly sworn,
To telle þe trewth I haue no fer.
In Galelye I know þat he was born;
I can telle in what place and where.
Aȝens þis no man may answere,
For he was born in Bedlem Judé.
And þis ȝe knowe now all, and haue don here,
þat it stant in þe lond of Galelye.

f. 172v PYLAT
Weyl, serys, syn þat I knowe þat it is so,
þe trewth of þis I must nedys se.
I vndyrstand ryth now what is to do:
þe jugement of Jesu lyth not to me.
Herowde is kyng of þat countré,
To jewge þat regyon in lenth and in brede.
þe jurysdyccyon of Jesu now han must he;
þerfore Jesu in hast to hym ȝe lede.

In hall þe hast þat ȝe may, spede,
Lede hym to þe Herownde anon present;
And sey I comawnde me with worde and dede,
And Jesu to hym þat I haue sent.

PRIMUS DOCTOR
This erand in hast sped xal be,
In all þe hast þat we can do.
We xal not tary in no degré,
Tyl þe Herowdys presens we com to.

Here þei take Jesu and lede hym in gret hast to þe Herowde. And þe Herowdys scafald xal vnclose shewyng Herowdys in astat, all þe Jewys knelyng except Annas and Cayphas; þei xal stondyn, et cetera.

PRIMUS DOCTOR
Heyl, Herowde, most excyllent kyng!
We arn comawndyd to þin presens.

F. 172v marked 170   145 *lacks a capitulum*

Pylat sendyth þe be us gretyng,
And chargyth us be oure obedyens
SECUNDUS DOCTOR þat we xuld do oure dylygens
To bryng Jesus of Nazareth onto þe;
And chargyth us to make no resystens,
Becawse he was born in þis countré.

ANNAS We knowe he hath wrowth gret folé f. 173r
Ageyns þe lawe shewyd present.
Therfore Pylat sent hym onto þe
þat þu xuldyst gyf hym jugement.

HEROWDE REX Now be Mahound, my god of grace,
Of Pylat þis is a dede ful kende.
I forgyf hym now his gret trespace
And schal be his frend withowtyn ende,

Jesus to me þat he wole sende.
I desyred ful sore hym for to se.
Gret ese in þis Pylat xal fynde.
And, Jesus, þu art welcome to me.

PRIMUS JUDEUS My sovereyn lord, þis is þe case:
þe gret falsnesse of Jesu is opynly knawe.
þer was nevyr man dede so gret trespas,
For he hath almost dystroyd oure lawe.

SECUNDUS JUDEUS ȝa, be fals crafte of soserye
Wrowth opynly to þe pepyll alle,
And be sotyl poyntys of nygramancye,
Many thowsandys fro oure lawe be falle.

CAYPHAS Most excellent kyng, ȝe must take hede:
He wol dystroye all þis countré, both elde and ȝyng,
Yf he ten monthis more procede,
Be his meraclys and fals prechyng.

181 excellent] yng *canc. in dark brown and red after* excel

He bryngyth þe pepyl in gret fonnyng,
   And seyth dayly among hem alle
f. 173v That he is Lord, and of þe Jewys kyng,
   And þe Sone of God he doth hym calle.

REX HEROWDE Serys, alle þese materys I haue herd sayd,
   And meche more þan ȝe me telle.
Alle togedyr þei xal be layde,
   And I wyl take þeron cowncelle.

Jesus, þu art welcome to me!
   I kan Pylat gret thank for his sendyng.
I haue desyryd ful longe þe to se,
   And of þi meracles to haue knowyng.

It is told me þu dost many a wondyr thyng;
   Crokyd to gon and blynd men to sen;
And þei þat ben dede, gevyst hem levyng,
   And makyst lepers fayre and hool to ben.

These arn wondyr werkys wrougth of þe,
   Be what wey I wolde knowe þe trew sentens.
Now, Jesu, I pray the, lete me se
   O meracle wrougth in my presens.

In hast now do þi dylygens,
   And peraventure I wyl shew favour to the.
For now þu art in my presens,
   Thyn lyf and deth here lyth in me.

And here Jesus xal not speke no word to þe Herowde.

Jesus, why spekyst not to þi kyng?
   What is þe cawse þu stondyst so stylle?
Þu knowyst I may deme allthyng,
   Thyn lyf and deth lyth at my wylle.

f. 174r What! Spek, Jesus, and telle me why
   Þis pepyl do þe so here acuse.

214 s *canc. before* þe

Spare not, but telle me now on hey
  How þu canst þiself excuse.

CAYPHAS Loo, serys, þis is of hym a false sotylté.
  He wyl not speke but whan he lyst!
þus he dysceyvyth þe pepyl in eche degré—
  He is ful fals, ȝe veryly tryst.

REX HEROWDE What, þu onhangyd harlot, why wylt þu not speke?
  Hast þu skorne to speke onto þi kyng?
Becawse þu dost oure lawys breke,
  I trowe þu art aferd of oure talkyng.

ANNAS Nay, he is not aferde, but of a fals wyle,
  Becawse we xuld not hym acuse.
If þat he answerd ȝow ontylle,
  He knowyth he kannot hymself excuse.

REX HERO[WDE] What! Spek, I say, þu foulyng! Evyl mot þu fare!
  Loke up, þe devyl mote þe cheke.
Serys, bete his body with scorgys bare,
  And asay to make hym for to speke.

PRIMUS JUDE[US] It xal be do withoutyn teryeng.
  Come on, þu tretour, evyl mot þu þe!
Whylt þu not speke onto oure kyng?
  A new lesson we xal lere þe.

Here þei pulle of Jesus clothis and betyn hym with whyppys.

SECUNDUS JUDE[US] Jesus, þi bonys we xal not breke, f. 174v
  But we xal make þe to skyppe.
þu hast lost þi tonge, þu mayst not speke—
  þu xalt asay now of þis whippe!

TERCIUS JUDEUS Serys, take þese whyppys in ȝoure honde,
  And spare not whyl þei last,

228 hymself] y *written over another letter* (e?) 229 HEROWDE] Hero, *remainder cropped* 233 JUDEUS] Jude, *remainder cropped* 237 JUDEUS] Jude, *remainder cropped* 241 whyppys] h *written over a* y

And bete þis tretoure þat here doth stonde;
I trowe þat he wyl speke in hast.

And quan þei han betyn hym tyl he is all blody, þan þe Herownd seyth:

[REX HEROWDE] Sees, serys, I comawnde ȝou be name of þe devyl of helle!
Jesus, thynkyst þis good game?
Þu art strong to suffyr schame;
Þu haddyst levyr be betyn lame
Þan þi defawtys for to telle.

But I wyl not þi body all spyl,
Nor put it here into more peyn.
Serys, takyth Jesus at ȝoure owyn wyl
And lede hym to Pylat hom ageyn.
Grete hym weyl and telle hym serteyn
All my good frenchep xal he haue.
I gyf hym powere of Jesus, þus ȝe hym seyn,
Whether he wole hym dampne or save.

PRIMUS DOCTOR Sere, at ȝoure request it xal be do;
We xal lede Jesus at ȝoure demaw[n]de,
And delyver hym Pylat onto,
And telle hym all as ȝe comawnde.

f. 175r

31
[SATAN AND PILATE'S WIFE; THE SECOND TRIAL BEFORE PILATE]

Here enteryth Satan into þe place in þe most orryble wyse. And qwyl þat he pleyth, þei xal don on Jesus clothis and ouyrest a whyte clothe, and ledyn hym abowth þe place, and þan to Pylat be þe tyme þat hese wyf hath pleyd.

SATHAN Thus I reyne as a rochand with a rynggyng rowth!
As a devyl most dowty, dred is my dynt!

245 *s.h. supplied* 259 demawnde] demawde
[*Play 31*] 2 dyth *canc. in red before* dynt

Many a thowsand develys, to me do þei lowth,
Brennyng in flamys as fyre out of flynt!
Hoso serve me, Sathan, to sorwe is he sent,
With dragonys in doungenys, and develys fu[l] derke!
In bras and in bronston þe brethellys be brent
þat wone in þis werd my wyl for to werke!

With myschef on moolde here membrys I merke
þat japyn with Jesus, þat Judas solde!
Be he nevyr so crafty nor conyng clerke,
I harry þem to helle as tretour bolde!

But þer is o thyng þat grevyth me sore,
Of a prophete þat Jesu men calle.
He peynyth me every day more and more
With his holy meraclis and werkys alle.

I had hym onys in a temptacyon
With glotenye, with covetyse, and veynglorye.
I hasayd hym be all weys þat I cow[de] don,
And vttyrly he refusyd hem and gan me defye.

þat rebuke þat he gaf me xal not be vnqwyt!
Somwhat I haue begonne, and more xal be do.
For all his barfot goyng, fro me xal he not skyp, f. 175v
But my derk dongeon I xal bryngyn hym to!

I haue do made redy his cros þat he xal dye upon,
And thre nayles to takke hym with, þat he xal not styrte.
Be he nevyr so holy, he xal not fro me gon,
But with a sharpe spere he xal be smet to þe herte!

And sythyn he xal come to helle, be he nevyr so stowte.
And ȝet I am aferd and he come he wole do som wrake.

6 ful] fu 13 myn hert *canc. in red before* me 19 cowde] cownde
21 vnqwyt] q *written over another letter*

þerfore I xal go warnyn helle þat þei loke abowte,
þat þei make redy chenys to bynd hym with in lake.

Helle, helle, make redy, for here xal come a gest!
Hedyr xal come Jesus, þat is clepyd Goddys sone.
And he xal ben here be þe oure of none,
And with þe here he xal wone,
And han ful shrewyd rest.

Here xal a devyl spekyn in helle:

DEMON Out upon þe! We conjure þe
þat nevyr in helle we may hym se.
For and he onys in helle be,
He xal oure power brest.

SATHAN A, a, than haue I go to ferre!
But som wyle help, I have a shrewde torne.
My game is wers þan I wend here;
I may seyn my game is lorne!

Lo, a wyle ȝet haue I kast:
If I myth Jesus lyf save,
Helle gatys xal be sperd fast
And kepe stylle all þo I haue.

To Pylatys wyff I wele now go,
f. 176r And sche is aslepe abed ful fast,
And byd here withowtyn wordys mo
To Pylat þat sche send in hast.

I xal asay, and þis wol be,
To bryng Pylat in belef.
Withinne a whyle ȝe xal se
How my craft I wole go pref.

38 DEMON] o *blotted*

Here xal þe devyl gon to Pylatys wyf, þe corteyn drawyn as she lyth in bedde; and he xal no dene make, but she xal sone after þat he is come in makyn a rewly noyse, comyng and rennyng of þe schaffald, and here shert and here kyrtyl in here hand. And sche xal come beforn Pylat leke a mad woman, seyng þus:

VXOR PILATY
Pylat, I charge þe þat þu take hede:
Deme not Jesu, but be his frende.
Ȝyf þu jewge hym to be dede,
Þu art dampnyd withowtyn ende.

A fend aperyd me beforn
As I lay in my bed slepyng fast.
Sethyn þe tyme þat I was born
Was I nevyr so sore agast.

As wylde fyre and thondyrblast
He cam cryeng onto me.
He seyd þei þat bete Jesu or bownd hym fast,
Withowtyn ende dampnyd xal be.

Þerfore a wey herein þu se
And lete Jesu from þe clere pace.
Þe Jewys, þei wole begyle þe,
And put on þe all þe trespace.

PYLAT
Gramercy, myn wyf, for evyr ȝe be trewe; f. 176v
Ȝoure cowncel is good, and evyr hath be.
Now to ȝoure chawmer ȝe do sewe,
And all xal be weyl, dame, as ȝe xal se.

Here þe Jewys bryng Jesus aȝen to Pylat.

PRIMUS DOCTOR
Sere Pylat, gode tydandys þu here of me:
Of Herowd þe kyng þu hast good wyl,
And Jesus he sendyth aȝen to the,
And byddyth þe chese hym to save or spylle.

SECUNDUS DOCTOR
Ȝa, sere, all þe poer lyth now in þe,
And þu knowyst oure feyth he hath ner schent.

83 h *canc. before* knowyst oure] *a black line obscures part of* u

þu knowyst what myschef þerof may be—
We charge þe to gyf hym jwgement.

PYLAT
Serys, trewly ȝe be to blame
Jesus þus to bete, dyspoyle, or bynde,
Er put hym to so gret schame.
For no defawth in hym I fynde.

Ne Herowdys nother, to whom I sent ȝow,
Defawte in hym cowde fynde ryth non,
But sent hym aȝen to me be ȝow,
As ȝe knowe wel everychon.

Therfore vndyrstande what I xal say:
Ȝe knowe þe custom is in þis londe
Of ȝoure Pasche day, þat is nerhonde:
What þeff or tretore be in bonde
For worchep of þat day xal go fre away,

Without any price.
f. 177r Now þan methynkyth it were ryth
To lete Jesus now go qwyte
And do to hym no mo dyspyte.
Serys, þis is myn avyse.

I wolde wete what ȝe say.

Here all þei xul cryen:

Nay! Nay! Nay!

PRIMUS DOCTOR
Delyvere us þe þeff Barabas,
þat for mansclawth presonde was!

PYLAT
What xal I þan with Jesu do?
Whethyr xal he abyde or go?

94 *no capitulum* 98 ff (*?*) *canc. in red before* xal 99 *no capitulum*
Small capitula before stanzas from 104–13 *are rubricated*

SECUNDUS DOCTOR
Jesus xal on þe cros be don!
Crucifigatur, we crye echon!

PYLAT
Serys, what hath Jesus don amys?

Populus clamabit:

Crucifigatur, we sey atonys.

PYLAT
Serys, syn algatys ȝe wolyn so
  Puttyn Jesu to wo and peyn,
Jesus a wyle with me xal go;
  I wole hym examyne betwyx us tweyn.

Here Pylat takyth Jesu and ledyth hym into þe cowncel hous and seyth:

Jesus, what seyst now, lete se.
  This matere now þu vndyrstonde:
In pes þu myth be for me,
  But for þi pepyl of þi londe.

Busshoppys and prestys of þe lawe,
  þei love þe not, as þu mayst se;
And þe comoun pepyl aȝens þe drawe.
  In pes þu myth a be for me,

þis I telle þe pleyn.
  What seyst, Jesus? Whi spekyst not me to? f. 177v
  Knowyst not I haue power on þe cros þe to do?
  And also I haue power to lete þe forth go.
What kanst þu hereto seyn?

JESUS
On me poer þu hast ryth non
But þat my fadyr hath grawntyd beforn.

112 s.d. omnes *canc. in red in right margin* 127 spekyst not to me to *canc. in red after* not; me to *interl. above* *A capitulum stands before* 127

I cam my faderys wyl to fullfylle,
Þat mankynd xuld not spylle.

He þat hath betrayd me to þe at þis tyme,
His trespas is more þan is þine.

PRIMUS DOCTOR Ȝe pryncys and maysterys, takyth hed and se
How Pylat in þis matere is favorabyl.
And þus oure lawys dystroyd myth be,
And to vs alle vnrecurabyl.

Here Pylat letyth Jesus alone and goth into þe Jewys and seyth:

PYLAT Serys, what wole ȝe now with Jesu do?
I can fynde in hym but good
It is my cownce[l] ȝe lete hym go—
It is rewthe to spylle his blood.

CAYPHAS Pylat, methynkyth þu dost gret wrong
Aȝens oure lawe þus to fortefye.
And þe pepyl here is so strong
Bryngyng þe lawful testymonye.

ANNAS Ȝa, and þu lete Jesu fro us pace—
Þis we welyn upholdyn alle—
Þu xalt answere for his trespas,
And tretour to þe emperour we xal þe kalle!

f. 178[r] PYLAT Now þan, syn ȝe wolne non other weye
But in alwyse þat Jesus must deye,

Artyse, bryng me watyr, I pray þe,
And what I wole do ȝe xal se.

Hic vnus afferet aquam.

The rubricated sign [sign] *stands at left of* 133 *and* 135 *in place of capitula* 143 cowncel] cownce 145 m *written in left margin* 146 Aȝens] A *written over another letter* 153–54 *and all subsequent couplets in this play preceded by rubricated small capitula*

As I wasche with watyr my handys clene,
So gyltles of hese deth I mut ben.

PRIMUS DOCTOR
þe blod of hym mut ben on vs,
And on oure chyldyr aftyr vs.

Et clamabunt, 'Ʒa! Ʒa! Ʒa!' þan Pylat goth aȝen to Jesu and bryng[*yth*] *hym, þus seyng:*

PYLAT
Lo, serys, I bryng hym here to ȝoure presens,
þat ȝe may knowe I fynde in hym non offens.

SECUNDUS DOCTOR
Dylyuere hym, delyvere hym, and lete us go,
On þe crosse þat he were do!

PILAT
Serys, wolde ȝe ȝoure kyng I xulde on þe cros
don?

TERCIUS DOCTOR
Sere, we seyn þat we haue no kyng but þe
emperour alon.

PILAT
Serys, syn algatys it must be so,
We must syt and oure offyce do.

Brynge forth to þe barre þat arn to be dempt,
And þei xal haue here jugement.

Here þei xal brynge Barabas to þe barre, and Jesu, and ij þewys in here shertys, bareleggyd, and Jesus standyng at þe barre betwyx them. And Annas and Cayphas xal gon into þe cowncell hous quan Pylat sytty[*th*].

PYLAT
Barabas, hold up þi hond,
For here at þi delyveré dost þu stond.

And he halt up his hond.

160 s.d. bryngyth] bryng, *with contraction for* ys *altered to* t *remainder cropped* 170 s.d. syttyth] sytty, 172 he (?) *erased before* dost

f. 178^v

Serys, qwhat sey ȝe of Barabas, thef and tretour bold?
Xal he go fre or [xal he] be kept in holde?

PRIMUS DOCTOR
Sere, for þe solennyté of oure Pasche day,
Be oure lawe he xal go fre away!

PYLAT
Barabas, þan I dymysse þe,
And ȝeve þe lycens to go fre.

Et curret.

Dysmas and Jesmas, theras ȝe stondys,
Þe lawe comawndyth ȝou to hald up ȝoure hondys.

Sere, what sey ȝe of þese thevys tweyn?

SECUNDUS DOCTOR
Sere, þei ben both gylty, we seyn.

PYLAT
And what sey ȝe of Jesu of Nazareth?

PRIMUS DOCTOR
Sere, we sey he xal be put to deth.

PYLAT
And kone ȝe put aȝens hym no trespas?

SECUNDUS DOCT[OR]
Sere, we wyl all þat he xal be put upon þe crosse.

Et clamabunt omnes voce magna, dicentes, 'Ȝa! Ȝa! Ȝa!'

PYLAT
Jesu, þin owyn pepyl han dysprevyd
Al þat I haue for þe seyd or mevyd.

I charge ȝou all at þe begynnyng,
As ȝe wole answere me beforn,
Þat þer be no man xal towch ȝoure kyng
But yf he be knyght or jentylman born.

Fyrst his clothis ȝe xal of don,
And maken hym nakyd for to be.

174 xal he] he xal 178 s.d. *not underscored* 186 *underscored in red* DOCTOR] Doct, *remainder cropped* 191 kyng] k *malformed*

Bynde hym to a pelere as sore as ȝe mon,
  þan skorge hym with qwyppys þat al men may
    se.

Whan he is betyn, crowne hym for ȝoure kyng; f. 179r
And þan to þe cros ȝe xal hym bryng.

And to þe crosse þu xalt be fest,
And on thre naylys þi body xal rest:

On xal thorwe þi ryth hand go,
Anothyr thorwe þi lyfte hand also;

þe thred xal be smet þour bothe þi feet,
Whech nayl þerto be mad ful mete.

And ȝet þu xalt not hange alone,
But on eyther syde of þe xal be on.

Dysmas, now I deme þe,
þat on hese ryth hand þu xalt be.

And Jesmas on þe left hand hangyd xal ben,
On þe Mownth of Caluerye, þat men may sen.

Here Pylat xal rysyn and gon to his schaffald, and þe busshoppys with hym; and þe Jewys xul crye for joy with a gret voys and arryn hym, and pullyn of his clothis, and byndyn hym to a pelere and skorgyn hym, on seyng þus:

PRIMUS JUDEUS
Doth gladly, oure kyng,
For þis is ȝoure fyrst begynnyng.

And quan he is skorgyd þei put upon hym a cloth of sylk, and settyn hym on a stol, and puttyn a kroune of þornys on hese hed with forkys; and þe Jewys knelyng to Cryst, takyng hym a septer, and skornyng hym; and þan þei xul pullyn of þe purpyl cloth and don on ageyn his owyn clothis, and leyn þe crosse in hese necke to beryn't, and drawyn hym forth with ropys. And þan xal come to women wepyng and with here handys wryngyn, seyng þus:

f. 179v

32
[THE PROCESSION TO CALVARY; THE CRUCIFIXION]

PRIM[A] MULIER
Allas, Jesus! Allas, Jesus! Wo is me!
  þat þu art þus dyspoylyd, allas!
And ȝet nevyr defawth was fownd in the,
  But evyr þu hast be fole of grace.

SECUND[A] MULIER
A, here is a rewful syth of Jesu so good,
  þat he xal þus dye aȝens þe ryth.
A, wykkyd men, ȝe be more þan wood
  To do þat good Lord so gret dyspyte!

Here Jesus turnyth aȝen to þe women with his crosse, þus seyng:

JESUS
Dowterys of Hierusalem, for me wepyth nowth,
  But for ȝoureself wepyth, and for ȝoure chyldyr also.
For þe days xal come þat þei han aftyr sowth,
  Here synne and here blyndnesse xal turne hem to wo.

þan xal be sayd, 'Blyssyd be þe wombys þat bareyn be';
  And wo to þe tetys tho days þat do ȝevyn sokyng.
And to here faderys þei xul seyn, 'Wo to þe tyme þat þu begat me',
  And to here moderys, 'Allas, wher xal be oure dwellyng?'

þan to þe hyllys and mownteynes they xal crye and calle,
  'Oppyn and hyde us from þe face of hym syttyng in trone;

Play 32 follows immediately upon Play 31
1 PRIMA] 1 *us*   5 SECUNDA] ij *us*

Or ellys ovyrthrowyth and on us now come falle,
  þat we may be hyd from oure sorweful mone'.

Here Jesus turnyth fro þe women and goth forth; and þer þei metyn with Symonem in þe place, þe Jewys seyng to hym:

PRIMUS JUDE[US]
Sere, to þe a word of good:
  A man is here, þu mayst se,
Beryth hevy of a rode
  Whereon he xal hangyd be.

Therfore we prey all the   f. 180^r T quire
  þu take þe crosse of þe man;
Bere it with vs to Kalvarye,
  And ryth gret thank þu xalt han.

SYMON
Serys, I may not in no degré:
  I haue gret errandys for to do.
þerfore I pray ȝow excuse me,
  And on my herand lete me go.

SECUNDUS JUDEUS
What! Harlot, hast þu skorne
  To bere þe tre whan we þe preye?
þu xalt beryn't haddyst þu sworn,
  And yt were ten tyme þe weye!

SYMON
Serys, I prey ȝou, dysplese ȝou nowth.
  I wole help to bere þe tre;
Into þe place it xal be browth
  Where ȝe wole comawnde me.

Here Symon takyth þe cros of Jesus and beryth it forth.

VERONICA
A, ȝe synful pepyl, why fare þus?
  For swet and blood he may not se.
Allas, holy prophete, Cryst Jhesus,
  Careful is myn hert for the.

21 JUDEUS] Jude, *remainder cropped*   þerfore we prey *written in bottom margin of f. 179^r as catchword*   33 skorne] k *blotted*   38 *letters erased above* þe

And sche whypyth his face with here kerchy.

JESUS
Veronyca, þi whipyng doth me ese.
My face is clene þat was blak to se.
I xal þem kepe from all mysese
þat lokyn on þi kerchy and remembyr me.

f. 180v *þan xul þei pulle Jesu out of his clothis and leyn them togedyr; and þer þei xul pullyn hym down and leyn hym along on þe cros, and aftyr þat naylyn hym þeron.*

PRIMUS JUDEUS
Come on, now here we xal asay
Yf þe cros for þe be mete.
Cast hym down here, in þe devyl way;
How long xal he standyn on his fete?

SECUNDUS JUDEUS
Pul hym down, evyl mote he the!
And gyf me his arm in hast;
And anon we xal se
Hese good days, þei xul be past.

TERCIUS JUDEUS
Gef hese other arm to me,
Another take hed to hese feet,
And anon we xal se
Yf þe borys be for hym meet.

QUARTUS JUDEUS
þis is mete, take good hede,
Pulle out þat arm to þe sore.

PRIMUS JUDEUS
þis is short—þe deuyl hym sped!—
Be a large fote and more.

SECUNDUS JUDEUS
Fest on a rop and pulle hym long,
And I xal drawe þe ageyn.
Spare we not þese ropys strong,
þow we brest both flesch and veyn.

45 JESUS] Je *written over* Ve 63 þe] þ *written over a* d John *written in black by another hand above* 65

TERCIUS JUDEUS Dryve in þe nayl anon, lete se,
And loke and þe flesch and senues well last.
QUARTUS JUDEUS þat I graunt, so motė I the!
Lo, þis nayl is dreve ryth wel and fast.

PRIMUS JUDEUS Fest a rop þan to his feet, f. 181r
And drawe hym down long anow.
SECUNDUS JUDEUS Here is a nayl for both, good and greet;
I xal dryve it thorwe, I make avow.

Here xule þei leve of and dawncyn abowte þe cros shortly.

TERCIUS JUDEUS Lo, fela, here a lythe, takkyd on a tre!
QUARTUS JU[DEUS] ȝa, and I trowe þu art a worthy kyng.
PRIMUS JUDEUS A, good sere, telle me now, what helpyth þi prophecy þe?
SECUNDUS JUDEUS ȝa, or any of þi fals prechyng?

TERCIUS JUDEUS Serys, set up þe cros on þe hende
þat we may loke hym in þe face.
QUARTUS JUDEUS ȝa, and we xal knelyn onto oure kyng so kend,
And preyn hym of his gret grace.

Here quan þei han set hym up, þei xuln gon before hyn seyng eche affter other þus:

PRIMUS JUDEUS Heyl, Kyng of Jewys, yf þu be!
SECUNDUS JUDEUS ȝa, ȝa, sere, as þu hangyst þere flesche and bonys,

lo þis nayl is dreve ryth *copied from* 72 *in black by another hand in bottom margin of f. 180*v 75 greet] g *written over an* r 76 dryve] r *written over a* y 78 JUDEUS] Ju, *remainder lost in damage to leaf* 79 helpyth] *initial* h *malformed, possibly written over another letter* 85 kyng] kyn *faintly written over an erasure*

TERCIUS JUDEUS Com now down of þat tre,

QUARTUS JUDEUS And we wole worchepe þe all atonys!

Here xul poer comonys stand and loke upon þe Jewys iiij or v; and þe Jewys xul come to them and do them hange þe þevys.

PRIMUS JUDEUS Come on, ȝe knavys, and set up þise ij crosses ryth,
And hange up þese to thevys anon.

f. 181v SECUNDUS JUD[EUS] Ȝa, and in þe worchep of þis worthy knyth,
On eche syde of hym xal hangyn on.

Here þe sympyl men xul settyn up þese ij crossys and hangyn up þe thevys be þe armys. And þerwhylys xal þe Jewys cast dyce for his clothis, and fytyn and stryvyn. And in þe menetyme xal oure Lady come with iij Maryes with here and Sen Johan with hem, settyng hem down asyde afore þe cros, oure Lady swuonyng and mornyng, and [*be*] *leysere seyng:*

MARIA A, my good Lord, my sone so swete!
What hast þu don? Why hangyst now þus here?
Is þer non other deth to þe now mete
But þe most shamful deth among þese thevys fere?

A, out on my hert—whi brest þu nowth?
And þu art maydyn and modyr, and seyst þus þi childe spylle!
How mayst þu abyde þis sorwe and þis woful þowth?
A, deth, deth, deth! Why wylt þu not me kylle?

Here oure Lady xal swonge aȝen, and ore Lord xal seyn þus:

JESUS O Fadyr Almythy, makere of man,
Forgyff þese Jewys þat don me wo.

and hange up, *copied from* 90 *in black by another hand, written in bottom margin of f. 181v*
89 þise] i *malformed* 91 JUDEUS] Jud, *remainder cropped* 92 s.d. swuonyng] *a minim blotted between* w *and* u be] *supplied, following D* 102 wo *canc. before* wo

Forgeve hem, fadyr, forgeve hem þan,
For thei wete notwh what þei do.

PRIMUS JUDEUS
ȝa! Vath! Vath! Now here is he
þat bad us dystroye oure tempyl on a day,
And withinne days thre
He xulde reysyn't aȝen in good aray.

SECUNDUS JUDEUS
Now and þu kan do swech a dede, f. 182r
Help now þiself, yf þat þu kan;
And we xal belevyn on þe withoutyn drede,
And seyn þu art a mythty man.

TERCIUS JUDEUS
ȝa, yf þu be Goddys sone, as þu dedyst teche,
From þe cros come now down.
þan of mercy we xal þe beseche
And seyn þu art a lord of gret renown.

JESTES
Yf þu be Goddys sone, as þu dedyst seye,
Helpe here now both þe and vs.
But I fynde it not al in my feye
þat þu xuldyst be Cryst, Goddys sone Jesus.

DYSMAS
Do wey, fool! Why seyst þu so?
He is þe Sone of God, I beleve it wel!
And synne dede he nevyr, lo,
þat he xuld be put þis deth tyl.

But we ful mech wrong han wrowth.
He dede nevyr þing amys!
Now mercy, good Lord, mercy, and forgete me nowth
Whan þu comyst to þi kyngham and to þi blysse!

JESUS
Amen, amen, þu art ful wyse.
þat þu hast askyd I grawnt þe:

105 w *canc. in brown and red before first* Vath   121 Do] *Hal* Go   126 *an erasure before* dede *and* He *written in left margin*

þis same day in paradyse
With me, þi God, þu xalt þer be.

f. 182v MARIA

O my sone, my sone, my derlyng dere!
What! Haue I defendyd þe?
þu hast spoke to alle þo þat ben here,
And not o word þu spekyst to me.

To þe Jewys þu art ful kende:
þu hast forgove al here mysdede.
And þe thef þu hast in mende:
For onys haskyng mercy, hefne is his mede.

A, my sovereyn Lord, why whylt þu not speke
To me þat am þi modyr, in peyn for þi wrong?
A, hert, hert, why whylt þu not breke,
þat I wore out of þis sorwe so stronge!

JESUS

A, woman, woman, beheld þer þi sone,
And þu, Jon, take her for þi modyr.
I charge þe to kepe here as besyly as þu kone;
þu, a clene mayde, xal kepe another.

And, woman, þu knowyst þat my fadyr of hefne me sent
To take þis manhod of þe, Adamys rawnsom to pay.
For þis is þe wyl and my faderys intent,
þat I xal þus deye to delyuere man fro þe develys pray.

Now syn it is þe wyl of my fadyr, it xuld þus be.
Why xuld it dysplese þe, modyr, now my deth so sore?
And for to suffre al þis for man I was born of the,
To þe blys þat man had lost, man aȝen to restore.

F. 182v marked 180 *at right of an erased mark* (160?) 146 take] a *altered from another letter?* 152 develys] l *written over an* r

Her oure Lady xal ryse, and renne, and halse þe crosse.

MARIA MAGDALENE
A, good lady, why do ȝe þus? f. 183r
Ȝoure dolfol cher now cheuyth us sore.
And for þe peyne of my swete Lord Jesus,
Þat he seyth in ȝou, it peyneth hym more.

MARIA VIRGO
I pray ȝow alle, lete me ben here,
And hang me up here on þis tre
Be my frend and sone þat me is so dere,
For þer he is, þer wold I be.

JOHANNES
Jentyl lady, now leve ȝoure mornyng,
And go with us now, we ȝou pray;
And comfort oure Lord at hese departyng,
For he is almost redy to go his way.

Here þei xal take oure Lady from þe crosse. And here xal Pylat come down from his shaffald with Cayphas and Annas and all here mené, and xul come and lokyn on Cryst. And Annas and Cayphas xul skornfully sey[n]:

CAYPHAS
Lo, serys, lo, beheldyth and se,
Here hangyth he þat halpe many a man.
And now yf he Goddys sone be,
Helpe now hymself, yf þat he kan!

ANNAS
Ȝa, and yf þu Kyng of Israel be,
Come down of þe cros among us alle.
And lete þi God now delyuere the,
And þan oure kyng we wole þe calle.

Here xal Pylat askyn penne and inke, and a tabyl xal be take hym wretyn afore 'Hic est Jesus Nazarenus, Rex Judeorum'. And he xal make hym to wryte, and f. 183v *þan gon up on a leddere and settyn þe tabyl abovyn Crystys hed. And þan Cayphas xal makyn hym to redyn and seyn:*

158 cheuyth] cheu 168 s.d. seyn] sey, *remainder cropped*

CAYPHAS Sere Pylat, we merveylyth of þis,
Þat ȝe wryte hym to be Kyng of Jewys.

Þerfore we wolde þat ȝe xuld wryte þus,
Þat he namyd hymself Kyng of Jewus.

PYLAT Þat I haue wretyn, wretyn it is.
And so it xal be for me, iwys.

And so forth all þei xal gon aȝen to þe skaffald and Jesus xal cryen:

[JESUS] Heloy, Heloy, lamazabathany?
My fadyr in hevyn on hy,

Why dost þu me forsake?
The frelté of my mankende,
With stronge peyn yt gynnyth to peynde!
Ha, dere fadyr, haue me in mende,
And lete deth my sorwe slake.

SECUNDUS JUDEUS Methynkyth he this doth calle Hely.
Lete us go nere and aspy,
And loke yf he come preuely,
From cros hym down to reve.

JESUS So grett a thrust dede nevyr man take
As I haue, man, now for þi sake;
For thrust asundyr my lyppys gyn crake,
For drynes þei do cleve.

TERCIUS JUDEUS Ȝoure thrust, Sere Hoberd, for to slake,
Eyzil and galle here I þe take.
What! Methynkyth a mowe ȝe make.
Is not þis good drynk?

177, 179, *and* 181 *preceded by rubricated small capitula* 182 s.d. Jesus *looped in red like a s.h.* 183 *s.h. supplied* lamazabathany *preceded by brown double virgule and followed by red double virgule* 184–5 *written as one line, divided by a red virgule* *No capitulum before* 185 *Ink is lighter and writing smaller with* 184 193 cros] r *written over an* o

To crye for drynke ȝe had gret hast,
And now it semyth it is but wast;
Is not þis drynk of good tast?
Now telle me how ȝe thynk.

QUARTUS JUDEUS
On lofte, Sere Hoberd, now ȝe be sett,
We wyl no lenger with ȝou lett.
We grete ȝou wel on þe newe gett,
And make on ȝou a mowe.

PRIMUS JUDEUS
We grete ȝou wel with a scorn
And pray ȝou bothe evyn and morn,
Take good eyd to oure corn,
And chare awey þe crowe.

JESUS
In manus tuas, Domine, f. 184r
Holy Fadyr in hefly se,
I comende my spyryte to þe,
For here now hendyth my fest.
I xal go sle þe fende, þat freke,
For now myn herte begynnyth to breke.
Wurdys mo xal I non speke.
Nunc consummatum est.

MARIA
Alas! Alas! I leve to longe,
To se my swete sone with peynes stronge
As a theff on cros doth honge,
And nevyr ȝet dede he synne!
Alas, my dere chyld to deth is dressyd!
Now is my care wel more incressyd!
A, myn herte with peyn is pressyd—
For sorwe myn hert doth twynne!

JOHANNES
A, blyssyd mayde, chaunge ȝoure thought,
For þow ȝoure sone with sorwe be sought,
3itt by his owyn wyl þis werk is wrought,
And wylfully his deth to take.

206–13 *written two lines as one, divided by single red virgules* *Ff. 184 and 185 consist of different paper from the rest of T quire, and the scribal characteristics are also different from those in the rest of the gathering*

Ȝow to kepe he chargyd me here,
I am ȝoure servaunt, my lady dere;
Wherfore I pray ȝow, be of good chere,
And merthis þat ȝe make.

MARIA
Thow he had nevyr of me be born,
And I sey his flesch þus al to-torn,
On bak behyndyn, on brest beforn,
Rent with woundys wyde,
f. 184v
Nedys I must wonyn in woo,
To se my frende with many a fo
All to-rent from top to too,
His flesch withowtyn hyde.

JOHANNES
A, blyssyd lady, as I ȝow telle,
Had he not deyd, we xuld to helle,
Amongys fendys þer evyr to dwelle,
In peynes þat ben smert.
He sufferyth deth for oure trespace,
And thorwe his deth we xal haue grace
To dwelle with hym in hevyn place.
Þerfore beth mery in hert!

MARIA
A, dere frende, weel woot I this,
Þat he doth bye us to his blys.
But ȝitt of myrth evyrmor I mys
Whan I se þis syght.

JOHANNES
Now, dere lady, þerfore I ȝow pray,
Fro þis dolful dolour wende we oure way;
For whan þis syght ȝe se nought may,
Ȝoure care may waxe more lyght.

MARIA
Now sythe I must parte hym fro,
Ȝit lete me kysse, or þat I go,
His blyssyd feyt þat sufferyn wo
Naylid on þis tre.
So cruelly with grett dyspyte
Þus shamfully was nevyr man dyghte.
Þerfore in peyn myn hert is pyghte—
Al joye departyth fro me.

Hic quasi semi-[m]ortua cadat prona in terram. Et dicit Johannes:

JOHANNES Now, blyssyd mayd, com forthe with me, f. 185^{r}
No lengere þis syght þat ȝe se.
I xal ȝow gyde in þis countré
Where þat it plesyth ȝow best.

MARIA Now, jentyl Johan, my sonys derlyng,
To Goddys temple þu me brynge
þat I may prey God with sore wepynge
And mornynge þat is prest.

JOHANNES All ȝoure desyre xal be wrought;
With herty wyll I werke ȝoure thought.
Now, blyssyd mayde, taryeth nowth,
In þe temple þat ȝe ware.
For holy prayere may chaunge ȝoure mood
And cawse ȝoure chere to be more good.
Whan ȝe se notȝ ȝoure childys blood,
þe lasse may be ȝoure care.

Tunc transiet Maria ad templum cum Johanne, et cetera.

MARIA Here in þis temple my lyff I lede,
And serue my Lord God with hertyly drede.
Now xal wepynge me fode and fede,
Som comforte tyll God sende.
A, my Lord God, I þe pray,
Whan my childe rysẹth þe iij^{de} day,
Comforte thanne thyn handmay,
My care for to amende.

269 s.d. semi-mortua] *D; MS* seminor tua 284 *A letter canc. before* childys

33
[THE HARROWING OF HELL (PART I)]

ANIMA CHRISTI Now all mankende in herte be glad
With all merthis þat may be had!
For mannys sowle, þat was bestad
In þe logge of helle,
f. 185v Now xal I ryse to lyve agayn,
From peyn to pleys of paradyse pleyn.
þerfore, man, in hert be fayn,
In merthe now xalt þu dwelle!

I am þe sowle of Cryst Jesu,
þe which is kynge of all vertu.
My body is ded—þe Jewys it slew—
þat hangyth ȝitt on þe rode.
Rent and torn al blody red,
For mannys sake my body is deed.
For mannys helpe my body is bred,
And sowle-drynk my bodyes blode.

þow my body be now sclayn,
þe thrydde day, þis is certayn,
I xal reyse my body agayn
To lyve, as I ȝow say.
Now wole I go streyth to helle
And feche from þe fendys felle
All my frendys þat þerin dwelle,
To blysse þat lestyth ay.

The sowle goth to helle gatys and seyth: 'Attollite portas principes vestras, et eleuamini, porte eternales, et introibit Rex Glorie'.

Play 33 follows immediately upon Play 32

18 certayn] *an erased* e *above the* y   24 s.d. *Latin words not underscored. The red mark for versicle stands at left (used elsewhere only to mark Latin versicles in Play 41)* Nota anima latronis *written in black in left margin, possibly by Scribe C*

Ondothe ȝoure ȝatys of sorwatorie!
On mannys sowle I haue memorie.
Here comyth now þe Kynge of Glorye,
These gatys for to breke.
Ȝe develys þat arn here withinne,
Helle gatys ȝe xal vnpynne.
I xal delyvere mannys kynne;
From wo I wole hem wreke.

BELYALL Alas, alas! Out and harrow!
Onto þi byddynge must we bow.
þat þu art God now do we know—
Of þe had we grett dowte!
Aȝens þe may nothynge stonde;
Allthynge obeyth to thyn honde;
Bothe hevyn and helle, watyr and londe,
Allthynge must to þe lowte.

ANIMA CHRISTI Aȝens me it wore but wast f. 186r
To holdyn or to stondyn fast.
Helle logge may not last
Aȝens þe Kynge of Glorye.
þi derke dore down I throwe;
My fayr frendys now wele I knowe.
I xal hem brynge reknyd be rowe
Out of here purcatorye.

34
[THE BURIAL; THE GUARDING OF THE SEPULCHRE]

CENTURIO In trewth, now I knowe with ful opyn syght
That Goddys dere sone is naylid on tre.
These wundyrful tokenys aprevyn ful ryght
Quod vere Filius Dei erat iste.
ALIUS MILES 2 The very childe of God I suppose þat he be,
And so it semyth wele be his wundyrful werk:

Play 34 follows immediately upon Play 33

þe erth sore qwakyth, and þat agresyth me;
With myst and grett wedyr it is woundyr dyrk.

ALIUS MILES 3 Soch merveylis shewe may non erthely man!
þe eyr is ryght derke þat fyrst was ryght clere;
The erthqwave is grett, þe clowdys waxe whan.
These tokenys preue hym a lorde without any pere.
CENTURIO His fadyr is pereles kyng of most empere,
Bothe Lorde of þis World and Kynge of Hevyn hyȝe.
Ȝit out of all synne to brynge us owt of daungere,
He soferyth his dere sone for us all to dye.

NICHODEMUS Alas, alas, what syght is this,
To se þe Lorde and Kynge of Blys,
þat nevyr synnyd ne dede amys,
þus naylid vpon a rode!
Alas, Ȝewys, what haue ȝe wrought?
A, ȝe wyckyd wytys, what was ȝoure thought?
Why haue ȝe bobbyd and þus betyn owth
All his blyssyd blood?

f. 186v SENTURYO A, now trewly telle weyl I kan
þat þis was Goddys owyn sone.
I knowe he is both God and man
Be þis wark þat here is done.

þer was nevyr man but God þat cowde make þis werk
þat evyr was of woman born,
Were he nevyr so gret a clerk;
It passeth hem all, þow þei had sworn.

Hese lawe was trewe, I dare wel saye,
þat he tawth us here amonge.
þerfore I rede ȝe, turne ȝoure faye,
And amende þat ȝe han do wronge.

12 any] a *written over another letter* 29 cowde] *a stroke, perhaps accidental, over* e

JOSEPH OF ARA[MATHIE]

O good Lord Jesu, þat deyst now here on rode,
  Haue mercy on me and forgyf me my mys.
I wold þe worchep here with my good,
  þat I may come to þi blysse.

To Pylat now wole I goon
  And aske þe body of my Lord Jesu.
To bery þat now wold I soon
  In my grave, þat is so new.

Heyl, Sere Pylat, þat syttyth in sete!
  Heyl, justyce of Jewys men do þe calle!
Heyl, with helthe I do þe grete!
  I pray þe of a bone whatso befalle.

To bery Jesuis body I wole þe pray,
  þat he were out of mennys syth.
For tomorwyn xal be oure holy day;
  þan wole no man hym bery, I þe plyth.

And yf we lete hym hange þer stylle, f. 187r
  Some wolde seyn þerof anow.
þe pepyl þerof wold seyn ful ylle
  þat nother xuld be ȝoure worchep nor prow.

PYLAT

Sere Joseph of Baramathie, I graunt þe;
  With Jesuis body do þin intent.
But fyrst I wole wete þat he ded be,
  As it was his jugement.

Sere knytys, I comawnd ȝow þat ȝe go
  In hast with Josepht of Baramathie;
And loke ȝe take good hede þerto
  þat Jesu suerly ded be.

Se þat þis comawndement ȝe fulfylle
  Without wordys ony mo.

27 ARAMATHIE] Ara, m *partially lost in hole in leaf, remainder cropped* 41 god *canc. in brown and red before* goon

And þan lete Joseph do his wylle,
What þat he wyl with Jesu do.

Here come to knytys beforn Pylat atonys, þus seyng:

PRIMUS MILES Sere, we xal do oure dylygens,
With Joseph goyng to Caluerye.
Be we out of þi presens,
Sone þe trewth we xal aspye.

JOSEPH AB [ARAMATHIE] Gramercy, Pylat, of ȝoure jentylnesse,
þat ȝe han grawntyd me my lyst.
Anythyng in my province
ȝe xal haue at ȝoure [request].

f. 187v PYLAT Sere, all ȝoure lest ȝe xal haue.
With Jesuis body do ȝoure intent.
Whethyr ȝe bery hym in pyt or grave,
þe powere I grawnt ȝow here present.

The ij knygtys go with Joseph to Jesus, and stande and heldyn hym in þe face.

SECUNDUS MILES Methynkyth Jesu is sewre anow—
It is no ned his bonys to breke.
He is ded, how þinkyth ȝow?
He xal nevyr go nor speke.

PRIMUS MILES We wyl be sure or þan we go.
Of a thyng I am bethowth;
ȝondyr is a blynd knyth I xal go to,
And sone a whyle here xal be wrowth.

Here þe knyth goth to blynde Longeys and seyth:

Heyl, Sere Longeys, þu gentyl knyth.
þe I prey now ryth hertyly

73 ARAMATHIE *supplied* 76 request] resquest, *with* q *written over a* t
86 bethowth] *final* h *blotted, perhaps altered from another letter*

þat þu wylt wend with me ful wyth.
It xal be for þi prow, veryly.

LONGEUS Sere, at ȝoure comawndement with ȝow wyl I wende
In what place ȝe wyl me haue.
For I trost ȝe be my frend;
Lede me forth, sere, oure Sabath ȝou save.

PRIMUS MILES Lo, Sere Longeys, here is a spere
Bothe long and brood, and sharp anow.
Heve it up fast þat it wore þere,
For here is game. Show, man, show!

Here Longeys showyth þe spere warly; and þe blood comyth rennyng to his hand, and he auantorysly xal wype his eyn.

LONGEYS O good Lord, how may þis be, f. 188r
þat I may se so bryth now?
þis thretty wyntyr I myth not se
And now I may se, I wote nevyr how!
But ho is þis þat hangyth here now?
I trowe it be þe [maydonys] sone.
And þat he is. Now I knowe wel how
þe Jewys to hym þis velany han don.

Here he fallyth down on his knes.

Now, good Lord, forgyf me that
þat I to þe now don have.
For I dede I wyst not what.
þe Jewys of myn ignorans dede me rave.
Mercy! Mercy! Mercy, I crye!

[*þan*] *Joseph doth set up þe lederys, and Nychodemus comyth to help hym.*

106 maydonys] mayndonys 113 *is extra-metric, written at right of* 110 *without rhyme-brackets* 113 s.d. þan] þu *or* þn *with tittle above* u *or* n

NICODEMUS Joseph ab Aramathy, blyssyd þu be,
For þu dost a fol good dede.
I prey the, lete me help þe,
þat I may be partenere of þi mede.

JOSEPH Nychodemus, welcome indede.
I pray ȝow ȝe wole help þerto.
He wole aqwyte us ryth weyl oure mede,
And I haue lysens for to do.

Here Joseph and Nychodemus takyn Cryst of þe cros, on on o ledyr and þe tother on another leddyr. And quan [*he*] *is had down, Joseph leyth hym in oure Ladys lappe, seyng þe knytys turnyng hem, and Joseph seyth:*

JOSEPH Lo, Mary, modyr good and trewe,
Here is þi son, blody and bloo.
For hym myn hert ful sore doth rewe.
Kysse hym now onys eer he go.

f. 188v MARIA VIRGO A, mercy! Mercy, myn owyn son so dere,
þi blody face now I must kysse.
þi face is pale, withowtyn chere;
Of meche joy now xal I mysse.
þer was nevyr modyr þat sey this,
So here sone dyspoyled with so gret wo.
And my dere chylde nevyr dede amys.
A, mercy, Fadyr of Hefne, it xulde be so.

JOSEPH Mary, ȝoure sone ȝe take to me;
Into his grave it xal be browth.
MARIA Joseph, blyssyd evyr mot þu be
For þe good dede þat ȝe han wrowth.

Here þei xal leyn Cryst in his grave.

JOSEPH I gyf þe þis syndony þat I have bowth
To wynde þe in whyl it is new.

121 s.d. he *supplied*

NICHODEMUS Here is an onyment þat I haue browth
To anoynt withall myn Lord Jhesu.

JOSEPH Now Jesu is withinne his grave,
Wheche I ordeyn somtyme for me.
On þe, Lord, I vowche it save;
I knowe my mede ful gret xal be.

NICHODEM[US] Now lete us leyn on þis ston ageyn,
And Jesu in þis tombe stylle xal be.
And we wyl walke hom ful pleyn;
þe day passyth fast I se.
Farewel, Joseph, and wel ȝe be;
No lengere teryeng here we make.

JOSEPH Sere, almythy God be with þe;
Into his blysse he mote ȝou take.

MARIA Farewel ȝe jentyl princys kende. f. 189r
In joye evyr mote ȝe be.
þe blysse of hefne withowtyn ende
I knowe veryly þat ȝe xal se.

Here þe princys xal do reuerens to oure Lady and gon here way, and leve þe Maryes at þe sepulcre. Cayphas goth to Pylat, seyng þus:

CAYPHAS Herk, Sere Pylat, lyst to me.
I xal þe telle tydyngys new.
Of o thyng we must ware be,
Er ellys hereafter we myth it rewe.

þu wotyst weyl þat Jesu,
He seyd to us with wordys pleyn,
He seyd we xuld fynd it trew,
þe thryd day he wold ryse agey[n].

Four rubricated dots follow 141 146 NICHODEMUS] *abbreviation for* -us *mostly cropped* 157 s.d. go *canc. before* Cayphas nota *written at left of* 157 s.d., Incipit hic *and some rubbed words* (here þe . . . þ . . . Cay . . .) *written at right and below, all in black ink, possibly by Scribe C* 158 *s.h. in paler ink* 160 must] st *smudged, perhaps altered from other letters* 165 ageyn] agey

Yf þat hese dyscyplys come, serteyn,
And out of his graue stele hym away,
þei wyl go preche and pleyn seyn
þat he is reson þe thryd day.

þis is þe cowncel þat I gyf here:
Take men and gyf hem charge þerto
To weche þe grave with gret power
Tyl þe thryd day be go.

PYLAT Sere Cayphas, it xal be do,
For as ȝe say, þer is peryl in.
And it happend þat it were so,
It myth make oure lawys for to blyn.
Ȝe xal se, sere, er þat ȝe go,
How I xal þis mater saue,
And what I xal sey þerto,
And what charge þei xal haue.

Come forth ȝe, Sere Amorawnt
And Sere Arphaxat; com ner also,
Sere Cosdram and Sere Affraunt,
And here þe charge þat ȝe must do.
Serys, to Jesuis grave ȝe xal go
Tyl þat þe thryd day be gon,
And lete nother frend nor fo
In no wey to towche þe ston.

Yf ony of hese dyscipelys com þer
To fech þe body fro ȝou away,
Bete hym down! Have ȝe no fere—
With shamful deth do hym day!

In payn of ȝoure godys and ȝoure lyvys
þat ȝe lete hem nowth shape ȝou fro,

166–97 *written two lines as one, divided by two brown virgules surrounding one red one* Nota (*?*) hic hic *written in black at left of* 182, *possibly by Scribe C* 194 *lacks a capitulum*

And of ȝoure chyldere and ȝoure wyfys—
For al ȝe lese and ȝe do so.

PRIMUS MILES Sere Pylat, we xal not ses. f. 189v
We xal kepe it strong anow.
SECUNDUS MILES Ȝa, and an hunderyd put hem in pres,
Þei xal dey, I make avow!

TERCIUS MILES And han honderyd? Fy on an C and an C þerto!
Þer is non of hem xal us withstonde.
QUARTUS MILES Ȝa, and þer com an hunderyd thowsand and mo,
I xal hem kylle with myn honde!

PYLAT Wel, serys, þan ȝoure part ȝe do.
And to ȝoure charge loke ȝe take hede,
Withowtyn wordys ony mo,
Wysly now þat ȝe procede.

Here þe knytys gon out of þe place.

Lo, Sere Cayphas, how thynkyth ȝow?
Is not þis wel browth abowth?
CAYPHAS In feyth, sere, it is sure anow.
Hardely, haue ȝe no dowth.

ARFAXAT ij Let se, Ser Amaraunt, where wele ȝe be?
Wole ȝe kepe þe feet or þe hed?
AMERAUNT At þe hed, so mote I the.
And hoso come here, he is but ded.

ARFAXAT ij And I wole kepe þe feet þis tyde,
Þow þer come both Jakke and Gylle.
COSDRAM iij And I xal kepe þe ryth syde;
And hoso come, I xal hym kylle.

209 s.d. *a letter canc. before* out 214 *another hand, possibly C, has written in black* jus *before s.h. here and in* 218, ijus *before s.h. in* 216, iijus *before s.h. in* 220, *and* iiijus *before s.h. in* 222 so mote I the I wole be at þe h *canc. in red between* 215 *and* 216

AFFRAUNT 4 And I wole on þe lefte hand ben,
And hoso come here, he xal nevyr then.
Ful sekyrly his bane xal I ben
With dyntys of dowte.
f. 190r V quire
Syr Pylat, haue good day!
We xul kepyn þe body in clay.
And we xul wakyn wele þe way,
And wayten all abowte.

PYLATUS Now, jentyl serys, wele ȝe vowchsaffe
To go with me and sele þe graffe,
þat he ne ryse out of þe grave
þat is now ded?
CAYPHAS We graunte wel; lete us now go.
Whan it is selyd and kepte also,
Than be we sekyr, withowtyn wo,
And haue of hym no dred.

Tunc ibunt ad sepulcrum Pilatus, Cayphas, Annas, et omnes milites, et dicit:

ANNAS Loo, here is wax ful redy dyght;
Sett on ȝoure sele anon ful ryght.
þan be ȝe sekyr, I ȝow plyght,
He xal not rysyn agayn.
PILATUS On þis corner my seal xal sytt,
And with þis wax I sele þis pytt.
Now dare I ley he xal nevyr flytt
Out of þis grave, serteayn.

ANNAS Here is more wax ful redy, loo.
All þe cornerys ȝe sele also,
And with a lokke loke it too.
Than lete us gon oure way.

Syr pilat *written as catchword at foot of f. 189v* *With V quire, the paper is again YHS in a Sun, and the scribal characteristics again resemble those of the text prior to the Passion Plays* Nota *written in black by another hand at left of* 226 231 *a stroke canc. in dark brown and red before* graffe 245 grave] g *written over another letter* (r?)

And lete þese knytys abydyn þerby;
And yf hese dysciplys com preuyly
To stele awey þis ded body,
To vs they hem brynge without delay.

PILATAS On every corner now is sett my seale;
Now is myn herte in welthe and wele.
Th[er] may no brybour awey now stele f. 190v
þis body from vndyr ston.
Now, syr buschopp, I pray to the,
And Annas also, com on with me.
Evyn togedyr all we thre,
Homward þe wey we gon.

As wynde wrothe,
Knyghtys, now goht
Clappyd in cloth,
And kepyth hym well!
Loke ʒe be bolde
With me for to holde.
Ʒe xul haue gold
And helme of stele.

Pylat, Annas, and Cayphas go to þer skaffaldys, and þe knyghtys sey[n]:

AFFRAUNT 4 Now in þis grownnde
He lyth bounde
þat tholyd wounde
For he was fals.
þis lefft cornere
I wyl kepe here,
Armyd clere,
Bothe hed and hals.

254 PILATAS] *stroke through second* a *may represent change to* u Pilatus *written faintly by another hand in bottom margin of f. 190r* 256 Ther] This 262–301 *written two lines as one,* 302–25 *three lines as one, each divided by a red virgule and one or two brown virgules* 269 s.d. seyn] *the fourth letter blotted, perhaps partially cropped* 270 tyde *canc. in red before* grownnde 274 lefft] *second* f *written over a* t

COSDRAM 3

I wyl haue þis syde
Whatso betyde.
If any man ryde
   To stele þe cors,
I xal hym chyde
With woundys wyde,
Amonge hem glyde
   With fyne fors.

AMERAUNT/ PRIMUS

The hed I take
Hereby to wake.
A stele stake
   I holde in honde
Maystryes to make.
Crownys I crake,
Schafftys to shake
   And schapyn schonde.

ARFAXAT/ SECUNDUS

I xal not lete
To kepe þe fete;
They ar ful [wete],
   Walterid in blood.
      He þat wyll stalke
      Be brook or balke
      Hedyr to walke,
   þo wrecchis be wood.

f. 191r PRIMUS MILES

Myn heed dullyth,
Myn herte fullyth
   Of slepp.
      Seynt Mahownd,
      þis beryenge grownd
   þu kepp!

286 PRIMUS] jus *altered to* ijus *in black* 293 sle fre and bonde *interl. in black above* schapyn schonde, *apparently by Scribe C* 294 SECUNDUS] 2us *canc. and* 1us *written before it in black* 296 wete] *largely obliterated, though traces of* w..te *survive* white (?) *written over it in black, apparently by Scribe C* 298 stalke *partially obscured by erasure* (*of a word?*) *above* 302 *preceded by rubricated small capitulum*

SECUNDUS MILES
I sey þe same;
For any blame,
I falle.
Mahownd whelpe,
Aftyr þin helpe
I calle.

TERCIUS MILES
I am hevy as leed;
For any dred,
I slepe.
Mahownd of myght,
þis ston tonyght
þu kepe!

QUARTUS MILES
I haue no foot
To stonde on root
By brynke.
Here I aske
To go to taske
A wynke.

35
[THE HARROWING OF HELL (PART II); CHRIST'S APPEARANCE TO MARY; PILATE AND THE SOLDIERS]

Tunc dormyent milites, et ueniet Anima Christi de inferno cum Adam et Eua, Abraham, Johan Baptist, et aliis.

ANIMA CHRISTI
Come forthe, Adam, and Eue with the,
And all my fryndys þat herein be!
To paradys come forthe with me,
In blysse for to dwelle.
þe fende of helle, þat is ȝoure foo,

308, 314 *and* 320 *preceded by rubricated small capitula*

Play 35 follows immediately on Play 34

initial s.d. Eua] Eua

He xal be wrappyd and woundyn in woo.
Fro wo to welthe now xul ȝe go,
With myrthe evyrmore to melle.

ADAM

I thanke þe, Lord, of þi grett grace,
That now is forȝovyn my grett trespace.
Now xal we dwellyn in blysful place,
In joye and endeles myrthe.
Thorwe my synne man was forlorn,
And man to saue þu wore all torn,
And of a mayd in Bedlem born,
þat evyr blyssyd be þi byrthe.

f. 191v EUA

Blyssyd be þu, Lord of Lyff!
I am Eue, Adamis wyff.
þu hast soferyd strok and stryff
For werkys þat we wrought.
þi mylde mercy haht all forȝ[e]vyn;
Dethis dentys on þe were drevyn.
Now with þe, Lord, we xul levyn—
þi bryght blood hath us bowth.

JOHANNES BAPTISTA

I am þi cosyn, my name is Johan.
þi woundys hath betyn þe to þe bon.
I baptyzid þe in Flom Jordon,
And ȝaff þi body baptyze.
With þi grace now xul we gon
From oure enmyes everychon
And fyndyn myrthis many on
In pley of paradyse.

ABRAHAM

I am Abraham, fadyr trowe
þat reyned after Noes flowe.
A sory synne Adam gan sowe,
þat clad us all in care.

13 man] n *smudged* 21 h *canc. before* all forȝevyn] forȝovyn all] a *malformed* 31 fyndyn] *second* y *surmounted by tittle and followed by an* s *above a deleting dot*

A sone þat maydenys mylk hath sokyn,
And with his blood oure bonde hath brokyn.
Helle logge lyth vnlokyn—
Fro fylth with frende we fare.

ANIMA CHRISTI

Fayre frendys, now be ȝe wunne,
On ȝow shyneth þe sothfast sunne.
þe gost þat all grevaunce hath gunne,
Ful harde I xal hym bynde. f. 192r
As wyckyd werme þu gunne apere
To tray my chylderyn þat were so dere.
þerfore, traytour, heuyrmore here
Newe peynes þu xalt evyr fynde.

Thorwe blood I took of mannys kynde,
Fals devyl, I here þe bynde!
In endles sorwe I þe wynde,
þerin evyrmore to dwelle.
Now þu art bownde, þu mayst not fle.
For þin envyous cruelté,
In endeles dampnacyon xalt þu be,
And nevyr comyn out of helle.

BELIALL

Alas! Herrow! Now am I bownde
In helle gonge to ly on grounde.
In hendles sorwe now am I wounde,
In care evyrmore to dwelle.
In helle logge I lyȝ alone.
Now is my joye awey al gone,
For all fendys xul be my fone.
I xal nevyr com from helle.

40 nota anima caym *written in left margin, with erased words beneath it ending with* as folow fayere frendys, *all written in black by Scribe C* anima caym *written at right of* 40 (*by the same reviser?*) 56 thowght(?) *and other word or words erased in right margin* 58 on *interl. over an erasure* *Below* 64 *and in left and right margins, Scribe C has written in black:*

nota þe devyll thowght many et cetera
hens I wyll þe bere/
þan crist

Thowght many be gon I am glad et cetera

And þan / cayme / xall sey / his spech / And þan crist / xall sey / now ys / your foo / et cetera

ANIMA CHRISTI Now is ȝoure foo boundyn in helle,
þat evyr was besy ȝow for to qwelle.
Now wele I rysyn flesch and felle,
þat rent was for ȝoure sake.
Myn owyn body þat hynge on rode,
And, be þe Jewys nevyr so wode,
It xal aryse, both flesch and blode.
My body now wyl I take.

Tunc transiet Anima Christi ad resuscitandum corpus, quo resuscitato dicat Jesus:

f. 192v JESUS Harde gatys haue I gon
And peynes sofryd many on,
Stomblyd at stake and at ston
Nyȝ thre and thretty ȝere.
I lyght out of my faderys trone
For to amende mannys mone.
My flesch was betyn to þe bon,
My blood I bledde clere.

For mannys loue I tholyd dede,
And for mannys loue I am rysyn up rede.
For man I haue mad my body in brede,
His sowle for to fede.
Man, and þu lete me þus gone
And wylt not folwyn me anone,
Such a frende fyndyst þu nevyr none
To help þe at þi nede.

Salue, sancta parens, my modyr dere!
All heyl, modyr, with glad chere.
For now is aresyn with body clere
þi sone þat was dolve depe.
þis is þe thrydde day þat I ȝow tolde
I xuld arysyn out of þe cley so colde.
Now am I here with brest ful bolde;
þerfore no more ȝe wepe.

F. 192v marked 190 82 rede] r *interl. above an erased letter*

MARIA Welcom, my Lord! Welcom, my grace!
Welcome, my sone and my solace!
I xal þe wurchep in every place.
Welcom, Lord God of Myght!
Mekel sorwe in hert I leed
Whan þu were leyd in dethis beed.
But now my blysse is newly breed;
All men may joye þis syght.

JESUS All þis werlde þat was forlorn f. 193r
Shal wurchepe ȝou bothe evyn and morn.
For had I not of ȝow be born,
Man had be lost in helle.
I was deed and lyff I haue,
And thorwe my deth man do I saue.
For now I am resyn out of my graue,
In hevyn man xal now dwelle.

MARIA A dere sone, þese wurdys ben goode.
Þu hast wel comfortyd my mornyng moode.
Blyssyd be þi precyous bloode
Þat mankende þus doth saue.
JESUS Now, dere modyr, my leve I take.
Joye in hert and myrth ȝe make.
For deth is deed and lyff doth wake,
Now I am resyn fro my graue.

MARIA Farewel, my sone! Farewel, my childe!
Farewel, my Lorde, my God so mylde!
Myn hert is wele þat fyrst was whylde.
Farewel, myn owyn dere love!
Now all mankynde, beth glad with gle!
For deth is deed, as ȝe may se,
And lyff is reysed, endles to be,
In hevyn dwellynge above.

In ff. 193r–200r the ink-colour is (with some variations) unusually dark 106 ȝou *interl.* 111 am resyn] aresyn, *with tittle above* a *and a mark beneath it (to indicate an error?)* 113 *a letter* (d.?) *canc. in dark brown and red before* ben 123 is *interl.*

Whan my sone was naylyd on tre,
All women myght rewe with me;
For grettere sorwe myght nevyr non be
  Than I dede suffyr, iwys.
f. 193v   But þis joy now passyth all sorwe
    þat my childe suffryd in þat hard morwe.
    For now he is oure alderers borwe,
  To brynge us all to blys.

Tunc evigilabunt milites sepulcri, et dicit Primus Miles:

PRIMUS MILES
Awake, awake!
Hillis gyn quake
And tres ben shake
  Ful nere atoo!
    Stonys clevyd,
    Wyttys ben revid,
    Erys ben devid—
  I am servid soo.

SECUNDUS MILES
He is aresyn, þis is no nay,
þat was deed and colde in clay!
Now is he resyn belyve þis day,
  Grett woundyr it is to me!
    He is resyn by his owyn myght,
    And forth he goth his wey ful ryght.
    How xul we now us qwytte
  Whan Pylat doth us se?

TERCIUS MILES
Lete us now go
Pilat ontoo,
And ryght evyn so
  As we han sayn,
    þe trewth we sey:
    þat out of clay
    He is resyn þis day
  þat Jewys han slayn.

137–44 *written two lines as one, divided by virgules as earlier* 142 rewi *canc. in red before* revid 153–68 *written two lines as one, divided as above* 157 sey] e *malformed, perhaps an* a

QUARTUS MILES
I holde it best.
Lete us nevyr rest,
But go we prest,
þat it were done.
All heyl, Pilatt,
In þin astat!
He is resyn vp latt
þat þu gast dome.

PILAT
What? What? What? What?
Out upon the! Why seyst þu þat?
Fy vpon the, harlat,
How darst þu so say?
þu dost myn herte ryght grett greff! f. 194r
þu lyest vpon hym, fals theff!
How xulde he rysyn ageyn to lyff
þat lay deed in clay?

PRIMUS MILES
3a, þow þu be nevyr so wroth,
And of these tydandys nevyr so loth,
3itt goodly on ground on lyve he goth,
Qwycke and levynge man.
Iff þu haddyst a ben þer we ware,
In hert þu xuldyst han had gret care,
And of blysse a ben ryght bare,
Of colore bothe pale and whan.

PILATUS
Or ȝe come there
3e dede all swere
To fyght in fere
And bete and bynde.
All þis was trayn,
3oure wurdys wore vayn.
þis is sertayn—
3ow fals I fynde!

166 *followed by three red dots* 177 3 *canc. in dark brown and red before* MILES
181 ware] ar *malformed, perhaps written over other letters* 185–92 *written two lines as one, divided as above*

SECUNDUS MILES
Be þe deth þe devyl deyd,
We were of hym so sore atreyd,
þat for fer we us down leyd
Ryght evyn vpon oure syde.
Whan we were leyd upon þe grounde,
Stylle we lay as we had be bounde.
We durst not ryse for a thowsand pounde,
Ne not for all þis worlde so wyde.

PILATUS
Now fy upon ȝoure grett bost!
All ȝoure wurchep is now lost!
In felde, in town, and in every cost,
Men may ȝou dyspravyn.
f. 194v Now all ȝoure wurchep, it is lorn,
And every man may ȝow we[l] scorn,
And bydde ȝow go syttyn in þe corn
And chare awey þe ravyn.

TERCIUS MILES
Ȝa, it was hyȝ tyme to leyn oure bost.
For whan þe body toke aȝen þe gost,
He wold a frayd many an ost,
Kynge, knyght, and knave.
Ȝa, whan he dede ryse out of his lake,
þan was þer suche an erthequake
þat all þe worlde it gan to shake!
þat made us for to rave!

QUARTUS MILES
Ȝa, ȝa, herke, felawys, what I xal say:
Late us not ses be nyght nor day,
But telle þe trewth ryght as it lay
In countré where we goo.
And than I dare ley myn heed
þat þei þat Crystys lawys leed,
They wyl nevyr ses tyl they be deed
His deth þat brought hym too.

206 wel] *B; MS* we 213 d *canc. before* he, *a letter* (k.?) *canc. before* lake

PRIMUS MILES Be Belyall, þis was now wele ment.
To þis cowncell lete us consent.
Lett us go tellyn with on assent
He is resyn up þis day.
SECUNDUS MILES I grawnt þerto, and þat forthryght,
þat he is resyn by his owyn myght.
For þer cam non be day nor nyght
To helpe hym owte of clay.

PILATUS Now, jentyl serys, I pray ȝow all, f. 195r
Abyde stylle a lytyl thrall
Whyll þat I myn cowncel call,
And here of þer councell.
PRIMUS MILES Syr, att ȝoure prayour we wyl abyde
Here in þis place a lytel tyde.
But tary not to longe, for we must ryde—
We may not longe dwelle.

PILATUS Now, jentyl serys, I pray ȝow here
Sum good cowncel me to lere.
For sertys, serys, without dwere,
We stonnde in ryght grett dowte.
CAYPHAS Now trewly, sere, I ȝow telle,
þis matere is both fers and felle.
Combros it is þerwith to melle,
And evyl to be browth abowte.

ANNAS Syr Pylat, þu grett justyse,
þow þu be of wittys wyse,
Ȝit herke ful sadly with good devyse
What þat þu xalt do:
I counsel þe, be my reed,
þis wundyrful tale pray hem to hede;
And upon þis ȝeve hem good mede,
Bothe golde and sylver also.

And, sere, I xall telle ȝow why
In ȝoure erys prevyly

240 dwelle] w *written over another letter*

Betweyn us thre serteynly;
Now herk, serys, in ȝoure erys.

Hic faciant Pilatus, Cayphas, et Annas priuatim inter se consilium, quo finito dicat:

f. 195[v] ANNAS
For mede doth most in every qwest,
And mede is maystyr bothe est and west.
Now trewly, serys, I hold þis best—
With mede men may bynde berys.

CAYPHAS
Sekyr, sere, þis counsell is good.
Pray þese knyhtys to chaunge þer mood.
Ȝeve them golde, feste, and food,
And þat may chaunge þer wytt.

PYLATT
Sere, ȝoure good councel I xall fulfylle.
Now, jentyl knyhtys, come hedyr me tylle.
I pray ȝow, serys, of ȝoure good wylle,
No ferther þat ȝe flytt.

Jentyl knyhtys, I ȝow pray,
A bettyr sawe þat ȝe say.
Sey þer he was cawth away
With his dyscyplis be nyght.
Sey he was with his dyscyplis fett.
I wolde ȝe worn in ȝoure sadelys ssett.
And haue here gold in a purs knett,
And to Rome rydyth ryght.

QUARTUS MILES
Now, Syr Pylatt,
We gon oure gatt.
We wyll not prate
No lengere now.
Now we haue golde,
No talys xul be tolde
To whithtys on wolde,
We make þe avow.

264 berys] r *altered from another letter* 281–304 *written two lines as one,* 281–92 *divided by brown and red virgules as above,* 293–6 *by red virgules only,* 297–304 *by pointing*

PILATUS
Now, ȝe men of myth,
As ȝe han hyght,
Euyn so forthryght,
Ȝoure wurdys not falle.
And ȝe xul gon
With me anon,
All everychon
Into myn halle.

PRIMUS MILES
Now hens we go f. 196^{r}
As lyth as ro;
And ryght evyn so
As we han seyd,
We xul kepe counsel
Wheresoevyr we dwell.
We xul no talys tell—
Be not dysmayd.

36
[THE ANNOUNCEMENT TO THE THREE MARYS; PETER AND JOHN AT THE SEPULCHRE]

Hic uenient ad sepulcrum Maria Magdalene, Maria Jacobi, et Maria Salomé, et dicit Maria Magdalene:

MAGDALEN.
Swete systeryn, I ȝow besech,
Heryght now my specyal speche:
Go we with salvys for to leche
Cryst, þat tholyd wounde.
He hath us wonnyn owt of wreche.
The ryght wey God wyl us teche
For to seke my Lorde, my leche;
His blood hath me vnbownde.

289 men of *canc. in brown and red after* men of   finem 1^{a} die Nota *written in left margin below* 304 (*opposite s.d. preceding Play 36*), *possibly by C.*

Play 36 follows immediately upon Play 35

Vij develys in me were pyght.
My loue, my Lord, my God almyght,
Awey he weryd þe fyndys wight
With his wyse wurde.
He droff fro me þe fendes lees,
In my swete sowle his chawmere I ches,
In me belevyth þe Lorde of Pes.
I go to his burryenge boorde.

MARIA JACOBI My systerys sone I woot he was.
He lyth in here as sunne in glas.
Þe childe was born by oxe and asse
Vp in a bestys stall.
Thow his body be gravyd vndyr gres,
f. 196v Þe grete Godhede is nevyr þe lasse.
Þe Lord xal rysyn and gon his pas,
And comfortyn his frendys all.

MARIA SALOMÉ My name is Mary Salomé.
His modyr and I, systerys we be;
Annys dowterys we be all thre,
Jesu, we be þin awntys.
The naylis gun his lemys feyn,
And þe spere gan punche and peyn.
On þo woundys we wold haue eyn;
Þat grace now God graunt vs.

MARIA MAGDALEN Now go we stylle
With good wyll
Þer he is leyd.
He deyd on crowch,
We wolde hym towch,
As we han seyd.

Tunc respicit Maria Magdalene in sepulcro, dicens:

14 In *written in left margin* 22 lasse] a *altered from an* e Systerys dowterys bothe *canc. in brown and red between* 25 *and* 26

Where is my Lord, þat was here,
þat for me bledde bowndyn in brere?
His body was beryed rygh by þis mere,
þat for me gan deye.
þe Jewys, fekyll and fals fownde,
Where haue þei do þe body with wounde?
He lyth not upon þis grownde—
þe body is don aweye!

MARIA JACOBI To my Lorde, my love, my frende,
Fayn wolde I salve a spende,
And I myght aught amende
His woundys depe and wyde.
To my Lorde I owe lowlyté,
Bothe homage and fewté.
I wolde with my dewté
A softyd hand and syde.

MARIA SALOMÉ To myghtfful God omnypotent f. 197r
I bere a boyst of oynement.
I wold han softyd his sore dent,
His sydys al abowte.
Lombe of Love withowt loth,
I fynde þe not, myn hert is wroth!
In þe sepulcre þer lyth a cloth,
And jentyl Jesu is owte.

ANGELUS Wendyth forth, ȝe women thre,
Into þe strete of Galylé.
Ȝoure Savyour þer xul ȝe se
Walkynge in þe waye.
Ȝoure fleschly Lorde now hath lyff,
þat deyd on tre with strook and stryff.
Wende forth, þu wepynge wyff,
And seke hym, I þe saye.

33–8 *written three lines as one,* 33 *and* 34 *divided by a double brown virgule, the rest by pointing*
64 *an incomplete* g *canc. before* of

Now goth forth fast, all thre,
To his dyscyplys fayr and fre.
And to Petyr þe trewth telle ȝe—
þerof haue ȝe no dreed.
Spare ȝe not þe soth to say:
He þat was deed and closyd in clay,
He is resyn þis same day,
And levyth with woundys reed.

MARIA MAGDALEN A, myrthe and joye in herte we haue,
For now is resyn out of his graue
He levyth now oure lyff to saue,
þat dede lay in þe clay.
f. 197v MARIA JACOBY In hert I was ryght sore dysmayd
The aungel to us whan þat he sayd
þat Cryst is resyn; I was affrayd,
þe aungel whan I say.

MARIA SALOMÉ Now lete us all thre fulfylle
þe angelys wurde and Goddys wylle;
Lett us sey with voys wul shrylle,
Cryst, þat Jewys dede sle,
Oure Lord, þat naylyd was on þe rode,
And betyn out was his bodyes blode,
He is aresyn! þough they ben wode,
A, Lorde, ȝitt wele þu be.

Maria Magdalene dicit Petro et ceteris apostolis:

[MARIA MAGDALENE] Bretheryn all, in herte be glad,
Bothe blythe and joyful, in herte ful fayn.
For ryght good tydandys haue we had
þat oure Lord is resyn agayn!

79 MAGDALEN] g *altered from a* d 95 *s.h. supplied* 98 *Scribe C has made several revisions. He has written and canc.* and aperyd to us serteyne *in right margin, and has written longitudinally in left margin for insertion after* 98:
Lyk as he dyede nakyd as he was borne
and commande us to go[1] to Petyr and John and his dyscipulys all
and tell to yow he wolde apere in lyknes as he was befo[rn]

[1] to go] *interl.*

An aungel us bad ryght þus, sertayn,
To þe, Petyr, þat we xulde telle
How Cryst is resyn, þe which was slayn,
A levynge man evyrmore to dwelle.

MARIA JACOBI To lyve is resyn ageyn þat Lorde,
The qwych Judas to Jewys solde.
Of þis I bere ryght trewe recorde
By wurdys þat þe aungel tolde.
Now myrth and joye to man on molde;
Euery man now myrth may haue.
He þat was closyd in cley ful colde
This day is resyn owt of his grave. f. 198^{r}

PETRUS Sey me, systeryn, with wurdys blythe,
May I troste to þat ȝe say?
Is Cryst resyn ageyn to lyve
þat was ded and colde in clay?
MARIA SALOMÉ ȝa, trostyth us truly, it is no nay!
He is aresyn, it is no les.
And so an aungel us tolde þis day
With opyn voys and speche expres.

JOHANNES ȝa, þese be tydyngys of ryght gret blys,
þat oure maystyr resyn xulde be!
I wyl go renne in hast, iwys,
And loke my Lord yf I may se.
PETRUS For joye also I renne with the,
My brothyr Johan, as I þe say.

99 *C has placed deleting dots under* aungel *and* bad, *and interl.* bade *above* aungel 101 *the reviser has interl.* he *above* Cryst 105 *a stroke canc. in dark brown and red before* trewe 106 *the reviser has interl.* for *before* By *and has marked for insertion below* 106 *a passage he has written in the bottom margin of f. 197^{v}:*

for . . . aperyd to us with handys, fytte, and hert borde and ferre (*?*) he schowyd us his woundys fyve,
both handys and fytte, and þe wound in his syde—
and þerfor beleve us þat he is man (*?*) alyve

In darker ink the reviser (?) has canc. for *in the first line of this passage and written* allso *at the left; he has written* he *over the following word, canc. the last five words in this line, and interl.* with body bolde *above; he has also canc. the third line* 117 *in left margin C has written longitudinally:* and so he bade us tell yow þis daye. 119 be ȝ *canc. in dark brown and red before* þese

In hast anon evyn forth go we;
To his grave we renne oure way.

Hic currunt Johannes et Petrus simul ad sepulcrum, et Johannes prius venit ad monumentum, sed non intrat.

JOHANNES The same shete here I se
þat Crystys body was in wounde.
But he is gon! Wheresoever he be,
He lyth not here upon þis grownde.

Petrus intrat monumentum, et dicit Petrus:

PETRUS In þis cornere þe shete is fownde;
And here we fynde þe sudary
f. 198v In þe whiche his hed was wounde
Whan he was take from Calvary.

Hic intrat Johannes monumentum dicens:

JOHANNES The same sudary and þe same shete
Here with my syth I se both tweyn.
Now may I wele knowe and wete
þat he is rysyn to lyve ageyn!
Onto oure bretheryn lete us go seyn
þe trewth ryght hevyn as it is:
Oure maystyr lyvyth, þe whech was slayn,
Allmyghty Lorde and Kynge of Blys.

PETRUS No lengere here wyll we dwelle;
To oure bretheryn þe wey we take.
The trewth to them whan þat we telle,
Grett joye in hert þan wul þei make.

Hic Petrus loquitur omnibus apostolis simul collectis:

Beth mery, bretheryn, for Crystys sake!
þat man þat is oure mayster so good,

134 Calvary] v *altered in darker ink from another letter*

From deth to lyve he is awake,
þat sore was rent upon þe rood.

JOHANNES As women seyd, so haue we fownde:
Remevyd awey we saw þe ston!
He lyth no lengere vndyr þe grownde;
Out of his graue oure maystyr is gon.

[*Omnibus congregatis.*]

THOMAS We haue grett woundyr, everychon,
Of þese wurdys þat ȝe do speke.
A ston ful hevy lay hym vpon—
From vndyr þat ston how xulde he breke?

PETRUS The trewth to tellyn, it passyth oure witt! f. 199r
Wethyr he be resyn thorwe his owyn myght,
Or ellys stolyn out of his pitt
Be sum man prevely be nyght.
That he is gon we saw with syght,
For in his graue he is nowth.
We cannot tellyn in what plyght
Out of his graue þat he is browth.

37
[THE APPEARANCE TO MARY MAGDALENE]

Maria Magdalen goth to þe graue and wepyth, and seyth:

MARIA MAGDALEN For hertyly sorwe myn herte doth breke.
With wepynge terys I wasch my face.
Alas, for sorwe I may not speke—
My Lorde is gon þat hereinne wase.

154 s.d. Omnibus congregatis] *B; MS* Omnes congregaꝑ; *this s.d. precedes* 155 *s.h.*
161 out] t *altered from another letter*

Play 37 follows immediately upon Play 36
1 sorwe] o *blotted and an* o *interl. above*

Myn owyn dere Lorde and Kynge of Gras
þat vij deuelys fro me dyd take.
I kannat se hym, alas! Alas!
He is stolyn awey owt of þis lake.

AUNGELUS Woman þat stondyst here alone,
Why dost þu wepe, and morne, and wepe so sore?
What cawse hast þu to make such mone?
Why makyst þu such sorwe, and wherefore?

MARIA MAGDALEN I haue gret cawse to wepe evyrmore:
My Lord is take out of his grave,
Stolyn awey and fro me lore.
I kannot wete where hym to haue.

Hic parum deambulet a sepulcro, dicens:

Alas, alas, what xal I do?
My Lord awey is fro me take.
f. 199v A, woful wrecche, whedyr xal I go?
My joye is gon owth of þis lake.

JESUS Woman, suche mornynge why dost þu make?
Why is þi chere so hevy and badde?
Why dost þu sythe so sore and qwake?
Why dost þu wepe so sore and sadde?

MARIA MAGDALEN A grettyr cawse had nevyr woman
For to wepe bothe nyth and day
Than I myself haue, in serteyn,
For to sorwyn evyr and ay.
Alas, for sorwe myn hert doth blede—
My Lorde is take fro me away.
I muste nedys sore wepe and grede.
Where he is put I kannot say.

But, jentyl gardener, I pray to the,
If þu hym took out of his graue,

7 kannat] se *canc. after* kan 28 And *canc. in red before* For

Telle me qwere I may hym se,
  þat I may go, my Lorde to haue.

Spectans:

JESUS M. A. R. I. A.

MARIA MAGDALEN
  A, maystyr and Lorde! To þe I crave,
    As þu art Lord and Kynge of Blys,
  Graunt me, Lord, and þu vowchesave,
    Thyn holy fete þat I may kys.

JESUS
Towche me not as ȝett, Mary,
  For to my fadyr I haue not ascende.
But to my bretheryn in hast þe hyȝ,
  With these gode wurdys here care amende:
  Sey to my bretheryn þat I intende f. 200r
    To stey to my fadyr and to ȝowre,
  To oure Lord, both God and frende;
    I wyl ascende to hevyn towre.

In hevyn to ordeyn ȝow a place,
  To my fadyr now wyl I go;
To merth, and joye, and grett solace,
  And endeles blys to brynge ȝow to.
  For man I sufferyd both schame and wo—
    More spyteful deth nevyr man dyd take.
  Ȝit wyl I ordeyn for al this, lo,
    In hevyn an halle for mannys sake.

MARIA MAGDALY[N]
Gracyous Lord, at ȝoure byddyng
  To all my bretheryn I xal go telle
How þat ȝe be man levynge,
  Quyk and qwethynge, of flesch and felle.
  Now all hevynes I may expelle,
    And myrth and joy now take to me!
  My Lord, þat I haue louyd so wele,
    With opyn syght I dede hym se.

58 MAGDALYN] n *mostly cropped* *The ink-colour becomes paler with* 58

Whan I sowght my Lord in grave,
I was ful sory and ryght sad,
For syght of hym I myght non haue;
For mornynge sore I was nere mad.
Grettere sorwe ȝit nevyr whith had
Whan my Lord awey was gon.
f. 200v But now in herte I am so glad,
So grett a joy nevyr wyff had non.

How myght I more gretter joye haue
Than se þat Lorde with opyn syght,
The whiche my sowle from synne to saue
From develys sefne he mad me qwyght.

There kan no tounge my joye expres
Now I haue seyn my Lorde on lyve.
To my bretheryn I wyl me dresse,
And telle to hem anon-ryght belyve.
With opyn speche I xal me shryve,
And telle to hem with wurdys pleyn
How þat Cryst from deth to lyve,
To endles blys is resyn ageyn.

Bretheryn, all blyth ȝe be,
For joyful tydyngys tellyn I kan!
I saw oure Lord Cryst, lyste wel to me,
Of flesch and bon quyk levynge man.
Beth glad and joyful as for-than,
For, trost me trewly, it is ryght thus:
Mowth to mowth, þis [is] sertayn,
I spak ryght now with Cryst Jesus.

PETRUS A woundyrful tale, forsothe, is this.
Evyr onowryd oure Lorde mote be.
We pray þe, Lord and Kynge of Blys,
Onys þi presence þat we may se.
f. 201r Ere thu ascende to thi magesté,
Gracyous God, if þat ȝe plese,

69 *a stroke canc. before* mornynge 92 is *supplied*

Late us haue sum syght of the,
  Oure careful hertys to sett in ease.
      Amen

Explicit Apparicio Marie Magdale[n]

38 f. 202^{r}

[CLEOPHAS AND LUKE; THE APPEARANCE TO THOMAS]

Hic incipit Aparicio Cleophe et Luce.

CLEOPHAS My brothir Lucas, I ȝow pray,
  Plesynge to ȝow if þat it be,
To þe castel of Emawus a lytyl way
  þat ȝe vowchesaf to go with me.
LUCAS All redy, brother, I walke with the
  To ȝone castell with ryght good chere.
Euyn togedyr anon go we,
  Brother Cleophas, we to in fere.

Final Latin line Magdalen] n *mostly cropped* *Remainder of f. 201^{r} filled with scribblings.* Amen Amen *appears at right opposite* 99, *and* Explicit *is written below final Latin line. Below this is a copy of the text on f. 200^{r}, roughly written by another hand:*

But noow in herte I am so glad
so grete a jooy [*first* o *blotted*] nevyr wyff had non
how myght I more gretter haue than se
þat lorde with opyn syght the wyche my soule
from synne to saue from develys sefne
he mad me qwyght there kan no tounge [haue *written at right*]
my joy expres now I haue seyn my lorde
on lyve to my brethryn I wyll me dresse
and thell to hem with wurdys pleyn hwow
þat cryst from deth to lyve to endles blys
ys resyn agayen [*letter blotted*] bretheryn all bllyth
ye be for joyfull tydyngys tellyn y kan I saw
oure lord cryst lyste wel to me of flesch and bon
quyk levyng man beth glad and joyfull as for than
for trost me trewly it ys ryght thus
Mowth to mowth þis is sartayn I [*letters canc.*] spak rght now with cryst Jesus

F. 201^{v} blank, except for marks at foot of page

CLEOPHAS A, brother Lucas, I am sore mevyd
Whan Cryst, oure mayster, comyth in my mynde.
Whan that I thynke how he was grevyd,
Joye in myn herte kan I non fynde.
He was so lowlye, so good, so kynde,
Holy of lyf and meke of mood.
Alas, þe Jewys, þei were to blynde
Hym for to kylle þat was so good.

LUCAS Brothyr Cleophas, ȝe sey ful soth:
They were to cursyd and to cruell.
And Judas, þat traytour, he was to loth,
For golde and sylvyr his maystyr to selle.
The Jewys were redy hym for to qwelle,
With skorgys bete out all his blood.
Alas, þei were to fers and felle;
Shamfully thei henge hym on a rood.

CLEOPHAS Ȝa, betwen to thevys—alas, for shame—
They henge hym up with body rent.
Alas, alas, they were to blame!
To cursyd and cruel was þer intent.
f. 202v Whan for thurste he was nere shent,
Eyzil and galle þei ȝovyn hym to drynke.
Alas, for ruthe, his deth thei bent
In a fowle place of horryble stynke.

LUCAS Ȝa, and cawse in hym cowde they non fynde.
Alas, for sorwe, what was here thought?
And he dede helpe bothe lame and blynde,
And all seke men þat were hym browght.
Aȝens vice alwey he wrought;
Synfull dede wold he nevyr do.
Ȝit hym to kylle þei sparyd nought.
Alas, alas, why dede they so?

17 sey] se *smudged* *F. 202v marked* 200 33 LUCAS] a *partially rubbed*

JESUS Well ovyrtake, ȝe serys in-same.
To walke in felachep with ȝow I pray.
LUCAS Welcom, ser[e], in Goddys name;
Of good felachep we sey not nay.
JESUS Qwat is ȝoure langage, to me ȝe say,
That ȝe haue togedyr, ȝe to?
Sory and evysum ȝe ben alway—
Ȝoure myrthe is gon; why is it so?

CLEOPHAS Sere, methynkyth þu art a pore pylgrym
Here walkynge be þiselfe alone,
And in þe ceté of Jerusalem,
Þu knowyst ryght lytyl what þer is done.
For pylgrymys comyn and gon ryth sone;
Ryght lytyl whyle plygrymes do dwelle.
In all Jerusalem, as þu hast gone,
I trowe no tydyngys þat þu canst telle.

JESUS Why, in Jherusalem what thynge is wrought? f. 203r
What tydyngys fro thens brynge ȝe?
LUCAS A, ther haue they slayn a man for nought,
Gyltles he was, as we telle the.
An holy prophete with God was he,
Myghtyly in wurde and eke in dede;
Of God he had ryght grett pousté.
Amonge þe pepyl his name gan sprede.

He hyght Jesu of Nazareth,
A man he was of ryght grett fame.
The Jewys hym kylde with cruel deth,
Without trespas or any blame.
Hym to scorne they had grett game,
And naylid hym streyte ontyll a tre.
Alas, alas, methynkyth grett shame
Without cawse þat this xulde be.

42 p *canc. before* I 43 sere] serys 59 *a letter canc. in red before* ther
64 gan] a *written over an* r

CLEOPHAS
Ʒa, sere, and ryght grett troste in hym we had,
All Israel countré þat he xulde saue.
The thrydde day is this þat he was clad
In coold cley and leyd in grave.
Ʒitt woundyrful tydyngys of hym we haue
Of women þat sought hym beforn daylyth.
Wethyr they sey truthe or ellys do raue,
We cannot telle þe trewe verdyth.

When Cryst in grave þei cowde not se,
They comyn to us and evyn thus tolde:
f. 203v How þat an aungell seyd to them thre
That he xuld leve with brest ful bolde.
Ʒitt Petyr and Johan preve this wolde:
To Crystys graue they ran, thei tweyne.
And whan they come to þe graue so coolde,
They fownde þe women ful trewe, serteyne.

JESUS
A, ȝe fonnys and slought of herte
For to beleve in Holy Scrypture!
Haue not prophetys with wurdys smerte
Spoke be tokenys in signifure
That Cryste xuld deye for ȝoure valure
And syth entre his joye and blys?
Why be ȝe of herte so dure
And trust not in God, þat myghtful is?

Bothe Moyses and Aaron, and othyr mo—
In Holy Scrypture ȝe may rede it—
Of Crystis deth thei spak also,
And how he xuld ryse out of his pitt.
Owt of feyth than why do ȝe flitte
Whan holy prophetys ȝow teche so pleyne?
Turne ȝoure thought and chaunge ȝoure witte,
And truste wele þat Cryst doth leve ageyne.

LUCAS
Leve ageyn? Man, be in pes.
How xulde a ded man evyr aryse?
I cowncell þe such wurdys to ses
For dowte of Pylat, þat hyȝ justyce.

100 how] o *altered from another letter* (u?)

He was slayn at þe gre[t] asyse f. 204ʳ
  Be councell of lordys many on.
Of suche langage take bettyr avise
  In every company þer þu dost gon.

CHRISTUS Trewth dyd nevyr his maystyr shame.
  Why xulde I ses than trewth to say?
Be Jonas þe prophete I preve þe same,
  Þat was in a whallys body iij nyghtis and iij day.
  So longe Cryst in his grave lay
    As Jonas was withinne þe se.
  His grave is brokyn, þat was of clay;
    To lyff resyn aȝen now is he.

CLEOPHAS Sey nott so, man! It may not be,
  Thow thyn exaunple be sumdele good.
For Jonas on lyve evyrmore was he,
  And Cryst was slayn vpon a rood.
  The Jewys on hym, they wore so wood
    Þat to his herte a spere they pyght!
  He bled owt all his herteblood.
    How xulde he thanne ryse with myght?

CHRISTUS Take hede at Aaron and his dede styk,
  Which was ded of his nature.
And ȝit he floryschyd with flowrys ful thyk
  And bare almaundys of grett valure.
  The dede styk was signifure
    How Cryst, þat shamfully was deed and
        slayn,
  As þat dede styk bare frute ful pure,
    So Cryst xuld ryse to lyve ageyn.

LUCAS That a deed styk frute xulde bere, f. 204ᵛ
  I merveyle sore þerof, iwys.
But ȝitt hymsylf fro deth to rere
  And leve ageyn, more woundyr it is.

109 gret] gre

That he doth leve, I trost not this,
For he hath bled his blood so red.
But ȝitt of myrthe evyrmoor I mys
Whan I haue mende þat he is ded.

CHRISTUS Why be ȝe so harde of truste?
Dede not Cryste reyse thorwe his owyn myght
Lazare, þat deed lay vndyr þe duste
And stynkyd ryght foule, as I ȝow plyght?
To lyff Cryst reysid hym aȝen ful ryght
Out of his graue, þis is serteyn.
Why may nat Cryste hymself þus qwyght,
And ryse from deth to lyve ageyn?

CLEOPHAS Now trewly, sere, ȝoure wurdys ben good,
I haue in ȝow ryght grett delyght.
I pray ȝow, sere, with mylde mood,
To dwelle with vs all þis nyght.
CHRISTUS I must gon hens anon ful ryght
For grett massagys I haue to do.
I wolde abyde yf þat I myght,
But at þis tyme I must hens go.

LUCAS Ȝe xal not gon fro us þis nyght.
It waxit all derke, gon is þe day;
Þe sonne is downe, lorn is þe lyght.
Ȝe xal not gon from vs away.
f. 205r CHRISTUS I may not dwelle, as I ȝow say;
I must þis nyght go to my frende.
Þerfore, good bretheryn, I ȝow pray,
Lett me not my wey to wende.

CLEOPHAS Trewly, from vs ȝe xal not go!
Ȝe xal abyde with us here stylle.
Ȝoure goodly dalyaunce plesyth us so,
We may nevyr haue of ȝow oure fylle.

141 *a letter canc. before* this 142 d *canc. before* red 143 myrthe] y *written over an* r 160 hens] s *written over another letter* (y?)

We pray ȝow, sere, with herty wylle,
All nyght with us abyde and dwelle,
More goodly langage to talkyn vs tylle,
And of ȝoure good dalyaunce more for to telle.

LUCAS Ȝa, brothyr Cleophas, by myn assent,
Lete us hym kepe with strenth and myght!
Sett on ȝowre hand with good entent
And pulle hym with us þe wey well ryght.
The day is done, sere, and now it is nyght.
Why wole ȝe hens now from us go?
Ȝe xal abyde, as I ȝow plyght—
Ȝe xal not walke þis nyght vs fro.

CLEOPHAS This nyght fro us ȝe go not away!
We xal ȝow kepe betwen us tweyne.
To vs, þerfore, ȝe sey not nay,
But walke with us; þe wey is pleyne.
CHRISTUS Sythyn ȝe kepe me with myght and mayn,
With herty wyll I xal abyde.
LUCAS Of ȝoure abydyng we be ful fayn,
No man more welkom in þis werd wyde.

CLEOPHAS Off oure maystyr, Cryst Jesu, f. 205v
For ȝe do speke so mech good,
I loue ȝow hertyly, trust me trew.
He was bothe meke and mylde of mood,
Of hym to speke is to me food.
If ȝe had knowe hym, I dare wel say,
And in what plyght with hym it stood,
Ȝe wold haue thought on hym many a day.

LUCAS Many a day. Ȝa, ȝa, iwys.
He was a man of holy levynge.
Thow he had be þe childe of God in blys,
Bothe wyse and woundyrfull was his werkynge.
But aftere ȝoure labour and ferre walkynge,
Takyth þis loff and etyth sum bred.

175 langage] *second* g *written over another letter* 180 well] e *blotted*

And than wyl we haue more talkynge
Of Cryst, oure maystyr, þat is now ded.

CHRISTUS Beth mery and glad with hert ful fre,
For of Cryst Jesu, þat was ȝoure frende,
Ȝe xal haue tydyngys of game and gle
Withinne a whyle, or ȝe hens wende.

With myn hand þis bred I blys,
And breke it here, as ȝe do se.
I ȝeve ȝow parte also of þis,
This bred to ete and blythe to be.

Hic subito discedat Christus ab oculis eorum.

[CLEOPHAS] A, mercy, God! What was oure happ?
Was not oure hert with loue brennynge
f. 206[r] Whan Cryst, oure mayster, so nere oure lapp
Dede sitt and speke such suete talkynge?
He is now quyk and man lyvenge
þat fyrst was slayn and put in grave!
Now may we chaunge all oure mornynge,
For oure Lord is resyn his seruauntys to saue.

LUCAS Alas, for sorwe, what hap was this?
Whan he dyd walke with vs in way,
He prevyd by Scripture ryght wel, iwys,
þat he was resyn from vndyr clay.
We trustyd hym not, but evyr seyd nay—
Alas, for shame, why seyd we so?
He is resyn to lyve þis day;
Out of his grave oure Lord is go!

CLEOPHAS Latt us here no lengere dwelle,
But to oure bretheryn þe wey we wende.
With talys trewe to them we teḷle
That Cryst doth leve, oure maystyr and frende.

213 *lacks a capitulum* 217 *s.h. supplied*

LUCAS
I graunt þerto with hert ful hende:
  Lete us go walke forthe in oure way.
I am ful joyfull in hert and mende
  þat oure Lord levyth, þat fyrst ded lay.

CLEOPHAS
Now, was it not goodly don
  Of Cryst Jesu, oure mayster dere?
He hath with us a large wey gon,
  And of his vprysyng he dede us lere.
  Whan he walkyd with us in fere, f. 206v
    And we supposyd hym bothe deed and colde,
  þat he was aresyn from vndyr bere
    Be Holy Scripture þe trewth he tolde.

LUCAS
Ryght lovyngely don, forsothe, this was.
  What myght oure mayster tyl us do more
Than us to chere, þat forth dede pas?
  And for his deth we murnyd ful sore;
  For loue of hym oure myrthe was lore;
    We were for hym ryght hevy in herte.
  But now oure myrth he doth restore,
    For he is resyn bothe heyl and qwert.

CLEOPHAS
That he is þus resyn I haue grett woundyr!
  An hevy ston ovyr hym þer lay.
How shulde he breke þe ston asoundyr
  þat was deed and colde in clay?
  Euery man þis mervayle may,
    And drede þat Lorde of mekyl myght.
  But ȝit of þis no man sey nay,
    For we haue seyn hym with opyn syght.

LUCAS
That he doth leve, I woot wel this;
  He is aresyn with flesch and blood.
A levynge man, forsothe, he is,
  þat rewly was rent upon a rood.
  All heyl, dere brothyr, and chaunge ȝoure mood,
    For Cryst doth levyn and hath his hele!

264 hym] y *blotted, perhaps written over an incomplete letter*

We walkyd in wey with Cryst so good
And spak with hym wurdys fele.

f. 207r CLEOPHAS

Evyn tyll Emawus, þe grett castell,
From Jerusalem with hym we went.
Syxti furlonge, as we ȝow telle,
We went with hym evyn passent.
He spak with us with good entent;
þat Cryst xuld leve he tolde tyll us,
And previd it be Scripture, verament.
Trust me trewe, it is ryght thus.

LUCAS

Ʒa, and whan he had longe spokyn vs tylle,
He wold from vs a gon his way.
With strenght and myght we keptyn hym stylle,
And bred we tokyn hym to etyn, in fay.
He brak þe loff as evyn on tway
As ony sharpe knyff xuld kytt breed.
þerby we knew þe trewth þat day:
þat Cryst dede leve and was not deed.

PETRUS

Now trewly, serys, I haue grett woundyr
Of these grete merveylis þat ȝe vs telle!
In brekynge of bred ful evyn asoundyr
Oure mayster ȝe knew and Lord ryght well.
Ʒe sey Cryst levith, þat Jewys dyd qwelle.
Tyll us glad tydyngys þis is, serteyn!
And þat oure maystyr with ȝow so longe dede dwelle,
It doth wel preve þat he levith ageyn.

A, brother Thomas, we may be ryght glad
Of these gode novell þat we now haue.

Vade Worlych (?) *written and smudged at bottom right of f. 206v* Vade worlych, nota worlych *written in right margin opposite 279–80, apparently by C* 286 be *canc. before* breed nota wōlych *written by Scribe C (?) in right margin opposite* 290, *and canc.*

þe grace of oure Lorde God is ouyr vs all sprad;
Oure Lord is resyn his se[r]uauntys to saue.

THOMAS
Be in pes, Petyr, þu gynnyst to rave! f. 207v
Thy wurdys be wantowne and ryght vnwyse.
How xulde a deed man þat deed lay in grave
With qwyk flesche and blood to lyve ageyn ryse?

PETRUS
ȝis, Thomas, dowte þe not oure maystyr is on lyve.
Record of Mawdelyn and of here systerys too;
Cleophas and Lucas, þe trewthe for to contryve,
Fro Jerusalem to Emaws with hym dede they go.

THOMAS
I may nevyr in hert trust þat it is so!
He was ded on cros and colde put in pitt,
Kept with knyhtys iiij, his grave sealyd also.
How xulde he levyn ageyn þat so streyte was shitt?

PETRUS
Whan Mawdelyn dede tell us þat Cryst was aresyn,
I ran to his graue, and Johan ran with me.
In trewth, þer we fownde he lay not in presyn—
Gon out of his grave and on lyve þan was he.
Therfore, dere brother Thomas, I wole rede the,
Stedfastly þu trust þat Cryst is not deed.
Feythffully beleve a qwyk man þat he be,
Aresyn from his deth by myght of his godhed.

THOMAS
I may nevyr beleve these woundyr merveles
Tyl þat I haue syght of euery grett wounde,
And put in my fyngyr in place of þe nayles.
I xal nevyr beleve it ellys for no man on grownnde.
And tyll þat myn hand þe sperys pytt hath fownnde,
Which dede cleve his hert and made hym sprede his blood,
I xal nevyr beleue þat he is qwyk and sownde,
In trewth whyl I knowe þat he was dede on rood.

300 seruauntys] seuauntys 315 presyn] y *written over an* o
324 grownnde] *or* growunde 325 fownnde] *or* fowunde

f. 208r PETRUS Cryst be þi comforte and chawnge þi bad witt,
For feyth but þu haue, þi sowle is but lorn.
With stedfast beleve God enforme þe ȝitt,
Of a meke mayde as he was for us born.
CHRISTUS Pees be amonge ȝow! Beholde how I am torn.
Take hede of myn handys, my dere brothyr Thomas.
THOMAS My God and my Lorde, nyght and every morn
I aske mercy, Lorde, for my grett trespas!

CHRISTUS Beholde wele, Thomas, my woundys so wyde,
Which I haue sufferyd for all mankynde.
Put þin hool hand into my ryght syde,
And in myn hertblood þin hand þat þu wynde.
So feythffull a frend were mayst þu fynde?
Be stedfast in feyth, beleve wel in me.
Be þu not dowtefful of me in þi mynde,
But trust þat I leve, þat deed was on a tre.

THOMAS My Lord and my God, with syght do I se
þat þu art now quyk, which henge deed on rode.
More feythful þan I ther may no man be,
For myn hand haue I wasch in þi precyous blode.
CHRISTUS For þu hast me seyn, þerfore þi feyth is good.
But blyssyd be tho of þis þat haue no syght
And beleve in me. They, for here meke mood,
Shall com into hefne, my blysse þat is so bryght.

THOMAS As a ravaschyd man whos witt is all gon,
Grett mornynge I make for my dredfful dowte.
f. 208v Alas, I was dowteful þat Cryst from vndyr ston
Be his owyn grett myght no wyse myght gone owte.
Alas, what mevyd me thus in my thought?
My dowtefful beleve ryght sore me avexit.
The trewthe do I knowe þat God so hath wrought:
Quod mortuus et sepultus nunc resurrexit.

333 *a letter canc. in red before* torn 336 ah (*?*) *canc. in dark brown and red before* aske
360 resurrexit] re- *slightly cramped as if added later*

He þat was bothe deed and colde put in grave
 To lyve is aresyn by his owyn myght.
In his dere herteblood myn hand wasch I haue,
 Where þat þe spere-poynt was peynfully pyght.
 I take me to feyth, forsakynge all vnryght;
  Þe dowte þat I had ful sore me avexit.
 For now haue I seyn with ful opyn syght:
  Quod mortuus et sepultus nunc resurrexit.

I trustyd no talys þat were me tolde
 Tyl þat myn hand dede in his hertblood wade.
My dowte doth aprevyn Cryst levynge ful bolde
 And is a grett argument in feyth us to glade.
 Þu, man þat seyst þis, from feyth nevyr þu fade.
  My dowte xal evyr chere the, þat sore me avexit.
 Truste wele in Cryst, þat such meracle hath made.
  Quod mortuus et sepultus nunc resurrexit.

The prechynge of Petir myght not conuerte me
 Tyll I felyd þe wounde þat þe spere dyde cleve.
I trustyd nevyr he levyd, þat deed was on a tre,
 Tyll þat his herteblood dede renne in my sleve.
 Thus be my grett dowte oure feyth may we preve. f. 209r
  Behold my blody hand, to feyth þat me avexit;
 Be syght of þis myrroure, from feyth not remeve
  Quod mortuus et sepultus nunc resurrexit.

Thow þat Mary Magdalyn in Cryst dede sone beleve
 And I was longe dowteful, ȝitt putt me in no blame.
For be my grett dowte oure feyth may we preve
 Aȝens all þo eretykys þat speke of Cryst shame.
 Truste wel Jesu Cryst, þe Jewys kyllyd the same;
  The fende hath he feryd, oure feyth þat evyr avexit.

361 bothe] b *written over a* d 362 aresyn] n *partially obscured by a fleck of printed paper; other such fragments of paper appear between lines* 11 *or incomplete* w *canc. before* myght 388 eretykys] *second* y *written over an* i 390 feyth] feyyth, *with deleting dot under the first* y

To hevyn ȝow brynge, and saue ȝow all in-same
That mortuus et sepultus iterum resurrexit.
Amen.

f. 210^r
W quire

39
[THE ASCENSION; THE SELECTION OF MATTHIAS]

Hic incipit Ascencio Domini nostri, cum Maria, et vndecim discipulis, et duobus angelis sedentibus in albis; et Jesus dicit discipulis suis et cetera:

JESUS
Pax vobis. Amonge ȝow pes,
Bothe love, and reste, and charyté.
Amonge all vertues lete it not ses,
For amonge all vertues prynspal his he.

Ȝe be to blame I may wel preve,
For I wyl vse to ȝow wordys pleyn
Þat ȝe be so hard of herte to beleve
Þat from deth to lyve I am resyn ageyn.
Nottwithstondynge as ȝe knowe, serteyn,
To ȝow viij sythys aperyd haue I
Be soundry tymes, the trewth to seyn;
And þis is þe ix tyme, sothly,
Evyn and no mo.
But now sum mete
Anon doth gete;
For I wyl ete
With ȝow and goo.

My dyscyplis, here what I sey,
And to my wourdys ȝevyth attencyon.
From Jerusalem loke ȝe go nott awey,
But mekely abydyth my fadyres promiscyon,

Remainder of f. 209^r (112 mm) blank except for the words scribbled in another hand That mortuus et sse. *F. 209^v blank except for* hic incipit Ascencio, *scribbled by another hand*

[*Play 39*] 1 Pax vobis *written in Textura Quadrata* 5 *no capitulum*

Off whiche be my mowth ȝe haue had informacyon
  Whyll bodyly with ȝow I was dwellynge.
For Johan, sothly, for mannys saluacyon
  Onlye in watyr was me baptysynge.
    But I ȝow behete
      Withinne fewe days þat ȝe
      In þe Holy Goost xul baptyzid be. f. 210v
      Therfore rysyth up and folwyht me
    Onto þe Mownte of Olyvete.

JACOBUS MAJOR O Lord, vowchesaff vs for to telle
  Iff þu wylt now, withowte more delay,
Restoryn þe kyngdam of Israell
  And ȝeve vs þe joye, Lord, þat lestyth ay.
JESUS Serys, þe tymes and þe monthis knowe ȝe ne may
  Whiche my fadyr hath put in his owyn power.
But ȝe xul take within short day
  Of þe Holy Goost þe vertu cler,
    Thorwe whiche xul ȝe
      In Jerusalem and in Jury,
      And moreovyr also in Samary,
      And to þe worldys ende vttyrly,
    My wyttnes only be.

Lovyth no wrath nor no wronge,
  But levyth in charyté with mylde stevyn,
With myrthe, and melody, and aungell-songe.
  Now I stey streyte from ȝow to hevyn.

Hic ascendit ab oculis eorum, et in celo cantent et cetera.

ANGELUS Returnyth ageyn to ȝoure loggynge,
  To Jerusalem, for he wyl thus,
His promys mekely þer abydynge;
  For dowteles þis forseyd Jesus,
    Whiche from ȝow is take

37 short] t *blotted and a* t *interl. above* hic ascendit ab oculys *and* Joh *written by another hand in bottom margin of f. 210v*

f. 211r

In a clowde, as ȝe hym seyn
Steyng vp, so xal comyn ageyn.
Of al mankynde, þis is serteyn,
Jugement xal he make.

[PETRUS] O ȝe bretheryn, attendyth to me,
And takyth good hede what I xal seyn:
It behovyth þe scripture fulfyllyd to be
Þat of Dauyd was seyd with wourdys pleyn
Of Judas, whiche was þe gyde, serteyn,
Of hem þat Cryst slow cruelly;
Which aftyr from deth ros vp ageyn,
And hath abedyn in erthe ful days fourty.
And aftyr all this,
Before oure eye
In a bryght skye
He dede up stye
To hevyn blys.

This seyd Judas was amongys us
Noumbryd apostyll, and had lych dygnyté.
But whan he betrayd oure Lord Jesus,
He hynge hymself vpon a tre;
In whos sted muste nedys ordeyned be
Another, oure noumbre for to restore,
On of þo whiche, as weel knowe we,
Han be conuersaunt here longe before
In oure company;
Whiche xal wyttnes
Berun expresse
To more and lesse
Of Crystys resurrexion stedfastly.

Hic statuent duos, Joseph Justum et Mathiam, et cetera.

An unusually large space follows 55; *the subsequent stanza is preceded by an elaborate capitulum* 57 *s.h. supplied* 66–9 *written two lines as one, divided by ticks and commas* 74 whos] h *malformed, possibly written over another letter* 79–82 *written two lines as one, divided by brown virgule, ticks and commas, and red strokes* 82 s.d. Justum] Justus

O sovereyn Lorde, whiche of every man f. 211v
The hertys dost knowe most inwardly,
With all þe lowlyness we may or kan,
To þe we prey ful benygnely
That þu vowchesaff thorwe þi mercy
Vs hym to shewe whiche in þis cas
þu lykyst to chesyn effectuously
To ocapye þe lott of Judas plas.

Hic dabunt sortes, et cadet super Mathiam, et cetera.

Now gramercy, Lord!
And to fulfylle
þin holy wylle,
As it is skylle,
We all accorde.

f. 212r

40
[PENTECOST]

Modo de die Pentecostes. Apostoli dica[n]t genuflectentes; Spiritus Sanctus descendat super eos, et cetera.

PETRUS Honowre,
ANDREAS wurchipp,
JACOBUS MAJOR and reverens,
JOHANNES Glorye,
PHILIPPUS grace,
JACOBUS MINOR and goodnes,
THOMAS Dygnité,
BARTHOLOMEUS vertu,
SYMON and excellence,

92–5 *written two lines as one, divided by brown and red virgules* *Remainder of f. 211v (118 mm) blank except for writing below* 95: modo de die *and* hic dabunt so

[Play 40] Initial s.d. dicant] *D; MS* dicat *s.h.s in* 1–4 *written in red, slightly larger than usual, three to each line* Playnumber 40] 4 *written over an erased s.h.* Johannes, *which followed* Jacobus major; *inside the* O *is an erased rubricated number (?) and a small red figure*

MATHEUS Bewté,
JUDAS blyssynge,
MATHEAS and bryghtnes
PETRUS Be to þat Lord [of] heye wurthynes,
ANDREAS Whiche hath performyd þat he vs hyght,
JACOBUS MAJOR And vs enbawmyd with suche swetnes,
JOHANNES Whiche to dyscrye fer passyth oure myght.
PHILIPPUS This we all wel kenne.
JACOBUS MINOR Now, gracyous Lord Jesu,
THOMAS Conferme us in þi vertu,
BARTHOLOMEUS And graunt us grace evyr it to sew.
SYMON Sey we all togedyr, amen. Amen.

Et omnes osculant terram.

PRIMUS JUDEUS Now, felawys, take hede, for be my trewthe,
Ȝondyr syttyth a dronkyn felachepp.
SECUNDUS JUDEUS To don hem good, it were grett ruthe.
TERCIUS JUDEUS Ȝa, I prey God ȝeve hem all shenschepp!
f. 212ᵛ PRIMUS JUDEUS Muste in here brayn so sclyly doth creppe
þat þei cheteryn and chateryn as they jays were.
SECUNDUS JUDEUS Ȝa, were they ony wel browth asclepe,
It wore almes to þe revere hem to bere,
There hem to baptyze!
PRIMUS JUDEUS þat were, as thynkyth me,
A jentyl sporte to se;
A bettyr game to be
Cowde no man devyse.

PETRUS Serys, alas, what do ȝe mene?
Why scorne ȝe now þus Goddys grace?
It is nothynge as ȝe do wene:
þer is no drunke man in þis place.

5 of *supplied* F. 212ᵛ *marked* 210 23–6 *written two lines as one, divided by two brown virgules and one red*

Wherefore ryght grett is ȝowre trespace.
But, syrys, lyst what it doth sygnyfye:
Fulfyllyd is now to mannys solace
Of Johel þe pregnaunt prophecye,
In whiche þat he
That ȝe han seyn
In wourdys pleyn
Declaryth serteyn.
Now blyssyd God be.
Amen.

f. 214r

41
[THE ASSUMPTION OF MARY]

Ad mea facta pater assit Deus et sua mater.

DOCTOR Ryht worchepful souereynes, liketh yow to here
Of the Assumpcion of the gloryous Moder Mary
That Seynt Jhon the Euangelist wrot and tauht, as I lere,
In a book clepid apocriphum, wythoutyn dyswary.
At fourten yer sche conseyved Cryste in hire matere clere,
And in the fiftene yer sche childyd, this avowe dar I;
Here lyvyng wyth that swete sone thre and thretty yere,
And after his deth, in erthe xij yer dede sche tary.
Now acounte me thise yeris wysely,
And I sey the age was of this maide Marye
When sche assumpte above the ierarchye
Thre score yer, as scripture dothe specyfye:
Legenda Sanctorum autorysyth this trewely.

39 amen *written by another hand below* Amen *of main scribe* *Remainder of f. 212v (67 mm) blank*

[*Play 41*] *Ff. 213–22 are interpolated. The hand and the Two-Wheeled Cart paper do not appear elsewhere in the codex. F. 213r is blank except for the roughly-written* The Lord be thanked for his g *near top of the page, and several scribbled letters and* amen *at the foot. F. 213v is blank except for* ad mea facta, *scribbled by another hand on top of page, and* John *and some scribbles at the foot*
1 Lu *written in left margin* 9 thise] s *malformed, possibly written over another letter*

She was inhabith in Juré by the Mounte of Syon
After the Assencion of hir sone, conseyved in
spoused.
Alle the holy placys in erthe that Criste duellyd on,
Devouthly sche went hem, honouryng the Godhed.
Ferste to the place there Criste cristenyd was, clepid
Flum Jordon;
There he fastyd and takyn was by malicious falshed;
There he beryed was, and roos victoryously alon;
There he assendid alle hevenys, God in his
manhed.
Thus was sche ocupyed, I rede,
And meche sche was in the temple preyand.
Now blissid mot sche be, we owe to be seyand.
How sche was assumpte, here men schul be
pleyand,
Preyng you of audience; now ses and tak hede.

f. 214ᵛ MI....
Pes now youre blaberyng, in the develis name!
What, lousy begchis, mow ye not se,
Owre worthy prynsis, lo, are gaderid in-same
That are statis of this lond, hye men of degré.
By there hye wisdam they schal now attayne
How alle Juré beste gouernyd may be.
And of this pillid prechouris that oure lawis defame,
They schul ben slayn as they say, or fayn for to fle!
Wherfore in pes be ye,
And herkenyth onto hem moste stilly.
For what boy bragge outh, hym spill[e] I!
As knave wyth this craggyd kna[g], hym kylle I!
Now herkenyth oure pryncis alle kneland on kne.

EPISCOPUS LEGIS
Now, ye pry[n]sis, I, prest of the lave,
Of this demaunde responcyon: I aske here anon,

16 duellyd] e *interl.* 19 F *written in left margin* 20 victoryously] *B* vittoryously 26 G *written in left margin* 27 MI] *remainder cropped* 33 oure] u *altered by erasure from an* r 36 stilly] y *altered to or from* e, *altered to or from* i *an* I *added, evidently after the drawing of the rhyme-bracket, which passes through it* 37 outh] u *and* h *seem to be corrections, perhaps associated with marks under* o *and* t spille] *G; MS* spilly 38 knag] knad 40 prynsis] *G; MS* prysis I, prest] *Hal* i-prest

Ys there ony renogat among vs, fer as ye knawe,
Or ony that peruertyth the pepil wyth gay eloquens alon?
Yif there be, we muste onto hem set awe,
For they feyne falsly oure feyth—hem preve I houre fon!
Sweche schul ben bounden vp be the beltys til flyes hem blawe,
And gnaggyd vp by the gomys tyl the deuyl doth hem grone!
We may not won
To sweche harlotis settyn reddure
That geynseyn oure lawe and oure Scripture.
Now let sere pryncis in purpure,
In savynge of owre lawys now telle on.

PRIMUS PRINCEPS Sere, syn we slew hym that clepid hym oure kyng
And seyde he was Goddis sone, lord ouyr all,
Syn his deth I herd of no maner rysyng.
And lo, yif he hadde levyd, he had mad vs his thrall.
EPISCOPUS Therfore oure wysdam was to schortyn his endyng; f. 215r
Whoso clyme ouyrhie, he hath a foule fall.
SECUNDUS PRINCEPS Ya, yit of on thing I warne yow at the gynnyng:
His dame is levyng, Mary that men call;
Myche pepil halt hire wythall.
Wherfore, in peyne of reprefe,
Yif we suffre hyre thus to relefe,
Oure lawys sche schal make to myschefe,
And meche schame don vs sche schall.

EPISCOPUS A, sere, ye ben bolde inow! Art thou ferd of a wenche?
What trowyste thou sche myht don vs agayn?
TERCIUS PRINCE[PS] Sere, there are other in the contré that clenche
And prechyn he is levyng that we slewe, they seyn.
And yif they ben sufferyd thus, this will bredyn a stench,
For thorow here fayre speche oure lawys they steyn.

In 53–6 *rhyme-brackets are rubricated* 53 PRIMUS] m *obscured by inkstain* 67 thou] *B* that; *this word altered from* that, *or vice versa* 68 *s.h.* iij Prince, *remainder cropped* 70 this] is *written over an erasure* will *interl.*

And therfore devyse we now vpon this pleyn bench
What is beste for to do, hem for to atteyn.
We are but loste yif they reyn.
EPISCOPU[S] Why, let se, than; sey me youre ententis.
PRIM[US] Let vs preson hem til here myht schent is!
SECUND[US] Bettyr is to slen hem wyth dentis!
TERC[IUS] Nay, best is to hang hem wyth peyn!

EP[ISCOPUS] Nay, seris, nowth so. [You] bettyr avyse;
Haue in syth before what after may tide.
Yif we slewe hem, it wolde cause the comownys to ryse,
And rathere the devyl sle hym than we schulde that abi[de].
f. 215v But be that seustere ded, Mary, that fise,
We shal brenne here body and the aschis hide,
And don here all the dispith we can here devise,
And than sle tho disciplis that walkyn so wyde,
And here bodyes devyde.
Halde ye not this beste as is sayde?
PRIMUS Wyth youre wysdam, sere, we are wel payed.
EPISCOPUS Than, ye knyhtis, I charge yow, beth arayed;
And ye turmentouris, redy that tyde

When Mary is ded.
And but she deye the sunere, the devyl smyte of here hed!

Hic est Maria in templo orans et dicens:

MARIA O hye Wysdam in youre dygne deyté,
Youre infynyth lovnesse mad oure saluacyon.

75 EPISCOPUS] Ep, *remainder cropped* 76 PRIMUS] Prim, *remainder cropped* 77 SECUNDUS] Secund, *remainder cropped* 78 TERCIUS] Terc, *remainder cropped* 79 EPISCOPUS] Ep, *remainder cropped* seris] *faint black ink spill over* se you] youre 81 slewe] s *lacks ascender, first* e *written over erased letter* (y?) 82 abide] abi *and part of* d *survive, remainder cropped* 83 seustere] *B* senstere *an erasure after* fise 90 arayed] yed *written over an erasure* *Rubricated small capitula precede* 92, 125, *and other couplets in this play, except as noted*

That it lyst you of me, sympilest, to take here humanité,
  Wyth dew obeschyauns I make you gratulacyon.
And, gloryous Lord and sone, yif it like youre benygnyté
  Nouth to ben displesid wyth my desideracyon,
Me longith to youre presense, now conj[u]nct to the Vnyté,
  Wyth all myn herte and my sowle, be natures excitacyon,
  To youre domynacyon.
    For all creaturis in you don affye.
    And myche more owe I, youre moder be alye,
    Syn ye wern born God and man of my bodye,
  To desyre yowre presens, that were oure ferste formacyon.

SAPIENTIA My suete moderis preyere onto me doth assende;
  Here holy herte and here love is only on me.
Wherfore, aungyl, to here thou schalt now dyssende,
  Seyinge here sche schal comyn to myn eternyté.
Myn habundaunt mercy on here I extende, f. 216r
  Resseyuynge here to joye from worldly perplexité.
And in tokyn therof, this palme now pretende,
  Seyinge here sche fere no maner of diuercyté.

ANGELUS i By youre myth I dissende to youre moder in virginité.
ANGELUS ij For qwyche message injoyeth the hefnely consorcyté.

Hic discendet angelus ludentibus citharis, et dicet Marie:

PRIMUS A[NGELUS] Heyl, excellent prynces, Mary moste pure!
  Heyl, radyant sterre, the sunne not so bryth [is]!

100 conjunct] *an extra minim before* ct; *B suggests the minim was canc.* 104 *a letter canc. before* myche 106 ferste] s *written over another letter* 111 *preceded by a capitulum* 115 *no capitulum* 116 s.d. ludentibus citharis] *Hal, B; MS* ludent' cithar' 117 ANGELUS] A, *remainder cropped* 118 is (*?*) *erased and* is *interl. after* sunne *in slightly paler ink*

Heyl, Moder of Mercy and mayde most mure!
The blessyng that God yaf Jacob vpon you now lyth [is].
MARIA Now wolcom, bryth berde, Goddis aungyl I seuer!
Ye ben messager of Allmyhty; wolcom wyth my myhtis.
I beseke you now, say me, vpon youre hie nortur,
What is the very name that to youre persone dith is?

ANGELUS What nedith you, lady, my name ben desyrand?
MARIA A yis, gracyows aungyl, I beseke you requyrand.

ANGELUS My name is gret and merveylous, treuly you telland.
The hye God, youre sone, abidyth you in blis.
The thrydde day hens ye schul ben expirand,
And assende to the presense there my God, youre sone, is.
MA[RIA] Mercy and gromercy, God, now may I be seyand,
Thankyng you, suete aungyl, for this message, iwys.
ANG[ELUS] In tokenyng whereof, lady, I am here presentand
A braunce of a palme—owth of paradis com this.

Before youre bere God biddith it be bore.
MARI[A] Now thanke be to that Lord of his mercy euyrmore.

ANGEL[US] Yowre meknesse, youre lovnesse, and youre hie lore
Is most acceptable in the Trynité syth.
Youre sete ryall in hefne apparaled is thore;
Now dispose yow to deye, youre sone wyl thus rith.
f. 216v MAR[IA] I obbeye the commaundement of my God here before.
But on thyng I beseke that Lord of his myth:
That my brether, the appostelis, myht me be before,
To se me and I hem or I passe to that lyth.

120 is (*?*) *erased and* is *interl. after* now
133 ANGELUS] Ang, *remainder cropped*
137 ANGELUS] Angel, *remainder cropped*
131 MARIA] Ma, *remainder cropped*
136 MARIA] *most of final* a *cropped*
141 MARIA] Mar, *remainder cropped*

But they ben so deseverid, methynkyth it nyl be.
ANGELUS A yis, lady, inpossible to God nothyng trowe ye.

For he that sent Abbacuc with mete to Babylonye from Juré
Into the lake of lyonys to Danyel the prophete,
Be an her of his hed, lo, so myhty was he,
[B]e the same myht God make may the appostolis here mete.
And therfore abasche you not, lady, in yowre holy mende.
MARIA No more I do, glorious aungyl in kynde.

Also, I beseke my sone I se not the fende
What tyme outh of this word I schal passe hens.
His horible lok wold fere me so hende;
Ther is nothyng I dowte but his dredfull presens.
ANGELUS What nedith it to fere you, empres so hende,
Syn be the fruth of youre body was convycte his vyolens?
That horible serpent dar not nyhyn youre kende;
And yowre blosme schal make hym recistens
That he schal not pretende.
Desyre ye outh ellys now rythis?
MARIA Nouth but blessyd be my God in his myhtys.
ANGELUS To yow I recomaunde me than, moste excellent in sithis,
And wyth this ageyn to God I assende.

Hic ascendit angelus.

MARIA Now, Lord, thy swete holy name wyth lovnesse I blysse,
Of qwyche hefne and erthe eche tyme pshalmodyeth.
That it lykyth youre mercy me to you to wysse,

150 *and* 149 *inverted and marked* b *and* a *respectively in left margin* 150 Be] *G; MS* Se *Atypically, a large capitulum precedes the couplet in* 151–2 157 yow lady *canc. before* it 165 ageyn] e *altered from an* a 165 s.d. ascendit] it *written over a letter* 168 *a letter canc. before* mercy

My sympil sowle in serteyn youre name magnefyeth.
Now, holy maydenys, the seruauntis of God, as I gysse,
I schal passe from this world, as the aungyl sertefyeth.
Therfore to my sympil habitacyon, I telle you now this,
I purpose me to go, besekyng yow, replyeth,

f. 217r And assedually wachith me be dayes and nythis.

PRIMA VIRG[O] We schal, gracyous lady, wyth alle oure mythis.
Schul ye from vs passe, swete sonne of socoure
That are oure sengler solas, radyant in youre lythis?
Youre peynful absence schal make me doloure.
VIRGO SECUNDA Moste excellent prynces, in all vertu that dith is,
Alle hefne and erthe, lady, you doth honure.
We schal wachyn and wake, as oure dewe ryth is,
Into the tyme ye passe to that hye toure
Wyth. . . .
MA[RIA] God thanke you, and so do I.
Now I wyl dispose me to this jurné redy;
So wolde God my brether were here me by
To bere my body, that bare Jesu, oure Savyoure.

Hic subito apparet Sanctus Johannes Euangelista ante portam Marie.

JOHANNES A, myrable God, meche is thy myth!
Many wonderis thou werkyst, evyn as thi wyll is.
In Pheso I was prechyng, a fer contré ryth,
And by a whyte clowde I was rapt to these hyllys!
Here duellyth Cristis moder, I se wel in syth.
Sum merveylous message comyn that mayde tyll [is].

174 *is preceded by a red sign as are other single concatenated lines in this play, except as noted* 175 VIRGO] Virg, *remainder cropped* 179 is *erased after* dith *and interl. in fainter ink after* that 181 is *erased after* ryth *and interl. after* dewe 183 *remainder of line after* Wyth *cropped* 184 MARIA] Ma, *remainder cropped* 187 body] d *blotted* 188 *a word* (now?) *erased after* myth; *here and later in this stanza, rhyme-brackets extend through erasures* 190 now (?) *erased after* ryth 192 now (?) *erased after* syth 193 is (?) *erased after* tyll *and* is *interl. in fainter ink after* message

I wyl go saluse that berde that in vertu [is] moste brith.
  And of my sodeyn comyng wete what the skele
      [is].

Hic pulsabit super portam intrante domum Marie, sibi dicente:

Heyl, Moder Mary, maydyn perpetuall!

MARIA A, wolcome, mayde Johan, wyth all myn herte in
      specyall!
  For joye of youre presence myn herte gynnyth
      sweme.
Thynke ye not, Johan, how my child eternall
  When he hynge on cros sayd vs this teme:
'Lo, here thy sone, woman', so bad he me you call,
  And you me moder, eche othir to queme.
He betok you the gouernayl there of my body
      terestyall,
  On mayde to another, as convenyens wold seme.

And now that gracyows Lord hath sent me yow, sone. f. 217v

JOHANNES Now, good fayr lady, what is ther to done?
  Tellyth the cause why I am heder sent.
MARIA Swete sone Johan, so wyll I anone.
  Owre Lord God sent to me an aungyl that glent
And sayde I schulde passe hens, where thre were
      in one.
  Tho I askyd the aungyl to haue you present.
JOHANNES A, holy moder, schul ye from vs gone?
  My brether of this tydyngis sore wyl repent
  [þat ȝe schuld ben absent]!

194 is *erased after* brith *and interl. in fainter ink after* vertu (*see note*) 195 is *erased after* skele *and interl. in fainter ink after* what 195 s.d. sibi] s viiv *written in top margin of f. 217v* 205 sone] *a letter canc. in red after* n 207 Tellyth] e *obscured by smudge* 209 aungyl] y *written over another letter?* 211 aungyl] y *written over another letter* (e*?*) 212 A *malformed* from] m *altered from* n 214 *written in right margin opposite* 213 *by another hand whom G and B identify as the main scribe* ye schuld . . . bsen *written in left margin by scribe of this play, canc. in red with remainder cropped*

Euyr trybulacyon, Lord, meche þu vs sendyst:
Thou, oure maystyr and oure comfort, fro[m] vs ascendist,
And now oure joye, thy moder, to take thou pretendist.
Thanne all oure comfort is from vs detent.

But what seyde [the] aungyl, moder, onto you more?

MARIA He brouth me this palme from my sone thore,
Qwyche I beseke, as the aungyl me bad,
That aforn my bere by you it be bore,
Saynge my dirige devouthly and sad.

For, Johan, I haue herde the Jewys meche of me spelle.

JOHANNES A, good lady, what likyth it you to telle?

MARIA Secretly they ordeyne in here conseytis felle
When my sowle is paste, where Godis liste is,
To brenne my body and schamly it quelle,
For Jesu was of me born, that they slew wyth here fistis.
And therfore I beseke you, Johan, both flech and felle
Helpe I be beryed, for yn yow my tryst is.

JOHANNES Fere yow not, lady, for I schal wyth you duelle.
Wolde God my brether were here now and wyst this.

Hic subito omnes apostoli congregentur ante port[a]m mira[n]tes.

PETRUS A, holy brether, wyth grace be ye met here now.
Lord God, what menyth this sodeyne congregacyon?
Now, swete brother Powle, wyl ye take this vpon yow?
Preye to God for vs all we may haue relacyon.

215 þu] *G* yn   217 *and* 216 *inverted and marked* b *and* a *respectively in left margin*   216 from] *G; MS* fron   219 the] *G; MS* then   227 wyll *canc. in red and marked with deleting dots after* Godis, *and* liste *interl. above*   233 s.d. portam mirantes] portum mirates   Petrus *written as s.h. before s.d., then canc. in red and marked with deleting dots*

PAULUS Good brother Peter, how schuld I here pray now, f. 218r
That am lest and most vnworthy of this congregacy[o]n?
I am not worthy to ben clepyd apostle, sothly I say yow,
For as a woodman ageyn Holy Cherche I mad persecucyon.

But neuyrtheles, I am [by] the grace of God that þat I am, lo.
PETRUS A, gret is youre lownesse, Powle, brother, euyrmo.

PAULUS The keyes of hevene, Peter, God hath you betake,
And also ye ben peler of lith and prynce of vs all.
It is most sittyng to you this preyere to make,
And I, vnworthy, wyth yow preyen here schall.
PETR[US] I take this vpon me, Poule, for youre sake.
Now almythty God that sittiste aboue cherubyn halle,
In sygne of thyn holy cros oure handis we make,
Besekyng thy mercy may vpon vs falle;

And why we ben thus met, yif it lyke, vs lare.
JOHANNES A, holy brether alle, welcom ye are.

Why ye be met here I schal you declare:
For Mary, Goddys moder, by message is sent
That from this wrechid world to blysse sche schal fare,
And at here deying sche desyryth to haue vs present.
PETRU[S] A, brother Johan, we may syhyn and care,
Yif it displese not God, for these tydyngis ment.
PAULUS Forsothe, so we may, Peter, hevyin euyrmare
That oure moder and oure comfort schuld ben vs absent.

238 Powle *canc. in red and marked with deleting dots before* Peter 239 congregacyon] congregacyn 242 by *supplied;* in *deleted after* God The final word erased in 244, 246, 248, *and* 250; *the rhyme-brackets pass through the erasures* 246 pre *canc. before* preyere 248 PETRUS] Petr, *remainder cropped* 254 sent *canc. before* met 258 PETRUS] Petru, *remainder cropped* 260 hevyin] v *written over another letter?*

But neuyrtheles, the wyl of God fulfyllid mot be.

JOHANNES That is wel seyd, Poule, but herof bewar ye
That non of you for here deth schewe hevy speche.
For anon to the Jewys it schuld than notyd be
That we were ferd of deth, and that is ageyn that we teche.
For we seyn all tho belevyn in the hol Trynyté,
They schul euyr leve and nouth deye; this truly we preche.
And yif we make hevynesse for here, than wyl it seyd be,
'Lo, yone prechouris to deye they fere hem ful meche'.

f. 218v And therfore in God now beth glad euerychon.

PETRUS We schal don as ye sey vs, holy brother Johan.
Now we beseke you, let vs se oure moder Marie.
JOHANNES Now in Goddys name, to here than all let vs gon.
Sche wyl ben ful glad to se this holy companye.
PETRUS Heyl, moder and maydyn! So was neuyr non,
But only ye, most blissid treulye.
PAULUS Heyl, incomparabil quen, Goddis holy tron!
Of you spreng salvacyon and all oure glorye.

Heyl, mene for mankynde and mendere of mys!

MARIA A, wyth all myn hol herte, brether, ye are wolcom, iwys.
I beseke you now to telle me of youre sodeyne metyng.
PETRUS In dyueris contreys we prechid of youre sone and his blis,
Diueris clowdys eche of vs was sodeynely curyng.

266 is *interl.* 267 holl] *for* holy? iv *written by another hand in top margin of f. 218r* 273 y (?) *canc. before* moder 274 let *canc. before* than *A large capitulum erased before* 280

W[e] in on were brouth before youre yate here,
iwys;
The cause why, no man cowde telle of oure comyng.
MARIA Now I thanke God of his mercy. An hy merakle is this!
Now I wyl telle yow the cause of my sonys werkyng.

I desyrid his bodily presence to se.
JOHANNES No wonder, lady, thow so dede ye.

MARIA Tho my sone Jesu of his hye peté
Sent to me an aungyl, and thus he sayd,
That the thredde nyth I schuld assende to my sone in
deité.
Thanne to haue youre presence, brether, hertly I
prayed,
And thus at my request God hath you sent me.
PETRUS Wys gracyous lady, we are ryth wel payed.
MARIA Blissid brethere, I beseke you than, tent me.
Now wyl I rest me in this bed that for me is rayed.

Wachith me besily wyth youre laumpys and lithtis.
PAULUS We schal, lady. Redy allthyng for you dith is.

MARIA Now sone schul ye se what Godis myth is.
My flech gynnyth feble be nature.

Hic erit decenter ornatus in lecto.

PETRUS Brether, eche of you a candele takyth now rithis, f. 219r
And lith hem in haste whil oure moder doth dure.
And bisyli let vs wachyn in this virgyne sythis,
That when oure Lord comyth in his spoused pure
He may fynde vs wakyng and redy wyth oure lithtis.
For we knowe not the hour of his comyng now sure,

And yn clennesse alle loke ye be redy.

285 We] *G; MS* W 286 Why] h *altered from a* y *A line mistakenly drawn under* 294 302 s.d. *not underscored* 305 sythis] i *written over a* t*?*

MARIA A, swete sone Jesu, now mercy I cry.
Ouyr alle synful thy mercy let sprede.

Hic dissendet Dominus cum omni celest[*i*] *curia et dicet:*

DOMINUS The voys of my moder me nyhith ful ny.
I am dyssend onto here of whom I dede sede.

Hic cantabunt organa.

MARIA A, wolcom, gracyous Lord Jesu, sone and God of mercy!
An aungyl wold a ssuffysed me, hye Kyng, at this nede.
DOMINUS In propire persone, moder, I wyl ben here redy,
Wyth the hefnely quer yowre dirige to rede.

Veni tu, electa mea, et ponam in te thronum meum,
Quia concupiuit rex speciem tuam.

MARIA Paratum cor meum, Deus, paratum cor meum,
Cantabo et psalmum dicam Domino.

APOSTOLI Hec est que nesciuit thorum in delictis,
Habebit requiem in respectu animarum sanctarum.

MARIA Beatam me dicent omnes generaciones,
Quia fecit michi magna qui potens est, et sanctum nomen eius.

DOMINUS Veni de Libano, sponsa mea; veni, coronaberis.
[MARIA] Ecce, venio quia in capite libri scriptum est de me,
Vt facerem voluntatem tuam, Deus meus,
Quia exultauit spiritus meus in Deo salutari me[o].

Hic exiet anima Marie de corpore in sinu[*m*] *Dei.*

311 s.d. celesti] *G; MS* celester 313 s.d. organa] *or* organis 314 *preceded by a capitulum* 318, 320, 322, 324, *and* 326 *preceded by the rubricated versicle mark as are* 343, 345, 369, *and* 370 327 *s.h. supplied* 329 meo] *G; MS* mes 329 s.d. sinum] *G; MS* sinu

DOMINUS
Now com, my swete soule in clennesse most pure, f. 219v
And reste in [m]y bosom, brithtest of ble.
Alle ye, myn apostelis, of this body takyth cure.
In the Vallé of Josephat there fynde schul ye
A grave new mad for Maryes sepulture.
There beryeth the body wyth all youre solempnité;
And bydyth me there stylle thre dayes severe,
And I schal pere ageyn to yow to comfort youre aduercyté.

Wyth this swete soule now from you I assende.

PETRUS
In oure tribulacyouns, Lord, thou vs defende;
We haue no comfort on erthe but of the alon.
O swete soule of Mary, prey thy sone vs defende;
Haue mynde of thy pore brether when thou comyst to þi tron.

CHORUS MARTYRUM
Que est ista que assendit de deserto
Deliciis affluens, innixa super dilectum suum?

ORDO ANGEL[ORUM]
Ista est speciosa inter filias Jerusalem sicut vidistis eam,
Plenam caritate et dilectione; sicque in celum gaudens suscipitur,
Et a dextris filii in trono glorie collocatur.

Hic cantabit omnis celestis curia.

PRIMA VIRGO
Now, suster, I beseke you, let vs do oure attendaunce
And wasche this gloryous body that here in oure sith is,
As is the vse among vs, wythoutyn ony varyaunce.
Now blessid be this persone that bar God of Mythtis.

vii (?) *written above* clennesse *in top margin* 331 my] *G; MS* ny brist *canc. before* brithtest 338 *and* 339 *lack capitula* 340 on] *or* in 345 ANGELORUM] *G; MS* Angels 348 Prima Virgo *written as s.h. before* 347 s.d., *then canc. in red and marked with deleting dots*

SECUNDA VIRGO I am redy, suster, wyth all myn hol affyaunce,
To wesche and worschepe this body that so brith is.
Alle creaturys therto owyn dew obeschaunce,
For this body resseyved the Holy Gostis flithtis.

Et osculabunt corpus Marie.

JOHANNES Now, holy brother Peter, I hertely you pray
To bere this holy palme before this gloryous body.
For ye ben prince of apostelis and hed of oure fay;
Therfore it semyth you best to do this offis, treuly.

PETRUS Sere, and ye slept on Cristis brest, seyng all
f. 220r celestly;
Ye are Goddis clene mayde, wythoutyn ony nay.
This observaunce is most like you to do dewly;
Wherfore tak it vpon you, brother, we pray.

And I schal helpe for to bere the bere.

PAULUS And I, Peter, wyth oure brether in fere,
This blessid body schal helpe to the ground.
This holy cors now take we vp here,
Seyng oure observaunce wyth devouth sound.

Hic portabunt corpus versus sepulturam cum eorum luminibus.

PETRU[S] Exiit Israel de Egipto, domus Jacob de populo
barbaro. Alleluia!

APOSTOLI Facta est Judea sanctificacio eius, Israel potestas
eius. Alleluia!

Hic angeli dulciter cantabunt in celo, 'Alleluia!'

EPISCOPUS Herke, sere princys, what noyse is all this?
The erthe and the eyer is ful of melodye!

359 tru (*?*) *canc. before* treuly 361 clene] l *altered from an* h 365 *s.h. not looped in red* 369 PETRUS] Petru, *remainder cropped*

I herde neuyr er swyche a noyse now, iwys.
Con ye outh say what they signefye?

PRIMUS PRINCEPS
I not, be my God, that of myht meche is.
Whatsumeuyr they be, hougely they crye!
I am aferd there wyll be sumthyng amys;
It is good prevely among vs we spye
Wythowte.

SECUNDUS PRINCEPS
Now I haue levyd this thre skore yer,
But sweche another noyse herd I neuyr er.
Myn herte gynnyth ogyl and quake for fer—
There is sum newe sorwe sprongyn, I dowte.

TERCIUS PRIN[CEPS]
Ya, that there is, sothly I say yow:
The prophetis moder, Mary, is ded!
The disciplis here beryn in gret aray now,
And makyn alle this merthe in spyth of oure hed.

EPISCOPUS
Fy on yon lousy doggys, they were bettyr nay!
Outh! Harrow! The devyl is in myn hed!
Ye dodemvsyd prynces, faste yow aray,
Or I make avow to Mahound, youre bodyes schul blede,
Now that quene is ded! f. 220v
Ye coward knytys in plate,
And ye tormentours, thryfe schul ye late!
Faste, harlotys, go youre gate,
And brynge me that bychyd body, I red!

PRIMUS PRINCEPS
Dowte you not, sere byschop; in peyne of repref,
We schal don schame to that body and to tho prechours.

SECUNDUS
Sere, I schal geyne tho glabereris or gramly hem gref!
Tho teynt tretouris schul tene yif my loke on hem louris.

375 PRINCEPS] nc *blotted* 381 *miswritten* another, *with* o *interl. after* n, *canc. in red before* another 384 PRINCEPS] Prin, *most of* c *and remainder of word cropped* 385 is *canc. in red and marked with deleting dots before* Mary 388 *a word erased after* nay 390 *a word erased after* aray vii iv *written in top margin of f. 220r*

TERCIUS PRINCEPS
To hurle wyth tho harlotys me is ful lef!
I schal snarle tho sneveleris wyth rith scharp schouris.

EPISCOPUS
Hens than, a devylis name, and take me that thef,
And br[y]nge me that bygyd body evyn tofore these touris!
And here disciplis ye slo!
Hye you hens, harlotis, atonys!
The devyl boyes mot breke youre bonys!
Go stent me yone body wyth youre stonys!
Outh! Harrow! Al wod now I go!

Hic discendunt principes cum suis ministris vt feroci percucientes petras cum eorum capitibus.

SECUNDUS PRINCEPS
What devyl, where is this mené?
I here here noyse but I se ryth nouth.
Allas, I haue clene lost my posté;
I am ful wo, mad is my þowth!

TERCIUS PRINCEPS
I am so ferd I wold fayn fle!
The devyl hym spede hedyr me brouth!
I renne, I rappe, so wo is me,
Wyndand wod wo hath me wrouth!
To deye I ne routh.

PRIMUS PRINCEPS
A, cowardis, vpon you now fy!
Are ye ferd of a ded body?
I schal sterte therto manly;
Alle that company fere I ryth nouth!

f. 221r *Hic saltat insanus a[d] feretrum Marie et pendet per manus.*

Allas, my body is ful of peyne!
I am fastened sore to this bere!
Myn handys are ser bothe tweyne.
O, Peter, now prey thy God for me here.

402 snrle *canc. in red and marked with deleting dots before* snarle 404 brynge] brnge 409 Al wod] alwod 409 s.d. percucientes] *G*; *MS* percucienƋ 422 s.d. ad] *G; MS* af 425 hōdys *or* hādys (*?*) *canc. in red and marked with deleting dots before* handys

In Cayfas halle when thou were seyne
And of the, Peter, a mayde acusid there,
I halpe the tho; now helpe me ageyne,
That I were hol, outh of this fere—
Sum medycyn me lere.

PETRUS I may not tend to the, sere, at this hour
For ocupacyon of this body of honour.
But neuyrtheles, beleue in Jesu Criste, oure Saveyour,
And that this was his moder that we bere on bere.

[PRIMUS PRINCEPS] I beleue in Jesu, mannys saluacyon.

PETRUS In Goddis name, go doun than, and this body honure.

PRIMUS PRINCEPS Now mercy, God, and gromercy of this savacyon!
In Jesu and his moder to beleve euyr I seuere.

PETRUS Than take yone holy palme and go to þi nacyon,
And bid hem beleve in God yif they wyl be pure.
And towche hem therwyth, both hed, hand, and facyon,
And of her sekenesse they schal haue cure—
And ellis in here peynys indure.

PRIMUS PRINCEPS Gromercy, holy fader Peter.
I schal do as ye me teche her,
Thankyng God euyr in my speche her,
Wyth hye repentaunce and herte most mure.

Hic portabunt feretrum ad locum sepulture.

PETRUS Now, holy brether, this body let vs take,
And wyth alle the worschepe we may, ley it in the graue,
Kyssyng it alle atonys for here sonys sake.
Now insence ye, and we schal put here in this cave.

Hic ponent corpus in sepulcrum insensantes et cantantes.

435 mder (?) *canc. in red and marked with deleting dots before* moder 436 *s.h. supplied* 444 *a letter canc. before* indure

f. 221v JOHANNES De terra plasmasti me et carne induisti me;
Redemptor meus, Domine, resuscita me in novissimo die.

Now God blysse this body and we oure synge make.

Hic vnanimiter benedicent corpus in nomine Patris, et Filii, et Spiritus Sancti.

The fruth that it bar oure soules schal saue.
Now reste we vs, brether, vpon this pleyn lake.
Tyl from oure God and oure Lord tydyngis we haue,
Here muste we belave.

PAULUS So muste we, Johan, as ye say.
Thanne byde we here and pray,
Besekyng hym of comfort that best may,
Restyng here abowtyn this graue.

Hic vadit princeps ad Judeos cum palma.

PRIMUS PRINCEPS Ye Jewys that langour in this gret infyrmyté,
Belevyth in Crist Jesu and ye schal haue helthe.
Throw vertu of this holy palme that com fro the Trinyté,
Yowur sekenesse schal aswage and restore you to welthe.

SECUNDUS PRINCEPS I beleve in Crist Jesu, Goddis sone in vnyté,
And forsake my mavmentryes, fals in here felthe.

Hic tangat credentes cum palma et sanati sunt.

A, I thanke the, gracyous Lord, and thy moder of peté.
Now are we hol of oure seknesse and of oure foul belthe.

vv *written in top margin of f. 221v* 453 *preceded by capitulum* 455 s.d. *words after* corpus *not underscored* 457 brether] *or* brother 458 d *canc. before* Lord

TERCIUS PRINCEPS
What, harlotys, forsake oure lawe?

SECUNDUS PRINCEPS
So hald I beste the do.

TERCIUS PRINCEPS
Hens fro me in the develis name ye go!
I deye! Outh, outh! Harro!
The wylde develys mot me to-drawe!

PRIMUS DEMON
Herke, Belsabub and Belyal, Sere Sathan in the herne,
Vs fettyn oure servauntis to this preson!
Blow flamys of fer to make hem to brenne;
Mak redy ageyn we com to this, demon!

SECUNDUS DEMON
Faste for tho harlotis now let vs renne,
To caste hem in this pet here that depe is adon.
They schul brenne, and boyle, and chille in oure denne!
Go we now, a dewelys name, as faste as we mon.
Harrow, harrow, we com to town! f. 222r

PRIMUS DEMON
Drag we these harlotis in hye
Into the pet of helle for to lye!

SECUNDUS DEMON
Go we now, helle houndis, ye crye;
Sere Sathan may heryn oure son!

DOMINUS
Now, aungyl and alle this court celestyall,
Into herthe now discendith wyth me
To reyse the body of my moder terestyall,
And bryng we it to the blysse of my deyté.

Assent ye hereto now [in] vnyté?

ANGELI
Ya, for yowre hye mercy, Lord, al hefne makyth melodé.

Hic discendit et venit ad apostolos dicens:

478 preson] n̄ *may indicate a contracted* -un, *also in the rhyme-words in* 482, 484, *and* 489; *but it does not occur in the rhyme-word* demon *in* 480, *and appears to be otiose in* town̄ *in* 485
488 houndis] hon̄dis 494 in] *G; MS* the

DOMINUS Pes be to yow alle, my postelis so dere.
Lo me here, yowre Lord and youre God, now rythtis.
PETRUS A, wolcom, Criste, oure comfort, in thy manhed clere!
Gret merveylous God, mekyl now thy myth is.
DOMINUS What worschepe and grace semyth you now here
That I do to this body, Mary that hytht is?
JOHANNES Lord, as thou rese from deth and regnyst in thyn empere,
So reyse thou this body to thy blysse that lyth is.
Vs semyth this ryth is.
MYCHAEL Ya, gloryous God, lo, the sowle here prest now
To this blissid body likyth it you to fest now;
Hefne and erthe wold thynke this the best now
Inasmyche as sche bare you, God in youre mythtis.

Hic vadit anima in corpus Marie.

DOMINUS Go thanne, blyssid soule, to that body ageyn.
Arys now, my dowe, my nehebour, and my swete frende,
Tabernacle of joye, vessel of lyf, hefnely temple, to reyn.
Ye schal haue the blysse wyth me, moder, that hath non ende.
For as ye were clene in erthe of alle synnys greyn,
So schul ye reyne in hefne clennest in mend.
MARIA A, endles worchepe be to you, Jesu, relesere of peyn.
I and alle erthe may blisse ye, com of owre kend.
f. 222v Lo me, redy wyth yow for to wend.
DOMINUS Abouen hefnys, moder, assende than we,
In endles blysse for to be.
MICHAEL Hefne and erthe, now injoye may ye,
For God throw Mary is mad mannys frend.

501 hytht is] hythtis 509 ageyn] e *written over another letter* v *written in top margin of f. 222r*

Et hic assendent in celum cantantibus organis.

Assumpta es, Maria, in celum.

DOMINUS Yow to worchepe, moder, it likyth the hol Trinyté.
Wherfore I crowne you here in this kyndam of glory.
Of alle my chosyn, thus schul ye clepyd be:
Qwen of Hefne and Moder of Mercy.

MICHAEL Now blysid be youre namys, we cry!
For this holy assumpcyon alle hefne makyth
melody.
Deo gracias.

42
[JUDGEMENT DAY]

f. 223v

Hic incipit Dies Judicii, et Jesu descendente cum Michaele et Gabriele Archangelis; et Michael dicit et cetera:

MICHAEL Svrgite! All men aryse!
Venite ad Judicium!
For now is sett þe hyȝ justyce
And hath assygnyd þe Day of Dom.
Rape ȝow redyly to þis grett assyse,
Bothe grett and small, all an sum!
And of ȝoure answere ȝow now avyse,
What ȝe xal sey whan þat ȝe cum,
Ȝowre ansuere for to telle.
For whan þat God xal ȝow appose,
Ther is non helpe of no glose.
The trewth ful trewlye he wyl tose
And send ȝow to hevyn or helle.

A capitulum precedes 522 523 *no capitulum* 527 *no capitulum* blysid] y *roughly drawn over an* s, *or vice versa* *Remainder of f. 222v (110 mm) blank except for* Deo gracias *written by another hand and enclosed within flourished lines*

[*Play 42*] *Ff. 223–5 are again YHS in a Sun paper, written by main scribe. F. 223r blank except for* lo me redy with yow to wend, *copied by another hand from* 41/517 *F. 223v marked* 220
1 *s.h. written in Textura Quadrata*

GABRYELL Bothe pope, prynce, and prysste with crowne,
Kynge, and caysere, and knyhtys kene,
Rapely ȝe renne, ȝoure resonys to rowne!
For this xal be þe day of tene.
Nowther pore ne ryche of grett renowne,
Ne all þe develys in helle þat bene,
From þis day ȝow hyde not mowne;
For all ȝoure dedys here xal be sene
Opynly in syght.
Who þat is fowndyn in deedly gylte,
He were bettyr to ben hylte!
In hendeles helle he xal be spylte.
His dedys his deth xal dyght.

f. 224r *Omnes resurgentes subtus terram clamau*[*erunt*], *'Haaa, haaa, haaa!' Deinde surgentes dica*[*n*]*t, 'Haaa', et cetera:*

Haaa! Cleue asundyr, ȝe clowdys of clay,
Asundyr ȝe breke and lete us pas!
Now may oure songe be 'weleaway',
þat evyr we synnyd in dedly trespas!

Omnes demones clamant:

Harrow and owt! What xal we say?
Harraw, we crye, owt and alas!
Alas! Harrow! Is þis þat day
To endles peyne þat vs must pas?
Alas, harrow, and owt, we crye!

Omnes anime resurgentes dicant et cetera:

A, mercy, Lorde, for oure mysdede,
And lett þi mercy sprynge and sprede!
But, alas, we byden in drede—
It is to late to aske mercye.

14 prysste] sst *written over* ne 26 s.d. clamauerunt] *D; MS* clamauit Haaa, haaa, haaa . . . Haaa] *B* ha aa ha aa ha aa . . . ha aa; *also in* 27 dicant] *D; MS* dicat *Several letters erased at right of s.d.*

DEUS
Venite, benedicti, my bretheryn all,
Patris mei ȝe childeryn dere!
Come hedyr to me, to myn hyȝ hall,
All þo myn suterys and servauntys [were]!
All þo fowle wyrmys from ȝow falle.
With my ryght hand I blysse ȝow here.
My blyssynge burnyschith ȝow as bryght as berall;
As crystall clene it clensyth ȝow clere,
All fylth from ȝow fade.
Petyr, to hevyn ȝatys þu wende and goo;
þe lokkys þu losyn and hem vndo.
My blyssyd childeryn þu brynge me to,
Here hertys for to glade.

PETRUS
The ȝatys of hevyn I opyn þis tyde. f. 224v
Now welcome, dere bretheryn, to hevyn, iwys!
Com on and sytt on Goddys ryght syde
Where myrthe and melody nevyr may mys.

OMNES SALUATI
On kne we crepe, we gon, we glyde
To wurchepp oure Lorde, þat mercyfful is.
For thorwe his woundys, þat be so wyde,
He hath brought us to his blys.
Holy Lorde, we wurchepp þe!

DEUS
Welcome ȝe be in hevyn to sitt!
Welcum, fro me xul ȝe nevyr flitt,
So sekyr of blys ȝe xul be ȝitt;
To myrth and joye welcum ȝe be.

ANIME DAMPNANDUM
Ha! Ha! Mercy! Mercy, we crye and crave!
A, mercy, Lorde, for oure mysdede!
A, mercy, mercy! We rubbe, we rave!
A, help us, good Lord, in þis nede.

DEUS
How wolde ȝe wrecchis any mercy haue?
Why aske ȝe mercy now in þis nede?
What haue ȝe wrought ȝoure sowle to saue?
To whom haue ȝe don any mercyful dede,
Mercy for to wynne?

40 benedicti] *or* beneditti   *Two dark brown virgules and one red after* benedicti *and after* mei *in* 41   43 were] *B; MS* be   50 lokkys] kk *written over another letter*   *Two scribbled figures in left margin of f. 224v*   67 ore *canc. before* oure

PRIMUS DIABOLUS
Mercy? Nay, nay, they xul haue wrake!
And þat on here forehed wyttnes I take.
For þer is wretyn with letteris blake
Opynly all here synne.

f. 225r DEUS
To hungry and thrusty þat askyd in my name
Mete and drynke wolde ȝe ȝeve non;
Of nakyd men had ȝe no shame;
Ȝe wold nott vesyte men in no preson;
Ȝe had no peté on seke nor lame—
Dede of mercy wold ȝe nevyr don.
Vnherborwed men ȝe servyd þe same;
To bery the deed pore man wold ȝe not gon.
These dedys doth ȝow spylle!
For ȝoure love was I rent on rode,
And for ȝoure sake I shed my blode.
Whan I was so mercyfull and so gode,
Why haue ȝe wrought aȝens my wylle?

SECUNDUS DIABOLUS
I fynde here wretyn in þin forheed
Þu wore so stowte and sett in pryde
Þu woldyst nott ȝeve a pore man breed,
But from þi dore þu woldyst hym chyde.

TERCIUS DIABOLUS
And in þi face here do I rede
Þat if a thrysty man com any tyde,
For thrust þow he xulde be deed,
Drynk from hym þu woldyst evyr hyde.
On covetyse was all thy thought.

PRIMUS DIABOLUS
In wratth þi neybore to bakbyte,
Them for to hangere was þi delyte.
Þu were evyr redy them to endyte.
On þe seke man rewyst þu nought.

f. 225v SECUNDUS DIABOLUS
Evyrmor on envye was all þi mende:
Þ[u] woldyst nevyr vesyte no presoner;
To all þi neyborys þu were vnkende;
Þu woldyst nevyr helpe man in daunger.

76 forehed] r *blotted, altered from a* y? *F. 225v, outside leaf of final gathering, worn and stained* 106 þu] *second letter obscured by stain and rubbing*

TERCIUS DIABOLUS

The synne of slauth þi sowle xal shende!
Masse nore mateynes woldyst þu non here,
To bery þe deed man þu woldyst not wende.
þerfore þu xalt to endles fere.
To slowth þu were ful prest.

PRIMUS DIABOLUS

Thou haddyst rejoyse in glotonye,
In dronkeshepp and in rebawdye!
Vnherborwyd with velonye
þu puttyst from here rest.

SECUNDUS DIABOLUS

Sybile Sclutte, þu ssalte sewe,
All ȝoure lyff was leccherous lay.
To all ȝoure neyborys ȝe wore a shrewe,
All ȝoure plesauns was leccherous play.
Goddys men ȝe lovyd but fewe;
Nakyd men and febyl of array
Ȝe wolde nott socowre with a lytel drewe,
Nott with a thred, þe soth to say,
Whan they askyd in Godys name.

OMNES DAMPNANDI

A, mercy, Lord, mekyl of myght,
We aske þi mercy and not þi ryght;
Not after oure dede so us quyth.
We haue synnyd. We be to blame.

DEUS.

atque . . . I must go to þe most (?) *written by another hand in right margin opposite* 121–4
123 array] ar *interl.* 129 quyth] h *malformed, perhaps altered from another letter*
The play is incomplete